Bernard Stiegler

Nanjing Lectures 2016–2019

Edited and translated by Daniel Ross

CCC2 Irreversibility

Series Editors: Tom Cohen and Claire Colebrook

The second phase of 'the Anthropocene,' takes hold as tipping points speculated over in 'Anthropocene 1.0' click into place to retire the speculative bubble of "Anthropocene Talk". Temporalities are dispersed, the memes of 'globalization' revoked. A broad drift into a de facto era of managed extinction events dawns. With this acceleration from the speculative into the material orders, a factor without a means of expression emerges: climate panic.

Bernard Stiegler

Nanjing Lectures 2016–2019

Edited and translated by Daniel Ross

O

Open Humanities Press is an international, scholar-led open access publishing collective whose mission is to make leading works of contemporary critical thought freely available worldwide. More at http://openhumanitiespress.org

Contents

2016 Lectures
Reading Marx and Heidegger in the Anthropocene

1. Introduction to Questions Concerning Automatic Society 9
2. Functions of the Mind in Automatic Society 16
3. Retentions, Protentions and Knowledge 20
4. Technological *Epokhē*, the Anthropocene and the Neganthropocene 28
5. Organology, Economy and Ecology 36
6. Thermodynamics, *Gestell* and Neganthropology 41
7. Organology of Limits and the Function of Reason 50
8. Final Lecture 64

2017 Lectures
Heading Upstream from 'Post-Truth' to the Birth of Platonic Metaphysics

1. Introduction 71
2. The New Conflict of the Faculties and the Functionalist Approach to Truth 79
3. Socrates and Plato in the Tragic Age and the Inauguration of the Western Individuation Process 92
4. The Tragic Spirit 109
5. From *Meno* to *Phaedrus*: The Constitution and Crisis of Public Space 120
6. Tragic *Krisis* and Adoption 138
7. Against the Current 151
8. Conclusion? 162

2018 Lectures
Organology of Platform Capitalism

1. Introduction: From Biopower to Neuropower 169
2. From Psychopower to Neuropower 182

3. From Writing to Digital Writing: On the Brain and the Soul 194
4. The Pharmacology of Technological Memory 205
5. Neuroscience, Neuroeconomics, Neuromarketing 215
6. On Automatisms and Posthumanism 224
7. Automation and Automatisms 233
8. The Future of Neurotechnology 242
Anniversary Lecture: On the Need for a Hyper-Materialist Epistemology 258

2019 Lectures
Elements of a Hyper-Materialist Epistemology

1. Introduction 269
2. Specification of the Context in which there Arises the Need for a Hyper-Materialist Epistemology: The Reign of the 'Notion of Information' 277
3. On Technological Performativity and Its Consequences for the 'Notion of Information' 286
4. The Noetic Faculties and Functions in Exosomatization 295
5. Entropy, Negentropy and Anti-Entropy in Thermodynamics, Biology and Information Theory 303
6. Critique of Simondon's 'Notion of Information' 312
7. Critique of Sohn-Rethel and the Need for a Hyper-Materialist Epistemology 325
8. Sohn-Rethel, Vygotsky, Meyerson 334

Notes **345**

2016 Lectures

Reading Marx and Heidegger in the Anthropocene

FIRST LECTURE

Introduction to Questions Concerning Automatic Society

During this seminar, we will try to read, think and interpret Marx and Heidegger in the same movement of thinking. What will lead us through this double reading and questioning is the question of exosomatization – exosomatization being another name for what one calls more generally technics. But considered in terms of exosomatization, technics appears as a stage of the organogenesis to which the evolution of life amounts. In such a view, technics is not the opposite of life, but its evolution, a continuation of life by means other than life.

A living being is an organism, as Lamarck said, and the evolution of these organisms is an organogenesis. Hominization, which begins between two and three million years ago, is also the beginning of an exosomatization in which the human body begins to produce exosomatic organs, which are artificial organs: non-organic organs, which I call also *organological* organs.

This is what is generally called technics. Now, if we agree to say that everything that is the product of such an exosomatization, of such an ex-teriorization, or ex-ternalization, is technical, then we must say that language, as a social production, belongs to exosomatization, and, in this sense, belongs to technics. Technics is what I try to think with the concepts of what I call:

1 General organology

2 Pharmacology

As a stage of evolution, as the pursuit of organogenesis, and, in this sense, as the continuation of life – that is, an organization of matter as organic matter – by an organization of matter as organized inorganic matter, technics necessarily belongs to this process that, since Erwin Schrödinger, has been called negative entropy, or negentropy. Now, to think negentropy, we must first understand what entropy is and, second, understand whether organized inorganic matter opens the possibility of something that is different, not just from entropy, but also from negentropy.

Here, it is very important to notice that Marx, unlike Heidegger, could not have known the concept of negentropy. Now, even if Engels will talk about entropy in his *Dialectics of Nature*, he will not really take its novelty into account. As for Heidegger: he never gives consideration to entropy and negentropy in his thought of being and becoming.

The goal of this seminar is to rethink political economy, in order to conceive a new critique of political economy, and to do so in the context of what has come to be called the Anthropocene (that is, a vast and rapid increase of the rate of entropy in the biosphere), as well as from the perspective of what I will call the Neganthropocene. The goal is to reach such a concept through a new reading of Marx and Heidegger in light of the questions opened up by entropy and negentropy in the sphere of the exosomatic form of life that is ours – as humankind living on the Earth and in the Anthropocene era, which is also to say, in the age of disruption, which is the age of the concretization of what Heidegger called *Gestell*.

▪ ▪ ▪

The Anthropocene is a geological era, which appeared two hundred and fifty years ago, with industrialization and capitalism, this being also a new stage in the history of exosomatization. I will try to show you why and how this era can and must be overcome. As a vast, systemic and extremely rapid process of increasing entropy, the Anthropocene necessarily leads to the destruction of all kinds of life, and firstly, of human life. Furthermore, as the digital disruption that is currently destroying all kinds of social systems, in the sense of Bertrand Gille and Niklas Luhmann, replacing them with hyper-control technologies of what has been called algorithmic governmentality, the end of the Anthropocene is also the attempt to impose a new ideology, which is called transhumanism.

Transhumanism is a discourse that concerns a new stage of exosomatization, which is also a new kind of endosomatization, using, for example, neurotechnology to transform the interior of the brain from the exterior (I will come back to this topic later). But transhumanism is not only an ideology: it is also a new kind of marketing, which has its own university, called the University of the Singularity, which wants to turn the market into the sole source of criteria for exosomatic evolution.

To overcome the Anthropocene means to oppose such an ideology, such a marketing, and then, to respond to such a market of exosomatization with a revolutionary movement in economy that I call the advent of the Neganthropocene. And I will try to show you that it is possible and necessary to interpret Heidegger's concepts of *Gestell* and *Bestand* as exosomatization in the Anthropocene, and to interpret *Ereignis* as the Neganthropocene.

The Neganthropocene is a new way of understanding economy. In such an economy, the primordial value is negentropy – that is, organization inasmuch as it is based on increasing diversity – biodiversity as well as noodiversity, that is, knowledge. Knowledge is indeed, at least, negentropic. But we will see that perhaps we should say that knowledge is not just negentropic, but *neganthropic*.

Marx and Engels were the first thinkers of exosomatization: this is what they describe in *The German Ideology*, and we will come back to this text in subsequent lectures. Now, exosomatization, as a continuation of organogenesis, that is, of life, and hence of negentropy, is not *organic*, but *organological*, and this means that the artificial organs that are produced by and as exosomatization are both negentropic *and* entropic.

This double-sided structure of the exosomatic organs means that these organs are *pharmaka*, as was said in ancient Greece by Socrates. And here, two questions arise. How is it possible to reinterpret Marx,

1. in the light of negentropy – or even as neganthropy – that is, exosomatization?
2. in terms of the pharmacological question posed by the double-sided character of artificial organs insofar as they are also entropic – and which is sometimes also called anthropization?

We will examine the fragment on machines and automation in the *Grundrisse* to situate these questions in relation to our context of the rise of full and generalized automation. And I will talk now about this context, in order to introduce the historical and *geschichtlich* situation in which we must read Marx today.

All of this will lead us to read Heidegger in a new light.

▪ ▪ ▪

Hurrying at the last moment to finish the preparations for this seminar, I have decided to slightly rearrange its schedule – to be specific, I have decided to change the order of the opening sessions, and to begin with a description of the main features of the context within which I am proposing the topics that will here be addressed – with the aim of introducing my audience to a specific proposal: to undertake the transdisciplinary work that is required as a result of those technological mutations brought about by the Anthropocene, the industrial revolution and capitalism.

This proposal is for what I call a *general organology*, itself understood as a theoretical platform specifying the terms of an agreement between the disciplines in every field of knowledge. This platform defines the rules for analysing, thinking and prescribing human facts at three parallel but indissociable levels:

1 the psychosomatic, which is the endosomatic level of organic organs;

2 the artefactual, which is the exosomatic level of organological organs;

3 the social, which is the organizational level of institutional organisms or of corporations.

Hence this involves an analysis of the relations between organic organs, technical organs and social organizations – given that our point of departure consists in the claim that a human psychosomatic organ always exists in a relationship with artificial organs, and that this relationship is always prescribed by social organizations, where the latter are themselves over-determined by those same artificial organs and their arrangement with human psychosomatic organs.

I must add here – and I will of course develop this in the coming sessions – that it is always possible for the arrangements between these psychosomatic and artefactual organs to become toxic and destructive for the organic organs, and hence also for the body within which they dwell. In other words, a general organology is a pharmacology. This having been said, and before explaining these points any further, let's engage ourselves with a specification of our current context, as humans who belong to an era that since Crutzen has been referred to as the Anthropocene.

I argued ten years ago that we have entered the hyper-industrial age, that ours is an epoch of great symbolic misery, and that this leads to the structural destruction of desire, that is, it ruins the libidinal economy: speculative marketing, having become hegemonic, systematically exploits the drives, which are divested of every attachment.[1] Symbolic misery derives from what, with Nicolas Donin, we call the mechanical turn of sensibility, that is, an organological change, that places the sensory life of the individual under the permanent control of the mass media.

The causes of symbolic misery and the destruction of desire are both economic and organological: it is a matter both of the consumerist model and of those instruments that capture and harness consumer attention, implemented by the culture industries and the mass media at the beginning of the twentieth century. These instruments, controlled by marketing, bypass and short-circuit the *savoir-vivre* of consumers, their knowledge of how to live.

Consumers are thereby proletarianized, just as producers had been proletarianized in the nineteenth century by instruments that short-circuited their *savoir-faire*, their knowledge of how to make and do, this being fully accomplished at the beginning of the twentieth century. In production as well as in consumption, this industrial capture of attention also deforms attention:

1 Attention is formed through education, via processes of identification (in Freud's sense, that is, as primary and secondary identification), an education that constitutes the intergenerational relations at the core of which the knowledge of how to live is elaborated.

2 To raise a child is to singularly transmit a form of *savoir-vivre*, which he or she will singularly transmit in turn – to his or her comrades, friends, family and peers, both near and distant.

3 What is formed through all the pathways of education – including teaching – is that which the industrial capture of attention systematically de-forms.

The economy of desire is formed through processes of identification and transindividuation, woven in the course of intergenerational relations as the set of capacities to bind the drives by diverting their aims towards social investments. The industrial deformation and diversion of attention short-circuits and bypasses these processes of identification and transindividuation. As such, the symbolic misery imposed by consumer capitalism, which amounts to de-symbolization, leads *inevitably* to the destruction of the libidinal economy.

During the second half of the twentieth century, there was a continual decrease of the age at which attention was captured in an industrial way: in the 1960s, *juvenile* 'available brain time' constituted the prime target of the audiovisual mass media, but by the end of the century, it was *infantile* brain time that was being targeted and diverted from its affective and social environment, via all manner of programs and specialized channels – like Baby First, a channel belonging to Fox TV.

The object of desire is *desired* to the point of inverting the goals of the drives that support it, but this is so only because it does *more than just exist*: it *consists*, and, as such, it *infinitizes itself*, that is, it *exceeds all calculation*. To desire is to invest in an object, and to experience its consistence, and hence, to destroy desire is to liquidate all attachment and all fidelity, that is, all trust and confidence – without which no economy is possible. And ultimately, it is to liquidate *all belief*, and therefore, all *credit*.

The object of desire gives rise to a spontaneous belief in life that presents itself through this object as its *extra-ordinary* power. All love is phantasmal in the sense that it gives life to that which is not – to that which is ordinarily not. But because the fantasy of love, and of what Abdelkebir Khatibi called '*aimance*' (translated into English as 'lovence'[2]), is that which grants to civilizations their most durable forms, the literally *fantastic* sentiment in which love *consists* is the incarnation of a knowledge of the *extra-ordinariness of life* that constantly *surpasses* life – whereby life *invents* itself by going *beyond* life, and as the pursuit of life by means other than life, through the incessant and ever-increasing profusion and evolution of artifices.

This is how I have interpreted the movement of exteriorization, that is, of exosomatization, described by the anthropologist André Leroi-Gourhan in order to analyse the process of hominization as an invention of life by means other than life – that is, as a technological, organological and pharmacological evolution that constitutes the human problem of life on Earth, and the responsibility that we have not to evade this problem, which is constantly being remade by technical invention.

Love, as we all know, is strictly speaking the experience of artifice: it is essential to fetishize the one we love, and when we *stop* loving them, we are confronted with the artificiality of the amorous situation, as we are brought brutally back to the ordinariness of quotidian life. Two or three million years ago, life began to pass through the non-living artifice – there first appears what Aristotle referred to as the noetic soul, that is, the soul that loves (as we learn from Diotima in Plato's *Symposium*).

The non-living artifice conserves *for* life a trace of what, in the biological economy that Simondon called *vital individuation*, would previously have been lost forever in death. The *inventive power* of life that amazed Gilles Clément thus becomes what Paul Valéry described as the *life of the mind (or spirit)* – which, with modernity and capitalism itself, becomes the *political economy* of spirit, founded on industrial technology that has today become essential to an *industry of traces*. The proletarianization of consumers, their de-symbolization, their dis-identification and their confinement within drive-based misery, subjects all singularities to a calculability that turns the contemporary world into a desert in which one feels, paradoxically and increasingly, that as industry innovates more and more, it somehow turns out that life is being invented less and less – a situation that takes to the extreme what Paul Valéry described in 1939 as the decline in the value of *esprit*.[3]

The decline of the state, replaced by the hegemony of strategic marketing and financialization, was imposed throughout the entire world, and in every part of society, beginning in the 1980s. Along with these changes came drive-based misery and disinvestment, ruining desire and introducing forms of disbelief, miscreance and discredit that continue to afflict every form of authority, every institution and every business, eventually leading to the insolvency that the collapse of 2008 exposed for all to see.

The current and much more recent hegemony of the industry of traces tries to take control of the drives, through automation and automatisms founded on social networks. The drives are, however, ultimately uncontrollable, and hence, to try and channel the drives in this way, using mathematical algorithms to exert an automated form of social control, will in the end do nothing but carry the drives to an extremely dangerous level, by *dis-integrating* them, turning them into what Félix Guattari and Gilles Deleuze called 'dividuals' – and I may come back to this topic latter.

SECOND LECTURE

Functions of the Mind in Automatic Society

With the advent of reticular reading and writing via globally accessible networks that use those web technologies whose implementation commenced around 1993, digital technologies have led hyper-industrial societies towards a *new stage of proletarianization*. In this new stage, the hyper-industrial age has turned into an era of systemic stupidity.

Across networks of tele-action (and *tele-objectivity*), production centres can be de-localized, huge markets can be formed and then remotely controlled, industrial capitalism and financial capitalism can be structurally separated, and electronic financial markets can be continuously interconnected, directing in real time the automatisms that are derived from the application of mathematics to the 'finance industry'. *Processes of automated decision-making* can then be functionally tied to the *drive-based automatisms* that control consumer markets – initially through the mediation of the mass media, and, today, through the industry of traces that is also known as the data economy (that is, the economy of *personal data*).

Digital automata have succeeded in bypassing the deliberative functions of the mind, and a systemic stupidity has been established between consumers and speculators, *functionally based in the drives*, and pitting each against the other – going well beyond what Mats Alvesson and André Spicer have called 'functional stupidity'.[4] In the last few years, however, and specifically after 2008, a state of *generalized stupefaction* seems to have arisen that accompanies this systemic *bêtise*, this functional stupidity.

The resulting stupor is caused by the most recent *series of technological shocks* that emerged from the digital turn of 1993, that is, with the web – and not only with the internet. The revelation of these shocks, and of their major features and consequences, has brought about a state that is almost literally that of being stunned – in particular in the face of the 'four horsemen of the Apocalypse' (Google, Apple, Facebook and Amazon), *who appear literally to be dis-integrating those industrial societies* that emerged from the *Aufklärung*.

One result has been what, at a public meeting of Ars Industrialis in Paris, we have referred to as 'net blues', suffered by those who had believed or do believe in the promises of the digital era (including my friends at Ars Industrialis and myself).

The hyper-industrial societies that have risen from the ruins of the industrial democracies constitute the third stage of completed proletarianization: in the nineteenth century, we saw the loss of *savoir-faire*, and in the twentieth the loss of *savoir-vivre*. In the twenty-first century, we are witnessing the dawn of the age of the loss of *savoirs théoriques*, of theoretical knowledge – as if the cause of our being stunned was an *absolutely unthinkable development*. With the *total automation* made possible by digital technology, theories, those most sublime fruits of idealization and identification, have been deemed obsolete – and along with them scientific method itself. So at least we are told by Chris Anderson, in 'The End of Theory: The Data Deluge Makes the Scientific Method Obsolete'.[5]

Founded on the *self-and-auto-production* of digital traces, and *dominated by automatisms* that exploit these traces, hyper-industrial societies are undergoing the proletarianization of theoretical knowledge, just as broadcasting analogue traces via television resulted in the proletarianization of *savoir-vivre*, and just as the submission of the body of the labourer to mechanical traces inscribed in machines resulted in the proletarianization of *savoir-faire*. Just like the written traces in which Socrates already saw the threat of proletarianization that any exteriorization of knowledge brings with it – the *apparent paradox* being that *the constitution of knowledge depends on the exteriorization of knowledge* – so too digital, analogue and mechanical traces are what I call tertiary retentions, and I will explain these terms later.

When Gilles Deleuze referred to what he called 'control societies', he was already heralding the arrival of the hyper-industrial age.[6] The destructive capture of attention and desire is what occurs in and through those control societies that Deleuze described in terms of the non-coercive modulation exercised by television on consumers at the end of the twentieth century. These control societies appear at the end of the consumerist epoch, and what they do is make way for the transition to the hyper-industrial epoch.

In the automated society of which Deleuze could hardly have been aware, but which he and Félix Guattari anticipated (in particular when they referred to *dividuals*), control undertakes the mechanical liquidation of discernment, which comes from the Greek *to krinon* – from *krinein*, a verb that has the same root as *krisis*, decision. Discernment, which Kant called the understanding (*Verstand*), has been automated and automatized as *analytical* power that has been delegated to algorithms, algorithms that convey formalized instructions through sensors and actuators but outside of any intuition in the Kantian sense, that is, outside of any experience (this being the situation that occupies Chris Anderson).

The proletarianization of the gestures of work amounts to the proletarianization of the conditions of the worker's *sub*-sistence. The proletarianization of sensibility, of sensory life, and the proletarianization of social relations, all of which are being replaced by conditioning, amounts to the proletarianization of the conditions of the citizen's *ek*-sistence. The proletarianization of minds or spirits, that is, of the noetic faculties enabling theorization and deliberation, is the proletarianization of the conditions of scientific *con*-sistence (including the human and social sciences).

In the hyper-industrial stage, *hyper-control* is established through a process of generalized automation. It thus represents a step beyond the control-through-modulation discovered and analysed by Deleuze: now, the noetic faculties of theorization and deliberation are being short-circuited by the *current operator of proletarianization*, which is *digital tertiary retention*, or the mnemotechnical artefact – just as analogue tertiary retention was in the twentieth century the operator of the proletarianization of *savoir-vivre*, and just as mechanical tertiary retention was in the nineteenth century the operator of the proletarianization of *savoir-faire*.

By *artificially retaining something through the material and spatial copying of a mnesic and temporal element*, tertiary retention modifies the relations between the psychic retentions of *perception* that Husserl referred to as *primary* retentions, and the psychic retentions of *memory* that he called *secondary* retentions. What is called 'reason', and more generally what is called thinking, is a form of attention, and that attention is itself an arrangement operating between what Husserl referred to as retentions (R, memories) and protentions (P, expectations), via the intermediary of technical retentions, that is, mnemotechnics, which I call *tertiary* retentions (this is not Husserl's views of course, except in 'The Origin of Geometry').

A = R3 (R/P)

Alphabetical writing, like digital writing, is a type of tertiary retention. Attentional forms, which constitute ways of thinking, are arrangements of retentions and protentions made possible by mnemotechnical forms of memorization.

Thinking, in all its forms, is a temporal fabric woven from what Husserl called *primary and secondary* retentions and protentions. A temporal flux or flow, such as for example a speech that you might listen to, as in fact you are doing at this very moment, can constitute itself as such only because it is an aggregation of what Husserl called primary retentions. In the course of this speech that I am delivering before you, and that you seem to be listening to, you retain in a 'primary' way each of the elements that are presented. 'Primary' here means that each element that presents itself in each instant aggregates itself to the element that follows it in the next instant, and is retained in it, with which it forms the 'now' of the temporal flow: hence phonemes that aggregate to form a word, words that aggregate to form a sentence, sentences that aggregate to form a paragraph and so on – so that a unity of meaning is formed. These aggregations that accumulate one upon the other form what Husserl called primary retentions.

These primary retentions are, however, selections: they are *retained* only on the basis of retentional *criteria*, criteria that are formed in the course of my prior experience. And my experience is, precisely, an accumulation of *secondary retentions*, which are former primary retentions that have subsequently become past, and which constitute the stuff of my memory.

THIRD LECTURE

Retentions, Protentions and Knowledge

Each and every one of you who are currently listening to me will be hearing in what I say something different, and this is so because what I say is a flow of primary retentions from out of which each of you make a different selection, to the degree that each of you have different memories composed of different secondary retentions, resulting in different criteria for retaining and understanding what I tell you. We can summarize and formalize this by saying that, if the relationship between retention and protention, and between primary retention and secondary retention, is conditioned by what I called last week tertiary retention, then we can say that each one of you pays *attention* to what I say, therefore, in a singular way. But what nonetheless *unites* your different ways of hearing what I say, and thus ensures the possibility of forming an *agreement* between all your various understandings of what I tell you, is a *rational attentional form*.

The latter is formed through apodictic experience (of which geometry is the canonical example) – on the basis of which my speech tries to bring about an agreement between you. According to Husserl, in 'The Origin of Geometry',[7] this is made possible by alphabetical writing, which is what, in *Technics and Time, 1*,[8] I myself call literal tertiary retention (composed of letters). Literal tertiary retention contains a specific property: its capacity for synthesizing orthothetically, which is to say that it can reproduce an oral linguistic statement with exactitude – for example, this oral linguistic statement that I am now myself producing.

The term 'orthothetic' come from two Greek words, *orthos* and *thesis*. In his text dedicated to Plato's understanding of truth as it appears in *The Republic*, Heidegger claims that Plato forgot the meaning of *alētheia* by interpreting it as *orthotēs*, that is, exactitude. I personally believe that:

- this was made possible by the specific orthothetic character of literal tertiary retention;
- this also produced the opposite, because of what I call différantial identity.

Différantial identity is what happens when, for example, rereading a book, or an article, or notes I took the week before, I interpret it differently from the first time I read it.

I believe that the specificity of the cumulative knowledge that is apodictic geometry – where the word apodictic, coming from the Greek word *apodeixis*, means that it is based on a strictly formalized condition of demonstration – is what provides the sense of the Greek experience of *alētheia* in general. And so I believe that all this comes from the experience of literal tertiary retention, insofar as it constitutes, *firstly*,

an *orthothesis*

that is, an exact transmission of the logical reasoning of a thinker, and does so word by word, which is also to say, step by step, letter by letter, logic referring here firstly to the linguistic, that is, made of the stuff of words, and insofar as this experience of literal tertiary retention also constitutes, *secondly*, and at the same time,

a *différantial identity*

that is, a recording the repetition of which always produces a difference. How a repetition of the reading of a text that has not changed is able to produce a difference is also the issue at stake in Deleuze's book, *Difference and Repetition*.[9] This production of differences amounts to a process of interpretation that, in Greece, is called *hermēneia*, a word coming from the name of a God, Hermes.

What kind of tertiary retention is involved with a Chinese character, and what type of differentiation in repetition does it make possible? For me, this is a mystery, because I am not able to read and write Chinese characters. Now, I feel sure that the issue of the origin of algebra in Chinese mathematics arises from this type of ideographic tertiary retention. This is what was said by Nicolas Fréret, an eighteenth-century French sinologist:

> Chinese characters are immediate signs of the ideas which they express. One would think that the system of writing was invented by mutes, ignorant of the use of speech. We may compare the characters of which it is composed to the algebraic signs which express relations in our mathematical books. Let a geometrical demonstration, expressed in algebraic characters, be presented to ten mathematicians of different countries, they will all understand it alike, and yet they will not understand the words by which those ideas are expressed in speech. The same thing takes place in China; the

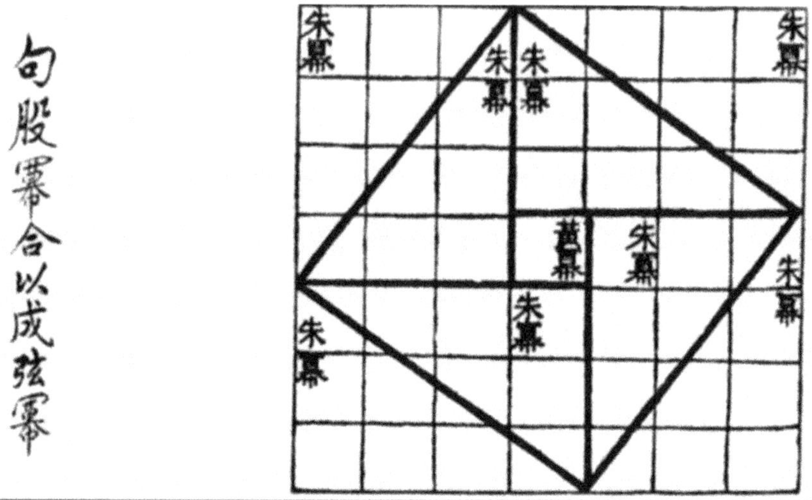

Figure 1, Figure of the hypotenuse from which we can deduce
c2 = 4(ab)/2 + (b – a)2 or also, (a + b)2 – 4(ab)/2 = c2

> writing is not only common to all the inhabitants of that great country, who speak dialects different from each other, but also to the Japanese, the Tonquinese, and the Cochinchinese, whose languages are entirely distinct from the Chinese.[10]

So, we could say that Greek alphabetical letters, which are literal tertiary retentions, made possible the apodictic development of Greek geometry, whereas Chinese ideographic characters made possible the algebraic development of mathematics.

Here I must make clear that there is a debate in the West concerning Chinese geometry, which begins with Mo Jing. This debate turns around the status that we can and must give to the geometrical object in Figure 1 coming from Chinese geometry, and if the figural explanation of the geometrical reasoning, as we can see it in Figure 2, can be considered as a demonstration, and, more precisely, as an apodictic demonstration. This is, for example, the issue at stake here:

> The Pythagorean theorem is generally held to be one of the most important results in the early history of mathematics. From it came important discoveries in theoretical geometry as well as practical mensuration. We saw in chapter 4 how the Mesopotamians' understanding of geometry, based on similar triangles and circles, was enhanced by the discovery of the Pythagorean result, and how their algorithmic procedure for extracting square roots of 'irregular' (irrational) numbers was also based on this result. In China too, a study of the

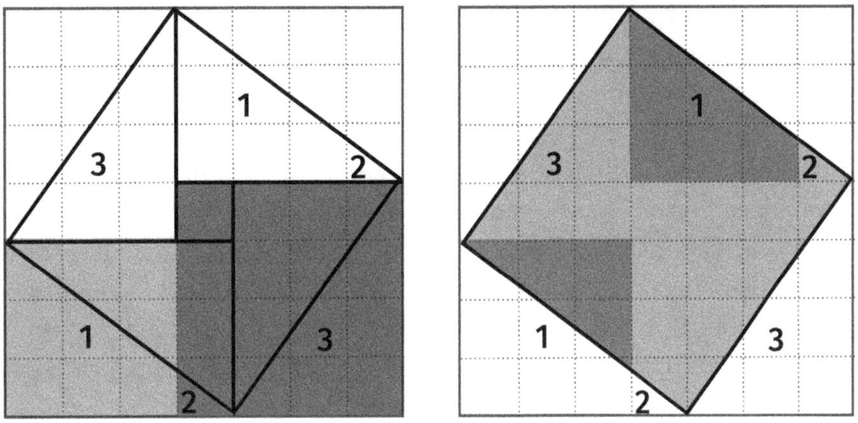

Figure 2a, The pieces form two squares whose dimensions are those of the sides of the right-angled triangle.

Figure 2b, The pieces outside the square of the hypotenuse have come to be placed inside.

> properties of the right-angled triangle had a considerable impact on mathematics.
>
> The earliest extant Chinese text on astronomy and mathematics, the *Zhou Bi*, is notable for a diagrammatic demonstration of the Pythagorean (or *gou gu*) theorem.[11]

This passage discusses diagrammatic demonstration, and refers to Joseph Needham, who claimed that in Chinese geometry, there was no demonstration properly speaking.

Anyway, let's continue our analysis of tertiary retention, and why this stuff is so important to the goals of this seminar.

Literal (that is, lettered) *tertiary retention*, which emerged around eight hundred B.C. in the Mediterranean Basin, made possible an attentional form through which a *rational and logical – in the Greek sense – transindividuation process* is produced. To clarify this point, I must introduce concepts that derive from Gilbert Simondon, who showed in *L'individuation à la lumière des notions de forme et d'information* that to individuate *psychically is always to contribute to a collective individuation*, and that this psycho-social individuation generates the *transindividual*, that is, shared *meanings*, which are, equally, collective secondary retentions, and which always themselves presuppose *supports*, or carriers, that enable them to be transmitted through time. These supports or carriers are technical objects in general, and hypomnesic technics in particular – hypomnesic tertiary retentions.

Hypomnesic technologies make possible the transmission of mental contents, beginning with rupestral drawings in the caves of the Upper Palaeolithic, hypomnesic technologies such as writing, whether ideographic or alphabetical, all of which amount to *spatial projections* of events that are firstly psychic, and *as such temporal*. More generally, all technical supports, objects and practices are the results of a process of *technical individuation*. This is why psychic and collective individuation is always *also* a technical individuation.

Technical individuation is concretized as a technical system, in the meaning given to this latter expression by Bertrand Gille in *The History of Techniques*, where a technical system is, then, also the concretisation of exosomatization. This means that noetic psychic individuation, that is, thinking, is *conditioned* by technical individuation – but not determined by it: the technical artefact always opens up a field of indefinite possibilities. This field of possibilities ranges from the worst to the best, because the technical artefact – for example, writing – is a *pharmakon*: a poison that can become a remedy, or vice versa.

Over time, tertiary retention evolves, for example, rupestral or low relief tertiary retentions become written tertiary retentions, and this leads to modifications of the *play* between primary retentions and secondary retentions, resulting in *processes of transindividuation* that are each time specific, that is, specific epochs of what Simondon called the *transindividual*. In the course of such an evolution, analogue technologies such as photography, or phonography, and then cinematography and television, are analogue orthothetic recordings, whereas computers and digital networks are digital orthothetic tertiary retentions.

Over the course of processes of transindividuation, founded on successive epochs of tertiary retention, shared meanings are formed by psychic individuals who thereby constitute collective individuals, and what we call 'societies'. The meanings formed during transindividuation processes, and shared by psychic individuals within collective individuals of all kinds, constitute the transindividual as the set of collective secondary retentions through which collective protentions are formed – that is, the *expectations* that typify that epoch.

If, according to the Chris Anderson article previously referred to, so-called 'big data' heralds the 'end of theory' – big data technology designating what is also called 'high-performance computing', 'intensive computing' or 'supercomputing', carried out on massive amounts of data, whereby the treatment of data in the form of digital tertiary retentions occurs *in real time* (at two thirds of the speed of light) and on a *global scale* and at the level of billions of gigabytes of data, operating through data-capture systems that are located everywhere around the planet and in almost every relational system that constitutes a society – it is because digital tertiary retention and the algorithms that allow it to be both produced and exploited thereby also make it possible for *reason as a synthetic faculty to be short-circuited* thanks to the extremely high speeds at which this automated analytical faculty of the *understanding* is capable of operating.

Because as we already saw last week, in the *Critique of Pure Reason*, Kant explains how and why the understanding, that is, *Verstand*, and reason, that is, *Vernunft*, are two different and irreducible dimensions of knowledge, understanding being analytic, and reason synthetic.

Now, let us examine how these questions appear if we go back to the first and main claim made by Engels and Marx, which, in my view, concerns the exosomatic situation of human beings. Hegel saw and showed that the development of mind and spirit, of what in German is called *Geist*, is a process of exteriorization of the mind, externalized in what he called 'objective spirit', based on objective memory – which I myself call tertiary retention. But for Hegel, this 'moment' of externalization was only a moment, which could be overcome by the dialectic as the moment of *Aufhebung*, which Hegel understood as the moment of re-interiorization of the exteriority, dissolving this exteriority into what Hegel called 'absolute spirit'. All of this was for Hegel the result of what he presented as a speculative dialectic based on what he called the speculative proposition.

For Engels and Marx, as they tell us in *The German Ideology*, Hegel's philosophy belongs to what they call German idealism, which inherits the 'ideological' concepts of Platonic and more generally Greek idealism, based on the theory of ideas proposed by Plato in *Republic*. The *materialist* version of the Hegelian speculative dialectic then understands exteriorization as *materialization*, and the latter as the *technical self-production* of humanity by its 'means of production', for the first time raising in an explicit way the question of *proletarianization*, that is, the question of the *destruction of knowledge that results from its exteriorization*, the latter being nevertheless the *fundamental condition of the constitution of all knowledge*.

In *The Communist Manifesto*, indeed, the proletarianization of manual workers is described as a loss of their knowledge, where the latter passes into the means of production that are machines. And Engels and Marx state that this process of proletarianization will progressively reach into all the layers of the population. Showing that the externalization of knowing is a proletarianization, a loss of knowledge, dialectical materialism rediscovers the initial question of the *pharmakon*, through which Socrates showed that writing, as an externalization of memory, can be also a loss of memory, even if the externalization is the condition of the constitution of knowledge and of the memory in which it consists as the transmission across generations of their experience as accumulated knowledge. As perhaps you can anticipate, we will rediscover these questions in the *Grundrisse*.

So: in this interpretation, the question of proletarianization would amount to a new version of the Socratic question of the *pharmakon*. And yet, *this materialism produced no pharmacology*: it continued to understand technics as a means, through which 'toxic' processes (such as proletarianization, or its consequence, pauperization) are only reflections of the class struggle as relations of production, where these processes would be able to be overcome, meaning that the toxicity of the *pharmakon* could be eliminated. What I believe, however, is that this can *never* be eliminated. But we can fight against it - and this combat is a struggle of knowledge. But we are not yet in a position to truly see this question, to which we will return later.

In the *Grundrisse*, the process of exteriorization, as we shall see, is described in Marx's work as *grammatization*, that is: as a process of analytical formalization, discretization, reproduction and automation, just as is the case with machine tool in general, and as these will be systematically developed by Taylorism, particularly with the assembly line. But in the *Grundrisse*, this *grammatization* is not thought *as such*.

Grammatization is a concept that comes from Sylvain Auroux, a French philosopher who is also a specialist of the history of sciences of language, and who used this word to describe how alphabetical writing appeared. But I myself use this concept of grammatization to describe how all human movement and behaviour can be analysed, discretized and reproduced – hence not only oral language. Gestures, for example, are discretized and reproduced in a tool machine, while analogue technologies such as photography, phonography and so on can reproduce perception, and digital technologies can reproduce the process of analytical understanding, for example, with big data or like AlphaGo. I will come back to this, of course.

The process of grammatization is the process of exosomatization and the artificial reproduction of human noetic experience itself, that is, of noetic experience, where noetic means mental, which becomes reproducible and then transmissible. Or in other words, which constitutes forms of knowledge based on the accumulation of tertiary retentions. Such an accumulation is based on recordings, which are the result of grammatization and which amount, indeed, to tertiary retentions.

But even though the *Grundrisse* describes the *materialization of knowledge* in the form of what I call tertiary retention, *the general question of knowledge in industrial society is not truly posed by dialectical materialism*: technics is not thematized as a *factor in knowledge as well as non-knowledge*, nor is there an *organology* of knowledge, or an *economy* of knowledge in the sense of a libidinal economy – that is, in the sense of the sublimation of desire.

Here, it is important to stress that we must connect Marx's philosophy to Freud's psychoanalytic account of libidinal economy – if we can agree that knowledge, insofar as it is constituted by desire, as was claimed by Socrates and Diotima in *Symposium*, is always the result of a connection between the libidinal economy and the economy of exosomatization that is the production of goods in general. And this connection must be formalized in the framework of the bio-economics that Nicholas Georgescu-Roegen tries to conceive by utilizing the concepts of entropy and exosomatization.

FOURTH LECTURE

Technological *Epokhē* the Anthropocene and the Neganthropocene

Proletarianization in and by digital tertiary retention is a *fact*. Is it inevitable? Is it unavoidable? In his article on the 'end of theory' (which is what I myself call generalized proletarianization), Chris Anderson claims that the destruction of attention is fatal. What Nicholas Carr suggests in *The Shallows* is more or less the same – although he at least puts it in less celebratory terms. I myself hold a contrary view: the *fact of proletarianization* is *caused* by the digital, which, like *every* new form of tertiary retention, constitutes a new age of the *pharmakon*. It is inevitable that this *pharmakon* will have toxic effects if new therapies, new therapeutics, are not prescribed.

Such prescriptions are the responsibility of the scientific world, the artistic world, the legal world, the world of the life of the spirit in general, and the world of citizens – and, in the first place, of those who claim to represent them. Much courage is required: it is a struggle that must face up against countless interests, including those who partly suffer from this toxicity and partly feed off it. It is this period of suffering, which is akin to the stage of the chrysalis in the allegory of metamorphosis, that we are now living everywhere in the world under the impact of digital tertiary retention.

All new tertiary retention is and will remain a poisonous *pharmakon* if it does not create *new transindividual arrangements* between psychic and collective primary retentions and secondary retentions, and therefore between retentions and protentions (expectations, through which objects of attention appear, and as such sources of desire) – which constitute new attentional forms, new circuits of transindividuation, new meanings and new capabilities of bringing about the horizons of meaning that are what I call consistences.[12] I say new transindividual arrangements because the new *pharmakon* to which a new tertiary retention amounts appears in a society where a *previous pharmakon* (for example, printed alphabetical writing) had produced circuits of transindividuation and forms of attention based in previous forms of tertiary retention.

Instead of creating *new transindividual arrangements* between psychic and collective primary retentions and secondary retentions, the new *pharmakon* that is digital tertiary retention can on the contrary *substitute itself* for psychic and collective retentions insofar as the latter can produce significance and meaning *only* insofar as they are *individuated by all and shared* on the basis of psychic individuation processes, through processes of social transindividuation that create relationships of solidarity, on which can be built, durably, and intergenerationally, *social systems*.

Last Monday, I told you that Bertrand Gille developed the concept of technical system for thinking the evolution of technics and technology. I would now like to add that he showed how any technical system is always adjusting itself in relation to what he called social systems, and we can represent this adjustment process like this:

ST/SS

Now, Bertrand Gilles also shows that:

1. Over the course of the history of technics, that is, of technical systems, and of the societies that, adjusted to theses technical systems, are constituted by social systems, there are periods in which the adjusted technical system enters into a transformation, and changes into a new technical system.
2. During this period of change, there occurs a disadjustment, which is the result of a change that unfolds in social systems and that begins as forms of disturbance, of trouble: conflicts and often revolutions or civil wars, or religious wars.
3. Since the end of the eighteenth century, first in Europe, and then in the United States, and today throughout the world, the industrial technical system, based on technology and not only on technics, that is, based on scientific knowledge and mathematical formalisms and not only on empirical experience, this industrial technical system is changing in an ever-faster way, constantly producing situations of disadjustment between the technical system and the social systems.

A technical system is always based on what Bertrand Gille calls a dominant technology – such as, at the beginning of the industrial revolution, the steam machine. Now, such a dominant technology is itself the result of a form of knowledge based on hypomnesic tertiary retention, which supports and carries it, and which is, in the case of the knowledge at the origin of the industrial revolution, printed alphabetical writing, itself having made possible, after the Renaissance, the so-called Republic of Letters.

Social systems, which structure collective individuals, are themselves formed on the basis of circuits of transindividuation, themselves founded on forms of knowledge and discipline. These forms of knowledge and discipline are what I call the therapeutics with which it is possible to take care of the new *pharmakon*, and, with such a therapeutic use of the *pharmakon*, to *take care of the society*, and of the people who constitute such a society composed of psychic individuals and collective individuals.

▪ ▪ ▪

What I described last Monday as a process of generalized proletarianization is the result of the disadjustment produced by digital tertiary retention insofar as it provokes what has been referred to as disruption. Disruption is the situation in which the speed of the evolution of technology is strategically exploited with the aim of creating legal and theoretical vacuums – which is to say, a structural lack of knowledge. Digital tertiary retention thus creates a very specific state of proletarianization. Now, each type of hypomnesic *pharmakon* provokes such short-circuits, such a bypass of knowledge.

It is always possible for a *pharmakon* to short-circuit and bypass the circuits of transindividuation of which it is nevertheless the condition. It is always possible to do so, even though it is this *pharmakon* that itself makes it possible for psychic individuals, through their psychic retentions, to ex-press themselves, to form collective individuals founded on these traces and these facilitations, that is, on the secondary retentions and collective protentions emerging from this pharmacology. And this is because exosomatization is the condition of noesis, of thought, of knowledge of every kind – *savoir vivre*, how to live (life-knowledge), *savoir faire*, how to do or make (work-knowledge), and how to think (conceptual or spiritual knowledge).

Nevertheless, and generally speaking, a new *pharmakon* may well start out by short-circuiting the psychosocial process. But the short-circuiting of psychic and collective individuation that is being caused today by automatized transindividuation processes, based on automation in real time and occurring on an immense scale, requires detailed analyses capable of taking account of the *remarkable novelty* of the digital *pharmakon*. These analyses belong to what I, along with the Institute de recherche et d'innovation, call 'digital studies' – which means not just digital humanities but a new paradigm for every kind of knowledge, constituting a new *epistēmē* in the sense of Michel Foucault, requiring a new epistemology in the sense of Gaston Bachelard, and itself belonging to what in the following sessions of this seminar I will call general organology.

To achieve socialization, that is, a process of collective individuation, every new *pharmakon* – in this instance a new form of tertiary retention – always requires the formation of *new knowledge*, which always means new therapies or therapeutics for this new *pharmakon*, through which are constituted new ways of doing things and reasons to do things, to live and to think, that is, to project consistences, which constitute at the same time new forms of existence, and, ultimately, new conditions of subsistence. This new knowledge is the result of what I call the second moment of an epokhal redoubling – that is, the *second moment* of the technological shock that is always provoked whenever a new form of tertiary retention appears. Because of this second moment, I describe the accomplishing of technological change as a doubly epokhal redoubling.

In making this claim, I affirm that technological change is always provoking:

- an *epokhē* in the philosophical sense, that is, an interruption of belief and knowledge, a break in this knowledge that had hitherto constituted the previous era, which is also what, in historical terms, we call an 'epoch', a suspension of behavioural programs constituting the culture of such an epoch; and
- the reconstitution of new knowledge, new forms of behaviour, new culture, new circuits of transindividuation – and then new social systems, themselves constituting a new society.

The problem, today, in the period of what we call disruption, is that it seems impossible to reconstitute any knowledge, and that forms of behaviour are now produced, not by social systems, cultures and knowledge, but by marketing that exploits 'big data' and digital tertiary retentions insofar as these are calculable, computable and as such constitute the worldwide data economy.

Chris Anderson claims that the contemporary fact of proletarianization is insurmountable. I disagree. Anderson claims that, in relation to what I have just described as a doubly epokhal redoubling comprised of two moments, the first consisting of the technological shock provoked by the new *pharmakon* and the second consisting of the production of new knowledge, there is *no longer any way* to bring about this *second moment*.

But what lies behind his taking of this position is the fact that Chris Anderson himself happens to be a businessman who defends an ultraliberal and ultra-libertarian perspective. He remains faithful to the ultra-liberalism implemented in all industrial democracies after the conservative revolution that occurred in the early 1980s, a 'revolution' that short-circuited processes of transindividuation via the analogue mass media, creating what Deleuze described as control societies.

For Chris Anderson, as for us, and as for the global economy, the problem is that the development, or rather the becoming, that leads to this stage of proletarianization is inherently entropic: it *depletes* the resources that it exploits and consumes – resources that, in this case, are psychic individuals and collective individuals. This stage of proletarianization leads, in the strict sense of the term, to the dis-integration of these psychic individuals and collective individuals.

In automatic society, those digital networks that are referred to as 'social' networks channel such expressions by submitting them to mandatory protocols to which psychic individuals bend because they are drawn to do so by the so-called *network effect*, which, with the addition of social networking, becomes an *automated herd effect*, that is, a highly mimetic situation – and one that constitutes a new form of *artificial crowd* in the sense given to this phrase by Freud.

Ten years ago, I compared TV or radio programs and channels to the constitution of artificial and conventional crowds such as they are analysed by Freud. The constitution of crowds, and the conditions under which they can take shape, are the subjects of analyses by Gustave Le Bon, on which Freud commented at length:

> The most striking peculiarity presented by a psychological crowd (in German: *Masse*) is the following. Whoever be the individuals that compose it, however like or unlike be their mode of life, their occupations, their character, or their intelligence, the fact that they have been transformed into a crowd puts them in possession of a sort of collective mind which makes them feel, think, and act in a manner quite different from that in which each individual of them would feel, think, and act were he in a state of isolation. There are certain ideas and feelings which do not come into being, or do not transform themselves into acts except in the case of individuals forming a crowd. The psychological crowd is a provisional being formed of heterogeneous elements, which for a moment are combined, exactly as the cells which constitute a living body form by their reunion a new being which displays characteristics very different from those possessed by each of the cells singly.[13]

On the basis of Le Bon's analysis, Freud showed that there are also 'artificial' crowds, which he analyses through the examples of the Church and the Army.

The program industries, too, however, also form, every single day, and specifically through the mass broadcast of programs, such 'artificial crowds'. The latter become, as masses (and Freud refers precisely to *Massenpsychologie* – the psychology of masses), the permanent, everyday mode of being of the industrial democracies, which are at the same time what I call, in *La télécratie contre la démocratie*, industrial tele-cracies. Generated by digital tertiary retention, net-connected artificial crowds constitute an economy of 'crowdsourcing' that must be understood in manifold ways –of which the so-called 'cognitariat' would be one dimension. 'Big data' is one very large component of those technologies that exploit the potential of crowdsourcing in its various forms, of which social engineering is a major element.

Through the network effect, through artificial crowds that the network effect allows to be created (such as the billions of psychic individuals who are now on Facebook), and through crowdsourcing that allows these crowds to be exploited, including through the use of 'big data', it is possible:

- to stimulate the production and self-and-auto-capture by individuals of those tertiary retentions we call 'personal data', which spatialize their psychosocial temporalities;
- to intervene, by circulating this personal data at the speed of light, in the processes of transindividuation that are woven through circuits that are formed automatically and *performatively*;
- through these circuits, and through the collective secondary retentions that they form automatically, and no longer transindividually, to intervene in return, and almost immediately, on psychic secondary retentions, which is also to say, on protentions, expectations and ultimately personal behaviour: it becomes possible to *remotely control, one by one,* each of the members of a network – this is so-called 'personalization'.

The internet is a *pharmakon* that can thus become a technics of hypercontrol and social dis-integration. Without a new politics of individuation, that is, without a formation of attention geared towards the specific tertiary retentions that make possible the new technical milieu (and every associated milieu, beginning with language), it will inevitably give rise to dissociation.

The hyper-industrial situation takes what Deleuze called control societies, founded on modulation by the mass media, to a stage of hyper-control generated by self-produced personal data, self-collected and self-published by people themselves – whether knowingly or otherwise – and exploited by applying high-performance computing to these massive data sets. This *automatized modulation* establishes what Thomas Berns and Antoinette Rouvroy have called algorithmic governmentality.[14]

The digital allows all technological automatisms to be unified (mechanical, electromechanical, photo-electrical, electronic and so on), by implanting the producer into the consumer, through the production of all manner of sensors, actuators and related software. But the truly unprecedented aspect of digital unification is that it allows articulations *between* all these automatisms: technological, social, psychic and biological – and this is the main point of neuromarketing and neuroeconomics. This integration, however, leads inevitably to total automatization, but it is not just public authority, social and educational systems, intergenerational relations and psychic structures that thereby find themselves disintegrated: for mass markets to be formed, and for all the *commodities* secreted by the consumerist system to be absorbed, wages needed to be distributed so as to supply purchasing power, but it is this very economic system that has disintegrated and that is becoming *functionally insolvent*.

The pharmacological character of the digital age has become more or less clear to those who belong to it, resulting in what I am calling 'net blues' – particularly after Edward Snowden's revelations, and also with the increase of social networking based on Facebook's strategy, which consists in exploiting the network effect in order to short-circuit the web: the state of fact constituted by this new age of tertiary retention has failed to provide a new state of law. *On the contrary*, it has liquidated the rule of law as produced by the retentional systems of the bygone epoch. Property law, for example, was directly challenged by activists through their practices in relation to free software, and through reflecting on the 'commons' – including some young artists who attempted to devise a new economic and political framework for their thinking. But this was never concretized by a new state of law.

These questions must, however, be seen as elements of an *epistemic* and *epistemological* transition from fact to law, and by canonical reference to what I described last Monday as an apodictic experience – that is, the way by which Greek citizenship succeeded in projecting law beyond fact. The passage from fact to law is firstly a matter of discovering *in facts* the *necessity* of interpreting *them*, that is, of projecting beyond *the facts* themselves, but also *on the basis of facts* that are not themselves self-sufficient – onto another plane towards which they beckon: that of a consistence through which and in which we must 'believe' (and here I take up terms used by Deleuze in *Cinema 2: The Time-Image*[15]).

This other plane is that of negentropy. Negentropy is an object of belief because it is the improbable possibility of a bifurcation – improbable because not calculable. On the contrary, systems of computation are structurally entropic, where this means: toxic. So, a *pharmakon,* as a product of exosomatization, always opens up two opposite possibilities: entropic possibilities, which are toxic possibilities, and negentropic possibilities, which are capable of inscribing a bifurcation in becoming, such a bifurcation transforming becoming [*devenir*] into future [*avenir*] – and I will try to show you later how it is possible and necessary to refer to Heidegger in order to think this difference between future and becoming, but also why we must overcome Heidegger and the ontological difference on which this notion of future is based, and to introduce the questions of exosomatization and negentropy into his existential analytic.

We will also see that from such a standpoint, it is possible and necessary to reinterpret what Heidegger called *Gestell, Bestand* and *Ereignis.*

If we are now living in the Anthropocene, this state of fact is not sustainable: we must pass to a state of law in which negentropy becomes the criterion of every type of value, the value of values, and this is why we must enter into the Neganthropocene. The context of this task of thinking conceived as a therapeutics is one in which automatisms of all kinds are being technologically integrated by digital automatisms. The unique and very specific aspect of this situation is the way that digital tertiary retention succeeds in totally rearranging assemblages or montages of psychic and collective retentions and protentions. The challenge is to invert this situation towards a new idea of dis-automatization that would arise from out of today's dis-integrating automatization. And this is the issue at stake in my reading of the *Grundrisse* – but we will see that later.

FIFTH LECTURE

Organology, Economy and Ecology

Today, we will begin to address questions coming from Heidegger, in order to understand better the questions that we previously asked with Marx. And this will permit us to take into account the urgent question of ecology in the age of absolutely computational capitalism.[16]

In 'A Thousand Ecologies: The Process of Cybernetization and General Ecology',[17] Erich Hörl takes up a proposition wherein the French poet Michel Deguy, who is also a philosopher, makes ecology the 'task of thinking'. And he points out that a phrase such as the 'task of thinking' owes something to Martin Heidegger. On the basis of this remark, he explains why Heidegger could not himself assume such an ('ecological') task *in our epoch*, that is, inasmuch as it posits that *the ecological dimension of humanity is what, above all, today reveals its primordially artificial constitution* – and its 'artifacticity'.[18]

Furthermore, Erich Hörl himself refers to Gilbert Simondon to show that, in addition to the fertility of the terms and analyses proposed by this thinker of relation, ecology, insofar as it is above all a relational form of thinking, must be conceived starting from cybernetics and from Simondon's critique thereof (in the Kantian sense of 'critique'), and by taking up this program on new bases (other than those of Norbert Wiener).

This is what leads Hörl to conceive of a general ecology capable of assuming the task of thinking on the basis of a techno-logical perspective in which cybernetics, which was for Heidegger, too, the science characteristic of 'modern technology',[19] constitutes the new conceptual framework that opens the way for a new 'encyclopedism' in Simondon's sense – that is, forming the new horizon of the transindividual (which in Simondon constitutes meaning) insofar as it bears the promise of a reconciliation between 'culture' and technics.

I have myself argued for about thirteen years that cybernetics must be understood as the most recent stage of a process of grammatization – a question I addressed in the previous session of this seminar – that can be thought only through the perspective of what I call a 'general organology', which I believe to be a more apt way of approaching these questions than through what, in *L'individuation à la lumière des notions de forme et d'information*, Simondon himself called a 'mechanology' (although he did occasionally use the term 'organology').[20]

General organology, which as we saw last week uses Bertrand Gille's concepts of technical system and social systems, is a method of thinking, at one and the same time, technical, social and psychic becoming, where technical becoming must be thought via the concept of the technical system, as it adjusts and is adjusted to social systems, themselves constituted by psychic apparatuses, that is, by psychic individuals. We saw that a technical system like the one based on network engineering can also short-circuit social systems and then psychic individuals.

We also saw last week that there is no human society that is not constituted by a technical system. A technical system is traversed by evolutionary tendencies that, when they concretely express themselves, induce a change in the technical system. Such a change necessitates adjustments with the other systems constituting society – those systems that Bertrand Gille called social systems, in a sense that should be specified in confrontation with Niklas Luhmann.

These adjustments amount to a suspension and a re-elaboration of the socio-ethnic programs or socio-political programs that form the unity of the social body. This re-elaboration, which in the previous sessions I called the doubly epokhal redoubling, is a selection from among possibilities, effected across what I call retentional systems, themselves constituted by mnemo-techniques or mnemo-technologies that I call hypomnesic tertiary retentions, the becoming of which is tied to that of the technical system, and the appropriation of which permits selection criteria to be elaborated in a way that constitutes a metastable motif and motive, that is, a characteristic stage of psychic and collective individuation.

Here, I must reintroduce the theme of exosomatization, which is the core of Georgescu-Roegen's conception of economy. Across several papers and lectures, Georgescu-Roegen showed that the question opened by the exosomatic form of life that is human life is that of the selection criteria operating in the exosomatic becoming of the artificial organogenesis to which human evolution amounts. The selection involved in this case is artificial, and here we should revisit the definition of ideology given by Engels and Marx, as well as the definition of class struggle from such a standpoint.

I claim that such a selection is overdetermined by the hypomnesic tertiary retentions that are the fruits of the process of grammatization wherein all the fluxes or flows [*flux*] through which symbolic and existential acts are linked can be discretized, formalized and reproduced. The most well-known of these processes is written language. And digital tertiary retention is the most recent of these processes.

General organology defines the rules for analysing, thinking and prescribing human facts at three parallel but indissociable levels of the psychosomatic, which is the endosomatic level, the artifactual, which is the exosomatic level, and the social, which is the organizational level. It is an analysis of the relations between organic organs, technical organs and social organizations.

Social organizations are social systems that define and prescribe the therapies and therapeutics of the *pharmaka* that compose the technical system. Such therapies and therapeutics are forms of knowledge, criteria of artificial selections between the possibilities of evolution opened up by the most recent stage of exosomatization, that is, by the most recent stage of individuation of the technical system, insofar as it is also a doubly epokhal redoubling.

The prescription of such criteria is called politics. Marx showed that such a politics is also and firstly a political economy, in which a conflict is always at work, and which today is the political economy of capitalism – which is based on a process of grammatization. Marx described this grammatization in the *Grundrisse* as an exteriorization of knowledge into automatons.

> In machinery, objectified labour materially confronts living labour as a ruling power and as an active subsumption of the latter under itself, not only by appropriating it, but in the real production process itself; the relation of capital as value which appropriates value-creating activity is, in fixed capital existing as machinery, posited at the same time as the relation of the use value of capital to the use value of labour capacity; further, the value objectified in machinery appears as a presupposition against which the value-creating power of the individual labour capacity is an infinitesimal, vanishing magnitude; the production in enormous mass quantities which is posited with machinery destroys every connection of the product with the direct need of the producer, and hence with direct use value; it is already posited in the form of the product's production and in the relations in which it is produced that it is produced only as a conveyor of value, and its use value only as condition to that end. In machinery, objectified labour itself appears not only in the form of product or of the product employed as means of labour, but in the form of the force of production itself. The development of the means of labour into machinery is not an accidental moment of capital, but is rather the historical reshaping of the traditional, inherited means of labour into a form adequate to capital.[21]

Here, one can see why knowledge cannot be thought today if such a thought is not capable of understanding what a tertiary retention is, which is also called, here, fixed capital:

> The accumulation of knowledge and of skill, of the general productive forces of the social brain, is thus absorbed into capital, as opposed to labour, and hence appears as an attribute of capital, and more specifically of *fixed capital,* in so far as it enters into the production process as a means of production proper. *Machinery* appears, then, as the most adequate form of *fixed capital,* and fixed capital, in so far as capital's relations with itself are concerned, appears as *the most adequate form of capital* as such. In another respect, however, in so far as fixed capital is condemned to an existence within the confines of a specific use value, it does not correspond to the concept of capital, which, as value, is indifferent to every specific form of use value, and can adopt or shed any of them as equivalent incarnations. In this respect, as regard's capital's external relations, it is *circulating capital* which appears as the adequate form of capital, and not fixed capital.
>
> Further, in so far as machinery develops with the accumulation of society's science, of productive force generally, general social labour presents itself not in labour but in capital. The productive force of society is measured in *fixed capital,* exists there in its objective form; and, inversely, the productive force of capital grows with this general progress, which capital appropriates free of charge.[22]

Nevertheless, we will soon see that Marx himself forgets this question, which is absent from Capital, when he writes about the difference between the bee and the architect. We will return to these questions.

As it is always possible for the arrangements between the psychosomatic and artefactual organs to become toxic and destructive for the organic organs, general organology is a pharmacology. Now, today, we must project these perspectives into a broader, more encompassing, more clearly urgent and 'relevant' (as one says in English) consideration of what, for the last sixteen years, since Paul Crutzen proposed it, has been referred to as the Anthropocene, which I would like to consider from the point of view of what I provisionally call, with regard to Alfred North Whitehead, a 'speculative cosmology'.

The speculativity of such a cosmology, which would also be performative, leads to the theoretical and practical prospect and program of a passage from the Anthropocene to what I propose naming the Neganthropocene – all these issues being placed in the context of the cosmological stakes of thermodynamics, with the notion of entropy that is its second law, and of the analysis of life *and technics* as negentropic inversions and bifurcations that nevertheless do not oppose entropy but divert it, *by deferring it*, in a process resembling what Derrida called 'différance', with an 'a'.

This diversion, which is also a postponement, is, in the case of technics (that is, organology), a pharmacology, and it constitutes a *future*, an *avenir*, within the irreversible law of entropic becoming, *devenir* – a becoming that, insofar as it is inherently entropic, then becomes the law of what had hitherto and without major objection been referred to as 'being': that is, until 1924, the year of the discovery by Edwin Hubble of the expansion of the universe, opening the era of what Ilya Prigogine calls the evolutionary perspective in physics.

SIXTH LECTURE

Thermodynamics, *Gestell* and Neganthropology

What does the adjective 'general' mean in the expressions *general ecology* used by Erich Hörl and *general organology* as I try to think it? Is it the same as what Georges Bataille was referring to in his thought of general economy in *The Accursed Share*?[23] Does this 'generality' inevitably lead us back to a *metaphysica generalis* – or to a *metaphysica speculativa*? That is, does it lead us back to *idealism*?

These questions must be explored in dialogue with Whitehead and Simondon, that is, with, respectively, *concrescence* as that process which is the subject of Whitehead's *Process and Reality,* and the process of *concretization,*[24] which is one of the main concepts of Simondon's *On the Mode of Existence of Technical Objects*[25] – by raising the question of the generality of the point of view of process, and as passage from abstraction to concretion, or to concrescence, *the abstract and the concrete* being conceived here, therefore, from a fundamentally and primordially processual point of view.[26]

In addition, these questions lead us back to that *cosmology* which passes through Simondon and Whitehead – beyond the rational cosmology of Kant, who could not, precisely, take into account the *organological* question (any more than could philosophy in general, with the exception of Marx). The ideas of a rational cosmology are in Kant those of reason (see 'The Transcendental Dialectic', chapter 2, 'The Antinomy of Pure Reason'), and we shall see that Whitehead sees himself in some respects from a similar perspective. Nevertheless, it is impossible to think with this apparatus alone the thermodynamic question such as it was constituted with Sadi Carnot as the *theory of the steam engine.*[27]

Kantianism, in fact, is constituted by a denial of the organological conditions of the formation of reason as well as of understanding. This does not allow for any thought of entropy such as Carnot understands it on the basis of the artefact that is the steam engine as closed thermodynamic system. Nor does it allow for consideration, therefore, of those regimes of negative entropy or negentropy that were uncovered by Erwin Schrödinger, preceded by Henri Bergson[28] and followed by Nicholas Georgescu-Roegen, who, unlike his predecessors, insisted on the issue of exo-somatic organs.

I have tried to show, in *Technics and Time, 3,* why the Kantian schematism, fruit of the transcendental imagination, did not allow Kant to think the organological (that is, tertiary retention) and its consequences for any idea of reason (including the idea of rational cosmology).[29] From the organological perspective I defend here, the schematism originally comes from technical exteriorization and the artefactualization of the world as the condition of the constitution of the world, that is, as condition of the projection in the world of concepts *constituting* the given data of intuition of this world such as it is *ordered* in the *cosmos* – and it is the consideration of the cosmos itself (and not just of the world) that hence finds itself affected: we access the cosmos as cosmos on the basis of hypomnesic tertiary retentions in all their forms, from the shaman's instruments to Herschel's telescope.

Since the time of ancient philosophy, the *kosmos*, as an arrangement [*disposition*] of *physis*, through which it lets itself be seen and thus appear (phenomenalize itself) as this very arrangement, and as an *order*,[30] this *kosmos* has been conceived in terms of spheres and cycles closed in upon themselves as a fundamental and absolute equilibrium. In Aristotle's *Metaphysics*, which localizes the sublunary world in the fixed sphere, technics, which constitutes the organological condition, is in relation to the sublunary as the region of contingency and of 'what can be otherwise than it is' (*to endekhomenon allōs ekhein*), whereas the *eide*, conceived in relation to cosmic fixities, opposes to this facticity the necessity of *to on*. This division will be maintained in Kant, and this is particularly clear in 'Theory and Practice'.

And we can see how Engels, even if he introduces a kind of dynamics into the universe, cannot understand how and why the issue at stake with entropy is the expansion of the universe as its cooling.

> Such an assumption denies indestructibility of motion; it concedes the possibility that by the successive falling into one another of the heavenly bodies all existing mechanical motion will be converted into heat and the latter radiated into space, so that in spite of all 'indestructibility of force' all motion in general would have ceased. (Incidentally it is seen here how inaccurate is the term 'indestructibility of force' instead of 'indestructibility of motion'.) Hence we arrive at the conclusion that in some way, which it will later be the task of scientific research to demonstrate, it must be possible for the heat radiated into space to be transformed into another form of motion, in which it can once more be stored up and become active. Thereby the chief difficulty in the way of the reconversion of extinct suns into incandescent vapour disappears. [...] [T]he eternally repeated succession of worlds in infinite time is only the logical complement to

> the coexistence of innumerable worlds in infinite space – a principle the necessity of which has forced itself even on the anti-theoretical Yankee brain of Draper.[31]

The advent of the thermodynamic machine, which Heidegger does not take into account, nevertheless constitutes, with the automation of machines, what Heidegger refers to as the *Ereignis* of 'modern technology' (that is, of the industrial revolution) and its *Gestell* – and this is also the advent (*Ereignis*) of what today we refer to as the Anthropocene, but not as an *Er-Eignis*, that is, a co-propriation, as the French translators of Heidegger wrongly claimed, but rather as an ex-propriation, wherein the human world appears to constitute a *fundamental disruption* of the cosmos, and of its local (planetary) equilibriums.

The thermodynamic *machine*, however, is *also* what introduces the question of an irreducible processuality of the cosmos itself, of the irreversibility of becoming, and, if not the instability, then at least the processuality in which this becoming consists, and it introduces all this at the heart of physics itself. This question seems, however, to have remained hidden in Heidegger due to his fixation on cybernetics.

The thermodynamic machine – which in *physics* raises the specific and new problem of the dissipation of energy and, more generally, of the irreversibility of the 'arrow of time' oriented towards disorder, that is, the irreversible increase of entropy – is also an industrial technical object that, arranged with the first automatisms and establishing *proletarianization* (that is, loss of knowledge) as the *fundamental principle of productivity*, fundamentally disrupts *social* organizations, and at the same time radically alters 'the understanding that Dasein has of its being'.

If proletarianization radically disrupts social organization, the thermodynamic machine also transforms the scientific point of view. Consisting essentially in a *combustion*, this technical object – an element of which, the flyball governor, will prove critical for conceiving cybernetics – introduced, on both the physical plane and the ecological plane, *the question of human fire and of its pharmacology*, which is thereby inscribed at the heart of the thought of the cosmos *as cosmos* (both from the perspective of physics and from that of anthropological ecology), the play between them being both cosmic and mundane: this is what the Promethean myth of fire means in Greek tragedy.

The notion of the Anthropocene can appear as such only from the moment when the question of the cosmos reveals itself to be that of combustion, accomplishing the transformation of cosmology into an astrophysics of combustion, and as emerging from the thermodynamic question opened and posed by the steam engine – that is, by the techno-logical conquest of fire. Only within this perspective can there occur the kenosis of the 'death of God'.

As a problem of physics, the techno-logical conquest of fire (which is the *Ereignis* of *Gestell* on the basis of which proletarianization arises as *Bestand*) placed *anthropogenesis at the heart of concrescence*, that is, organological organogenesis (what Georgescu-Roegen therefore calls the exosomatic), and as *the local technicization of the cosmos* – local and therefore *relative*. But this leads to a *complete rethinking* of the cosmos from an astrophysical perspective, *starting from this position and from this local opening of the question of fire*, and as a *pharmakon* of which we must take care (which is, in Greek mythology, the role of the goddess Hestia), and such that the question of the *energy* it harbours constitutes the *matrix of the thought of life as the play of entropy and negentropy.*[32]

The cosmos certainly becomes the universe well before this, with Nicolas of Cusa and Giordano Bruno. But it is only with thermodynamics that the cosmos becomes not only the infinite universe, but the astrophysical 'consumption' of becoming.

The discovery of the notion of entropy natively presupposes the experience of anthropic fire, so to speak, as the entropy of physical combustion, then as the negentropy of vital combustion, if we can put it this way, through which the living finds its place, its locality and its *ēthos* in the universe that is carried along in the dissipative movement of its disorder. Here, the living, insofar as it is not immortal, nor therefore divine, *always returns* to cosmic entropy[33] – including as the production of methane by animals, which can lead to the biospheric disequilibrium of the ozone layer and so on, that is, well before their return to inertia.

It is doubtful whether the full dimension of the question of entropy and negentropy among human beings, as a *question*, has ever truly been grasped.[34] We could show, for example, that the works dedicated to entropy by Henri Atlan and Edgar Morin take no account whatsoever of the specificity of organological (exosomatic) negentropy, nor obviously of the equally specific entropy that it generates – in particular since the advent of the Anthropocene. And we could also show that the theory of information conceived as regime of entropy and negentropy is itself thereby fundamentally weakened (Simondon included).

At the beginning of the nineteenth century, technics establishes, scientifically but also socially (as standardization and proletarianization), the *question* of entropy and negentropy as the crucial problem of the everyday life of human beings and of life in general, and, ultimately, of the universe as a whole, which once again becomes the *kosmos* insofar as it invites, hosts and in some way houses the negentropic, that is, the living, including *noetic* life, which we therefore ought call the *neganthropo-logical*.

As such, that is, as the organogenesis of this *anthropos* that is not self-sufficient, technics – which is also anthropic in the sense that it extends and accelerates the entropy of anthropization in the Anthropocene – constitutes the matrix of all thought of the *oikos*, of habitat and of its law as *ecology* as well as *economy*, which is also to say, as *oikonomia* (which can here be 'general' only in Georges Bataille's a-theological sense).

This is also what was going on with what was at one time conceived as hermeneutic knowledge of the mind. This eventually became, with the utilization by cognitivism of the concept of information – as it will be thought by information theory and computationalist cybernetics – a new 'science of the mind' (as well as *spirit*, *Geist*), in which mind and spirit find themselves folded back into 'cognition'.

In this new metaphysics that is cognitivism, the organological question that *makes possible* such a perspective (where the computer, assumed to be a 'Turing machine', as it is also in the movie fiction of *The Imitation Game*, but where also many people today contest this use and interpretation of Turing, notably Jean Lassègue and David Bates, becomes the model of the mind) is never posed.[35] 'Organological' means here: that which causes the living to pass from the organic stage to the organological stage, which requires radically new terms with which to think the organization of that of which this new organogenesis is the condition.

Technics – as the advent and event of what Ernst Kapp[36] and then Friedrich Engels called 'organ projection' or 'organ extension', but which more precisely is an *organological* extension, an extension that is *not* organic – is the pursuit of life by means other than life. And this is also the opening of what Heidegger believed should still be called the 'question of being' as the advent of Dasein, that is, of the 'being who questions':

> This being [*Seiende*], which we ourselves in each case are and which has questioning among the possibilities of its being, we formulate terminologically as *Dasein*.[37]

Contrary to this Heideggerian perspective, we posit that if Dasein questions, it can only be insofar as *technics challenges it, puts it into question* – and does so starting from the fact that it is required to *formulate* this challenge, that is, to exteriorize it, which is very often (if it is indeed a question and not a fantasy or chatter) the starting point for a new technical exteriorization and a new putting in question, a new challenge, and so on. Such a vicious circle is the issue at stake in Freud's civilizational discontent.

As this organogenesis that is at once anthropic and neganthropic, technics is the *post-Darwinian* evolution of life that has become *essentially technical and organological,* and not just organic. This technical form of life poses in completely new terms the problem of what Canguilhem called the infidelity of the milieu, which confronts living things in general each time their milieu changes, but which, in the case of technical life, constitutes a technical milieu that introduces a new type of infidelity, in which it is organological and not just organic life that ceaselessly disrupts its milieu, and does so structurally and ever more rapidly: structurally to the extent that this disruption is vital to it, but tragically to the extent that it is always also toxic – insofar as it constitutes a phase difference *that cannot be transindividuated,* that is, adopted, in the sense that it must be individuated both psychically and socially (this is what Niklas Luhmann, it seems to me, does not see).

In other words, this organological milieu poses in completely unprecedented terms the question of the relations between what Claude Bernard called the interior milieu and the exterior milieu. *New conditions of fidelity are required in order to overcome the shocks of infidelity,* so to speak, that are provoked by what I call the *doubly epokhal redoubling.* This study of milieus and infidelities constitutes the field of what we can refer to as a general ecology inasmuch as it inscribes in the cosmos the perspectives of a general organology. It is also the pathway to a new understanding of the dynamics and statics of religion.

When life becomes organological, and not just organic, and when the 'external' technical milieu conditions and in so doing constitutes the interior milieu of collective individuation and of the social systems in which it consists, as well as of psychic individuation (which results, as we now know, in an organological re-organization of the organic organization in which the cerebral organ primarily consists, and through the psycho-synaptic internalization of the exosomatic and the social relations which it weaves, as the work of Maryanne Wolf shows[38]), organological and pharmacological beings encounter the infidelity of the technical milieu, which as such constitutes them as *noetic* beings, for whom noesis is always both the repercussion [*contre-coup*] and the aftershock [*après-coup*] of an *epokhal technological shock.*

Technological shock is epokhal inasmuch as it makes an epoch, that is, it is a suspension, an interruption, a disruption, and as such *stupefaction.* Epokhal technological shock (such as the thermodynamic machine in partnership with discretization and the reproduction of the gestures of work by mechanical and automatic tertiary retention) is stupefying (and generates stupidity in a thousand ways) in that it disrupts the organological arrangements established by a prior and metastabilized stage of transindividuation – forming what Heidegger called 'the understanding that there-being has of its being'.

Such an 'understanding' is trans-individuated between the psychosomatic organs, technical organs and social organizations (that Gille and Luhmann both call, but in two very different senses, 'social systems'), and engenders a new 'understanding that there-being has of its being' formed by the new circuits of transindividuation that form between the initial technological shock and a second moment that amounts to a noetic fulfilment (that is, a circuit of transindividuation) through which stupor becomes surprise and ultimately eventuates in an understanding.

General ecology, general economy and general organology are attempts to form such circuits in our epoch. This 'generality' is indicative of an attempt to respond to the generality (and to the planetary, and as such locally cosmic, globality) of the shock *that is thought-provoking for us*, and this requires us to trans-form this thinking into action – that is, into *decision*, a decision that *slices into* becoming, that carves *into* it in order to carve *out* a future, that is, a protention that is *desirable* and that would not be reducible to becoming: becoming, *devenir*, is entropic, whereas the future, *avenir*, is negentropic. Such a program is necessarily also a neganthropology.

Stupefaction, which is the condition of noesis (just as stupidity is the condition of thinking, as say Nietzsche and Deleuze), is that of which one always finds an echo, more or less near or distant, in what I call surprise, a sur-prised ap-prehension, a *sur-prehension* [*surpréhension*], which would be irreducible to under-standing [*compréhension*], and where this relates to reason, to that reason which Kant distinguished from understanding.

It is as *reconstitution of a fidelity to the milieu, and, in this milieu, to psychic individuals, technical individuals and social individuals* (via social systems), that a *libidinal economy* (in Freud's sense) is established that would also be a *general* economy and a general *ecology*. In this libidinal and as such general economy, psychic, technical and social individuals take care of one another through *transductive* relations, relations in which one side (for example, psychic individuals) cannot exist without the others (for example, technical individuals or social individuals), even though technical and social individuals *pre-cede* psychic individuals, and do so as the condition of formation of their preindividual funds (as Simondon shows), funds that were previously constituted as circuits of transindividuation for those who are now dead.

In principle, and because reason is rooted in what Kant called transcendental apperception as the *spontaneous coming together that occurs between the noetic order and the cosmic order*, care (that is, *Sorge*), insofar as it is inherently negentropic, and as such derives from a neganthropology, is also that care taken of ecology insofar as the cosmic milieu is locally neganthropic and must be protected from anthropic disequilibriums, in this sense where what geography calls anthropization – for example, as anthropization of the sea, leads, when it is not a special object of care, *Sorge*, to entropy that is the destruction of the milieu.

To what extent and in what economic conditions the coming together, the agreement, that founds Kantian transcendental apperception is possible in the Anthropocene epoch is the entire issue at stake in bringing together general ecology, general organology and general economy – that is, libidinal economy as the possibility of moving beyond the drive-based stage of consumerist capitalism and as constituting an economic system founded on the valorization of negentropy translated into neganthropology.

The precedence of technological shock constitutes what Simondon described as a *phase difference*, and it finds its point of departure in the *originary default of origin* that is retold in Plato's *Protagoras*. The allegory of Prometheus and Epimetheus is in this way the mythical formulation of what the archaeology of André Leroi-Gourhan describes as a process of exteriorization, after Canguilhem thought it as technical life, and that I myself call the pursuit of life – that is, of *negentropogenesis* qua exosomatization – by means other than life.

This shock through which life mortifies itself by secreting what I have described as an epiphylogenetic memory that constitutes the possibility of what we today call culture, and which is the unthought ground of what Dilthey called the science of spirit,[39] is also what constitutes libidinal economy insofar as, as artefact, it constitutes the fetish and hence the organological body as object of desire, as was shown by Winnicott. In this way, the instinct becomes the drive, that is, the capacity for detachable fixations,[40] which is also to say, for perversion, and ultimately desire, via the binding of these drives through what Freud described as identification, idealization and sublimation – which is always a neganthropic process.

Such a libidinal economy implements, through *various causal chains arising from the cosmos and the biosphere*, a *positive quasi-causality*.[41] And as such it inverts the arche-event or *Ereignis* of organological facticity into a therapeutic necessity, and does so to the benefit not only of psychic, technical and social individuals, but also vital, terrestrial and cosmic individuals: to take care of psychic and collective individuation, that is, of the organological biosphere (that we currently call the Anthropocene), is *also* to take care of what constitutes the general ecological condition.

SEVENTH LECTURE

Organology of Limits and the Function of Reason

Last week, I proposed to articulate general ecology, general economy and general organology, and I will not specify how I conceive this arrangement as a libidinal economy that is itself essentially a behaviour of care. The object of such an articulation is the process of a negentropogenesis specified as an exosomatization, which it would be better to write, then, as *neganthropogenesis*.

Here it is absolutely essential to read and critique *The German Ideology,* and then to reread the *Grundrisse* on the basis of this rereading of *The German Ideology.* I have tried to open up this work in *States of Shock,* where I discuss the following passage:

> Nature builds no machines, no locomotives, railways, electric telegraphs, self-acting mules etc. These are products of human industry, natural material transformed into organs of the human will over nature, or of human participation in nature. They are *organs of the human brain, created by the human hand*; the power of knowledge, objectified. The development of fixed capital indicates to what degree general social knowledge has become a *direct force of production,* and to what degree, hence, the conditions of the process of social life itself have come under the control of the general intellect and been transformed in accordance with it. To what degree the powers of social production have been produced, not only in the form of knowledge, but also as immediate organs of social practice, the real life process.[42]

This passage is a kind of continuation of the opening statements in *The German Ideology*:

> Men can be distinguished from animals by consciousness, by religion or anything else you like. They themselves begin to distinguish themselves from animals as soon as they begin to *produce* their means of subsistence, a step which is conditioned by their physical organisation. By producing their means of subsistence men are indirectly producing their actual material life.
>
> The way in which men produce their means of subsistence depends first of all on the nature of the actual means of

> subsistence they find in existence and have to reproduce. This mode of production must not be considered simply as being the production of the physical existence of the individuals. Rather it is a definite form of activity of these individuals, a definite form of expressing their life, a definite *mode of life* on their part. As individuals express their life, so they are. What they are, therefore, coincides with their production, both with *what* they produce and with *how* they produce. The nature of individuals thus depends on the material conditions determining their production.[43]

As they express their life, so they are. With Marx, as Heidegger says, being becomes production. But such a production, which is also and firstly a reproduction, is not simply an economy: it is the continuation of life insofar as it is itself reproduction – but in the case of biological reproduction, it is endosomatic, whereas human reproduction is exosomatic.

In this regard, Georgescu-Roegen claims that we must understand economy as a new law of relation between organs, and of selection in a process of evolution, that is – as a bioeconomy. In this economy, exosomatic organs are detachable limbs, and they can create the possibility of exchanging organs – and hence the possibility that these can become goods in the sense of trade.[44]

Only on the basis of such a critique of what in Marx and Engels amounts to the first philosophical formulation of the organological question (engendering and pre-ceding as it does the question of class struggle) is it possible and necessary to constitute general ecology on the basis of a general economy (here I continue my discussion with Erich Hörl's project), that is, a libidinal economy, itself conceived on the basis of a general organology, and to do so as a new political thinking, founded on a critical reinterpretation of Marx – for example, concerning the dialectic of master and *Knecht*. To quote from *States of Shock*:

> For to inherit the Hegelian dialectic is, for Marx [and Engels], firstly to inherit the dialectic of master and slave – itself founded on the dialectic of the *desire for recognition*. Now, what leads to the dialectical inversion of the master by the slave, the latter having become 'consciousness in itself and for itself', is, in Hegel, the slave's pursuit *of knowledge*. That is, the slave achieves this inversion by conquering *determinations of the understanding*, and *through work*, by *putting technics to work* – the worker (who is the slave) gives himself an art, that is, a form of *knowledge* and an *individuation*, and

> ultimately a *property*, which *is* his individuation, that is, his existence *recognized*:[45]

Hegel:

> Work [...] is desire held in check, fleetingness staved off; in other words, work forms [...]. This [...] formative *activity* is at the same time the singularity [*die Einzelnheit*] or pure being-for-self of consciousness which now, in the work outside of it, acquires an element of permanence.[46]

Now, this slave is not a slave, but a *Knecht*, that is, a servant, and such a *Knecht* is not at all a proletarian, if it is true that his dialectical and revolutionary power is based on the increasing of his knowledge by work and by technical and technological practices: he is a craftsman, that is, a future bourgeois, whereas a proletarian is defined as the one who has lost his knowledge – this knowledge having passed into the machine.

Back to *States of Shock*:

> Work is exteriorization par excellence, that is, as individuation [that is, as exosomatization]. As such, it is also the exteriorization of the for-itself of consciousness: it is the *retaining* of consciousness outside of itself, and the element of its permanence – [his] *retention* is permanent only because it has become *tertiary*.
>
> Through this conquest of self in the exteriorization of self, and for the master, [*Knecht*] consciousness achieves consciousness in itself and for itself, that is, beyond the master. And through the moments of this dialectic: [47]

Hegel again:

> In the master, being-for-self is an 'other' for the *Knecht*, or is only *for* him [that is, is not his own]; in fear [that of the *Knecht* who has become the *Knecht* through his recoil in the face of death, which the master does not fear, who as a result of this becomes the master], being-for-self is present in the *Knecht* himself; in fashioning the thing [in the work imposed by slavery as the stage of a *Bildung*], he becomes aware that being-for-self belongs to *him*, that he himself exists essentially and actually in his own right. The shape does not become something other than himself through being made external [*hinausgesetzt*, placed outside, as Hyppolite puts it, *pros-thetized* in some way] to him; for it is precisely this shape that is his pure being-for-self, which in this externality is seen by him to be the truth. Through this rediscovery of

> himself by himself, the *Knecht* realizes that it is precisely in his work wherein he seemed to have only an alienated existence that he acquires a mind of his own.[48]

Actually, here, Hegel says already what *The German Ideology* will say against... Hegel, that is, against idealism. Why? Because Hegel will say that this exteriorization or this externalization is only a moment in a phenomenology of the spirit that will, having become absolute, totally re-interiorize its previous exteriority.

This dialectic of work and workers, which is obviously the foundation of Marxism, is in Hegel not a question of the *worker becoming proletarian* as much as it is about the *artisan becoming an entrepreneur,* that is, bourgeois. In other words, the reappropriation of this dialectic by Marxism is based on a misunderstanding.[49]

Such a reinterpretation of Hegel and Marx is possible only on the basis of a conjoined rereading of Marx, Freud, Husserl, Heidegger, Canguilhem, Leroi-Gourhan, Derrida, Deleuze and many others. And a rereading, too, of Nicholas Georgescu-Roegen – through an investigation of the fundamental question of the difference between the organic and the organological, which is also their mutual différance(s), and thereby opens a new age of that différance that is noesis (by tracing new circuits of transindividuation) in relation to the différance that is life.

Such an investigation, such an instruction, is itself possible only by adopting a method that will coordinate the diverse knowledge that constitutes the theory of general organology, but that will also, and as organological practice, invent negentropic instruments at the service of all forms of knowledge – *savoir faire, savoir vivre, savoir théoriser* (knowledge of how to do, live and theorize) – and that take the digital as their object insofar as 1) the digital is an affair of digits, which are also fingers, and 2) it is conceivable only on the condition of rethinking all forms of knowledge starting from the organogenesis of artefacts, societies and psychic individuals that has occurred since the origin of hominization.

Or in other words, from the beginning of human evolution and up until 'big data' and the 'data economy', and, even beyond, as medicine 3.0 and eventually as that new stage of exosomatization of which transhumanism is the ideology, which is also to say that transhumanism is the strategic marketing of the disruption of the rules of life itself, some people claiming that, through this, Google itself becomes totalitarian, and where the question of fingers as digits arises anew and in a new perspective, which, in my view, means the perspective of the

Anthropocene and the bifurcation we must provoke within it, thereby opening the possibility of the Neganthropocene.

▪ ▪ ▪

Insofar as I can imagine it, the general ecology invoked by Erich Hörl is both a scientific and a political ecology, and it must as such tightly articulate the questions of *selection* and of *decision* – in the epoch of the digital trace and its algorithmic treatment, as well as in debate with Nietzsche. It is, in other words, a fundamental critique that poses the question of the *criteria* of selection, formed in such a way that they become criteria *of decision*, that is, *critical categories*, rather than merely biological, psychic or technical automatisms.

The *passage* from *psycho-biological automatic selection* to its *disautomatization* as *decision* is possible only when *organic* organs combine with, and form a *system* with, the organological organs that are tertiary retentions, that is, with the epiphylogenetic supports of collective memory, opening up an *interpretive play* (a différance) through which criteria of selection become criteria of decision, that is, of *psychosocial individuation*, and not just vital individuation.

The outcome of this interpretive play is the production of circuits of transindividuation, that is, the continuous formation of new knowledge – such as thermodynamics emerging from the steam machine – arising from the unfurling of organogenesis, generating new *pharmaka* from the circuits of transindividuation deriving from constituted knowledge, in turn requiring new forms of knowledge, placing into crisis those from which they stem, and provoking more or less stupefaction from this *pharmakon* that is always stunning and astounding. In this regard, artificial intelligence seems to represent some kind of a limit. But what kind, and to what extent?

Hence is produced the transformation of techno-epokhal shock into a surprise, a sur-prehension that eventually becomes a com-prehension – which is less the understanding that there-being has of its being than that through which psychosocial individuation takes care of its organological and pharmacological condition, as *Sorge*, by trans-forming *technical becoming* at a single stroke into a *noetic future*, that is, into the *desire to live in quasi-causality* (in Deleuze's sense), and therefore *by default*, and as a fault *that is necessary* – and on the basis of which, and because it has become banal, a new and always surprising pharmacology can arise.

It is in the context of this normativity that we must interpret Canguilhem when he posits that knowledge of life is the specific form of life capable of caring for itself (as in *The Normal and the Pathological*), treating itself – particularly as *biology* (as in *Knowledge of Life*) – and in the same way we must understand *ecology* as this same form of life caring for itself through the knowledge of the milieus, systems and processes of individuation through which the concrescence of the cosmos generates processes of individuation such that entropic and negentropic tendencies play out in different ways in each of the different forms of infidelity of these milieus.

The questions about life and negentropy that arise with Darwin and with thermodynamics must in this sense be reinterpreted in the organological context, given that natural selection gives way to artificial selection, and that the passage from the organic to the organological displaces the play of entropy and negentropy.[50] Thought in this way, technics is an *accentuation of negentropy*, since it is an agent of *increased differentiation*, but it is *also* an *acceleration of entropy* – not just because it is a process of combustion and of the dissipation of energy, but because *industrial standardization* seems today to lead to the destruction of life as the burgeoning and proliferation of differences: biodiversity, cultural diversity and the singularity of psychic individuations as well as collective individuations – and this is what we call the Anthropocene.

Only from this perspective do the questions of *Bestand*, *Gestell* and *Ereignis* make sense for us – that is, for those in the Anthropocene who question the epokhal singularity in which this age, which is a period that presents itself as the probability of the end of ages, fails to consist, so to speak. But if so, *Bestand*, *Gestell* and *Ereignis* take on a meaning that is in a way the epoch of the default of epoch, which is possible only according to a twist of meaning that is incompatible with Heideggerian thought – even less so given that the epokhal dimension of thermodynamics is in no way taken into account in the writings of the *Kehre*.

In addition, the *perspective and the prospect* (that is, the future) that I propose here (as the epoch still to come), in terms of general organology with respect to a Neganthropocene that calls for a neganthropological conception of noetic life, that is, of life that studies and knows life in order to care for it (as biology, ecology, economy, organology and everything that this entails, namely, every form of knowledge understood in terms of its cosmic tenor) – this perspective and prospect also functionally and primordially involves a libidinal economy, and of libidinal economy rethought in organological terms and as general economy in Georges Bataille's sense (that is, as we will see, an economy of gift, that is of potlatch), this general economy requiring a complete redefinition of phenomenology in general and the existential analytic in particular.

Such a redefinition passes through the inscription of the Freudian shock within an organological perspective, thereby going beyond

Freud himself. It means asking the organological question of tertiary retention as that which constitutes the possibility of the dis-automatization of instinct – in a vein not foreign to the questions raised by Arnold Gehlen, who must be read here with John Bowlby and Donald Winnicott. The dis-automatization of instinct comes at the cost of the formation of other automatisms, artificial (that is, psychic, technical and social) automatisms, which as a general rule require an economy: that which sets the rules in any society and does so through various forms of regulation (rituals, education, law, institutions) governing the processes of exchange resulting from the dis-automatization of the instincts insofar as this makes possible and necessary the detachability of artificial organs, which can then become objects of exchange, as well as the detachability of the drives, which, precisely insofar as they themselves become detachable, must be bound together so as not to become entropic. It is this entropic possibility that constitutes the horizon of *Beyond the Pleasure Principle* in terms of the dimension through which the death drive enters noetic life.

General economy, general ecology and general organology are a salvage effort with respect to the conditions of a libidinal economy today ruined, which it is a matter of rethinking from the perspective of neganthropology starting from the fetish, the transitional object and the artefact as condition of all consistence beyond subsistence and existence (in the sense I explained in the first lecture) – and in the sense where Whitehead inscribes this dimension of consistence at the heart of concrescence.

General economy, ecology and organology thus conceived with Georges Bataille, together call for Vladimir Vernadsky's concept of 'biosphere', later replaced with that of 'global ecosystem', and revived in France by René Passet, a concept with which we can explore the *paradox of technology*, which is another name for what Ivan Illich called counterproductivity. When, *as a system*, the growth of technology reaches a certain point, its *effects are inverted* – and as such it becomes paradoxical, which Passet described as a 'passage to limits'.[51] We must relate this concept of counterproductivity to the *pharmakon* in general, and the diverse counterproductive effects of the prevailing organological condition should be seen as entropic and negentropic pharmacological effects.

The automotive *pharmakon*, the car, created to augment mobility, engenders urban congestion. The computerized *pharmakon*, created to *assist with decision-making*, engenders cognitive overflow syndrome and paralysis (confounded with stupefaction and consolidated with the systemic and functional stupidity wrought by drive-based capitalism, to which is added, in France, the institutional stupidity generated by the

Ecole nationale d'administration, an institution responsible for training, for example, François Hollande and most of his advisers: hence France hurtles towards its current fate, one in which stupidity reaches extreme levels). This paradox can also be seen with *medicines* that, if poorly prescribed (not just in the wrong doses), poison the patient, or may even produce what in pharmaceutical science is called a 'paradoxical reaction', that is, where the medicine acts in such a way that it causes the very thing against which it is intended to fight.

The pharmacological paradox equally afflicts the social organizations that are institutions and corporations insofar as they always make use of political technologies, governmentality and management, in the sense in which Foucault placed these political technologies at the heart of his thought of power in general under the umbrella of biopower (which should be related back to Weber, and read alongside Polanyi). This issue should also be explored with Gille and Luhmann with respect to the concept of social system, where all of these things constitute specific cases of the pharmacology that conditions and limits any organology and therefore any human ecology.

We must, then, also examine more closely the general conditions of emergence of these paradoxical effects, and we must do so alongside a reading of Passet's *L'Économique et le Vivant* (1979), in which the problem of sustainable development is examined from the perspective of systems theory, in terms of passages to limits in various domains, domains that are understood as systems or elements of systems:

> Sustainable development is not a question like others, or just one among others. This question reveals a passage to limits through which it is the interplay of economic laws that is transformed.[52]

These limits raise the question of new equilibriums and disequilibriums, establishing new general conditions of *intersystemic metastability*:

> Beginning in the eighties, in fact, with the issue of global damage to the biosphere..., it is no longer specific resources or environments that are threatened, but the regulatory mechanisms of the planet itself.[53]

The biosphere is defined here, following Vladimir Vernadsky, as a complex

> and self-regulating system, in the adjustments and evolutions of which life – and thus the human species – plays a fundamental role. Two logics confront each other here: that which presides over the development of economic systems

> and that which ensures the dynamic reproduction of natural environments.[54]

The question raised here is that of the Anthropocene – more than twenty years before its more or less official recognition – at the level of natural milieus. But this question also arises today, and perhaps especially, and certainly *firstly*, at the level of organological milieus *themselves*, and of *social systems and social environments* – that is, mental environments, as these occur in the so-called 'knowledge society'.

For if it is true that the question is care, its organization, its culture, one might even say its worship [*culte*] – care as the formation of attention through circuits of transindividuation that cultivate reason through reasons to live and to take care of life in quasi-causality – *then the question of mental ecology precedes the question of environmental economy.* And this is so, even though mental ecology is conditioned by organology and pharmacology, so that from Plato to Marx and up until ourselves, it presents itself as the question of *stupor*, or of *torpor*: I employ this latter term that Adam Smith used in his analysis of the extremes of the industrial division of labour – 'torpor' was used by Smith to describe the effects of mechanization on the minds of those who were in the course of becoming proletarian.[55]

And such torpor becomes, in our time, a stupor – and our stupefaction in the face of the state of shock provoked by digital technology leads not only to functional stupidity, but to a catastrophic and dis-astrous (losing the light of the stars, the stars that in French are 'asters', and losing them for lack of a *therapeutics of computation* based on a new cosmology) destruction of noesis itself by automatic proletarianization.

As for development, in Passet's terms, this involves growth that is both complexifying and multi-dimensional:

- this growth is complexifying through a dual movement of diversification and integration, allowing the system to grow by reorganizing itself yet without losing its coherence;
- it is multi-dimensional to the extent that, beyond the economic in the strict sense, it takes into account the quality of the relations established between human beings within the human sphere, and their relations with the natural environment.[56]

This duality is a source of conflict because

> while nature maximizes its stocks (biomass) on the basis of a given flow (solar radiation), the economy maximizes market flow by depleting natural (non-market) stocks, the decrease

> of which is noted in no economic records and produces no corrective action.[57]

Hence there arises a question of nature and culture. I would have liked to show that to address Passet's question we must overcome this opposition, but I will be able to do no more than give an outline of this in my concluding remarks.

Be that as it may, this conflict has today reached a threshold that amounts, precisely, to a passage to limits. Now, in reaching its limits, any system in 'phase transition' undergoes changes in the way it functions:

- the limit of the saturation of needs...
- the limit of the reproducibility of a natural resource...
- the limit of rhythms of assimilation and self-purification...[58]

Such a passage to limits is a sudden return to entropy. At stake is therefore the power to provoke bifurcations in this entropic becoming, reopening unknown pathways to come, to the future – and I argue (in agreement, I think, with the perspective of Erich Hörl) that such pathways are organological, and must above all consider the still unknown possibility of the most recent stage of grammatization, that is, of digital tertiary retention inasmuch as it makes possible new and unprecedented neganthropic works.

The latter pass through a fundamental economico-political change, which takes account of automation and its ruinous effects on employment, and installs a new mechanism to redistribute productivity gains, in the wake of the analyses of Oskar Negt and André Gorz, in the form of time allocated for the development of individual and collective capabilities (in Amartya Sen's sense): it is for this reason that Ars industrialis advocates the creation of a contributory income, modelled on the law of the '*intermittents*' (casual or freelance workers in the performing arts sphere) in France, and IRI is developing contributory research platforms with a view to designing a new architecture of the World Wide Web at the service of an economy that values negentropy and fights entropy at the same time. These perspectives are developed in my two last books and I will return to these questions in the next session.

▪ ▪ ▪

Let us conclude by turning to Whitehead. When he introduces the concept of process, he at the same time establishes that the *opposition* between natural phenomena and cultural phenomena has become outdated. This obviously does not mean that the *distinction* between nature and culture would be outdated. In this way, a general economy is outlined that is not yet a general organology, but that calls for the latter and requires it.

In Whitehead, with regard to cosmology, it is no longer a question of spheres, but of process, that is, more precisely, of dynamic interlocked spirals materialized by regimes of speed – and where there is such a thing as *infinite speed*, which is that of thought: the power to *disrupt* and to *dis-automatize*, that is, *to change the rules* – a power that is knowledge, which Whitehead, in his 'Introductory Summary' to *The Function of Reason*, also called history, and which is par excellence the *function* of reason (Whitehead here inherits something from the Kantian framework that I recalled at the beginning of my remarks):

> History discloses two main tendencies in the course of events. One tendency is exemplified in the slow decay of physical nature. With stealthy inevitableness, there is degradation of energy. The sources of activity sink downward and downward. Their very matter wastes. The other tendency is exemplified by the yearly renewal of nature in the spring, and by the upward course of biological evolution. In these pages I consider Reason in its relation to these contrasted aspects of history. Reason is the self-discipline of the originative element in history. Apart from the operations of Reason, this element is anarchic.[59]

This discipline that is reason, the privilege of noetic beings in Aristotle's sense, is obviously a specific negentropic capacity to 'realize' an order in struggling against this 'anarchic element'. I myself argue that such a faculty is neganthropological and constitutes the *Neganthropos* that we strive to be in actuality.

More often, however, we are entropic, in particular since the advent of consumer capitalism: this capacity to change the rules that is neganthropological reason brings with it a danger of intersystemic conflict (highlighted by von Bertalanffy in the introduction to his *General System Theory*, and as this theory's justification[60]). The pharmacological question is in this way inscribed at the heart of cosmology and as the 'anthropo-technical', bio-spheric and local consequence that follows from the initial combustion and its universal thermodynamic law.

To be able to change the rules is to have the power to move faster than the speed of light, insofar as the latter has become, as the speed of digital automatons, the horizon of the calculation and computing industry: it is to move *infinitely* fast, to escape established circuits regardless of their speed, and to introduce a bifurcation – at the speed of desire, that is, of *idealization, through which neganthropy passes onto the plane of consistence*, making the noetic economy of desire the line of flight of any neganthropology that can be realized only organologically, that is, pharmacologically, and this is the issue at stake in what Whitehead called the function of reason:

> The function of Reason is to promote the art of life.[61]
>
> The higher forms of life are actively engaged in modifying their environment. In the case of mankind this active attack on the environment is the most prominent fact in his existence.[62]
>
> The primary function of Reason is the direction of the attack on the environment.[63]

Clearly, this should be considered together with Canguilhem.

Such a power, however, presupposes knowledge, knowledge that is always the knowledge of powerlessness (and of a 'non-knowledge'). The question then arises of the laws of the universe conceived as constituting the field of what we call physics, a body of rules for a game that we cannot change – but that we can localize and, through this localization, which is also an augmentation, interpret. That is, we can *organize* this inorganic, entropic and sidereal play or game, and this is what we do with nanophysics and quantum technology, at the risk of bringing about, in return, dis-organizations, such as for instance via that new toxicity imposed on organisms by the nanometric infidelity of new milieus of life. And this is so only because the universe is incomplete, unfinished, as Whitehead claims.

Given that technics consists above all in the *organization of inorganic matter* (which was the main issue of *Technics and Time, 1*), leading in turn to the *organological reorganization of cerebral organic matter*, which modifies the play of every somatic organ, and thus gives rise to a new form of life (that is, a new form of negentropy) that is nevertheless also, as technical, an accelerator of entropy on all cosmic planes (and it is this two-sidedness that characterizes the *pharmakon*), there remains a cosmic question of technics: that is, of a technical epoch of a cosmos within which nanophysics amounts to a transformational inscription (in the sense of Jean-Pierre Dupuy and Françoise Roure when they refer to transformational technologies[64]), at the quantum level, of reorganization, one that operates via the intermediary of the scanning tunnelling microscope.

The scanning tunnelling microscope is itself a computer capable of simulating, that is, of schematizing. This arrangement between the cerebral organ and the quantum scale of hyper-matter is a stage of concrescence that is also a process of concretization in the broader Simondonian sense – in that it operates on all planes of the cosmos at the same time: sidereal, vital and psychosocial, that is, technical. This localization can act retroactively on the play of the whole biosphere, into which it can in a way spread itself generally (through a process of amplification[65]), and this has now engendered that specific stage of concrescence that we refer to in our epoch as the Anthropocene.

Technics obviously respects the laws of physics, since otherwise it would not function. But technics, as 'matter that functions' organologically (and constituting as such what I propose calling hyper-matter), locally trans-forms the cosmic order in ways that are not predictable. Hence the concretization of the technical individual as a mode of existence, the functioning of which cannot be dissolved into the laws of physics, tends to give rise to associated techno-geographical milieus. It was for this reason that Simondon claimed the need for a mechanology that I prefer to understand as an organology – given that mechanology does not enable us to think pharmacologically, or to think the links between psychic, technical and collective individuation.

Processes, concrescence, disruptions, infidelities of milieus, and metastable equilibriums (and thus disequilibriums) all form what, in our epoch, presents itself to us as what we are causing *within* ourselves, *around* us, and *between* us, as projections of a becoming that we are no longer able to trans-form into a future on the basis of our organological and pharmacological condition, that is, as the play between the processes of psychic, technical and collective (that is, social) individuation, processes through which and in which we always find ourselves tied to these three dimensions by their mutual organological condition.

It seems today that this play and this game is turning into a massacre, wherein psychic individuation and collective individuation are being killed off by a technical individuation that is slave to a self-destructive economy – because it is destructive of the social milieus without which no technical milieu is possible that does not at the same time destroy the physical milieus of the biosphere.

The *general ecological* question poses and imposes on this tripartite division the question of biological, geographical and cosmic systems and processes, such that they thoroughly infuse, constantly, locally, and in conditions of locality that remain totally to be thought, the processes of psychic, technical and social individuation. In addition to analysing the condition of transindividuation through co-individuation of the processes of psychic, technical and social individuation, general organology studies the conditions of returning to vital biological sources, and of doing so in the cosmic, entropic and sidereal conditions of negentropy, insofar as these are made possible by scientific and noetic instruments.

Through this dual approach, general organology investigates the conditions of possibility of a political and noetic *decision*, a decision that is made possible by grammatization. And at the same time, it investigates the specific regime of the *pharmakon* that is established by grammatization, which is haunted by the question of proletarianization. The realities of the latter, in terms of subsistence and existence, must be studied for each epoch of the 'history of the supplement', given that, failing the development of therapies and therapeutics, proletarianization has the effect of eliminating the possibility of decision, that is, of neganthropogenesis.

EIGHTH LECTURE

Final Lecture

Last week I tried to show you why and how Marx misinterpreted the famous dialectic of the master and the slave, and why the latter is *not* a slave, because he is a *Knecht*, that is, a servant.

Another issue arises from the fact that Marx doesn't question the ambiguous status of technology insofar as it is a *pharmakon* – and this is one of the reasons that has meant that Marxism has so often been considered to be a determinism.

What I wanted to show you, today, are the systemic limits of capitalism, which is now known as the Anthropocene, but we no longer have time and, since you have the text that addresses this question, I prefer to let you read it. So, instead, I will finish this seminar by proposing a few comments on the *Grundrisse*, drawn from *States of Shock*.

It is the failure to pose either the question of the *toxicity* of the *pharmakon*, or that of its *curativity* and the therapeutics this presupposes (which is always a system of de-proletarianization) that leads the *negativity* of the Marxist dialectic to the doctrine of the dictatorship of the proletariat rather than to a political project of de-proletarianization, that is, to a reacquisition of knowledge in the service of the individuation of citizens.

This outcome was due less to the fact that Marx was wrong than to the fact that philosophy is collective work, and those who contribute to its individuation are able to do so *only in their time* – and *as* their time becomes *the time of everyone*.

Marx, of course, could not have conceived any of this or the way that it would and should come to modify his own concepts. Because these concepts were unavailable to him, and because exteriorization itself had not yet reached the stage that would require thinking grammatization as such (as the pharmacological spatialization of time in the form of tertiary retention), Marx was not able to pose the question of a curative pharmacology, that is, a positive pharmacology. The failure of poststructuralism to pose this question, on the other hand, seems to lie rather in the fact that it is unaware of the scope of the Marxist understanding of technics, despite the analyses of Kostas Axelos.[66] As for Marx, he could not envisage this curativity as techno-logical and industrial individuation, reconstituting knowledge and participating in the struggle against proletarianization.

As I said in the last lecture, this dialectic of work and workers, which is obviously the foundation of Marxism, is in Hegel not a question of the *worker becoming proletarian* as much as it is about the *artisan becoming an entrepreneur*, that is, bourgeois. In other words, the reappropriation of this dialectic by Marxism is based on a misunderstanding.

What Hegel nevertheless does not think here – when he analyses the becoming of objective spirit by and in work, and as a stage of the 'work of the concept' – is the *machine's* work, which deprives the worker of his singularity, that is, of his work. Work is for the worker then reduced to a job (a salary), a negativity that turns it into a pure force of labour that is no longer work properly speaking, given that work, as Hegel explains, is an individuation process in which the worker is individuated at the same time as the object, which is thereby individuated technically (this is what I have tried to describe as work in an associated milieu).

It is for this reason that, in Marxist economico-political theory, the dictatorship of the proletariat, supposedly grounded in this dialectic, is in fact based on a profound misinterpretation. For Marx himself showed in the *Grundrisse* that the determination carried out by exteriorization in machines, and as grammatization, is what structurally and materially deprives the slave of all knowledge – the slave whom the worker becomes, a wage labourer, a status destined to be extended to 'all layers of the population' via wage labour, as Marx and Engels would write in the *Communist Manifesto*.[67]

In *Das Kapital*, Marx's gesture consists, on the one hand, in making the concept of the proletariat synonymous with the concept of the working class, and, on the other hand, in taking the negativity of the proletarian condition as an unsurpassable horizon and in never posing the question or the hypothesis of de-proletarianization – a Marxist leaning that extends Hegelian metaphysics.

Now, we know that the free software movement as an organization of work, for example, is based on de-proletarianization, itself being based on the contributory possibility enabled by the contributory technologies that appeared with the internet and especially the Web – Wikipedia being a prime example. In other words, Marxist philosophy has proven incapable of anticipating the evolution of technology that occurred with digital tertiary retention.

What Hegel never thinks is technics as that which bypasses and short-circuits the knowledge of the *Knecht*. Marx does attempt to think machine technology, but he does so without drawing any consequences for the master-*Knecht* dialectic. This is why (because he 'forgets' to think the positive and negative pharmacology of the organology that is constituted by the process of exosomatization) he turns the negativity of the universal subject of history (that would be the proletariat) into the revolutionary principle, whereas it is in fact the curative positivity of the pharmacological supplement deriving from work that inverts the logic of disindividuation, and as technique of the self, and that must make possible a new age of individuation, that is, of knowledge. And it must do so as a new history of the love of knowledge, its savours, as knowing how to do and to live, and also how to theorize.

Marx and Engels described the process of proletarianization in *The Communist Manifesto* (1848), and they described it as the loss of knowledge resulting from exteriorization, and, as we have seen, this is a viewpoint that would be further developed in the *Grundrisse* (1857). The proletariat *is not* the working class, but the *non-working* class [*la classe des désoeuvrés*], that is, the downgraded, the class of those who are *de-class-ified*. They are those who *no longer know*, but *serve without knowledge*, because they serve not a master, but systems, systems that exteriorize knowledge *even for the 'masters'*.

The Hegelian and 'idealist' definition of the *understanding* was inverted by Marx when he proposed that exteriorization, in which the understanding essentially consists, is first and foremost that of the means of production: such is his 'materialism'. But in so dismissing idealism, Marx lost sight of the question of ideality, that is, idealization as that which is at work in all investment and in all knowledge of the object of desire. And poststructuralism, too, leaves this in the shadows by tending to confound desire and drive: the misunderstanding in relation to the proletariat is at the same time a misunderstanding of desire.

In *The German Ideology* (1845), Marx's materialism initially consists in identifying the first 'historical act' of noetic beings with their technical capacity. As we saw, non-inhuman beings

> begin to distinguish themselves from animals as soon as they begin to *produce* their means of subsistence, a step which is conditioned by their physical organisation.[68]

The Hegelian question of exteriorization is thus 'put back on its feet', to some extent as a question of general organology, where the materialist dialectic assigns *being* (and its becoming) to *doing*, that is, to *production*:

> As individuals express their life, so they are. What they are, therefore, coincides with their production, both with *what* they produce and with *how* they produce. The nature of individuals thus depends on the material conditions determining their production.[69]

As we have already seen, this definition of being as pro-duction and re-pro-duction, that is, as exo-somatization, is based on a process of artificial selection.

That this exteriorization can lead to the proletarianization of workers is explained in the *Grundrisse* in terms of the passage from the tool to the machine, that is, to a new stage of exteriorization:

> the means of labour passes through different metamorphoses, whose culmination is the *machine*, or rather, an *automatic system of machinery* (system of machinery: the *automatic* one is merely its most complete, most adequate form, and alone transforms machinery into a system) [...]; this automaton consisting of numerous mechanical and intellectual organs, so that the workers themselves are cast merely as its conscious linkages.[70]

Here, the labourers are no longer workers, because a worker works, where this means: opens a world, in French, *oeuvre*. Those labourers have themselves become organs of this machinery, exactly like software, or like a horse or a slave that is not at all, here, precisely, a *Knecht*.

And Marx continues:

> In no way does the machine appear as the individual worker's means of labour. Its distinguishing characteristic is not in the least, as with the means of labour, to transmit the worker's activity to the object; this activity, rather, is posited in such a way that it merely transmits the machine's work, the machine's action, on to the raw material – supervises it and guards against interruptions. Not as with the instrument, which the worker animates and makes into his organ with his skill and strength, and whose handling therefore depends on his virtuosity. Rather, it is the machine which possesses skill and strength in place of the worker, is itself the virtuoso, with a soul of its own in the mechanical laws acting through it.[71]

This analysis forms the basis of Simondon's argument in *On the Mode of Existence of Technical Objects*. The process of disindividuation that Simondon describes paraphrases the above statements by Marx:

> The technical individual becomes at a certain point man's adversary, his competitor, because man had, when there were only tools, centralized all technical individuality within himself; the machine then takes the place of man because man gives to the machine the function of tool-bearer.[72]

Marx does indeed emphasize that this industrial division of labour, and the replacement of workers and tools by machines, is also a change in the status of knowledge and of the science that it brings. Scientific knowledge is placed at the service of the process of exteriorization, whereby it is knowledge itself, and in general, that is exteriorized. And this machinic exteriorization is the new regime of exosomatization that characterizes our age as one of disruption, which short-circuits and bypasses social systems, even including the Chinese communist party. And it is, as well, the concretization of the ultimate consequences of the Anthropocene – but these consequences are self-destructive, and here we can see why we must reinterpret the philosophy of Marx and Engels, as well as reconsider the very question of what politics is, faced with digital economy.

Next year, we will try to go deeper into the question of truth, knowledge, capitalism and digital technology in the Anthropocene.

2017 Lectures

Heading Upstream from 'Post-Truth' to the Birth of Platonic Metaphysics

FIRST LECTURE

Introduction

At the end of the year just past, *Oxford Dictionaries* decided that 2016's 'word of the year' was 'post-truth'. They justified this choice – which, as we will see, involves a *performative gesture within a process of transindividuation* – first and foremost by pointing to current international politics, especially British and American:

> *Why was this chosen?*
>
> The concept of *post-truth* has been in existence for the past decade, but Oxford Dictionaries has seen a spike in frequency this year in the context of the EU referendum in the United Kingdom and the presidential election in the United States. It has also become associated with a particular noun, in the phrase *post-truth politics*. [...] *Post-truth* has gone from being a peripheral term to being a mainstay in political commentary, now often being used by major publications without the need for clarification or definition in their headlines.[73]

This is discussed in perhaps a more interesting and engaged way on an Indian blog:

> The bewilderment that followed Brexit and Trump was only to be expected. Less understandable, however, was the profound sense of denial that has gripped those who have toppled from their pedestals.
>
> Post-truth is a reworking of the much discredited Marxist notion of 'false consciousness' that was based on the notion that there is one living truth centred on the wisdom of those who are sufficiently enlightened.
>
> It assumes that there is only one objective truth and that the debate between the half-full and half-empty can be settled conclusively and objectively. To those who had never encountered a Trump voter or who couldn't think why anyone would endorse the UK's exit from the European Union, post-truth became a catch-all phrase to justify their limited exposure to their own societies.
>
> Rather than acknowledge the limitations of their own social reach, post-truth became a shorthand to argue that the others were ignorant fools, living in a world of delusion.[74]

This, too, emphasizes the Anglo-Saxon context, but also points out, by examining the 20–26 September 2016 cover of *The Economist* (whose headline states, 'Art of the Lie'), that the question of post-truth is also the question of *lying* in the epoch of social networks (Figure 3).

Being myself a Frenchman and a continental European, I would like to make very clear that the 'hexagonal' context (this is a term used in France as a way of referring to French domestic affairs) is just as 'post-truthy' as anything in America or Britain: lying has in France, too, become an everyday practice undertaken by those who take themselves to be the elites.

In French slang, 'c'est du flan' means: it's a lie, it's all just show. And 'Le changement', 'Change', obviously refers in this instance to the promises of François Hollande (Figure 3). Oxford adds that behind the concept of post-truth becoming the word of the year – if not the concept of the year (we should ask what the differences between these two may be), there lies a contemporary history, which must be reconstituted.[75] And the Indian blog inscribes this recent history into an older history: that of Marxism.

Now, as you will no doubt have noticed, *The Economist* cover directly relates the concept of post-truth, which it refers to firstly as lying, to so-called 'social' media ('Art of the Lie: Post-Truth in the Age of Social Media'). This direct connection between social media and lying is made by *The Economist* despite the fact that it utilizes this very same media itself, as do both the Indian blog and *Oxford Dictionaries*, given that what I have been showing you comes from their websites.

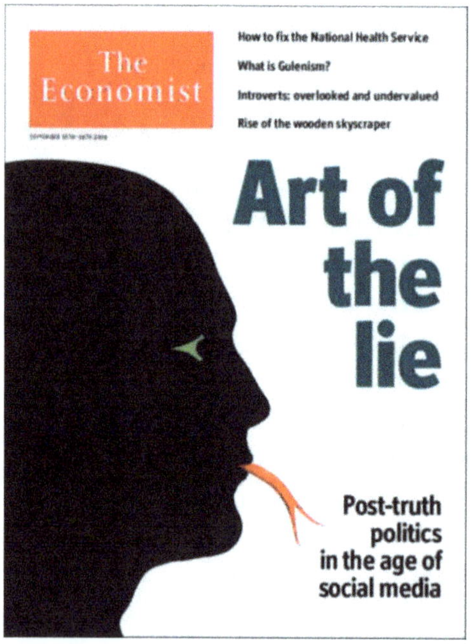

Figure 3. Cover of *The Economist*, Septempber 10-16, 2014.

In this course, we will reflect on this context by re-situating it in terms of the project of thinking opened in the twentieth century by Martin Heidegger, who proposed that truth has a history – and that the historicity of truth is the essence of truth, and that being is therefore time and time is being, so that the history of truth also amounts to a history of being, where the latter occurs through a privileged being that he calls Da-sein.

Obviously, we cannot ignore the fact that Heidegger himself, at the very moment he was studying what he would come to call the history of truth, was *deceived* by something like a first global experience of the 'post-truth' era,

Figure 4. Recreation of anti-Hollande message.

if it is *true* that Heidegger was clearly a Nazi, and if it is *true* that, long after his period as rector of a university under Nazism, he remained an anti-Semite, something which can be read into the frightening statements of *Discourse on Thinking*, which would put forward the concept of *Gelassenheit*. I tried to show in my last book, entitled *Dans la disruption. Comment ne pas devenir fou?*,[76] why and how *Discourse on Thinking*, in particular, is a *symptom* of this *illness of the West* that is anti-Semitism.

It is, however, precisely *with* Heidegger that we must try to think the possibility of a post-truth, and to understand what 'post' could mean here, without being content to hear in this 'post' an echo of so-called 'postmodernity', which is a rather catch-all concept, or to hear it in terms of what is variously referred to as post-phenomenology, post-structuralism, post-Marxism and so on. Here, it is perhaps a question of hearing in the 'post' of truth the *quasi-causal possibility* of a leap – *ein Sprung* – beyond this test or ordeal which is also that of the Anthropocene in its disruptive period – this link between the Anthropocene and post-truth obviously being more than just a coincidence.

Such a leap beyond post-truth must be attempted *with* Heidegger, and even, more particularly, by reconstructing the path along which Heidegger lost his way, but which, nevertheless, can cause us to think not only the possibility, but the imperative nature of a leap starting from what he called *Gestell*, and towards what he called *Ereignis* – which obviously does not mean that we should interpret Heidegger's last thoughts in the same way that Heidegger did himself.

Here, more than ever, what Heidegger said about limits in the famous *Kant and the Problem of Metaphysics*, which he did by quoting Kant, must not only be recalled, but *resolutely practised* – failing which we will sink either into idolatrous forms of reading or into sterile imprecation, which is, in the end, always an approach steeped in denial, *which inverts the denial by which we deny the necessity of thinking* [*penser*] – and of caring [*panser*].

▪ ▪ ▪

Let us now turn to the matter of what I propose we study together during this short seminar. Our main 'subject' will be Plato, inasmuch as he inaugurated philosophy itself – and where I will argue the paradoxical thesis that Socrates is himself, ultimately, 'at the limit', pre-Socratic, where this word, 'limit', will come to occupy the focus of our attention.

But we will study Plato with and through [à *travers*] Heidegger, Heidegger constituting here, too, just as much, one particular way [*un travers*], that is, a bias, but an inevitable bias, whose character *as* bias must be analysed as such. We will see why it is only in this way that it is possible to return (like salmon) to something that amounts to more than just a source, a 'spring', as we could say in English (and where the source of the Danube was an object of meditation in Heidegger's 1942 lecture course on *Hölderlin's Hymn 'The Ister'*), a spring, then, which is perhaps also a *Sprung* – if it is *true* that every source is always, in the history of *truth*, a kind of leap.

I have argued in *Technics and Time, 1* that, in *Sein und Zeit*, Heidegger comes very close to the question of what I call tertiary retention, which is the inscription in the world – that is, the trace, *Spur*, and in a technical, that is, *exteriorized*, form – of the past of Dasein. Tertiary retention is the inscription of a past that this Dasein has not lived, which has accumulated before it, and has accumulated as world, *Welt*, which this Dasein inherits, and does so actively, that is, through its education that begins from the first day of its coming into the world.

This past, accumulated and generally buried, but not erased, in this way constitutes a world. And in order to come into this world, education must not be content just to re-produce the past, but must, on the contrary, individuate it – in the sense developed by Simondon in *L'individuation psychique et collective* – that is, *interpret* it. Such an interpretation, as the individuation of the past, is also a 'worlding of the world' [*mondanéisation*]: a *making*-world, the question of which, too, is dealt with by Heidegger in *Holzwege*, and especially in relation to van Gogh's work, *Shoes* (1886), of which it is a matter of understanding what it opens up – a world.

And in order to interpret a past that has not been lived, and that Simondon describes as its preindividual background or funds, which Deleuze often referred to, including in *Logic of Sense*, and that I myself present in this way (see Figure 5), *individuation* – which, Simondon tells us, is always both psychic and collective (and we will need to discover to what extent this is also true of Dasein) – *needs knowledge*. This knowledge, which is the issue in *Theaetetus*, and which, as we will see, led Heidegger to revisit the presentation of this question in Plato's final period, if we follow Léon Robin's reconstruction of the Platonic corpus, this knowledge, in all its forms, is what provides the criteria of interpretation, that is, of selection. This is not Heidegger's point of view: it is the point of view that I will myself argue for by building on Socrates, Husserl, Nietzsche and Derrida, but at the same time by distancing myself from Husserl, Nietzsche and Derrida, if not from Socrates, of whom we have only the traces left to us by Plato and by those who copied his texts, which are what I call alphabetical hypomnesic and literal tertiary retentions.

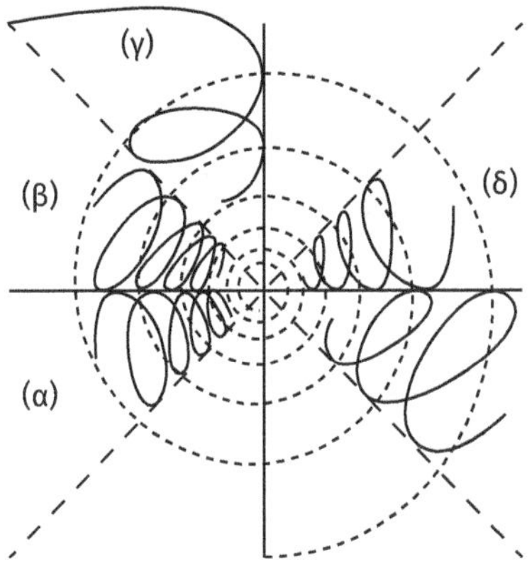

Figure 5. Idiotext by author.

In the course of my research, I have endeavoured to show that this process of selection begins with perception, so that – the latter being temporal, that is, constituting inner sense, which is also, for Kant, the form of time[77] that constitutes the transcendental aesthetic, the effective operation of which is the synthesis of understanding by the transcendental imagination – any perception is first and foremost the process of receiving or gathering what Husserl called primary retentions, which will be denoted here by **1R**. These are, ultimately, primary selections, which we will denote by **1S**, where these selections are effected on the basis of criteria, and where those criteria are secondary retentions, which we will denote by **2R**. Secondary retentions are former primary retentions, that is, former primary selections: former retentions that constitute, in a primary way, a phenomenon *as present* and in the time of its flowing through inner sense (in the Kantian sense). I insist on this question of the present because, as we will see, it *is*, in a certain way, *alētheia* – as *Anwesenheit* and *Gegenwart*. These are, then, former selections that have subsequently become memories, that is, something that comes 'from the past'. As such, they constitute what Hume, for example, described as habits.

2R, secondary retentions, are psychic, but there are 2Rs that become social, that is, collective. In so doing, they form knowledge – of how to live, do and conceive. These various kinds of knowledge are transmitted, and this transmission occurs mainly through the process of education, as we already saw – the latter being the sole pathway by which nascent Dasein can *enter into the world*. Consequently, I distinguish between psychic secondary retentions, **P2R**, and collective secondary retentions, **C2R**.

It is the sharing – in Greek, *moira* – of such collective secondary retentions, inasmuch as they engender collective expectations, or in other words collective protentions (which we will denote by **CP**), it is this sharing of collective retentions constituting a non-lived and yet inherited past, which is thus also a sharing of collective protentions constituting the horizon of a common and desirable future, that forms what we will call an epoch. Such an epoch is also what Heidegger called 'the understanding that there-being has of its being', where the latter is, as he says, shored up by an 'average and vague understanding of being'.[78] But, conceived in this way, an epoch is what implements, and at the same time invents, dis-covers and metastabilizes criteria, through crises in which former criteria disappear in favour of new criteria. This critical play of retentions and protentions through which an epoch is formed – and is formed as *Bildung* – constitutes what I call a process of transindividuation, which we will denote by **PTI**.

Technics and Time, 1 is the attempt to show that the play of the psychic and collective retentions and protentions that constitute an epoch is always conditioned, at every step, by tertiary retentions, which are the spatialized traces of conscious time – spatialized in the most diverse forms, firstly by tools and instruments, which appeared some three million years ago, then by the hypomnesic tertiary retentions (**R3H**) that appeared in the Upper Palaeolithic.

The critical play between (1) these tertiarized retentions and (2) primary and secondary retentions, engenders protentions, and falls within the scope of the process that Derrida called différance, which is, as you know, temporalization as spatialization, and vice versa.

But if différance constitutes epokhality, which Heidegger also named *Geschichtlichkeit*, it does so noetically, which means:

- on the one hand, that it stems from a process of exosomatization, a term I have borrowed from Alfred Lotka;
- on the other hand, that it is noetized as *praxis*, and not just as *poiēsis*, but most likely this is so only starting from the Upper Palaeolithic, where the latter constitutes the age of grammatization in the sense described by Leroi-Gourhan in *Gesture and Speech*,[79] and which is also the age of Lascaux, those caves that for Georges Bataille would signify *The Birth of Art*.[80]

If there is any necessity to what transpires during this course, it will be the experience of a *hermēneia* of that of which the world consists in the era of *post-truth*, an era that is *in truth* that of an absence of epoch. The path traced by Heidegger is something we will need to retrace, if not step by step then at least in its manifold sinuousness, because only *Being and Time* enables a close approach to the question of tertiary retention and of what ultimately constitutes its perpetually renewed problem, question and secret, namely, the *pharmakon*, which I represent here with this photograph taken by Aby Warburg in New Mexico in the late nineteenth century (See Figure 6), and which I argue symbolizes this *pharmakon* that haunted him from beginning to end – the end being the Kreuzlingen lecture where he discussed the snake, from the Hopi ritual to the bronze serpent of the Bible.

Heidegger's closest approach to these questions occurs in §76 of *Being and Time*, but this highly proximal approach is at the same time a distal recoil. Heidegger recoils from the very thing he approaches so closely, and this is precisely what opens up *Erstreckung* as the very possibility of the close and the distant.

It is starting from these questions in *Technics and Time, 1* that I have argued that the history of truth is the epiphylogenetic history of a form of life that, with Georges Canguilhem, I also call technical life, and more recently, with Lotka, exosomatic life. In what follows, I will try to convince you that thinking, conceiving and interpreting the history of truth requires us to also undertake a history of noesis, the latter being conditioned by the history of hypomnesic tertiary retention, that is, by the history of grammatization, this word deriving not from Derrida's grammatology but from the work of Sylvain Auroux.[81]

The question of the *pharmakon* – a question that Heidegger ultimately avoids, even though, in the final reckoning, and especially at the end of his thinking, he really speaks of nothing else[82] – is a question that obviously found its way to me through Derrida, but in what follows you will understand, I hope, why it is that I did not just stick to the latter's analysis, however original and decisive it may be in many respects.

Figure 6. Photo by Aby Warburg.

Finally, all this should be situated in the context without epoch of the end of the Anthropocene, which can also be called *Gestell*, that is, in the context of a disruption that fundamentally stems from cybernetics, which articulates sub-marine networks and satellite networks via data centres, and captures the data of the beings that we ourselves are, doing so in order to render calculable, and algorithmically treatable, all the forms of retention and protention in which consists what we call ek-sistence in exo-somatization, and where différance as noetic différance, and not only as vital différance, must be conceived as ek-sistance with an 'a'.

And we will also see that this means that we ought to conceive thinking [*pensée*] as that which consists in caring [*panser*], that is, in taking care – which is also to say, what *Being and Time* calls *Sorge*.

Let us summarize, before turning to the materials that we will work on tomorrow.

1 Heidegger raises the question of the history of truth by continuously circling around the question of the *pharmakon* and tertiary retention, which arise from the exosomatic condition of ek-sistence; yet, despite this, Heidegger never engages with this issue – for reasons that we will try to elucidate, and that have everything to do with his Nazi and anti-Semitic corruption.

2 It is Derrida who opens the path that leads to this rereading of Heidegger – and does so starting from the trace, the erasure of being and the *pharmakon* as hypomnesic condition of anamnesis – but Derrida did not himself follow this path out to the end, which is also that of *Gestell* as experience of disruption, which is also to say, of the Capitalocene that is the Anthropocene. While on this road, Derrida abandons the direction that aims at the *pharmakon*, changing course towards undecidability, without having delineated the polarity wherein the *pharmakon* is experienced precisely as the undecidable about which we must nevertheless decide.

3 All this rests, as well, on the question of the tragic in the Greeks that Nietzsche introduced in his Dionysian philology.

4 By introducing the concept of exosomatization, the rereading of Derrida with Simondon is immediately given a new depth and perspective, enabling différance to become something we can think, treat or take care of [*panser*], with the concepts of sidereal, vital and psychosocial individuation.

SECOND LECTURE

The New Conflict of the Faculties and the Functionalist Approach to Truth

Yesterday I tried to inscribe the planetary discussion around the topic of post-truth into what Heidegger called the history of truth. What I will develop during this seminar belongs to what I call a neganthropology. This word is a kind of reply to Levi-Strauss when he said that it would be better to spell anthropology as entropology.

I myself claim that Anthropocene should better be written Entropocene, and that we have to escape such an Entropocene by producing a new era of truth. And today, we will see that for this, a neo-functionalist approach to the history of truth is needed, and we will then see why and how it could and should lead to the so-called post-truth era. Now, the post-truth stage of this history could open the possibility of a new era of truth: the Neganthropocene, as a new era of truth defined as a new function of the exosomatic form of life, which is also the genuine issue at stake in what Heidegger called *Ereignis*, which is thinkable only by considering the age of *Gestell* as also amounting to the age of *Bestand*.

For this, we need:

- first, to reconsider the concepts of negentropic organogenesis, informational negentropy and exosomatization, issues that are addressed by Wiener, but in a vocabulary that remains that of metaphysics;
- second, to requalify the metaphysical terms in which those concepts were elaborated after thermodynamics – and for this, we must reread Plato and re-characterize Socrates' statements beyond and below Plato.

Now, recalling Heidegger's remarks about that moment in the history of truth that is *Politeia*, Plato's *Republic*, and to understand why the evolution of negentropic organogenesis that is described by Lamarck as well as by Schrödinger, and the relationship between exosomatization and entropy that is at stake in both Lotka's analysis and Georgescu-Roegen's work, to understand, then, why such an evolution is the condition of truth inasmuch as it is a history that is linked to the evolution of artefacts, we need to revisit Heidegger's deconstruction of this history from the new standpoint of the Anthropocene, and to connect this with Heidegger's considerations concerning *Gestell* and *Ereignis*.

Today, and in order to prepare us for such a course, I will introduce the topic of what Kant called the conflict of the faculties, but as a new such conflict, engendered by the evolution of tertiary retentions when they become digital and algorithmic. For this, it will be necessary to overcome the current concept of negentropy – noesis being itself, in my view, what produces neganthropic bifurcations, where this concept of bifurcation comes from Whitehead.

To enter into these topics, we should read Heidegger's 'Plato's Doctrine of Truth', and I also would like you to read his 'The Turn' or 'The Turning', about which I will talk a little bit next week.

▪ ▪ ▪

Before talking about what I will describe as the exosomatization of the faculties and functions of noesis, let's go back to the question of entropy, of which the ancient Greeks were ignorant, and which Heidegger, too, chooses to ignore.[83] The concept of entropy describes the thermodynamic process, and it has been extended to the field of biology as negative entropy – that is, as the *deferral* of entropy, which we might call its *différance* (in Derrida's sense), for, indeed, this leads to a spatialization of what we will describe in what follows as an organogenesis, whether this is endosomatic or exosomatic. There have also been *countless attempts to transplant* the concepts of entropy and negentropy to the fields of information theory, cybernetics, communication theories, systems theories and complexity theory, all in the pursuit, ultimately, of various attempts to formalize the human sciences and social sciences.

Furthermore, in the bio-economics of Nicholas Georgescu-Roegen, the increase in the rate of entropy, and its reduction (low entropy), that is, the *local slowing down* of the entropic process, become the nodal points of economics itself, which he approached in terms of the fact of exosomatic organogenesis (and where Leroi-Gourhan, for example, showed the growth of exosomatic organogenesis in the process of hominization). Exosomatic organogenesis distinguishes the *economic beings that we must be* from other living things, which are 'negentropic' thanks only to their endosomatic organogenesis, which is itself 'spontaneously' economic (so to speak) due to the 'pressures of selection'.

What after Heidegger we call *Gestell* constitutes the *contemporary infrastructures of knowledge*. These infrastructures are those of a *technological and industrial development of knowledge and of the faculty of knowing in general* that is also called the post-truth era. The post-truth stage of the history of truth is occurring in the context of the rise of what we now call 'big data', and the high-performance computing that makes its production possible, in the form of the production of *patterns* – the establishing of correlations. Also part of this context is the rise of a transhumanist ideology that anticipates a *point of bifurcation*, referred to – particularly by Ray Kurzweil – as the 'Singularity'. It is striking to observe that this discourse, which thus anticipates a tipping point, a singularity in the mathematical and physical sense of the term, by this *very gesture* puts forward two theses whose conjunction warrants serious consideration, but which I have time here only to mention:

- on the one hand, it asserts that a bifurcation is coming, when machines will become 'more intelligent' than their creators – ourselves, or our fellow human beings;
- on the other hand, it takes for granted that on the basis of this intelligence, we – or our fellows – will then be less intelligent than our exosomatic productions yet will be able to become immortals.

It is in light of this utterly fanciful twofold perspective, backed as it is by transhumanist ideology, that we should analyse and criticize the discourse of Chris Anderson, whose formal and fundamental errors, if I can put it like that, I have explained elsewhere and will not go into again here.[84] But following this, and complementary to it, I would like now to recall my argument in *Technics and Time, 3*, and to make a case for the addition of five theses.

1 What is at stake both in the Kurzweilian delirium and in the Andersonian entrepreneurial strategy involves the *faculties of knowing, desiring and judging*, in the Kantian sense. But to mobilize Kant against these ideologemes characteristic of the disruptive period into which the Anthropocene (that is, the Capitalocene) has entered,[85] and within which a 'shift' is readying itself that has nothing to do with the 'Singularity' in the transhumanist sense but everything to do with the end of theory in Anderson's sense, we must *critique Kant himself* by showing how he lacks an exosomatic conception of the schematism and of that imagination he referred to as transcendental. It was a critique of this sort that I tried to outline in *Technics and Time, 3*, by showing that artificial retention, or what I call *tertiary* retention, is the condition of any *noetic* retention or protention whatsoever, that is, of any rationality.

2 The faculty of knowing has evolved in the course of what Alfred Lotka named exosomatization, and as the progressive exteriorization (différance) – but as noetic différance, and not only vital différance – a progessive exteriorization and differance of the *functions* of the *faculty* of knowing,[86] in particular:

a of the *intuition*, through instruments of observation;

b of the *understanding*, through computing and information technologies;

c of the *imagination*, when instruments of observation become instruments for the production of behavioural programs via what Adorno and Horkheimer called the industry of cultural goods.

As you can see, what I am saying is that différance refers to the deferral of entropy, but this deferral can be either endosomatic, that is, negentropic, or exosomatic, that is, neganthropic. It is because the functions of the faculty of knowing are trans-formed by exosomatization that Heidegger was right to see Book VII of *Republic* as marking a *change in the meaning of truth for Plato,*[87] in which, as Heidegger said, *alētheia* comes to be understood in terms of *orthotēs* and *omoiosis*. But Heidegger did not see that what prepares itself through alphabetical exosomatization, that is, *hypomnesic and literal (lettered) tertiary retentions*, is what Kant described as the *division of the faculty of knowledge into functions*, where the understanding functions *analytically* and reason functions *synthetically* – that is, it is as such capable of *producing bifurcations*, in the sense suggested by Whitehead, and according to, or as a function of, the ideas (of reason) that constitute the kingdom of ends.

3 In the current stage of the exosomatization of the noetic faculties in general (of knowing, desiring and judging, if we keep to these Kantian metacategories), digital tertiary retention consists of information, that is, data, which can present itself only as *formatted in terms of its a priori calculability.* (By contrast, in the epoch of Kant, data was that which was 'given' to the intuition, and which is manifold, diverse, that is, characterized by the fact that it is precisely *not yet* 'formatted', which for Kant was the function of the concepts of the understanding.)

Through the *functional and algorithmic integration*[88] of the intuition (formatted by data-capturing interfaces), the understanding (the analytical functions of which are delegated to algorithms) and the imagination (which is reconfigured by the automated protentions extracted from the retentions accumulated by 'profiles'[89] and provoked by the interactions during which the schematization is itself delegated to the functions of the production of desire, in the sense denounced, wrongly, by Adorno and Horkheimer, as an exteriorization of the imagination, which Kant claimed to be transcendental), what occurs is that the *fixed capital* of capitalism becomes *fully computational*, and knowledge, which turns into information, becomes massively automated. This amounts, in other words, to the full realization of the 'fragment on machines' in Marx's *Grundrisse*.[90]

4 The 'data economy', high-performance computing and 'deep learning' are all based on analytical, statistical and probabilistic models that together form *reticulated artificial intelligence*, that is, a generalized connectivity that processes the traces systematically and systemically generated by feedback loops capable of operating at speeds between two and four million times quicker than the noetic body and its nervous system. This noetic body is noetic only to the extent that it is exosomatized, divided into the functions of the faculties of knowing, desiring and judging (if we retain these Kantian terms). These faculties are constituted by their exosomatization (their exteriorization in a supplementary différance), and coupled with a disorganization and reorganization of the cerebral organ, which thereby becomes not just organic but organological.[91]

This organology, which is the condition of the faculties and of their various functions, is pharmacological. This means that it can just as easily deepen and lengthen circuits of noetic transindividuation as it can short-circuit them, in the latter case by replacing them with automatisms (the clichés of sophistic thinking in the eyes of Socrates, the destruction of work-knowledge [*savoir faire*] by machinism according to Marx, the liquidation of life-knowledge [*savoir vivre*] by the culture industries according to Adorno, the obsolescence of scientific theory and method outstripped and overtaken by supercomputing according to Anderson, and so on).

5 Fifth thesis. The current development of *thoroughly computational fixed capital* leads to an *anthropic collapse*. To go beyond this point requires a new economy founded on a neganthropology. This neganthropology, which has the goal of enabling us to pass from the Anthropocene to the Neganthropocene, must be based on the constant critique of the limits of exosomatization insofar as it is pharmacological, and on the way it tends to perpetually (like the rock of Sisyphus, perpetually rolling back) intensify both entropy and negentropy. This intensification of tension constitutes what the Greeks called *hubris*, what Heidegger called *Gewalt*, and what Socrates described as a *pharmakon*.

I will not elaborate on these theses in what follows. Instead I will propose to reconsider the questions raised by entropy and negentropy in the anthropological and neganthropological fields such as I have tried to conceive them. But on the basis of these notions it will then become possible to put these five theses to the test.

In *Technics and Time, 2*, I argued that information, in the modern sense that appeared in the nineteenth century with press agencies and telecommunication networks, is first and foremost a commodity that *loses value with time* – in the course of that time during which it is disseminated into a space where it is broadcast or diffused, and which is also a *market*, a *computational milieu* that turns behaviours into *inherently* calculable objects.[92]

Information then becomes a *function*, and it has 'value' only inasmuch as it does so. During the nineteenth century – which will also be that of the appearance of mechanography in North America – the world entered into a process of constant transformation. It entered the Anthropocene as the age of *calculated exosomatization*, oriented towards what will become permanent innovation (or what Joseph Schumpeter described as creative destruction). The need for psychic individuals and collective individuals to orient themselves within this perpetual becoming, to find the way to a future, requires them to exercise not the faculty of orienting themselves in thought and the world starting from what Kant called the *subjective principle of differentiation*,[93] but the *everyday informational practice* that Hegel referred to in Jena between 1803 and 1806. Of course, in Hegel's time, and despite the 'absolute knowledge' to which he aspired and which he intended to embody, the concept of information as *function* was *yet to emerge*, and *he did not see it coming*.

In the *new* world, which will lead to what is precisely *not* absolute knowledge but the *complete opposite*, absolute *non-knowledge* – that is, computationally and functionally integrated de-noetization (noesis having been *functionally disintegrated*) – something that *informs* me is something that *matters* to me, something of material interest that I had not known, that I was unaware of. From the moment I *become* 'aware' of it, I gain an advantage, an advantage I begin to lose as soon as others also become aware of it and so able to gain the *same* advantage, which means that no one any longer has any advantage.

Knowledge, then, as 'being up-to-date', 'being aware', becomes confounded with 'the news' of the *new* world – and of the 'New World'.

This is so because, already in this epoch, what 'matters' is increasingly oriented by the market as the space of behavioural calculations according to calculable interests – which paves the way for the secularized age of what Nietzsche would call nihilism and Weber would call disenchantment. This calculability of interests gives rise to what Hölderlin called philistinism in what he saw as a time of distress, and it is what leads to the submission of *otium* (which orientates the *incalculability of the protentions* characteristic of what Kant called the kingdom of ends) to *negotium*. Through this process the bourgeoisie seizes hold of the noetic heritage of the aristocracy – who practised noesis precisely as this *otium cultivating* 'incalculables' as *freedom*, that is, as the possibility of effecting bifurcations.

This is how the question of information and of its value presents itself – and from this we can see that information is the *very opposite* of knowledge, given that the latter is cumulative, lasting *through* its transformations (Einstein does not erase Newton, Marx does not eliminate Hegel, and so on). For Charles-Louis Havas in 1835, four years after the death of Hegel, information was worth whatever the newspapers were willing to pay for his dispatches. And the more it is diffused, the less it is worth. Hence is fully established the nihilistic conception of value wherein everything tends towards equivalence – where 'everything is the same' and 'anything goes'.[94]

Consequently, the value of information evaporates. And along with its value, information itself evaporates, if by information we mean 'that which brings the "informed" person a disturbance that leads his or her behaviour to be transformed in a manner that is advantageous *so long as others are not advantaged*'.

Here we see why information can be said to amount to a negentropic potential based on which it is possible to produce a difference (a new regime of différance), but which is bound to evaporate. This evaporation of différance – this fundamentally entropic tendency of information as a commodity whose value is calculable on a market – is also what installs a new regime of repetition (in the Deleuzian sense).[95]

What is referred to in the new concept of 'information' in the market context has two main characteristics:

- on the one hand, information is a *signal*, a *temporal* signal – that is, a signal that is produced *in time* and within a stream that 'vectorizes' a space homogenized by a distribution network through which it is broadcast and 'disseminated' in the course of a time that thereby itself becomes calculable
- on the other hand, it is an *economy*, but an economy constituted by a calculability, an economy in the sense of the capitalist economy, a market economy where any use value can be transformed into exchange value, and so into a calculation. I can calculate and monetarize all things according to the calculability of information, which is itself the foundation of a theory of competition, of supply and demand, and so on, and *into which anything can be reduced and dissolved*, thereby becoming 'virtual' in the contemporary (and hollow) sense of this term.

Is the value of information really always calculable? Is its *entire* value reducible to calculation? Obviously the answer is 'no': the value of information is calculable only insofar as those who calculate this value belong to a space of distribution and therefore of calculability that is homogeneous. (This space amounts to a kind of phase space, in the sense of Henri Poincaré and Richard S. Hamilton – a space where calculation tends to eliminate time by totally spatializing it.)

If this tendentially Hamiltonian space and the time flowing through it are fragmented, and from this perspective disturbed, if in other words it forms *heterogeneous localities*, then to orient oneself it is not enough to have calculable information. One must trans-form this information by making it pass through the filter of a critical re-evaluation of its value, according to criteria that amount to some or other kind of knowledge. Here, and unlike with information, the value of knowledge does not evaporate over the time during which it is disseminated in what is no longer simply homogeneous space, *amounting instead to places*. The value of knowledge is precisely what is enriched by *new values of knowledge*, through the way in which the *diversity of places* enables a critique of purely and simply calculable information, a critique undertaken in order to detect an incalculable potential that we here call not negentropic, but neganthropological.

Information, defined for instance as the market exploited by Havas, can also be considered from a completely different standpoint. The newspaper I purchased this morning for €1.90, loses value so quickly that by tomorrow it will hardly be worth anything, and after tomorrow morning it will simply be tossed in the trash, or at least to the ragmen [*chiffonniers*], as paper recyclers used to be called. From such a standpoint, in twenty-four hours the value of the daily news contained in a daily newspaper evaporates for the reader of this newspaper. And yet...

And yet sometimes we read 'the paper' late and, in this lateness, suddenly discover what we could never find in mere 'information', namely, an element of comprehension: for example, we learn something about the way information *functions*. Or, again, there is an element of surprise [*surpréhension*], an element that *exceeds comprehension* (*Verstandnis*), or exceeds the understanding (*Verstand*) – a surpassing whereby we can begin to 'think for ourselves', to exercise the synthetic powers of reason to judge what we had hitherto tended rather simply to consume: what had been a commodity is turned into knowledge.

There are people who will sell you the newspaper that came out on the day you were born. Others salvage newspapers from flea markets or elsewhere, not because they are archivists, but because they see the newspaper as an archive that enables them to reconstruct the past, thereby bringing to light the question of hypomnesic tertiary retention. What we are dealing with is then no longer information but a document.

The document acquires its value not on some homogeneous market of information but within a local exploration, in the 'sur-prehensive' noodiversity of an inherent heterogeneity of knowledge, whose functions are divided into disciplines, in the service of the knowledge of the historian, the archivist, the palaeographer, the genealogist or the archaeologist. When Google provides us with analytical graphics, in order, for example, to make clear the evolution of co-occurrences – through the centuries, decades, years, months, weeks, thanks to 'Google Analytics' – the search engine facilitates an understanding of what is no longer exactly information, even if it mobilizes information technologies. Such tools are nevertheless luxuries for the Alphabet corporation: they do not fuel turnover.

One could define information as 'negentropic' by transferring the biological concept of negentropy to Shannon's theory of information, or by transferring the Shannonian concept of information to biology (with Henri Atlan – and by way of the feedback loop, the homeostasis of Ross Ashby and the theory of self-organization in dissipative structures). Insofar as it disrupts the system it penetrates, information could then be called negentropic in that it is what leads a system to change its state.

Let us, from a different standpoint, call this system an *idiotext*. In this case we are no longer talking about *information* but about the *given* [*donnée*] – not data in the sense used today by the information industries when they describe themselves as the designers, producers and managers of the data economy, which considers the informed system as a calculating or computing system, but rather *sense data*, as what provides to the understanding that which Kant called 'the manifold of intuition'.

Let us posit that this dynamic system, the idiotext, which is a *living* system, is also an interpretive system – more precisely, an open system that interprets, from within the functional instability and infidelity (in Canguilhem's sense) of its exosomatized milieu, the condition of its maintaining itself in this opening, namely: *truth* as the *power to bifurcate possessed by a system that, without this knowledge, would ineluctably become closed*, that is, be bound to destroy itself due to the inevitable increase in the rate of entropy within the locality in which it consists, eventually leading to the obliteration or effacing of this locality.

This living system that noetically differs and defers (which holds off [*temporise*], by spatializing) this effacement (even though ultimately 'everything must efface itself, everything will efface itself'[96]), this form of life that knows itself to be mortal and knows that concrescence is bound to be effaced, generally in the mode of nonknowing and denial; this open system is hermeneutic: it does not just calculate information.

I can, of course, mobilize analytical and as such computational techniques in the service of a certified understanding of the data that I receive and that must be interpreted – the data in relation to which I must decide. But I am *affected* by what, through what constitutes itself not as *information* but as the *given* in the Kantian sense, presents itself to me as a *motive* of reason, or as an echo of such a motive, the motive of my reason that expresses my desire insofar as it consists above all in a noetic activity that is itself inscribed within the neganthropological fate *maintaining* its archi-locality despite being bound to disappear in concrescence.

Data of this kind can present itself to the idiotext in a thousand ways – including getting slapped. When one takes a slap, it is the given: sense data. To receive a slap in the face, to suffer it, is to receive sense data in the form of a shock. To learn that one's father has died: this is to receive the given (which becomes not sense data but a data of sensibility, feeling, since the father is effaced, withdrawn from the sensible, and has become, if not 'spiritual' or 'suprasensible', at least *revenantial*: spectral). One does not (or not only) make calculations with this data that, received, we must *render* to those who have given it to us by having made it fruitful, that is, by having trans-formed it exosomatically and *intensified* the improbability that constitutes their power both to shock and to nourish.

This given data, which is not information, is an *event*. One tiny little event can affect my nervous system, and through my nervous system it can affect my isothermal regulation, which can generate in my body a reaction that is not a calculation but a *reflex* – which might, for instance, cause me to shiver, perhaps indicating to me that the ambient temperature is low compared to that of my body and that the temperature difference between my body and the surrounding environment could cause me to 'catch cold', as we say – could trigger within me a state of vulnerabililty, for example, to a virus that happens to pass nearby – so this reflex leads me to react by putting on more clothes or closing a window.

This little event need not involve my consciousness, or my unconscious, strictly speaking, yet it can contribute to the development of other events that do involve my unconscious – but let's leave that to one side.

Or consider some other sorts of events: I may, for example, be in the process of 'surfing the net' (or rather, the Web, and, through that, the net). I go to the Google website and activate the PageRank information algorithm by making a request: I complete a task, as ergonomists put it. Then I come across something completely different from what I was actually looking for: by 'browsing', I *happen upon* – by accident, by chance – something utterly different from what I was *expecting*. This different thing, which is a little accident, *a little event* – an accident is always an event that occurs in the stream of micro-actions or macro-actions, or, as we say, 'in the course of action' – this thing that happens so suddenly, and was therefore not planned or foreseen, no doubt *resembles* information.

This thing resembles information that comes along to disturb an existing system (me), which means that *the informational system with which I interact*, in the classical model of information as object of calculation, comes to disturb the informational system *that I am myself*, and comes to disturb me because I did not foresee, in my own calculations, the possibility of such an event, and, from this fact, *I learn something through this unforeseen thing* to which I then adapt myself.

Now, the *unforeseen* aspect of this serendipitous accident that occurs during my browsing Google with PageRank is not unforeseen in the sense of something not anticipated, that is, calculated by the dynamic system that I am – calculable by it, *anticipatable* by it. But that unforeseen-ness, that *unexpectedness*, which is *not* anticipatable, which was *totally* unexpected, perhaps proceeds nevertheleess *from what was most expected*, expected as the unhoped-for (*anelpiston*): the improbable, the incomparable, and the inestimable – the bifurcating.

The expectation of the unexpected is the horizon of the archiprotention of what is incalculable, and it is what opens every form of knowledge to that which exceeds the understanding. Heidegger called this expectation of the unexpected *Sein-zum-Tode*. But this 'originary' protention that stems from a default of origin must be reconceived today from a neganthropological perspective that passes through Freud. It must be reconceived by delineating what, in the drives and their vicissitudes, derives from entropy, what from negentropy, and what, as desire, neganthropologically exceeds both of these within the horizon of différance, as what Derrida called 'survival' or 'living-on'.

This *unforeseen* was *unexpected* because I was not expecting it at all. *I was not aware of it*, I did not organize my behaviour around it, according to it, in that direction. Yet when suddenly it happens to me – through what we call serendipity – it turns out that I *precipitated* this unexpectedness, and this precipitation, which is a crystallization where something bifurcates, reflects the fact that I did expect it, and even, perhaps, that I expected *only that*...without knowing it.

I thereby discover within myself a strange *expectation of the unexpected*: I find that the unexpected comes to echo what I expected *without knowing* that I was expecting it. This expectation is of a completely different order than calculable anticipation. It belongs to what *Being and Time* described as being inherently *indeterminate*, and it is therefore inscribed within the *Sein-zum-Tode* in which there-being consists insofar as it is *never completely there, not yet* completely there, *insofar as its locality is open*, because it *remains* always *improbably to come*, and *presents itself only in this expectation* – as 'pending' [*en attendant*] (which also means, *attentively*).

Calculable anticipation is always explainable: it is banal, routine and can always be made conscious, and as such it is completely formalizable, describable and transformable into an informational model where retentions and protentions can be reduced to calculations. The *long-awaited unexpected* [*inattendu tant attendu*], that which is *not yet* there, is something completely different: something I did not know yet expected. Freud, Heidegger and Lacan call this (in the diversity of their agreement) *das Ding*. And this refers us back to Plato's *Meno*.

What is in play, here, functions as a *circuit*, but it is not at all a circuit of calculable information, nor is it able to be related, therefore, to market value, any more than to an *adaptive balance sheet* – that is, to some homeostatic maintenance of the state of a system through a more or less adaptive process of metastable homeostasis, which it would then be a matter of maintaining. On the contrary, what occurs in this play does not have the function of adapting that which functions to a milieu; rather, what occurs has the function of enabling the *adopting* of a milieu through the occurrence of an event, and, in adopting it, of individuating oneself while individuating it – which relates to the questions of the milieu that Whitehead, Canguilhem and Leroi-Gourhan understood respectively as the *attack* on the environment, *infidelity and normativity* within the milieu, and the *technicity* of the milieu.

Through what I discover by accident, and as the long-awaited unexpected, I *individuate myself*: I transform myself 'from the ground up', not so as to produce by calculation a new homeostatic state, but, on the contrary, so as to overturn every dimension of my being, leading me to reformulate myself – to adopt new behaviours that are not summable, or comparable, or calculable: they are *singularities*. Having learned something of the unexpected, I am myself singularly reindividuated, which means that I have bifurcated *after having been disindividuated*, that I have become no longer comparable to what I had hitherto been, in my having been, in my *to ti en einai*. This can happen to me through a bullet that lodges in my lower back, as happened to Joë Bousquet, or by alcohol taking hold of my habits, as happened to Malcolm Lowry: such an individuation by incalculable accidents proceeds step by step according to what Deleuze called quasi-causality.

It might be asked, here, how this differs from what happens when I adapt, for example, to the informational bombardment of computing. For in that case, too, my behaviour changes: I adopt different behaviour, and so in this case, too, I am individuated. I am, however, *barely* individuated: I *adapt* myself to the milieu; in other words, I approach a *behavioural average* thanks to which I lose my singularity – I get closer to the mean. And this means: I disindividuate. Such are the stakes of nihilism.

THIRD LECTURE

Socrates and Plato in the Tragic Age and the Inauguration of the Western Individuation Process

In France, I try to teach my students to use a video platform to share their notes, those notes being inscribed in the temporal flux of a video recording. Hence I also teach those students how to use Google, search engines in general and the Web, but how to do so, not just with an 'informational' approach, but by practising journeys of knowledge via psychically and socially *individuating* approaches – and, in so doing, adding to the neganthropic enrichment of the world, that is, to its diversification. Such approaches would contribute to the enrichment of the world's *noodiversity*, where *wealth* is the opening of possibilities such that they are not reducible to becoming – and where becoming means being pulled by the arrow of time towards the probability of the Im-mense: the cooling down of the universe extending to perpetuity.

By individuating myself through a knowledge that, by this very fact, I in turn individuate, I contribute to a *diversification* that opens up the possibility of a deviation and through it of bifurcations punctuating a différance. Such bifurcations did not previously exist in the world where the occurrence of this accident was possible – where the possible is not a modality of being but a bifurcation in the stream of becoming through which it *makes* (the) différance, through an incalculable trans-formation, a completely singular transformation, one deviating from the averages that the information industry produces in systemic fashion. The latter is what Nietzsche already saw as the nihilism typical of his time, an age in which the first steps were being taken towards the establishing of what would become mass society.

Differing and deferring via what we call information and communication technologies, but also via writing, consists in producing *tertiary retentions* – formerly in a hieratic manner, conducted through sacralization and hierarchization via symbolic, magical or sacred powers; then, through schools, universities and academic or scientific powers, aiming to develop forms of knowledge, which are powers to act (first of the *polis*, then of theologico-political power, and, in the Anthropocene, of capital as the Capitalocene); and, today, through the information industries. The latter tend towards a *disruptive* takeover of power via control technologies, but in so doing they are heading straight for the wall of a 'big shift'. All this makes it *imperative* to rethink entropy and negentropy in terms that are *related to but different from* thermodynamics, biology or the attempted formalizations of cybernetics and the information sciences.

The knowledge produced by an event leads individuals to bifurcate, to transform themselves in order to increase their power to act – a transformation that in cybernetic theory is called feedback. This living feedback does not come from the outside of the living thing; it is, on the contrary, what the living thing projects outward onto the exterior – what Humberto R. Maturana and Francisco J. Varela call the *autopoiesis* produced in enaction.[97] But in the case of the *economic* beings that we *must* be, *insofar as we only exist exosomatically, affected and disaffected by the milieus that we ourselves produce,*

- either, this organogenesis produces an adaptation to the milieu by informational computation, in so doing sterilizing the capacity for invention;
- or, it produces normativity in the sense of Georges Canguilhem – transforming pathogenic elements into elements of meaning, into *pathos* in this sense, that is, into new kinds of affects, which will in turn generate other affects: affected, I affect others after that which has affected me, and that I *trans-form* – that is, I *transindividuate* – at the same time individuating the milieu according to and as a *function* of my affection, my *pathos*, which becomes a *normativity* through this process of transindividuation that is an *incalculable différance.*

This is the meaning of *Stimmung* in Heidegger's existential analytic. It is no longer a cybernetic feedback loop, which we can also conceive in terms of Jakob von Uexküll's circuit running between receptor organs and effector organs, a circuit within which the tick pursues its 'destiny'.[98] It is, on the contrary, a noetic 'destinerrance' where différance stands *between* noetic bodies, this *between* being, precisely, noesis *that is always missing, always in default, and that, from this fact, is necessary.*

The noetic loop is a spiral, and it forms the spiral of hubris within which is produced an exosomatic drift, a trans-formation of the world and the milieus of life by organological production (and not just organic production). This exosomatic drift gives rise to a new type of diversification by artificial selection, amounting not just to a *local différance of entropy* – that is, to negentropy – but to *neganthropy.*

Organological neganthropy is not negentropy: it is produced not by the living, but by the *nonliving* in the service of the *living* – clothes, tools, artificial organs, paths, roads, houses, cities, records, mail, computers, networks… The world is composed of such *pharmaka*, and one result of all this is always to produce an increase in the rate of entropy, for example, through the dissipation of energy and the destruction of vital milieus and of organisms themselves.

But organological transformation (exosomatic organogenesis) *also* produces neganthropy. Neganthropology and neganthropic production, which result from exosomatization, are concretized only through the knowledge that they require. These forms of knowledge [*savoirs*] produce tastes [*saveurs*], that is, differences, noodiversified nuances through which the exosomatic being constantly raises itself towards a noesis that is more than human, which is always sur-human (just as the cosmos is always sur-realist: the cosmos, which is not just the universe, is composed of places within which improbable possibilities – surreal possibilities – well up).

This tendency contained in exosomatization is nevertheless perpetually being destroyed by an inverse, anthropic, homogenizing tendency, dictating, to the great noetic diversity that noodiversity forms, *obligations* to which it must adapt, in particular after capitalism takes hold of Western knowledge in order to turn it into a function of production and a power of economic domination through calculation and computing. This has tended, ever since the advent of digital tertiary retention, to transform knowledge into systems of information, amounting to the concrete realization of what the 'fragment on machines' described as the materialization of automation via the total integration and absorption of knowledge into fixed capital. Yet what this leads to is, in reality, the disintegration of knowledge by absolute non-knowledge.

It is a question, therefore, of *cultivating the possibility of a neganthropological bifurcation* from computational exosomatization, and as its prescriptive therapeutics. This requires the organological invention of new architectures of data, conceived in direct relation to academic organizations, revisiting in the era of digital, computational and reticulated tertiary retention what Kant already described as the *conflict of the faculties*, with the advent of this conflict that is in reality also and first *a conflict of functions within exosomatization*. We must care about, that is, in French, *panser* (this verb being very close to *penser*), we must care about this conflict of functions (and of faculties) so as to reorient all this technology towards the neganthropological fate that is the only way out of the Anthropocene: by entering the Neganthropocene.

Thinking all this means building upon the work of Nicholas Georgescu-Roegen and affirming that:

- on the one hand, economics is necessitated by exosomatization inasmuch as it replaces biology – and inasmuch as it is therefore not reducible to the laws of biology;
- on the other hand, economics must be thought on the basis of the question of entropy.

And through these bioeconomic perspectives, we must give new sense to *The German Ideology* of Marx and Engels, as well as to *The Dialectic of Nature* of Engels.

This is not, *first of all*, a matter of finding some alternative to capitalism: it is a matter of finding an alternative to anthropy, and of doing so through an economy of neganthropy. It is this set of questions that the Digital Studies Network is attempting to consider.

Living knowledge, when it is mortified, becomes non-knowledge, that is, so-called information. This situation, this state of fact, demands that we cultivate a new state of law from an organological perspective, and according to the reality of contemporary exosomatization, that gives *place(s)* to *new knowledge*. And because knowledge is not simply calculable, this requires us to mobilize the function of reason according to and as a function of the possibilities and impossibilities opened up and closed off by automated understanding.

The function of this new reason, which can only be a new critique, is what, as a capacity for bifurcation and decision, activates and reactivates (in Edmund Husserl's sense) the data that high performance computing provides to interpretation, and does so as the power to bifurcate – the power to act, to trans-form.

Such a problematic, which therefore requires us to rethink the architectures of data, equally requires us to think 'digital studies' in the sense of this concept that we have argued for along with Franck Cormerais and Jacques Gilbert, namely, as the study of the fabrication functions of the 'digits' – the *digital* functions of exosomaticization, where 'digit' refers to both the digits that *make things* and the digits that *count*.

Hence the digital denotes that which *ties* calculation to fabrication and fabrication to calculation, but which always assumes the *surpassing* of calculation, which is to say, precisely, the power of bifurcating, given that only knowledge, insofar as it takes care of the *pharmakon* and thereby surpasses the anthropic dimension of exosomatic organs and their organizations, is capable of reopening prospects and perspectives for the future.

Within these new perspectives, the *duty* of the economic beings that we must be is no longer just moral: it is cosmic. Based on the noetic power of dreaming (and of realizing our dreams, which is the condition of exosomatization), we must, using every means at our disposal, make this duty serve a surrealist and serendipitous cosmology, a quasi-causal cosmology.

Now, let's see how these questions form both the issues at stake in the origin of philosophy, with Socrates and Plato, and in the denial of philosophy as it immediately becomes, with Plato, metaphysics. So now let's enter the matter of the seminar as such.

Socrates's notary

Maurice Blanchot writes that in *Phaedrus*,

> Plato evokes, in order to condemn it, a strange language: [...] this is indeed speech, but it does not think what it says [...]. To entrust it to truth is really to entrust it to death. Socrates proposes therefore that language of this sort should as much as possible be avoided, like some dangerous disease [...].

This extreme mistrust of writing, which is shared still by Plato, shows what doubts and problems were occasioned by the new use of written communication.[99]

In the twenty-first century, all these issues are revived by what I call digital hypomnesic tertiary retention, but such that they arise in an entirely new way. It is in order to think [*penser*] this novelty, and to position it in such a way that we can care for it [*panser*], that I have taken my cue from Marcel Détienne's observations in *Les savoirs de l'écriture en Grèce ancienne*,[100] written in the 1980s, during the same period in which telematics was being developed in France, which would prove to be an important step in the conception of the World Wide Web, out of which a vast global industry of memory would unfold, leading to what has been called 'disruption', a concept that must obviously be understood in several senses, which I will not do now but which you can find outlined in *The Age of Disruption*.

Ancient Greece was *transfixed* by the *highly polemical adoption of a new retentional apparatus* – in the sense I have given to this expression in *Technics and Time 3*. It was, originally, in being confronted with the emergence of ortho-graphic tertiary retention that the event of philosophy first took place. And this way of putting the impact of mnemotechnical change on trial was also the way in which the question of *technics* came to be discovered – and the way in which it was *repressed*: Socrates refused

> the impersonal knowledge of the book [this is still Blanchot, here, in 1953, inspiring the young Jacques Derrida]. *Such a*

> *body of knowledge is linked to the development of technology in all its forms,* and it treats speech, and writing, as a technique, as technics.[101]

If we can but admire Blanchot's reflections here, we should nevertheless take his words with a degree of caution, especially when he *takes it as self-evident* that in *Phaedrus* it is indeed the words *of Socrates,* recorded in *Plato's supposedly faithful writing,* that discuss and condemn writing. For if one must pay careful attention to this secretary of Socrates named Plato, and especially to his warnings about written recordings [*consignations*], this relates first and foremost to his own activity as a notary of this supposedly Socratic speech.

We will see in the second part of this seminar how and why Socrates remains tragic, despite Plato's erasing from memory the fact that Socrates belonged to what still constituted the thoroughly tragic dimension of this period, which we also call – on the basis of that 'Socrates' whom we receive through the writings of Plato – the pre-Socratic epoch. To show this, we must cast doubt on what Blanchot says, and what, after him, Derrida will say: in fact, neither Socrates nor Plato reject writing. Socrates emphasizes the pharmacological – that is, tragic – character of writing. The fate of mortals is pharmacological, and this is what the tragic tradition affirms, which is to say, the pre-Socratic tradition. That Plato wants to instrumentalize writing in order to subject it to the dialectic does not amount to a condemnation: it is a denial. The 'historial' name for and meaning of this denial is what Heidegger called metaphysics. But Heidegger himself did not escape that which he deconstructs. And this is, before anything else, what lies behind his Nazism and anti-Semitism.

This seminar will thus be a kind of inquiry carried out in dialogue with two of Heidegger's lecture courses:

- the 1924–25 course on the *Sophist* and, in order to introduce the reading of Plato, on Aristotle, in particular on the *Nicomachean Ethics*;
- the 1931 course on *Republic*, Books VI and VII, and *Theaetetus*.

At these two moments, Heidegger puts forward the analyses and hypotheses that will ultimately lead to 'Plato's Doctrine of Truth', where he will show how *alētheia* then becomes, for Plato, and to the exclusion of any other understanding, *orthotēs* and *omoiosis*.

Ideal retention

Before proceeding with our second point today, which is ideal retention, I should briefly recall the theses I developed in *Technics and Time, 1*, which were inspired by the French historian Bertrand Gille.

Gille shows that any society is always constituted by the local appropriation of a technical system that exceeds it, and that this appropriation occurs via the social systems. The technical system corresponds to the local state of development of what, in previous sessions, I have referred to as exosomatization. Over millennia, exosomatization accelerates, and, from the late eighteenth century, through the development of industrial machinism, the increased pace of this acceleration means that the social systems are constantly disadjusted and challenged – thrown into question. In the twentieth and twenty-first centuries, this acceleration intensifies still further, resulting, today, in so-called 'disruption'.

This revolutionary turning point in acceleration is the concrete reality of what has come to be called the Anthropocene, and the age of disruption is the period in which reason comes to be outstripped and overtaken by reticular (or network) digital technologies, leading to *Gestell*, at least according to the interpretation I am proposing here, in a way that is partially homogeneous with Heidegger's claims, and partially strives to take a step beyond Heidegger, and to do so by thinking what I call the Neganthropocene.

Let us now return to the age of ancient Greece in which literal (lettered) tertiary retention appeared, which was the mnemotechnical dimension of the Greek technical system. The advent of a new form of mnemotechnics constitutes, like the advent of a new technical system, a techno-logical *epokhē*, a suspension of the collective and behavioural programs currently in force, and their replacement by new ways of life. But this replacement requires that the techno-logical *epokhē* be redoubled by another *epokhē*, by a discourse and more generally by a protean *symbolic production* (pious, if not religious, juridical, moral, architectural, sculptural, in general artistic, but also scientific, and so on), which defines the conditions of the adjustment between the new technical system and the other systems that form the social unity.

The birth of the West is the elaboration of a form of thinking that defines, or tries to define, the *conditions of the adjustment* to a new retentional apparatus, that is, to a *new milieu of the spirit*, which at the same time takes the place of what this milieu had hitherto been. In *Technics and Time, 3*, I highlighted the great longevity of what will be called, including by Blanchot, the 'epoch of the Book', which in our epoch reaches its end, its terminus – which obviously does not mean that the book disappears (it has never been so pervasive), but that *the age of its spiritual hegemony has passed.*[102]

What I tried to show in *Technics and Time, 3* is that:

1 the retentional system, which is both analogue (constituting what Adorno and Horkheimer called the culture industries) and digital, is today fully integrated into the global technical system of industrial production;

2 retentional criteria are therefore hegemonically subject to market forces, resulting in a succession of transformations – especially with respect to adoption, and to the 'revenance' of the past and the projection of the future – on the basis of what I have analysed as a *process of the interiorization of substrata.*

In order to constitute an organological and pharmacological approach to the exosomatization currently underway – which operates under the pressure of transhumanist storytelling – our task will here be to *understand how the criteriological apparatus typical of the epoch of the Book will govern the conditions of this interiorization.*

This criteriological apparatus – whose organs of transmission and interiorization are universities, which themselves emerge from philosophy, and which constitute the history of truth – is currently undergoing massive change, if not complete disintegration and destruction. It is in this context that we can refer to 'post-truth'. But in order to evaluate the historical meaning of this symptomatic discourse, we need to begin by returning to the history of the exosomatization of hypomnesic tertiary retentions, that is, to what amounts to the history of grammatization, in relation to which I argue that:

- it begins in the Upper Palaeolithic, as Derrida too suggests, himself referring to Leroi-Gourhan;
- what occurs between the seventh and fifth centuries BCE is a crisis whose first episode is the tragic and pre-Socratic age, and whose second episode is the denial of the pharmacological dimensions which this age had asserted, and their replacement by Platonic metaphysics as the discourse of the mastery of the letter by the dialectic.

Hence begins what Blanchot calls the *epoch of the Book, which arises as a rupture with the world of spirits, the latter giving way to the Spirit.* And hence occurs the construction of the metaphysics of the One, which will be called into question by both Derrida and Deleuze, each in their own style.

To analyse Plato is therefore, here, to pay close attention to how this epoch ends, a period of about a century and a half, during which the 'doubly epokhal redoubling' occurs and stabilizes itself. It is, in other words, the period during which a new retentional system is adopted, and the preceding system abandoned. There is obviously much in common between this way of seeing the birth of philosophy and the theses put forward by Eric Havelock, as well as those of Walter Ong, which are taken up by Maryanne Wolf. But I have also tried to show why Havelock and Ong themselves misunderstand Plato's relationship to writing, because they do not identify the ambiguity of his relationship to Socrates and to the tragic age.

I refer to the epoch of *the* Book, and not of books, because, through the Platonic oeuvre – which consists of several periods, in some respects contradictory, unfolding over the course of more than fifty years – what comes to be constituted is *metaphysics*. From the birth of philosophy, metaphysics weaves itself as the *ideal text* or the *ideal library*, which is to say the text or the library that defines, *like a dictionary*, what are the *right criteria* to be deployed as principles of selection by and in the retentional system, and which, as foundational, would themselves be *indisputable*, that is, as we will see, non-textual, *and therefore non-hypomnesic*. This denial of textuality is what Derrida showed clearly in 'Plato's Pharmacy'.

But as we shall see, this denial still affects Heidegger, and this unawareness is the condition of Kantian metaphysics.

Platonic thought is a discourse on memory, in which it is a matter of purifying what he calls *anamnesis* of what he calls *hypomnesis*, and where the method of doing so is dialectics, which no longer has anything to do with what Socrates understood as the dialogical practice of putting truth to the test of conversation. The Platonic dialectic is a means of defining essences, on the basis of the work of analysis, then of synthesis, where work amounts to the elaboration of a fundamental ontology – in which essences constitute *good retentions*, or good retentional *criteria*.

And everything begins with this: *the* criterion that is posited as being in principle prior to any criteriology, given the possibly for the *mneme* to have a hypomnesic dimension, is the following: *a good criterion does not itself have a technical essence*. It must not be hypomnesic.

Now, this discourse on 'good retentions', which is thus also a discourse on those tertiary retentional systems that are therefore here called '*hypomnesic*', is constituted as the *construction* and *apology* of the *personage*, the *character*, through whom Plato expresses himself, haunted by this ghost who makes him speak: Socrates makes Plato speak to the extent that he, Plato, makes Socrates speak – he makes speak that Socrates whose oral statements he hypomnesically assembles, which he has retained from the past by tertiarizing them, *and through which he projects his own unity – just as*, as I argued in *Technics and Time, 3*, the *consciousness of Kant* is constituted by unifications and arrangements of primary, secondary and tertiary retentions, the last of which are, by definition, able to be adopted by inheriting them, and lie at the non-transcendental origin of what Kant called, in the first edition of the *Critique*, the schemas of the imagination.

In the history of Plato's Socratic inheritance – which is also a sumptuous *dilapidation*, and, as we will see, *a discourse on the conditions of adoption* – the Socrates *of Plato* comes, over the course of the dialogues, to cover over the *tragic* Socrates, with which metaphysics (of which, *therefore*, this is the birth) here settles its account, bringing the West in general (or its embryo) out of its tragic epoch. Instead, he installs and anchors metaphysics to the complex of oppositions that will bind it to what we call the epoch of the Book, which is also to say, the epoch *of what will become Christianity*, and where this is perhaps the true beginning of the West – that is, its definitive rupture with the last echoes of its Orient.

This complex of oppositions, *which begins by opposing the dead to the living* inasmuch as technical memory (or hypomnesis) is opposed to living memory (or anamnesis), necessarily and simultaneously posits the *immortality of the soul* – and thereby invents the soul itself. Metaphysics, as the beginning of the epoch of the Book, is constituted precisely *as the rejection of the hypomnesis* that is the technical artefact of *textualized and literalized* memory, that is, as the denial of its biblio-graphic character, for which is substituted an absolutization of its psychic origin. This absolutization begins with the allegory of the winged soul, the soul becoming the absolute origin of any criteriology, which is also to say, *that which is opposed to the body* – which, strange as it may seem, finds itself endowed with the very same defects and attributes as hypomnesic *tekhnē*. But we know why: it is a question of the exosomatic body.

For Plato, far from the living thing par excellence, the body is itself already mortification: it is in *Phaedrus* that Plato recounts *both* the myth of the fall of the winged soul and the myth of the invention of writing by Theuth. In other words, the retentional criteria defined by Plato through the dialectic, as the basis of any fundamental ontology, are also fashioned in such a way that they mask the retentional system for which they are to be implemented, including the body that it involves, and this is so *because this body is inevitably implicated in the prostheticity that affects it*: exosomatization always leads to endosomatic rearrangements, of which, as Maryanne Wolf shows, the brain is the key organ.

The hypomnesic system, however, thoroughly conditions the constitution of these Platonic criteria. This question of the need to *define* retentional criteria works its way through the whole of ancient Greece, in that, *through their implementation*, an absolutely *new We* emerges, under the name of the *polis* – and I have argued in *Technics and Time, 3* that it is only by sharing and interiorizing such criteria that a *We* can both maintain its unity and pursue its psychic and collective individuation, and where 'collective' means, *here*, and for the first time, *political*.

It is on the definition of these criteria that Plato focuses, like all the Greek thinkers. In the books of Plato, however, these criteria are forged inasmuch as they are implemented, above all, *as principles with which to select and edit the utterances of Socrates*. To the degree they are assembled into an original logical flow, through which Plato forges the unity of his own thought, which *is* this logical flow, these statements affect the *polysemic* possibilities that make them typical of the *tragic* speech of Socrates. Instead, new meanings are acquired, to the extent that Plato selects from among possibilities and eliminates those he finds bothersome or disconcerting [*embarrassment*]. The criteria founded in this way then become constitutive of any truthful dialectics – according to a new concept of truth that Plato produces in Book VII of *Republic*, as Heidegger argues (as we have seen). These criteria form, in other words, fundamental ontology, projected as the ideality of the intelligible – and amount to an exit from the tragic epoch. But this final point is something that Heidegger fails to see clearly, as a reading of *The Essence of Truth* will show.

Now, the veracity of these criteria is measured by how effectively they allow a literary figure to come together – that is, the dynamic unity of the work of Plato as a literal flow that narrates, as it were, the *dialectical adventures* of 'Socrates'. Here, we must reconstruct a sequence that is composed of several dramatic, theatrical twists and turns.

1. The 'Socrates' of Plato is *firstly*, in the period during which Plato writes his so-called 'Socratic' dialogues, *the one who constantly throws criteria into question, who challenges every criterion*.

2. But, through a series of successive shifts, some of the *crucial* questions stemming from this general putting into question are then *put out of question* (they are no longer in question, exonerated, in the clear, '*hors de cause*'), so that the initial thematization of criteriology becomes the writerly device

by which 'Socratic' statements are set into a logical flow, and through which Plato legitimates his own operation in order, *finally*, to put beyond debate the *foundations* of this criteriological apparatus, to remove from question the *archi-criteria* that support it, and hence to *restrain the diachronic as well as diacritical upsurge of spirits that characterizes the end of the tragic epoch in Greece*, and of which Socrates is the *final* representative.[103] In the works of Plato, this occurs during what Léon Robin calls the mature period, but which is, in my view, the dogmatic period, the phase that includes everything characteristic of metaphysics as a regression with respect to the tragic question of the *pharmakon*.

3 Towards the end of the work, yet another period appears, one that is, once again, aporetic, in particular with the *Timaeus* and its question of the *khōra*.

A question truly questions only to the extent that, being the implementation of a criterion that puts in question what it interrogates, what it *critiques*, it puts this criterion itself to the test, and to the question, by putting it to work. This is, in a way, what Plato does with the character of Socrates himself. But he does so in such a way that, over the years, some criteria are *a priori* placed beyond question [*mis hors de cause*], that is, *forgotten as* questions. This is concretely expressed, as we shall see, as a *dogmatization of what was initially an aporetic complex*. It is this criteriological occultation that allows the masking of the question of criteria insofar as they are always criteria *of retention* within an *originarily mnemo-technical* milieu, a milieu that is, in Plato's own terms, *hypomnesic*: metaphysics *is* this denial.

Hence the epokhal redoubling of the new retentional system, *that is, its adoption*, occurs, at the same time:

- as its quasi-discovery – Plato highlighted *the question of hypomnesis, which is to say, precisely, the question of what we call tertiary retention* – as the examination of his own practice of this *still new* retentional system that was alphabetical writing;

- by constructing a discourse of denial that is nevertheless immensely rich, obscuring the role of retention in his own textual construction: the *anamnesic* being an *ideal retention*, the *hypomnesic* being *mnemotechnical retention*, the difference between these two retentions also amounting, in Plato, to the difference between dialectics and sophistry.

As we shall see, however, *the dialectic is, in fact, an operation of the adoption, theorization and legitimation of what Sylvain Auroux calls grammatization.*

The spirit of Socrates

'Socrates' (inasmuch as he is accessible to us only through writings) is the premier instance of the *tertiarization of the mind* [*esprit*], or of the spirit that takes itself as its object *in its unity*, that is, *as Spirit*, but does so, as it were, in a hollowed-out way, or negatively. The tertiary establishes itself as a principle of the *negative of thought*, as heteronomy, irreducible supplementarity – and as what it is a matter, precisely, but at all costs, of reducing. And this includes: *at the cost of forgetting Socrates*, and at the cost, too, of his *invention*[104] – but of an invention that is an inversion.

The alibi of this inversion is that *Socrates did not write*.

It is this primordial Socratic non-writing that guides the dialectic as premier operation of grammatization, that is, as an explanation of how one should write – in the global war of spirits that is thereby initiated. And – as we will see by looking closely at reminiscence (ideal retention as anamnesis), which is precisely what, in the Platonic corpus, will contain both the greatest and the most beautiful questions, plus all the contradictions, aporias, denials and reversals of the most decisive propositions – it seems that the theory of reminiscence, which was firstly, as the myth of Persephone, the recollection (by the still tragic Socrates, responding to Meno) of the *revenance of spirits*, will later become, essentially with *Phaedrus*, the *theory of the pure origin of the unique Spirit*.

Anamnesis would then supposedly be pure of any hypomnesis *because it is a question of eliminating textuality, that is, interpretability*, the god of which is Hermes. It is, first and foremost, a question of *reducing the polysemy* of the words of Socrates, that is, the polysemy of their Platonic recording [*consignation*], and, through that, of *every possible type of veridical utterance*, that is, of *any 'reminiscent' production*, which is necessarily, *as* reminiscence, a *repro-duction*, in the sense of this notion that I have developed in *Technics and Time, 3*.

The textualization of Socratic speech, as tertiarization,[105] *in fact records* [*consigne*], *firstly, a primordial predicament* [*embarras*] *of the mind, questions and difficulties that arise as aporias*. This is, above all, the positive effectiveness of recording [*consignation*]. Now, Socrates died because the city stopped supporting this obstinate putting everything into question carried to the limits of questionability – which is, however, the only way to really investigate questions. The apologist who produces the archive and memory, Plato must celebrate *and reveal*, in this obstinacy, the *necessity of the discourse that he records* as the trace of this life, including and *especially in its final moments*, that is, in its *logical* and, through that, moral *exemplarity*. Just like Kant with his own flux, Plato is confronted with the problem of an *inadequation* in the logical flow of *Socrates*, which sublimates the enormity and immensity of the gesture by which Socrates *is brought to an end*.

Kant, when he rereads himself under pressure from public criticism – or as he himself wrote elsewhere, 'addressing the entire *reading public*'[106] – when he re-examines, to the letter, the 1781 version of the transcendental deduction, finds himself confronted with difficulties in unifying his reasoning, that is, unifying the flow of his own consciousness, which will lead to the new edition of 1787, which proves to be even more loaded with contradictions in that it claims to be able to maintain complete continuity with the first version. On this point, see the second chapter of *Technics and Time, 3*.

Now, *mutatis mutandis*, the same thing occurs between the life of Socrates and its written recording by Plato. Literalizing Socrates, Plato uncovers, 'addressing the entire *reading public*', and in the first place addressing himself as first reader of his own text, *difficulties of unification* that will lead him to continue this recording [*consignation*], to *add new episodes* that will end up concocting a completely different version, even though Plato takes it as perfectly compatible with the initial state of the problem.

The difference between the two cases is obviously that in the first, one flux (that of Plato) substitutes itself for another (that of Socrates), so that a *projection* is constituted *for an other*, and this occurs as if it were the beginning of cinema, of a great film being shown in the shadows of a cave, which has everything to do with the darkened world of a movie theatre [*salle obscure*], where consciousness, as I said in *Technics and Time, 3*, is immobilized, rendered unconscious, and so on.[107]

It is through the *purported resolution* of *Socratic inadequation*, which *makes Socrates speak, dia-logue and question*, and which means that Socrates always has something *more* to say, it is through this so-called resolution by *logical necessity understood as non-contradictory necessity*, that is, non-textual necessity, that Plato will settle his account with the tragic epoch, and through that with the spirit of Socrates – and with his *daimōn*. At the same time, he will invent the metaphysical basis of grammatization that will support the extension of what Auroux calls Extended Latin Grammar, and Derrida calls *mondialatinisation:*[108] the *statement*, as the first and shortest *logos* (*ton logon o protos te kai smikrotatos – Sophist* 262c).

What to retain of this heritage: the spirit of Socrates? What do we do with such a death? What can we say of death after Socrates, he 'who did not write'? What does this restraint with respect to written retention say about him, and about the *role of dead memory*, and about retention in general?

What in *Technics and Time, 3* I called the 'heritage' of 'completed inadequation'[109] is here truly *colossal*: at the heart of the inadequation stands that which comes to an end for Socrates while remaining intact for his apologist. What was death for Socrates? This question, from *Socrates's Apology* to *Phaedo*, and passing through *Crito*, but also, in a more subterranean way, through all the other dialogues, up to but not including the dogmatic period, and in particular through *Meno* and *Phaedrus*, this question, which little by little will stop mattering, will no longer be in *question*, remotely controls the entire Platonic archivization of characters, that is, their invention: over the course of this text, whose *interpretability* proves to be textually *ever more open and incomplete*, during this *interminable* apology, we must yet find a *terminus*, the *necessity of the end*, and invention is always constrained by the imperative to *produce a transcendental unity of the apperception in which this flow of speech will have consisted*, Socrates, *who inevitably becomes what Plato wrote*.

The transcendental unity of this interminable *logos*, which in that epoch was not yet called 'consciousness', will authorize some arrangements with their historical empiricality: *Socrates increasingly becomes Plato*. And, in the course of constructing the unifying fiction of the Socratic character, the aporetic dimension of this death is gradually lost and mourned – and by resolving tensions, contradictions and obstinate aporias, the *question*, which should have been left as that which *remains*, instead cedes its place to *edification*: the edification *of the character* will also be *that of the souls* that, for the occasion, Plato will *properly invent*, by promising to them, too, in certain conditions, transcendental unity – that of a *We* that founds justice on Earth, and which is the mirror of the Sovereign Good radiating in the *topos ouranios*.

Enclosed within the text as is the soul within the body, Plato's reader must know how to await liberation by projecting his or her transcendental unity beyond the tertiary contingency of this text, and by rediscovering within it, anamnesically, this kind of *absolute past* that is the contemplation of the Good 'and of all essences' (*Meno*), which is also its absolute future, that is, Being *insofar as it is not Time*, which is confounded, here, *in the work of Plato as still today*, with Becoming.

The *unifying fiction*, which is also the *confusion of the character with its author*, and, therefore, necessarily the *negation of the literality of the text*, is the price to be paid for the concelebration of the death of the philosopher – his founding *sacrifice*: to invent the speech of Socrates by recording it, co(n)-signing it, and, through that, to replace it by substituting text for speech, repro-ducing it. This invention is the law of memory as forgetting, as selection, as putting retentional criteria into play that are never purely adequate to that from which they are selecting, which enables the selection to be *reduced*.

How to do otherwise? To memorize is to forget, such is *time* – as Borges teaches us in 'Funes, the Memorious'.[110] The question of memory and forgetting is the very heart of Platonic metaphysics insofar as, faced with such aporias, it is forced, precisely, to produce a fable, which, because it is also the denial of this fabulation, thereby merits the name of metaphysics. For this fable to be credible, for it to reach its goal, *it must conceal that forgetting occurs during memorization and its operation, anamnesis.* Hence it must *efface time.* And at the same time:

- it must, precisely, *erase the question of the criteria* that it is obliged to implement, the law needed in order to invent his character;
- it must conceal that this *this character is an invention,* that it *is* a *character;*
- it must prove and demonstrate that *the truth has absolutely nothing to do with fiction,* just as Husserl had to insist that perception has *no* relationship with imagination.

And, into the bargain, this results in a *condemnation of stories* in general, and of *those told by the pre-Socratics in particular.* It is a question of effacing time *by erasing the textuality of the text,* and by definitively separating truth and fiction. And thus of 'realizing' the truth: this is what will be called the *realism of the Ideas.*

It is always a question of forgetting – of establishing the selection criteria on the basis of which, forgetting, we memorize and remember. As for the *search criteria sought by Plato* (such is the subject of *Meno* and the stakes of its aporia: how to *search* for the criteria of *research,* how, in other words, to go *faster than* the music – than this music that a dream invites Socrates to practise in the last days of his life, while awaiting his death?), these criteria must *account for a unity of the character of Socrates that does not exist,* which is a fantasy, and they must *establish it through the fantasy of an other,* and *as* the fantasy of this other, as the *unity* of this other, as the Same of Plato, who *is* this 'other', and not as the unity and fantasy of *Socrates, with whom the other is confused, but who preferred to die* (in the absence of Plato who, 'I believe, was ill':[111] the genius of a writer who *scrupulously* inscribes into his text that the author of the text, who records the last words of his character, was, precisely, absent at this fateful moment, and thus did not hear this final logical flow, which, nevertheless, overdetermines by its content – the one absent from this moment reporting having been the witness of those who witnessed it – the entire machine of writing).

In other words, *Plato is, in a sense, the supplement of a unity that Socrates lacked*, which he adds to him like the pedestal he indeed needs, as we will see: we will see that it is thanks to this literary operation that, as an after-effect, the words of Socrates will prove to be prophetic, those words he uttered having just been condemned, and which were addressed to the Athenians who had condemned him.

> What price would you not pay to keep company with Orpheus and Musaeus, Hesiod and Homer?[112]

Now, what is this price? This price is that of a death and sacrifice *that will be remembered*, and well beyond Athens – because, *in fact*, this will be recorded, tertiarized, in the libraries of the whole world. This *price* is the death of the personage and his dead memory, that is, the hypomnesic recording of his logical flux, in particular at the end, of which we must make an exegesis.

This kind of *prosthesis that is Plato* can function, however, only by concealing its prosthetic character. The writer, whose textual flux knits together only by inventing the words of a death that he ventriloquizes, but by which he is haunted, devotes himself to this task with an almost unimaginable tenacity and efficacy. The result is a magnificent oeuvre, which can only inspire immense admiration, and the greatest respect, and which has haunted philosophy from its birth – this haunting, this *spirit*, being, *precisely, its birth* – until today. But the dynamism of all this, the quasi-magnetic and *ionizing* power of Platonic writing,[113] is that which is owed to the spirit of Socrates *insofar as his ghost haunts the entire textual edifice* and as *the spirit of its letter*, which puts it, interminably, back into question.

FOURTH LECTURE

The Tragic Spirit

The question of criteria arises for the Greeks during a long *crisis of the mind, or of spirits*, which is also a revolution in the history of minds and spirits, as Eric Robertson Dodds strongly insisted when he introduced the concept of the 'Inherited Conglomerate', that is, of the *layered sedimentation of beliefs inherited from the past, which are at times incompatible with each other*, as a result of which a phase shift in collective individuation can occur, in the sense that Gilbert Simondon posits that psychic individuation and collective individuation are based on a dynamic engendered by such a *déphasage*, a dephasing, an inadequation of self to self that constitutes the psychic individual as well as the collective individual, that social group capable of saying '*We*'.

These *sometimes mutually incompatible beliefs, inherited from the past*, form an *over-loaded, over-stretched* [*sur-tendu*] *preindividual milieu*. And this is especially true of Greece, which, for this reason, enters into a chronic crisis, which is also the specific form of instability that we call history inasmuch as it follows on from protohistory, and from prehistory, which is itself composed of periods – a temporal process that unfurls what Heidegger called the history of truth, starting from the experience of and encounter with the *as such*. This history of truth, however, is what will eventually lead – in the age of *Gestell* – to 'post-truth'.

Concerning ancient Greece, Dodds writes:

> A new belief-pattern very seldom effaces completely the pattern that was there before: either the old lives on as an element in the new – sometimes an unconfessed and half-conscious element – or else the two persist side by side.[114]

The crisis of the mind, or what is here precisely the crisis of spirits, which we can still see in our own epoch in the accumulation of forms of urban tertiary retention, is a *process of individuation that, faced with a sudden intensification of becoming, and carried to its extremes, that is, an eminently inventive process, finds itself threatened with splits and failures*. Consequently, in the pre-Socratic and Socratic epochs, a *new spirit* of the *We* is mobilized, which tries to forge new criteria, to create new ways of sharing out the *We*, and to thus enable it to *project a future onto becoming*, that is, a *unity*. But this becoming is also a difficult problem, since it is initially experienced as a profound and tragic *division*:

> But in the period between Aeschylus and Plato [...] the gap between the beliefs of the people and the beliefs of the intellectuals, which is already implicit in Homer, widens to a complete breach, and prepares the way for the gradual dissolution of the Conglomerate.[115]

This crisis of the mind, in the history of spirits, is, according to Dodds, a kind of *Aufklärung*:

> Xenophanes denied the validity of divination [...]. But his decisive contribution was his discovery of the relativity of religious ideas. 'If the ox could paint a picture, his god would look like an ox'.[116]

This sudden challenge to tradition, putting it in question, a tradition within which, nonetheless, thinkers find an essential part of their inspiration, as we shall see in *Protagoras, Meno, Symposium* and *Phaedrus,* generates a *reaction* that will complicate still further the sophistic as such. It is in the context of this violent spiritual conflict that Socrates will be sentenced to death:

> But the most striking evidence of the reaction against the Enlightenment is to be seen in the successful prosecutions of intellectuals on religious grounds which took place at Athens in the last third of the fifth century. About 432 B.C. or a year or two later, disbelief in the supernatural and the teaching of astronomy were made indictable offences. The next thirty-odd years witnessed a series of heresy trials which is unique in Athenian history. The victims included most of the leaders of progressive thought at Athens – Anaxagoras, Diagoras, Socrates, almost certainly Protagoras also, and possibly Euripides. In all these cases save the last the prosecution was successful: Anaxagoras may have been fined and banished; Diagoras escaped by flight; so, probably, did Protagoras; Socrates, who could have done the same, or could have asked for a sentence of banishment, chose to stay and drink the hemlock.[117]

But however much these old beliefs *and their spirits* may seem opposed to this new spirit that is the *spirit of logos*, one epoch does not simply dispose of the other: their elements form a chain, a chain within which they *reindividuate themselves*, and this is particularly true of *daimōns* and other spiritual figures, whether they come from Olympus or from Hades. Contrary to the claims of Deichgräber, 'Aeschylus did not have to revive the world of the daemons: it is the world into which he was born'.[118]

Now, as we will see, it is a question of knowing whether what still haunts Socrates as his *daimōn* is only a residue, or whether, on the contrary, it is not, precisely, a matter of *that which remains yet to be thought with respect to the mind of Socrates*, and, through him, the mind in general, *that is, to spirits* and to their *wars*. The Socratic *daimōn* is, indeed, evidence of the perseverance of a certain *Greek spirit*, to which the Homeric *atē* also bears witness in *The Iliad*:

> Always, or practically always, *ate* is a state of mind – a temporary clouding or bewildering of the normal consciousness.[119]
>
> But the most characteristic feature of the *Odyssey* is the way in which its personages ascribe all sorts of mental (as well as physical) events to the intervention of a [...] daemon. [...] Whenever someone has a particularly brilliant or a particularly foolish idea; when he suddenly recognizes another person's identity or sees in a flash the meaning of an omen; when he remembers what he might well have forgotten or forgets what he should have remembered, he [...] will see in it [...] a psychic intervention by one of these anonymous supernatural beings.[120]

It is owing to this same spiritual structure that, for example, a poet knows what he does:

> 'I am self-taught', says Phemius; 'it was a god who implanted all sorts of lays in my mind'. [He] means [...] that he has not memorised the lays of other minstrels [...]; he sings 'out of the gods'.[121]

We shall see that these notes testify to the way Socrates belongs to the tragic age – *even though Plato, while playing on it, slowly erases it.*

Tragic Greece is a critical epoch, in which the question of criteria arises, the question of the *differences we must make in order to judge* (*krinein*), where we see the appearance of words such as *dikē, aretē, metron, aidōs, agathon, alētheia, kalon*, and so on, but where these all fall *under the authority of a difference that remains between Immortals and Mortals*, which remains, in, through and despite the profane-becoming that is the invention of the city, an *archi-difference*. It is this question of criteria that Socrates poses with unequalled force, and that he always introduces with his question, '*ti esti...?*', which in turn becomes an *archi-criterion, the criterion that enables criteria to be established*, that is, the criterion that allows 'what is' to be distinguished from 'what is not' (what is and what is not just, virtuous, measured, modest, good, true, beautiful and so on).

It is by this transformation initiated by *Socrates, which constitutes a hinge between the tragic and the metaphysical, but where Plato's reinterpretation represents the real break with the tragic*, it is by this path, therefore, that *the difference between being and non-being, and the difference between being and beings, comes to replace tragic difference*. In this way, the initial spirit of the Socratic question of being, which is always presented in the form of a question (what is…?), is warped into a *method of division*, of discretization, which Plato himself calls a butchery – into a method of *definition*: into a dialectic – this word no longer having much relationship with that *dialogos* about which Socrates speaks. That the '*what is?*' of Socrates could become the archi-criterion, *the criterion that enables criteria to be established*: this is what Plato would like us to believe. But we will investigate another aspect of the originality of the Socratic archi-question, ti esti…?, one that, certainly, prepares the way for the coming of archi-criteriology, ontology, the history of being and the difference between being and beings, but which may above all consist in *the contesting of every constituted criteriology*, of any *net* establishing of such a difference: ti esti…? is the radical instrument of questioning, the *organon* that can tear out by the roots, as Blanchot says, or that can *disinter* the radical questions (those that lie underground, *in Hades*), and which, *in advance, challenge and question the Platonic operation*.

Socrates is a radical. With him, dialogue *uproots* questions, *draws them out* from his interlocutors. It is this interminable, tireless and incessant questioning, which arouses mortal hatred, that it is a matter of *bringing to an end*: for the city, by the death sentence, and for Plato, by *literally im-mortalizing it*.

But at the same time, the notary, or the secretary, is scrupulous, and the letter certainly keeps something of the spirit: it is thanks to it that we are here, today, questioning, and the work is great. This is so on the condition that we see in it, as in any process of individuation, the *work of an inadequation – of what Simondon called dephasage, shifting phase – that we must inherit*, as Simondon explains. In this way, Simondon is quite close to Heidegger, whom in any case he read a great deal. This is so, then, on the condition that we see in it an expression of this irreducible being-in-default of the Platonic *corpus*, which thereby becomes a preindividual milieu for the continuation and pursuit of individuation – for us, for the *We* who are still, in however small a way, sufficiently Greek to be able to remake the difference, to *make it anew*. And this is so, then, except and unless we say the individuation has been completed, that there is no longer any future to seek, that we should abandon the search for new criteria for any new research, and submit to a becoming to which we must resolve simply to *adapt ourselves*, and where *there would then be nothing more to say.*

How could we fail to notice here that this possibility, a possibility we find so unacceptable, is obviously what everyone now thinks and fears? Is this not the very ordeal and experience of post-truth?

Let us return, however, to what Socrates provokes us to think, we who read him in the Anthropocene, and, more precisely, in the disruption, that is, in the experience of *Gestell*, and as the absence of epoch, as the impossibility of creating an epoch. Through new criteria, when an epoch is produced, when a collective individuation worthy of the name is metastabilized – for what we ourselves are living through is collective *dis*individuation, and if this is not the first time such a thing has happened, it may be the first time it has happened on a scale that is almost global – so, when a collective individuation worthy of the name is metastabilized, a spirit is constituted, is decided, as *krisis*, during a critical epoch, that is, *both*:

- as an epoch on the brink of self-destruction and yet of self-generation, as Gramsci enables us to think, and as was thought, too, in the Athenian context of the epoch of Socrates and Plato; *and*
- as a discerning, sifting, analysing epoch, which *suspends* something in order to make room for the new – but which, today, *perhaps*, leads to something that may indeed be new, but *frighteningly new.*

It is always – today as yesterday, at the beginning of what was, yesterday, this *We* that we call Western, and that *we* are still ourselves, at least at its edge, or its precipice – it is always a matter of a war of spirits. And it is a matter of these spirits inasmuch as they are essentially ghosts, *revenants*, it then being a question of knowing *what* returns, *how* it returns, and how to *make* it return precisely *as a difference* that is also (and here lies the paradox) an *invention*: this difference that returns, and that is called différance, must, indeed, be *made,*[122] and, in so doing, it does *not* return, in the sense that it thereby becomes *another* difference.

To put it another way, I would like to show that when Socrates passes through the Mysteries of Eleusis, the myth of Persephone, and the myth of Prometheus and Epimetheus, what is invented reveals itself, afterwards, and by the force and the necessity of its invention, to have always been already there: the most absolute past reappears as the most absolute future, and this resurgence, if not this resurrection, constitutes

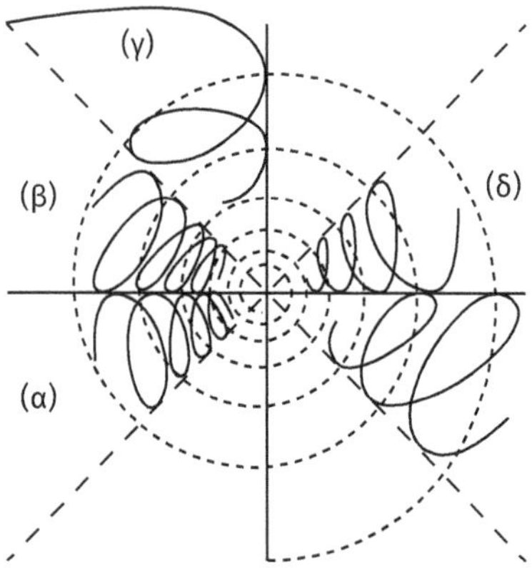

Figure 7. Idiotext by the author.

the *omnitemporality* of what, through time, maintains and supports time, like its riverbed, the rocks at the bottom of the raging torrent, *which the torrent excavates and exhumes, generating its forms and disposition in its torrential flow.*

It is these highly complex processes, which are the stakes of Heidegger's *Sein und Zeit*, but also of Simondon's processes of individuation and Derrida's différance, that I try to represent, figuratively, with these spirals (see Figure 7).

And it is as this process of the revenance of spirits that make the difference in the flux of Socratic dialogue that – from out of the ordinary that this dialogue keeps to scrupulously, refusing to be satisfied with the phantasmagoria of thaumaturges – there suddenly arises the extra-ordinary: that which passes onto this other plane that the *Republic* will describe as exiting the cave. But in the *Republic*, and after *Phaedrus*, which prepared the way for it, it is the demonic spirit of Socratic dialogue that will be lost, replaced by the dialectic as it is defined in both *Phaedrus* and *Republic*.

In the course of Socratic dialogue, of which *Meno* and *Symposium* are the peaks, the extraordinary arises as reminiscence, anamnesis, in a stroke of genius whose theatre is *Meno* – which I have quoted many times in *Technics and Time* – but before which Plato will *retreat*, and then get bogged down in, and ultimately *sink* into, the operation of pacifying the unity of the Socratic soul with *Phaedrus*. Anamnesis then takes on a completely different meaning.

We will now try to see how all this takes shape via *Protagoras, Meno, Symposium* and *Phaedrus*.

Protagoras, technics and neganthropology

The Greeks are mortals, and their mortality comes from the conflict between the Titans and the Olympians: this is what Hesiod tells, as well as Aeschylus. It is also what Vernant discusses,[123] and it is connected to the 'myth' told by Protagoras, who teaches us that the heirs of the theft of fire, mortals, who are the keepers of the flame stolen by Prometheus, are technicians.

We will return to Protagoras, but, before that, let us project this into what we know today thanks to archaeology, palaeo-archaeology and prehistory. Technics is our milieu, but we have naturalized it: we do not see it as such, as technics; we are immersed in technics as fish

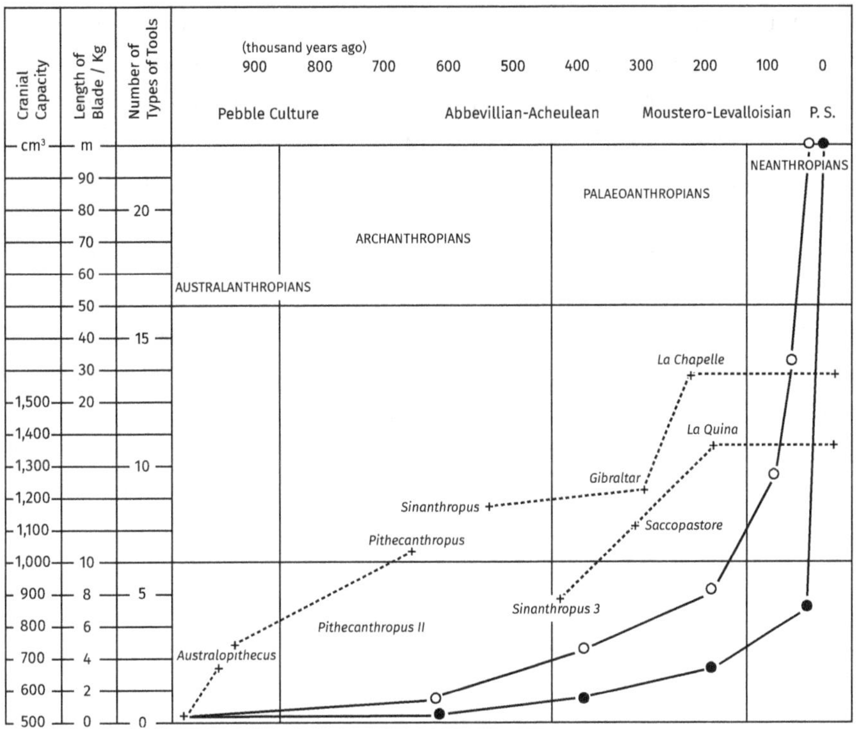

Figure 8. Cranial capacity compared to technical evolution. After André Leroi-Gourhan, *Gesture and Speech*, 1993.

are in water – except that technical innovation does not stop disrupting our milieu, and ourselves within this milieu, which thus changes constantly. But this is something we don't truly perceive until after the industrial revolution, which hugely accelerates the pace of this innovation, which at that time was referred to as 'progress' and which is now called the Anthropocene.

Nevertheless, our vital milieu, insofar as it is always constituted technically, never stops changing, and has been for between two and four million years (see Figure 8).

> In other words, it does seem as though the 'prefrontal event' had marked a radical turning point in our biological evolution as a zoological species governed by the normal laws of species behavior. In *Homo sapiens* technicity is no longer geared to cell development but seems to exteriorize itself completely – to lead, as it were, a life of its own.[124]

This is what Leroi-Gourhan calls the process of ex-teriorization, from which ek-sistence stems.

This technical exteriorization continues to accelerate, to the point that in 1995, Sony filed five thousand patents in a single year. But this acceleration of change is constant, and it is the material translation of the temporality of mortals – that is, of their relationship to death, inasmuch as they anticipate it, and, in order to defer it, work, transform their surroundings. For this transformation, they need tools, which they also transform, and which transform *them* in return.

If we consider these questions from a very general perspective, attempting to lay out very general principles, we can say that mortals, *oi thanatoi*, that is, *oi anthropoi*, are constituted by the fact that they know they will die, and that they live with this knowledge by developing forms of knowledge that also seek to *defer* this death, to postpone it, or even to surpass it, but we can add, with Leroi-Gourhan, that these mortals are living beings endowed not, like all higher living things, with two *memories*, but with three – and it is for this reason that we must go beyond the entropology of Lévi-Strauss and make a leap towards neganthropology.

Technical life, life that anticipates its death in the sense that, governed by the anticipation of its end, it trans-forms matter in order to defer this end, which is the fundamental constitution of Dasein, this technical life, this technical living thing, is endowed with a third memory – which Leroi-Gourhan called ethnic memory, but which itself presupposes a technical memory:

> In this book the term 'memory' is used in a very broad sense. It is not a property of the intelligence, but, whatever its nature, it certainly serves as the medium for action sequences. That being so, we can speak of a 'species-related memory' in connection with the establishment of behavior patterns in animal species, of an 'ethnic' memory that ensures the reproduction of behavior patterns in human societies, and similarly of an 'artificial' memory in its most recent form that – without referring to either instinct or thought – ensures the reproduction of sequences of mechanical actions.[125]

Technics, and the milieu it produces, forms a third memory, which is composed of what I call tertiary retentions, whose appearance amounts to a rupture in the history of life, and therefore in evolution. Lotka says the same thing, but in other terms.

There are all kinds of tertiary retentions, during the history of which there appear hypomnesic tertiary retentions, such as in decorated caves, which of course remind us of Book VII of the *Republic*. As the exteriorization of individual memory, hypomnesic tertiary retention has this peculiarity that when it appears to itself by exosomatizing itself, individual memory becomes transmissible to others, who become its heirs: hence it is that 'culture' arises from 'nature'.

Protagoras, eris and dikē

What Protagoras describes is a technical way of life, a way of life in groups traversed by an internal tension that tends to destroy the group as much as it constitutes its dynamic principle. This group life, which gathers together beings who are without qualities, incomplete beings, is constituted not by a unity of the species, not by genetic identity, as we would say today, but by an inventiveness that is a technicity, which is also to say a facticity, an artificiality, and, in that, a pharmacology.

This technicity, however, produces *eris*: this is what the dialogue *Protagoras* tell us through the appearance of Hermes, sent by Zeus, after the latter becomes concerned by seeing mortals killing each other, which they do because they cannot agree on what they should do to preserve their future. *Eris*: that is, firstly, discord. This discord returns in Greek mythology under the name of Eris, precisely as a goddess who sows conflict and disunity, but *eris* is also an agent of emulation: there is such a thing as 'good eris', which is what energizes mortals.

In other words, *eris* is two-sided: it is pharmacological – and it is so following the conflict between Zeus and Prometheus, where Zeus avenges himself on mortals for having been tricked by Prometheus, when during a sacrifice he was deceived into taking the bones for the meat (see *Theogony*). The role of *eris* in the life of mortals places Prometheus at the heart of their condition. Bad *eris* produces disindividuation, a condition of everyone for oneself, which leads to self-disgust and disgust for others, and, today, to the loss of the feeling of existing – that is, of individuating oneself, of becoming what one is – which in turn engenders the loss of the feeling that life is worth living.

This bad *eris* is what Socrates sees in the figure of the sophist Gorgias. In *Gorgias*, Socrates, in conversation with Polos, posits that to individuate oneself is to live by participating in the individuation of the group, *with* the group, *for* the group, and not against it. And this is so, even if we must die. This is why he says it is better to be a just victim than an unjust executioner. This is not a question of reaching happiness, *eudaimōnia*, in the sense of the enjoyment of oneself, but in the sense of the fullness of one's fate: achieving the happiness of being just.

It is obvious that this scene describes the fate of Socrates, and it is not the only time that Plato has Socrates speak of his own fate. But what does this involve for Socrates? Forgive me for quoting my own book, *Acting Out*, here:

> Socrates participates in the individuation of the City, and, right up until the end, and therefore *to the extreme*, he links his individual destiny to collective destiny: right up to his

> death, *which is at the same time the end of his individuation and the beginning of the* we *that is philosophy.* Socrates, by *tying his death* to the City in a certain manner, *inaugurates* the philosophical attitude that necessarily founds all philosophy, as an exemplary relation of the *I* and the *we*. Now, this end is also, therefore, an *infinitzation.*
>
> When Crito proposes that he escape, Socrates refuses, because if he did, he says, his children would become orphans – Socrates' children are the City's children, before they are Socrates' children. It is better they become orphans of Socrates than of their own city.[126] And this is why, he goes on, either it is necessary 'to bring the city around [to my point of view] by persuasion, or to do what it commands', upholding its laws without reserve, as it were 'in life and in death'. So, this *death* has the *legacy* of an *obligation*: that of *continuing to interpret* the laws of the City *beyond* the death of Socrates, just as much as *from* that death, a death that becomes also a kind of survival, a *kleos,* a posterity – even if not, as Plato will incorrectly try to demonstrate, an immortality.
>
> In that regard, Socrates' death *remains* incomplete – charged with 'potentials'. This is his genius.[127]

The question of justice is the constant concern of the Greek city, and it is the question of individuation insofar as it is always both psychic, which is to say individual (in the current sense), and collective. The psychic individual is not equivalent to the collective, which would be the rule for a totalitarian society. It is distinct, and this distinction is a chance. But this distinction is also a source of conflict. These conflicts must be subject to rules, which are called laws, and these should make possible a freedom that does not destroy the community, and it is in this sense that they must be just, and must make the freedom of the individual itself just, and make this individual just *through* his or her individuation, for this is what the word freedom means: individuation.

After the forgetfulness of Epimetheus and the theft of Prometheus that turns mortals into technicians, the latter become self-destructive, and so Zeus sends them Hermes, charged with giving to mortals the knowledge of political technique, *entekhnen politiken*: not Laws but the knowledge of how to create laws. Laws do not resolve the pharmacological problem that is posed here: they give it a framework, a mode of regulation, founded on the fact that all have access to this technical knowledge that is writing, which, after Vernant, Marcel Detienne shows to constitute the city in its juridical form. But these laws, in and of themselves, can never guarantee that mortals will never again sink into bad *eris*, since they must themselves be interpreted. Never will the pharmacological and poisonous character of these laws be erased: they can only constitute a framework for the metastabilization of these two tendencies that are good *eris* and bad *eris*.

Now, the problem is that this writing itself, which is the political technique par excellence, becomes a factor of discord: it is itself a *pharmakon*, says *Phaedrus*, one that is pressed into the service of the bad faith of the Sophists, whom Plato accuses of causing the degradation of the Athenian spirit insofar as they practise an *eristic*, that is, an *eris* expressed in *logos* – which is the very origin of reason and of what Plato will call the dialectic, but which, with the literal (lettered) instrument, becomes a logography, as Socrates says in *Phaedrus*, an *artificial logos*.

Process of individuation, excess and default

A process of individuation is what *happens to me* in such a way that, when something or other happens to me, I in a way arrive to myself through that which happens, of which I become the quasi-cause. When I myself arrive there, there where I arrive to myself, I discover through what happens to me that I *never finish* arriving to myself, and that 'I' am like the *horizon of myself*, always *ahead of myself*, which is also to say, *behind myself*, this 'self' [*même*] being what Freud called the *ego ideal*, and what Blanchot called, on a different register, the *incessant*. There where I arrive at by individuating myself, I find that I have still not arrived yet at what I am; I am still always in front of myself, in excess of myself, which is also to say, behind myself: in want of being, in default of being (of being myself: I am never completely my-*self*, and always already my-other). I who am always already more than the same, I find myself augmented by a new experience of this default of being through everything that happens to me, an augmentation *that makes me be* because it increases my 'power to act', if we can use here the language of Spinoza.

Mortals – being incomplete, inherently unfinished, because they are *deprived* of a quality that would be their own; being in impropriety, and as such proper to nothing, belonging to nothing, but where this means to nothing in particular and therefore to everything in potential – these mortals are capable of anything, of the worst and of the best.

FIFTH LECTURE

From *Meno* to *Phaedrus*: The Constitution and Crisis of Public Space

Reminders

We saw last week that the question of criteria is imposed upon the Greek city insofar as it is chronically in crisis. The chronic character of the *krisis* is called History. History is a *polemos*, a permanent conflict, but one that takes a variety of forms, including peaceful forms that constitute *logos* as *dialogos*. In *logos*, criteria are used in order to judge. In this way, every citizen, every member of the *politeia*, is a judge.

There is crisis, however, because there is a conflict between an Inherited Conglomerate (Dodds) and a new spirit, the spirit of *logos* as a new form of judgment founded on criteria and laws (*nomos*), which themselves interpret the divine injunction of *Dikē*, which is the condition of peace. The death sentence given to Socrates is part of this critical history. Socrates is host to both the old spirit, which lies at the source of the tragic spirit, and the new spirit, which, too, fosters the tragic spirit, but also tends to separate itself from it. The operator of this separation is named Plato, who embodies the spirit of *logos* that prepares the way for the 'logical' tendency, in the sense of formal logic, a tendency that leads, today, to those algorithms by which *logos* and spirit are reduced to calculation.

In the second session of this seminar we saw that all this occurs due to the exosomatization of the faculties of knowing, desiring and judging, and of their functions: intuition, understanding, imagination and reason. We are returning to the Socratic source, and to the tragic sources of Socrates himself, because we find ourselves in the age of post-truth, which is the time of the absence of epoch. To overcome this, to accomplish a leap beyond post-truth, we must recreate the history of truth, the question of which was opened up by Heidegger in his various courses and texts on Plato, from the course on the *Sophist*, then on the *Republic* and *Theaetetus*, and up until Heidegger returns to the cave allegory and identifies it as the turning point at the origin of philosophy, as the advent of a second stage in the history of being, preceded by the pre-Socratic epoch that passed through Parmenides.

We will try to show how, in this history, what is ultimately lacking in Heidegger is the very thing that he himself nevertheless makes clear, namely, the question of the spatialization of time in which what he himself names *Weltgeschichtlichkeit* consists, which is formed from what we are here calling tertiary retentions, which emerge from exosomatization – retentions that must themselves be differentiated across the ages, giving rise to a noetic turn and leading to what, for the Greeks, will be this new alphabetical and literal form of tertiary retention, to this *pharmakon*, which will be one of the three key questions in the *Phaedrus*. These three issues are:

1. the nature and origin of the soul;
2. dialectic beyond the *dialogos* of Socrates;
3. writing as *pharmakon*.

Both Eric Havelock and Walter Ong approach these questions, but I suspect that they never really grasp the true dynamics that are involved. And this is due to their confusion with respect to Socrates and Plato, the same confusion that will later be found in so many of our contemporaries, including Nicholas Carr.

That the spirit of Socrates still plays host to the tragic spirit is shown by his *daimōn*, which is an instance of Homeric *atē*. This, however, is the very thing that Plato will gradually erase. Socrates's *daimōn* is what inspires in him his question, '*ti esti…?*', which is the constant putting in question of everything that seems established, that is, the constant challenging of previously established criteria. The question that Socrates will be the one to raise, over and over again, is that of knowing how to judge.

The question '*ti esti…?*' will become, in Plato's reinterpretation, the operator of the *differentiation between being and non-being*, which then comes to replace the *tragic difference between immortals and mortals*. Surely Socrates himself was already some distance along the path to bringing about this change. But in the Socratic operation, it is, precisely, a matter of *preserving* the tragic source that, in the Platonic operation, it is a matter of eliminating – and this is the very meaning of Book III of the *Republic*. Socratic dialogue then becomes Platonic dialectic.

The tragic sources of the spirit of Socrates are twofold:

- on the one hand, they refer, in dialogue with Protagoras, to the founding mythology of the *relations between Prometheus and Zeus*;
- on the other hand, they evoke the mysteries of Eleusis: Eleusis, where, each spring, the Greeks come to ritually celebrate the myth of Persephone, and of her mother,

> Demeter, who is also the goddess of agriculture, and of the rebirth, each spring, of wheat and of life in all its forms, just as winter, each year, seems to lead to the disaster of death – death and life that we ourselves can relate to entropy and negentropy.

The myth of Persephone can be understood only on the basis of the Promethean mythology of the conflict between the Titans and Olympus, which is the background of the *Theogony.* The Olympians and the Titans are sons of Chronos, fraternal enemies who clash with each other during a conflict through which Zeus and the Olympians eventually triumph over Prometheus and the Titans. The dialogue in which Persephone appears is *Meno*, and it is to this dialogue that I would like to devote today's session. But before we turn to *Meno*, let's remind ourselves of *Protagoras.*

Eris and *aretē*

We saw at the end of the last session that the myth of Prometheus and Epimetheus comes from both Hesiod and Aeschylus. We say that this 'myth', told by Protagoras, teaches us that the heirs of the theft of fire, mortals, who are the keepers of the flame stolen by Prometheus, are technicians.

In other words, our vital milieu, insofar as it is always constituted technically, never stops changing, and has been doing so for between two and four million years. Technics and its milieu forms a third memory composed of tertiary retentions, amounting to a rupture in the history of life and therefore in evolution (as Lotka says in other terms). All kinds of tertiary retentions appear over the course of history, and in particular hypomnesic tertiary retentions, which first appear in caves that remind us of Book VII of the *Republic.* These hypomnesic tertiary retentions then make it possible for individual memory to be transmitted to those who inherit these tertiary retentions: hence culture arises.

The myth of Prometheus and Epimetheus ends with the intervention of Hermes, who, under instruction from Zeus, brings to mortals both *dikē* and *aidōs*, justice and shame, in order to contain *bad eris* and encourage *good eris*. *Eris*, which is highly pharmacological, is the dynamic principle of emulation and rivalry between mortals, through which they raise themselves above themselves, but it is equally what leads them to sink beneath themselves.

Eris is what constitutes psychic individuation *as* collective individuation. But it is what can also lead to *collective disindividuation*, and does so by unleashing *hubris*, which is itself the pharmacological lot of an exosomatic situation in which no criterion is given in advance, and where the *polis* is a political institution for the production of criteria that are both just and honourable, that is, contained and delimited by *aidōs*, the sense of shame and modesty.

In the epoch of Socrates and Plato, however, the Athenian city is not just in crisis: it is in civil war, which the Greeks call *stasis*. The *polis* itself rests on the generalized practice, by all citizens, of writing, that is, of literal tertiary retention, whose god is, once again, Hermes. This will be the subject of questioning and critique in *Phaedrus*, where, as you know, another god of writing, in this case Egyptian, will be evoked.

▪ ▪ ▪

Meno is the decisive text lying at the source of the history of philosophy. It is precisely in this text that the matrix appears of what will later become Plato's idealism, then German idealism, which will then be put into question by Marx and Engels in *The German Ideology*. In other words, it is the basis of transcendental philosophy in the sense of Kant, Husserl and Heidegger. Heidegger, however, does not seem to accord this text any great importance. At its core, this concerns a difference of interpretation about Plato's place in the history of philosophy, and about what Plato does and how Socrates should not be confounded with what Plato has him say in writings that present his primordial pharmacological dimension.

Unlike *Republic*, *Meno* is still a Socratic dialogue. The texts that will yield Platonic idealism, starting from the *Republic*, where an operation takes place that is first introduced in *Phaedrus*, these Platonic texts, which I call the dogmatic texts, represent a break with the kind of thing that appears in *Meno* with the question *ti esti...?*, inasmuch as it puts into question the idea that Meno forges – or fails to forge – of virtue, *aretē*.

Virtue is what allows mortals to live in respect to *dikē* and *aidōs*, and, in that, to tip *eris*, insofar as it is pharmacological, towards the side of good *eris*, of emulation that intensifies psychic individuation, but also collective individuation, which is the constant issue for the Greeks, as shown for instance in their sporting practice, but also in their theatrical and poetic encounters.

Socrates meets Meno

The Greeks ask themselves the question of *how to be virtuous*, or, in their own terms, *excellent*. They want to be taught how to be virtuous and, in that, excellent. These notions – *Aretē* and *Eris*, like *Lēthē*, *Dikē* and *Aidōs* – are also the names of goddesses. This is so for *Eris*, or, in the mythology of *Pandora*, for *Elpis*, which means both hope and fear, or, in other words, what, after Husserl, we will call protention.

Eris – which is both discord and emulation, a *dynamic* factor both *negative and positive* – is the socio-political translation of the pharmaco-logical and inherently unstable situation of mortals. *Elpis* is the psychic translation of this pharmaco-logical instability, which also involves mood, humour, *Stimmung, expectation* – both positive and negative. As well as all the fears of evil, all the misfortunes kept in the jar of Pandora, there is hope: this two-sided expectation, *as both hope and fear*, constitutes attention – in French we can more easily hear that it requires an *attente*, an expectation.

It is in this context that Socrates encounters Meno. We have seen that, according to Protagoras, who is a sophist, the question of virtue arises from the pharmaco-logical situation formed by the technicity of mortals, and where *what makes it possible that one may be virtuous, that is, sensitive to Dikē and Aidōs, is that one may not be*: it is the question of a *field of possibilities*, a field that is '*bipolarized*' between *two poles, which are virtue and non-virtue, aretē*, which is *excellence*, and *disgracefulness, unworthiness, indignity. Aretē* – virtue or excellence – becomes, with Socrates, essentially a *moral* question. It is this for which Nietzsche will reproach him – the terrible Nietzsche.

Virtue stems from the *technicity of mortals* insofar as they *have to be what they are*, as Protagoras says, since they are not *spontaneously* what they are. They are in *becoming*, and, in this becoming, they have to find and to *make* their future, to choose between future possibilities, to select what remains to come. All this implicitly raises the question of the *criteria* required for this transformation of becoming into future, and as the *critique* of this becoming.

For if they remain always yet to come in their becoming, and beyond becoming, and if they are therefore not simply *predestined* to be what they are, it is because the only way of existing is *in time*, they *are* only *in temporality*, thrown into the ek-stasis of what presents itself from the past and in view of the future, as attention, that is, as expectation. Mortals *are* only *in, after* and *as* a temporality whereby they must *make decisions, adopt orientations*, move *towards* their fate, find the *sense* of their path. But for this they need elementary criteria, criteria that last beyond all the transformations of the supplement, of *tekhnē*, of *logos*, of the *pharmakon*. These criteria, which are brought by Hermes, are named *Dikē* and *Aidōs*.

But these criteria are not, themselves, positively constituted: they must be interpreted. And virtue, *aretē*, is what stems from interpretations of these criteria. Virtuous are those who, faced with adversity, faced with accidentality and therefore the fundamental unpredictability of becoming, do not lose sight of *Dikē* and *Aidōs*, and always decide on the basis of these 'existentials' (if I can put it in Heideggerian terms), and, in so doing, interpret them according to the current *pharmacological* situation. The paramount question constantly posed to mortals, and posed insofar as they are exosomatic, is of knowing – and this is Socrates's question – what criterion makes, or what criteria make, individually or collectively, a decision, and make this decision *good*. Now, this criterion, or these criteria, must be founded on a sensibility formed by these *feelings* that are *aidōs* – which is the sense of honour and of its opposite, shame, but also of modesty, *verguenza* in Spanish, measure or reserve, which is also called *metron* – and *dikē*, the sense of justice, *that is, of adikia, injustice.*

What is *shame*? *It is not guilt. The Greeks knew nothing of guilt, only shame.* As for shame in modern Western society, the man who has suffered it, thought it and spoke about it like no other, is Primo Levi, which he thinks in terms of the shame of being human. More profoundly than guilt, shame constitutes the tragic basis of what presents itself in the epoch of *Meno* as the question of virtue in the Greek city. Virtue is possible only for those who already know the feelings of honour and shame as well as justice and injustice.

Honour and shame, and justice and injustice, are polarities that traverse all of us, as Simondon showed. Inhabited and constituted by these polarities that we host, of which we are the hosts, through *Elpis* as well as through *Eris*, we must *make the difference* between the poles they form, and we must make it in such a way that, as we do it, we invite others to do it. And this also means: *making the différance.*

In Christianity, but also in Simondon's thought, this difference that we must make, but which is so difficult to make, is also presented as the question of temptation – the *temptation of not making* this difference, of giving in to confusion, which leads, among Christians dominated by the imagery of Hell, that is, dominated no longer by shame but by guilt, to an iconology such as, for example, that of the temptation of Saint Anthony.

It is through the evolution of shame towards guilt, and on this theologico-religious foundation, that the history of truth leads to post-truth. This is what we learn from the terrible Nietzsche, who, even if he misunderstands the role of Socrates in this affair, must nevertheless be our guide, here, insofar as it is Nietzsche who thinks the history of truth as the nihilistic fate of the West, which is also to say, of capitalism. This is not something I can expand upon here, but you can find elements of it in *Automatic Society, Volume 1.*

What we see, in the representation of the temptation of Saint Anthony, is him giving in to the voice of the body, to the passions that haunt him as what, in his body, opposes itself to what would be the ordering of his soul. Such imagery, which is obsessed with sex, and which *in no way* belongs to tragic Greek culture, is founded, on the contrary, on the opposition of body and soul, whose metaphysical and onto-theological matrix begins to take shape in *Phaedrus*, in the allegory of the winged soul.

It is Freud who explains why guilt is tied to a specific relationship to sexuality, and therefore to the body. This guilt, however, has lost the feeling of shame, which belongs to a prior age, that of tragic Greece. Nevertheless, it is already with Plato that this transformation first gets underway. The contradictions I referred to earlier are of this order. And all this stems from the Inherited Conglomerate, that is, from the preindividual ground, the preindividual funds on the basis of which Socrates and Plato inaugurate the age of philosophy, and do so as *a specific understanding of truth*.

It is in order to resolve the tragic aporias left to him by Socrates – which, because they are tragic, are, precisely, not solvable – that Plato, after his failure in Syracuse, will gradually move towards the opposition of body and soul, and, through this opposition, towards the feeling of guilt. It is for this that Nietzsche will reproach Socrates, thereby mistaking his enemy.

You, Socrates, asks Meno, you know very well what virtue is – are you really going to make me believe that you do *not* know what virtue is? Are you really going to make me tell my fellow citizens that you are someone who is *ignorant*?

> Meno: I do not; but, Socrates, do you really not know what virtue is? Are we to report this to the folk back home about you?[128]

Socrates replies: neither I nor anyone knows, not even (and, in truth, especially not) your famous Gorgias:

> Socrates: Not only that, my friend, but also that, as I believe, I have never yet met anyone else who did know.
>
> Meno: How so? Did you not meet Gorgias when he was here?
>
> Socrates: I did.
>
> Meno: Did you then not think that he knew?
>
> Socrates: I do not altogether remember, Meno, so that I cannot tell you now what I thought then.[129]

As for yourself, says Socrates, tell me what virtue is *for you*:

> Socrates: [...] so you remind me of what he said. You tell me yourself, if you are willing, for surely you share his views.
>
> Meno: I do.
>
> Socrates: Let us leave Gorgias out of it, since he is not here. But Meno, by the gods, what do you yourself say that virtue is? Speak and do not begrudge us...[130]

Search by yourself and within yourself, Meno, and in dialogue with me, as to what virtue may be.

There follows the famous scene in which Socrates makes Meno understand that every time he responds by giving an example of virtue, he fails to say what, strictly speaking, virtue *is*, nor, therefore, what makes all these examples exemplary of the *same essence* of virtue. Socrates will not end up concluding that virtue cannot be taught. But through the question of knowing not only if it can be taught, but if we can know *what it is*, Socrates will posit that before we can claim to *teach* what it is, we must begin by posing the question of knowing *what it is*, in what it *consists*, and even whether it consists in anything at all: if it is a *true question*. And if something *is* a true question, perhaps we sometimes have to conclude that, in this regard, we do not know very much, and that we are unable to know much more – at least in the ordinary mode of knowledge.

Eris, Meno, virtue and the 'zazic clausule' of Socrates

All the dialogues pose the question of politics, law, justice and virtue – and they pose it against the theses of the sophists. What relations does virtue maintain with *dikē* and *aidōs*? Is it, for example, the unity of the two? Or the embodiment of both of them? Whatever answer we might come up with, it is, perhaps, impossible to say *what* virtue *is*. This is the conclusion reached by Socrates, for whom wisdom is always relative and limited: we can only experience its in-completion – which is concretely expressed in Greece as the experience of the in-finity of objects of projection and the idealization of this experience carried out à la lettre. The experience of this incompletion is what Socrates calls his non-knowledge, and he posits that it is above all this non-knowledge that, putting him *in* question, pushes him *to* question – this is the key issue in the *Apology*, that is, at the moment he decides to die so as to protect the city, so as to remain faithful to both *dikē* and *aidōs*.

Hippias, Gorgias and the Sophists in general, Socrates claims, do not ask themselves questions: they respond to something, but what they respond to is not a true question for them, but merely a pretext to make themselves look good, to make a show of their eristic art, which at the same time amounts to bad *eris*. How can one respond to a question if one is not oneself put *into* question?

Socrates's answer to their answers is: *ti esti…?* As for me, I tend to transpose (but not to translate) this phrase into what Roland Barthes called a zazic clausule.[131] What is this all about?

Barthes reads a book by Raymond Queneau, *Zazie in the Metro*. And he shows that Queneau, who became a poet in the wake of the surrealist movement, calls into question what Barthes calls Literature, where the latter designates, with its capital letter, the fabric of clichés, formulas, stereotypes and commonplaces, all of which pollutes the language of Zazie's uncle. Zazie is for this reason constantly making fun of her uncle. Hence there would be a *pharmacology of metalanguage*: the metalanguage of the sophists, who, according to Socrates, produce false thought, and prefer listening to their own chatter rather than listening to what this metalanguage tells them – this reflexive language. Now, this is also what adults do with their clichés, such as, for example, Zazie's uncle Gabriel.

Barthes argues that the Literature spoken about by Uncle Gabriel is a metalanguage, to which Zazie opposes her object language. She does this both by speaking of things without being emphatic or rhetorical, and by 'deflating' her uncle's tropes through what Barthes calls her 'murderous clausule',[132] in this case, 'my ass!', which she always appends to any responses she gives her uncle, thereby letting him know she does not believe a word of his metalanguage. For example, Gabriel talks to her about the 'actual tomb of the real Napoleon', saying he would like to take her to visit Les Invalides in Paris, to which Zazie responds: 'Napoleon my ass!'

So, at the risk of shocking this school, the scholarly institution and the entire institutional and academic apparatus – which comes to us from Plato, and to the source of which we are trying to return, and even to go back beyond this, by going back to Socrates, and, through Socrates, to his tragic sources, which is perhaps a way of doing speleology, of plunging into the spring in order to enter the underground, or into a cavern within which a river flows, the Styx for example, the river of Oblivion, of Forgetting, in the kingdom of Hades, which is also a cave of the kind we find discussed in the *Republic*, and which would be essential to terrestrial life – I will translate this phrase, in reference to Zazie, to her reading by Roland Barthes, and, as I say, at the risk of shocking the school, I will translate this interrogative statement,

Τι είναι η αρετή

by the following, exclamatory statement:

> Virtue my ass!

And I will justify this translation with the hypothesis that every time a sophist comes along and bores Socrates with his certainty of knowing what virtue is, this is how Socrates puts this certainty into question, through this 'murderous clausule', as Barthes said about Zazie, where *ti esti...?* signifies, to the one who pretends to question, the vanity of their vain talk, talk that, precisely, never really puts anything in question.

It is because Meno has been *spoiled* by the sophists that he responds to Socrates by saying:

> Meno: It is not hard to tell you, Socrates.[133]

Here is how Socrates replies, having been told by Meno that it's not hard to define virtue, and to do so by giving a succession of examples:

> Socrates: Even if they are many and various, all of them have one and the same form which makes them virtues.[134]

And so begins the discussion in which Meno will end up accusing Socrates of putting him into an embarrassing, perplexing position, into an aporia, which will in turn lead to Socrates's celebrated reply:

> Socrates: If I perplex others, it is that I am more perplexed than anyone.[135]

And this perplexity, this embarrassment, is due to the fact that what I believed I knew has been dissolved in dialogue, and, in this dissolution, this knowledge has been turned into non-knowledge.

It is at this point that Meno formulates his famous aporia:

> Meno: How will you look for it, Socrates, when you do not know at all what it is? How will you aim to search for something you do not know at all? If you should meet with it, how will you know that this is the thing that you did not know?[136]

To this aporia, Socrates responds by evoking Persephone and her myth:

> Socrates: For those who have, for their former miseries [*palaiou pentheos*], paid ransom to Persephone, she will, to the sun above, in the ninth year, restore their souls anew, from which noble kings, mighty in strength and great in knowledge, will arise, who will for all time as sacred heroes be honoured among mortals [*anthropon*].[137]

Of these verses from Pindar, Socrates gives this interpretation:

> Socrates: Hence, as the immortal soul has been many times reborn, and has seen all things here and in the underworld, in Hades, there is nothing that it has not learned; so it is in no way surprising that it can, whether to do with virtue or other things, recollect the things it knew before.[138]

This interpretation will be pursued further in *Phaedrus*, with the allegory of the winged soul, which I thank you for reading. We will not have time to analyse this crucial dialogue now, but you absolutely must read it in full, and especially:

- on the one hand, this allegory;
- on the other hand, the whole question of the *pharmakon*.

We will return to this briefly. For the moment, let's concentrate on what Socrates says in *Meno*, which I paraphrase in the following way: 'you tell me, Meno, that I cannot seek what I already know, since, if I know it, I don't have to look for it. As for myself, my answer is that I have forgotten it: what I seek has become latent, it belongs to *Lēthē*, which is a river in Hades'. To engage in dialogue is to recall, together, that which returns, and which is therefore a spirit, of which *atē*, like the *daimōn*, is an instance: they are apparitions, revenances, différances.

What returns does so via those who take care of *osiôtata*, sacred markers, those holy differences that separate mortals from immortals. In so doing, those who take care of *osiôtata*, that is, of that which returns through them, themselves become unforgettable, that is, those whose souls are '*athanatos*, and many times reborn' (*athanatos te ousa kai pollakis gegonuia*, from the verb *gignomai*, to become, to be born). They have learned everything, but, having returned from Hades, they have forgotten everything – this is what the mythology of *Lēthē* teaches us, which means both the goddess who is also the daughter of Eris, and *Lēthē*, the river.

We have no understanding of what is at stake, here, if we do not remember, on the one hand, what Dodds teaches us about *atē* and the *daimōn*, that is, what the Greece of Socrates received from the 'Inherited Conglomerate', and, on the other hand, what Vernant said about Hades, which stems from a separation between what is above, in Olympus and in the light, the kingdom of the Immortals, and what is below, in subterranean darkness, wherein lies the destiny and destination of mortal souls, that is, errant, wandering souls: this separation into places that mark out confines stems from the *hubris* of Prometheus, that Prometheus who dooms mortals themselves to the *hubris* of the *pharmakon*.

That the souls of heroes may return to haunt the earthly lives of noetic living beings, and to possess them, as with Homeric *atē* or Hamlet's ghost, is what makes knowledge possible, as that which returns, that which we remember as what come back to us from forgetfulness, *alētheia*, which is here called reminiscence, anamnesis.

And here, Socrates teaches Meno that when they come to agree on what they have to say about what virtue would be, when, at the end of the dialogue, they converge towards a truth that will appear to them with the force of knowledge returned from non-knowledge, and from the experience of overcoming this forgetfulness, then they will have learned something true.

The Greeks before Plato are tragic: they suggest that there is no eternal life. Yet Plato is led to this idea of an immortality of the soul, and he will oppose the soul, which would be immortal, to the body, which would be mortal. And it is in *Phaedrus* that he makes this opposition explicit.

But it is *Meno* that foreshadows this turning point. This change in the question of the relationship to death is directly tied to a crisis with respect to the technicity of mortals themselves. This crisis is also economic. And this technicity is also the factor that, on the one hand, challenges, puts into question, and, on the other hand, generates the capacity to *produce* questions, by passing through what writing, as orthothetic tertiary retention, makes possible in terms of the differentiation between analysis and synthesis, which is to say, both:

- Plato's transformation of the understanding of *alētheia* into *orthotēs* and *omoiosis*;
- the functional differentiation of the faculty of knowing, according to Kant, into the analytical function of the understanding and the synthetic function of reason.

All this, as we will see by reading *Phaedrus*, escapes Heidegger. And it is this misinterpretation that lies at the root of those temptations that are Heidegger's Nazism and anti-Semitism, from *Being and Time* to 'Time and Being'.

The constitution of public space as the space of a 'reading public'

All of this takes shape in an epoch that we must now understand in its broad historical outlines – and *as the very birth of historical understanding insofar as it is recorded ortho-graphically.* The city appears after a long period of obscurity following the Mycenaean epoch.

> The earliest Greek world, as the Mycenaean tablets conjure it up for us, is allied in many ways with the contemporaneous Near Eastern kingdoms. [...] But as one begins to read Homer, the picture changes.[139]

A *leap* occurs between the epoch of the *wanax*, the Mycenaean king, and that of the *polis*, and it is marked, notably, by a *difference of calendarity*. Already, in fact, the '*wanax* was responsible for religious life; he closely regulated the calendar'.[140] Mycenaean civilization is thus already composed around a scriptural mnemotechnics, a vast retentional apparatus for which calendarity is one key element: 'The whole system rests on the use of writing and the keeping of records'.[141] This civilization and its retentional system disappeared following the Dorian invasion,[142] at the end of which the *wanax* made way for the *basileus*:

> The term *wanax* [...] was replaced by the word *basileus* [...]. Writing itself disappeared, as though engulfed in the ruins of the palaces. When the Greeks rediscovered it toward the end of the ninth century, this time through borrowing from the Phoenicians, it was not only another type of script – a phonetic one – but a radically different cultural factor: no longer the specialty of a class of scribes, but an element of a common culture.[143]

With the adoption of a *new retentional system*, a *new space of individuation* is formed, in this case opening the era of public politics, of *publicité*, which is also a becoming-profane (*prophanes* meaning that which is 'visible to all, clear, manifest, evident', that is, public). In other words, this amounts to a brutal, radical displacement of what had hitherto governed the process of individuation: *the absolute difference between the sacred and the profane*. The becoming-profane of the collectivity is the movement of a new regime of *differentiations*, from which emerges a new social organization of tribes,[144] a shift for which Solon was a key figure. This new social organization then turns into the emergence of the *polis*, the city, where groups gradually merge and integrate, constantly and everywhere encountering the *question of adoption*. Now, confronted with this becoming-political, nascent ancient Greece for the first time experiences questions that will be repeated throughout pre-Socratic thought, and which are also, precisely, those of the conditions of what, with Simondon, we call a process of individuation:

> With the disappearance of the *wanax*, [...] new problems emerged. How was order to arise out of discord between rival

> groups and the clash of conflicting prerogatives and functions? How could a common life be founded on disparate elements? Or to apply the Orphics' formula, *how, on the social level, could one emerge from many and many from one?*[145]

Individuation, a metastable process, is 'strictured'[146] by a potential for conflict and a potential for union, which are composed together on the public stage formed by the new 'theatre of individuation'. It is a question of thinking that which *both* unites (*sun*) and separates (*dia*) as the necessity of the *sum-bole* (encounter, rapprochement, adjustment, interlocking, engagement, convention, contract, contribution, sharing) and the *dia-bole* (division, squabble, enmity, aversion, slander, disunion). Together, *sumbole* and *diabole* constitute the noetic regime of the *metabole*, and echoes of them can be found in Empedocles, as *Philotes* and *Neikos*, friendship and strife.

This necessity of the *sumbole* and the *diabole* reveals itself little by little in public space as *polemical oratory*, which will be called *eristic*. *Eris*, which is always at risk of sinking as *Neikos* into *diabole*, and *Philia*, which needs *sumbolon*, are

> two divine entities, opposed and complementary, [which] marked the two poles of society in the aristocratic world that followed the ancient kingships. An exaltation of the values of struggle, competition, and rivalry was associated with the sense of belonging to a single community, with its demands for social unity and cohesion. The spirit of *agon* [competition] that animated the *gene* [families] of the nobility was manifest in every sphere. [...] Indeed, politics, too, had the form of *agon*: an oratorical contest, a battle of arguments whose theatre was the agora.[147]

For the new retentional system, insofar as it is also the system of orthothetic *textuality*, is characterized by the principle of différant identity that I analysed in *Technics and Time, 2: Disorientation*, and which, as we shall see, results from a *tertiarization of linguistic temporal flows*, generating this paradox whereby the *literal identification* of utterances gives rise to the *proliferation of differences* between their interpretations. Now, *Eris* and *Philia* enter this world because *everything becomes 'literalizable'*, and thus open to literary interpretation, publishable in lettered form, textually legible and visible – and this is true, in the first place, for law:

> To read a text in cuneiform, whatever its size, it must be deciphered. The business of a scribe or a scholar is to interpret, to choose according to context, to confront the ambiguity

> of signs with ideographic and phonetic value. In Greece, no citizen capable of making a proposal to the assembly needs a 'writing expert' as mediator to read a decree cut to his intention.[148]

A paradoxical *différant identification* of utterances is enabled by the ortho-graphy that thereby emerges, and that Detienne is describing here, one that results

> from the tear in the context of enunciation, a paradoxical opacity of exposition in the effects of reading's (re)contextualization; it is as if although the indecision with regard to any reading's signification is reduced, the variability of its meaning has been proportionately increased, freeing up entirely new interpretive possibilities. This contextual wrenching, once accomplished, reveals *for itself* the play of textuality as such, emerging from any reading of the book, with a set of infinite contextual possibilities. What then offers itself for simultaneously original and radical discovery, if it is true that a context for reading can never be repeated, is an in-terminability of reading for any and every text; this is the very law of the here and now whose conjunction never occurs only once, all context being just such a conjunction.[149]

Everything becomes interpretable because *everything becomes literalizable*, that is, the object of organization in and by language, speech becoming the polemical and dialectical milieu wherein idiolectical difference is intensified, at the cost of a reduction of dialects.

> The system of the *polis* implied, first of all, the extraordinary preeminence of speech over all other instruments of power. [...] Speech was no longer the ritual word, the precise formula, but open debate, discussion, argument. [...] [Knowledge was] no longer preserved in family traditions as private tokens of power, and their exposure to public scrutiny fostered exegeses, varying interpretations, controversies, and impassioned debates.[150]

This literalization, which is therefore a textualization intensifying the interpretability of linguistic utterances, and, beyond that, of everything they aim at, is, at the same time:

- a *synchronization*, since language tends to unify itself, to identify itself in its publication, and, along with it, to unify ways of life and social relations;

- a *diachronization* of interpretations, a promise of History that weaves stories, and the birth of History – through these *Histories* that were written/recorded by Herodotus.

In fact, *synchrony never stops trans-forming itself through its interpretation*. Even as it secures the unity of groups and translates the process of individuation, it enters into an intense evolution of the *conditions of metastability*: the conditions of its equilibrium are perpetually threatened with disequilibrium (and this is then war, and the worst: *stasis*, when brothers turn upon and kill one another). In brief, the text, as synchronizer of the Law, and even though it is syn-chronic, remains textual, which means that it is potentially dia-chronic, always potentially interpretable: its justice lies precisely in its openness to interpretation, to judgment, *krinein*, which does not simply mean rules and regulations, a set of univocal instructions, a succession of algorithms, however syllogistic. It is a preindividual milieu, which the Greeks call *koine*, which, with Detienne, we translate as *publicité*, both public-ness and publicity, and which is constantly subject to evolutions through the jurisprudence of interpretations.

This literalization of laws 'not only ensured their permanence and stability; it also removed them from the private authority of the *basileis*, whose function was to "speak" the law'.[151] In other words, the literal publication of the law *has displaced the forum of interpretation, that is, of differentiation*, which is also to say, *the organizing of definition and the implementing of the retentional criteria constitutive of authority* – for the law is nothing but the sieve that enables the selection of facts to be sifted and judged. In relation to Mycenaean society, to Oriental empires and to the society of the *basileus*, therefore, what occurs is a vast 'transformation of the social status of writing'[152] insofar as it is the opening of both *the political and the epistemic* as interpretive activities, typical of this new process of individuation made possible by the ortho-graphic retentional system:

> Instead of being the privilege of one caste, the secret of a class of scribes working for the king, writing became the common property of all the citizens, an instrument for making things public. It made it possible to introduce into the public domain everything that goes beyond the realm of private life and is of interest to the community. Laws had to be written down. In this way they became truly the property of everyone. This transformation of the social status of writing was to have a fundamental effect on intellectual history. Writing made it possible to make public and reveal to everybody things that

> had always remained more or less secret in the Eastern civilizations, with the result that the rules of the political game – free debate, public discussion, and contentious argument – also became the rules of the intellectual game.[153]

So as to metastabilize the *We*, the city becomes a kind of monumental writing machine, through the buildings of which citizens, who are readers and writers, are exposed to surfaces that open onto and support the space of *publicité*:

> Solon 'writes the laws' in the midst of clashes, in the violence occurring between parties and to put an end to civil war. And writing is from the outset monumental, an architecture of letters. The laws are engraved onto a machine made of rectangular wooden beams, three or four sides of which are mounted on vertical frames and able to be rotated around an axis. A machine made to let see and let read, installed in the heart of the city, in the Prytaneum, close to Hestia, the power of the common hearth.[154]

This writing machine archives, stratifies and accumulates, and it does so *according to precise and explicit rules of rewriting*, themselves subject to being rewritten and interpreted, and which are no longer simply an empirical sedimentation: the *cumulative* character of laws constitutes a system that is also a *textual corpus, accessible à la lettre*, as is the case for philosophical debate, and this allows for jurisprudence:

> References from one law to another begin to appear around the late sixth century. [...] Justice created publicly and conforming to rules known to all; justice valid for all citizens, the letter of which can be verified both by the judge and by the accused.[155]

The great reformer, who, in 518 in Ionia, deposited power 'into the middle', is a *grammatist*:

> The gesture of Maeandrius was to offer the citizens of Samos the most democratic regime of the time. The regent chosen by Polycrates intended 'to show himself the most just of men'; Herodotus, however, describes the functions that come with being he who stands beside the tyrant: *grammatist*, scribe, not clerk or secretary of the antechamber, but, alongside Polycrates, the one responsible for all that is written.[156]

And, at the beginning of the sixth century, Solon, who writes the Laws, is also a poet – articulating oral tradition and written tradition:

> He is the first to refer to his legislative activity as a *graphein*. *Thesmous...esgraspa*: the laws, I have written them,[157]

even if, as Nicole Loraux writes, in this epoch it was still the case that

> the poetry of Solon could pass for *logos* without caring about the means of its transmission: the oral memory of the city was still alive enough to take it on board.[158]

It is after these analyses that we should reread Havelock and Ong.

Things will be different in the age of Pericles – whose speeches will be 'fixed' in place or 'reconstructed' by Thucydides, just as Plato will do with Socrates. *Writing then becomes the organon common to the political and the epistemic*, to *sophia* and to poetry, which, from then on, in Parmenides as in Empedocles, will be written down and thus no longer composed on the basis of its mnemonic function. What emerges from the *polis* and the *epistēmē* are the *fruits of one and the same process of individuation* under the impact of the rise of *one and the same retentional system*: political categories are found in the cosmological discourse of the Ionian physicists, and, ultimately, as the heart of pre-Socratic thought in general. It is hardly necessary to recall, say Lévêque and Vidal-Naquet,

> the influence properly political concepts had on the constitution of the image of the world in the representations of the philosophers of Ionia and Magna Graecia.[159]

SIXTH LECTURE

Tragic *Krisis* and Adoption

Tragic *krisis*

The *co-emergence of the political and the epistemic as adoption of a new retentional apparatus* for the psychic and collective individuation process proper to the Greek *polis* should be a subject of reflection for knowledge today – and, indeed, a serious concern: after the absorption of politics into the market through the integration of the *mnemotechnical system* into the global *techno-industrial system*, it is now the knowledge-form itself that has found itself under threat.

Thales, who with Solon was one of the Seven Sages, made

> a proposal to the assembly of the pan-Ionians in about 547. Thales proposed creating a single *bouleuterion* on the island of Teos because it was 'at the center of Ionia (*meson Iōniēs*)'.[160]

On the other hand, it was this same Thales who 'saw the unity of being, and, when he wanted to express it, he spoke of water!'[161] And it was this same geometer and astronomer who calculated the cosmic calendar, defined the number of days in a year, fixed the length of a month at thirty days and founded the theory of profane calendarity that Cleisthenes would institute as the law of the city. Thales is the very image of this double inscription of individuation, both political and epistemic, and of the tightly-bound co-emergence of its two dimensions. And this double inscription is marked in all the pre-Socratics.

To jurisprudence, whose conditions were at that time in the process of coalescing, is added the cumulative character of knowledge, all of which is part of a vast process of public interpretation made possible by the textuality of systematically 'literalized' statements:

> Thales rejoices in Pherecydes's wise decision not to keep his knowledge but to make it available *en koinōi*, to the community, thus the subject of public discussion. To put it another way: When a philosopher such as Pherecydes wrote a book, what was he doing? He was transforming private knowledge into a subject for a public debate similar to that which was becoming established for political matters. And, indeed, Anaximander discussed the ideas of Thales, and Anaximenes those of Anaximander, and through these discussions and arguments philosophy itself became established.[162]

The emergence of this publicness/publicity [*publicité*] occurs in the context of a crisis that is not only a crisis of beliefs: Greeks are confronted with the development, both on the mnemotechnical level and on the level of the overall technical system, with the new use of iron, which brought about the sudden growth of the artisan class. All 'systems' – in the sense in which I use this word in *Technics and Time, 1*, where it defined the tension that always ties the technical system to the other systems, which is to say the social systems, and always does so through the mediation of the mnemotechnical system – undergo change: religion, with the becoming profane and lessening significance of myth in the face of *logos*, as Dodds shows; trade and economics, with monetary and maritime development; the legal system, as we have just described in broad terms; the geographical system, with the extension of the space accessible by navigation and the birth of cartography; the education system, with the appearance of *grammatists*; the linguistic system, with the development of Attic language and grammatization in general; and so on.

It is in the seventh century that the conditions of this crisis appear, but they really

> unfolded in the sixth, a time of troubles in which we catch a glimpse of the economic conditions that gave rise to internal conflicts. On the religious and moral plane, the Greeks experienced this time as a questioning of their whole system of values, a blow to the very order of the world, a state of defect and defilement. [The] starting point of the crisis was economic [and bears witness to] the resumption and development of contacts with the East [...]. But in the last quarter of the seventh century the economies of European and Asian cities turned boldly outward [and] extended on the west as far as Africa and Spain, and on the east to the Black Sea.[163]

With this 'widening of the maritime horizon',[164] the space of life and the *relationship* to space are both transformed: spatiality as such, that is, cardinality as apparatus of orientation, was also affected by

> an acute demand for grain created by population pressure – a problem made all the greater by the fact that Hellenic agriculture tended now to favor the more profitable cultivation of vineyards and olive groves [...]. A search for land, for food, and for metal.[165]

As in other historical moments of great technical evolution, and in particular in the case of the industrial revolution, this process leads to feedback loops that in turn structure the process itself: the end of the seventh century, which is the moment when money is invented, coincides with the increased use of metals and with 'changes in social structure that were brought about by the orientation of a whole sector of the Greek economy towards overseas trade'.[166] The result of these changes is a 'concentration of landed property' and the 'subjugation of the greater part of the *demos*',[167] which in turn leads to tensions between the aristocracy and the other components of society:

> During the seventh century the tastes and manners of a Greek aristocracy that was attracted by luxury, refinement, and opulence were inspired by the ideal of *habrosyne*, of the magnificent and exquisite, which it found in the Oriental world. [...] And by becoming involved in the realm of wealth, the aristocratic *eris* introduced the ferment of alienation and division into Greek society.[168]

This is a general mutation of the social systems and of the articulation between them.

> Pierre-Maxime Schuhl emphasizes the scale of the social and political transformations that took place before the sixth century. He notes that the introduction of institutions such as money, the calendar, and alphabetical writing must have helped liberate men's minds, and that navigation and commerce tended to give a new, practical orientation to thought.[169]

But there is no doubt that, in this global process, the transversal role of the evolution of writing is not just one element among others: as an organization of retentions, which orders collective individuation, the ways that exchange is organized, the constitution of knowledge and the definition of laws, as well as individual acts and the construction of personal histories, it over-determines the conditions of evolution of the whole.

Now, this global evolution is a disadjustment, engendered here primarily by mnemotechnics, and it is thus an epoch characterized by the painful adoption of this revolution of the retentional apparatus and of the criteria that it always implements. The writing of the law tears the latter away from being implicit, and it is therefore also a sudden fragile weakening of customary law, undermining its authority. Nevertheless, implicit law remains: the Inherited Conglomerate is just that – this is what Sophocles puts on stage in *Antigone*.

Transformation reveals itself as a crisis of the unity of the *We*, and as the possibility of a failure of individuation, when it leads to the question of *hubris*, engendering 'bad *Eris*'. This is what occurs when *polemos*, on which the city is founded, and whose *dynamism* is a metastabilizing factor, which is to say the very principle of development, becomes the *destroyer* of the city, compromising its ability to maintain its unity:

> with the coming of the Iron Age, the powerful lost all decency, and *Aidos* [Shame] had to flee the world for the heavens. With the way thus left clear for the unleashing of individual passions and *hybris*, social relations were marked by violence, guile, despotism, and injustice.[170]

In *Antigone*, the character of Creon, and the speech he makes to *his son*, Haemon, show better than any other example that the question of *arbitrariness* profoundly marks the tragic epoch, as the threat of this *hubris* that is the absence of *aidōs*, that is, of humility, shame. With respect to shame, we have seen that, after Prometheus is forced to commit the theft of fire, that is, to give *tekhnē* to mortals (to repair the fault of Epimetheus, who forgot to endow mortals with any qualities), shame is the feeling that Zeus sends Hermes to bestow upon mortals, along with *dikē*, the feeling for justice. *Dikē* is the feeling of a *difference we must know how to make* between the just and the unjust. *Aidōs*, which we are translating as shame, *lies in the fact that faults in law can always be created insofar as, when the law is literalized, that is, when it becomes public, and through that profane, it can be inverted into a letter without spirit, into a convention that turns out to be arbitrary*, just as milk can turn.

The theatre of the polis as the there *of what convenes*

The Greek city is constituted on the basis of a convention: but we must understand this as an agreement elaborated by convening – through this coming-together, *co-venir* – that is a process of psychic and collective individuation. This convening that comes together as history, that is, as *Geschichte*, also *institutes* what will become the *polis* through the leap of a decision that is also a *sudden* [*subite*] *suspension of the state of things*, an *epokhē* that is also *suffered through* [*subie*]. Hence this convening is a dimension of the tragic, one that is instituted and inaugurated by a violent gesture that *breaks* the continuity of the already-there, *drawing, however, its movement and its impetus into that with which it breaks* – or, in other words, *along with what it breaks: the convening that establishes this convention also reinvents it.*

All of a sudden, individuation elaborates a series of new structures, but it is obviously from within its preindividual funds and as the resolution of the tensions it contains that the energy can be found with which to accomplish the 'quantum leap' that appears to us to constitute a rupture with this fund itself. This is the situation referred to as the Inherited Conglomerate. This inheritance could become that which bears within it its own potential for reversal, however, *only because this fund suddenly became accessible to the letter,* and because the revolution of individuation from which these new individuals called cities and citizens arose required *the retentional revolution that is the 'literalization' of preindividual funds,* which at the same time introduces new potentialities into the potential for individuation, and so gives rise to a newly 'super-saturated' age.

When Gilbert Kahn translates Heidegger's statement on the *polis* into French, in *Introduction à la métaphysique,* he renders *Geschichte* (which in everyday terms means history) as *'provention'*. This proventuality of history that begins with the literalization of retention means that the *law* of the *polis,* inasmuch as it is *instituted,* and instituted precisely as a suspension inaugurating an epoch by implementing that monumental writing and reading machine that is the city, is itself founded on what it inherits from the conglomerate, whose *spirits* it literalizes.

This literalization pursues, in the mode of rupture and as *epokhē,* a process of individuation in which *'we' recognize the unity of a history, one that we at the same time retro-project as being ours,* a unity both as *Geschichte* and as *Historie*: that of Greece, that of what, for all these reasons, we call the 'Greek miracle' – and, by the same token, our history and our 'unity', a we who are *still within literality* and yet right at its outermost edge, contemplating the abyss of its end – hence the temptation, sometimes, to refer to an 'end of history'.

Obviously, the history of Greece is not my own: I am French, not Greek. And obviously the history of Greece is not yours: you are Chinese, and not Greek. And yet, throughout this process of grammatization that unfolded in Greece, then in Western Europe, passing through the *mathesis univeralis,* which for Leibniz was partly inspired by Chinese writing, then in capitalism, which is, today, advancing more rapidly in China than anywhere else – throughout all of this, Greece has become *our* history, in *you,* who are Chinese, as in *myself,* a Frenchman.

This is why, together, we can and should read Plato with that German who was Martin Heidegger. *Geschichte* and *Historie* form a unity, the *unity of what breaks with that from which it breaks,* so that this convention that is the *polis* as the establishing of a law à la lettre can be call 'proventual' – in the sense that it is the *protention* of what comes [*vient*] and suitably agrees, what convenes [*convient*], everyone coming together there – insofar as it is forged in what *'pro-venes'* from out of the already-there that is woven from the *retentions* that this conglomerate constitutes: *its retentions, and the spirits of which they are the substrata.* Let's quote Heidegger:

> One translates *polis* as state [*Staat*] and city-state [*Staadstaat*]; this does not capture the entire sense. Rather, *polis* is the name for the site [*Stätte*], the Here, within which and as which Being-here is historically [*geschichtlich*]. The *polis* is the site of pro-venance [*Geschichte*], that 'here' *within* which, *out of* which and *for* which pro-venance provenes.[171]

This pro-vention, as this site that is the *polis*, is what allows Dasein to open itself to its historiality, which is certainly not created by the *polis*, but which is indeed its in-vention in the sense that it exhumes it as pro-vention of the already-there within which it remains concealed, and remains as if sealed by proto-historical authority, that of the *wanax*, then the *basileus* – just as I tried to show in *Technics and Time, 3* that the principle of contradiction, along with the categories in general and other *a priori* syntheses, are all invented in the transcendental unification of the flow of consciousness self-projecting itself as such, that is, as unified, in the epokhal consideration of its traces, even though all activity of consciousness is always the implementation of such a principle as the tendency to unification – as Kant describes in *Critique of Pure Reason.*

The *polis* is a new epoch of the process of psychic and collective individuation – its *historical* epoch properly speaking, which is therefore, inextricably, its *political* epoch properly speaking, that is, its *epokhē*: the interruption, the suspension of the conditions of the previous epoch, but in the mode of inheritance *by convention*, which is also to say, *in the mode of adoption*, which by the same token proves *to be the originary mode*, namely, *the tragic condition that is the originary default of origin*, through the discovery of what the *polis* pro-venes, which is also its *crisis* and its trans-*formation*, in particular *as the revelation, via institutionalization, of its always already conventional character inasmuch as it carries within it the danger of the arbitrary.*

With Greece, I adopt a past that is not mine: I am French, not Greek. But what does 'my' past really mean? My past is the past from out of which, having adopted it (since it never was mine: I have not lived it), I am *capable of projecting a future that is not just mine*. The danger *of arbitrariness* that results from this *facticity* constitutively stems from the *default of community* (of origin) that is also the *community of default* – that which *must* therefore be projected into a necessity, into a promise of a to-come [*a-venir*], a future of the community of the default that has been necessary *ever since the fault of Epimetheus.*

Now, this danger is the condition, in the widest possible sense of this word, of *freedom*: no freedom is possible that is not exposed to the possible withdrawal of any and all shame, to the *excess* of *hubris* that has lost *metron*, that is, the feeling of its retentional provenance, of the obligation to inherit, of the necessity of *adoption, which is always a question of adopting both that which advances itself as the new and that which greets it as its already-there.*

The default is also and immediately the possibility of *excess* – and the *necessity of the exception*, of which the heroes are symbolic figures. The *ariston* is obviously a figure of the exception, and *eris* presupposes the attraction of the *ariston* precisely insofar as it is exceptional. But this *excess in the default, of the default, this excess that is necessary*, is what is always also at the threshold of *hubris* insofar as *it is that which must not be*. Such is the political site, such is the *polis* as situation, as *tragic situation*: such is the abode [*séjour*] (*ēthos*) of mortals insofar as they are free.

In other words, the constitutively conventional character of being-together is what the *polis* discovers as the *question* of what convenes, of that which is fitting [*convenable*], with respect to the provenance of convention, and it is *in this question* that the major criteriological distinction made by the Greeks is revealed: the distinction between *phusis* and *nomos*.

> As a counterphenomenon [opposed to *phusis*] there arose what the Greeks call *thesis*, positing, ordinance, or *nomos*, law, rule in the sense of mores. But this is not what is moral but instead what concerns mores, that which rests on the commitment of freedom and the assignment of tradition; it is that which concerns a free comportment and attitude, the shaping of the historical Being of humanity, *ethos*, which under the influence of morality was then degraded to the ethical.[172]

Now, *ēthos*, the abode, the space of being-together, is also and firstly usage and habit. It is as *world* – and where a world is always a world of *uses*, structured by and forged in what, in *Technics and Time, 2*, I with Leroi-Gourhan called socio-ethnic programs – that the *ēthos* is conventional. The *ēthos*, as *polis*, can be the venue of *nomos*, of the law insofar as it is the subject of a debate, precisely to the extent that the law is a new mode of being of convention, of usage, of 'program': a critical mode of being where habits, no longer being simply those of custom, become reformable in the freedom of 'historiality', of a *Geschichte* that conceals in itself the already-there as pro-venance, but which presupposes the *pro*-grammaticity of the law.

This *pro*-grammaticity becomes possible through the process of grammatization that begins with the hypomnesic tertiary retentions appearing at the end of the Palaeolithic. It is then re-formable according to a political *pro*-grammaticity made possible by literal tertiary retention that amounts to a new stage of grammatization, in which heritage presents itself, in the *ēthos* that is the *polis*, in terms of the *freedom of adoption*. The place of this freedom is the *boulē*, the organ of public deliberation within which retentional criteria are forged, the physical space of which is named the *bouleutērion*, whereas *boulē* also means *will* in general – *determination*, both as commitment [*engagement*] and as deliberation.

Now, the provenance of the already-there, insofar as it gives the impetus that also allows the *rupture* with the already-there, is forged in *eris* and *eristikē*, and in *polemos*, which is to say, in the exercise of a *decision that never stops being taken*, a *krisis* in the initial sense (decision), being constantly subjected, in the publicness and publicity that is the *polis*, to the play of *logos* as exercise of what will later be called the *arbitrator* (Augustine), or, in other words, judgment, or again, to put it in the language of Aristotle's *On the Soul*, '*to krinon*' (426b17).

This originarily polemical situation of the *polis*, which is its ne-cessity insofar as it *never ceases* to constitute itself in and as the course of its individuation, is what the fault of Epimetheus reveals: left without qualities, mortals are confronted at every moment with the necessity of deciding – together – their future. It is necessary for them to find their bearings, to *orient themselves* – a possibility to which Zeus gave them access, but where he granted them only the *feeling* of the necessity of a *difference* that we must know how to *make*, which is the very expression of their having-to-be, of their having to become for the sake of a future, which is therefore the knowledge of a *criteriological necessity* that is also a critical necessity that shows two faces: *aidōs* and *dikē*, such that *without aidōs, there is no dikē*. We should go more deeply into this point by reading some verses from *Antigone*, but we will not have time.

What is thereby posed in all its dimensions is the question of adoption as I described in *Technics and Time, 3*: it is *posed* (*thesis*) from the moment of the earliest ortho-thetic retentional apparatus, which is the ortho-graphy born in ancient Greece, or what we also call *literal synthesis*.[173] Adoption, we said there, is the constitutive law of human groups, that is, of processes of individuation. But it is generally obscured by a narrative, a narrative that is a myth – in the strict sense of this word. The passage from the mythological society of the priest-king to the profane epoch of the city is literally a *discovery*: it is the uncovering of the conventional character of the community, which only in so doing becomes the invention of the *polis*, and which is instituted precisely by breaking down the links of traditional authority, including the *occlusion* of the process of adoption that had also constituted the *condition* of such forms of authority.

This certainly does not mean that, once uncovered, the process ceases to be mythologized: its mythologization is inevitable, and even indispensable – it is part of the *cinema of individuation*. And this has been shown by Nicole Loraux in her analysis of the Athenian myths of autochthony. Adoption having been laid bare, uncovered, means that its appearance of permanence is always threatened, just as it means that convention, which, as the *ēthos* proper to *nomos*, simultaneously recovers and suspends tradition, always risks falling suddenly into the arbitrary (this is the issue at stake in *Antigone*), that is, into finding its authority annihilated. The latter will in turn necessitate those re-mythologizations enabled by the *structure of revenances* in which the Inherited Conglomerate consists, the stratification and sedimentation of which are certainly not confined to ancient Greece, but are on the contrary characteristic of the already-there in general. Such is the *apparatus of political projection*, this constitutive cinema that is the cave, and that the city must at once critique and implement. In ancient Greece, this cinema is projected in the open air: it is a *theatre*.

We have said that the *polis* is also the birth of history as such, the latter being defined in terms of the *interpretability* of the already-there (in Heidegger's terms) or the preindividual (in Simondon's terms). This interpretability *to the letter* of the already-there is conferred by the literal and ortho-graphic synthesis in which this *textually re-elaborated* already-there henceforth presents itself, through which it is *contradictorily assigned to the law of this new textuality*, bearing these tensions within the preindividual potential from which ruptures emerge [*proviennent*], 'quantum leaps' and epokhalities of which individuation is the theatre – the already-there is never accessible otherwise than according to the conditions of some or other retentional apparatus.

From Heidegger's perspective, the birth of history is above all the revelation of *Geschichtlichkeit*, which is nothing but the dehiscence of the ontological difference, of being and beings, a difference *that is therefore made*, that is, *invented*, in the 'clearing' of the *polis* as inaugural site of the history of being. We ourselves adopt this analysis here. But with a few qualifications:

1 For Heidegger, strictly speaking, it is not a matter of an apparatus of adoption, at least as I have defined it in *Technics and Time, 3*, namely, as the simultaneous adoption of an already-there and of the techno-logical synthesis that makes

this already accessible and does so by *granting it its there* through the play of tertiary retentions.

2 Hence the question does not arise for Heidegger of the conditions of access to this already-there, that is, to this provention, no more than does the question of knowing how a 'flux' or a 'flow' that we are here calling 'historial' is constituted, which is a flux *of singularities*, of reflux and counterflow, a backwash through which a *We* is constituted that is also the epoch of being of an *I*, a dual constitution that amounts to what we call a process of individuation, for which it is a matter of thinking the common root of the *I* and the *We* in order, strictly speaking, to think. Thinking: which is all-the-more im-probable in that this *root* is nothing but the *default of origin, that is, of roots.* It is this that we are here calling the *tragic.*

3 Consequently, the *ontological difference* is not, for Heidegger, the presentation of the question of the *difference we must make* in the history of an *original disposition to adopt retentional systems* that Kant, in *Religion within the Bounds of Bare Reason*, calls a *predisposition to graft.*[174]

4 Heidegger, therefore, is unable to pose the *political question of interpretation*, the question of interpretation as the question of a politics of adoption and of the constitution of criteria of orientation through the elaboration of substrata, both by defining a retentional apparatus and by defining the conditions of its control and implementation. As provention, the *polis* is indeed, like Dasein, caught in a 'hermeneutic circle'. The latter, however in Heidegger's thought, has no *support*, no *medium*, and so could be neither, strictly speaking, worldly (within the ontic) nor originary (ontological). The reason for this is that Heidegger, as we have tried to show in *Technics and Time, 1*, has evacuated *Weltgeschichtlichkeit* of the constitutivity in which the ontological difference consists – the fact that its tertiary retentionality is what constitutes it as the play of its *crutches*, unfolding with the rhythm of a *limp*, at the pace of its *lameness*, that is, as the unfolding of its epochs.

Let us now explore this question of the hermeneutic circle, and, firstly, let us see what Heidegger has to say after he has explained how the question of being can be experienced only through an analytic of that particular being who is Dasein as the being *that we are ourselves*:

> But does not such an enterprise fall into an obvious circle? To have to determine beings *in their being* beforehand and then on this foundation first pose the question of being – what else is that but going around in circles? In working out the question do we not 'presuppose' something that only the answer can provide? Formal objections such as the argument of 'circular reasoning', an argument that is always easily raised in the area of investigation of principles, are always sterile when one is weighing concrete ways of investigating. They do not offer anything to the understanding of the issue and they hinder penetration into the field of investigation.[175]

How can we fail to notice that what is posed here is the question of *Meno*, the famous aporia that we have suggested was the *goad* to all philosophy, and just like the *gadfly* that Socrates saw himself as being for the city?

Now, this is precisely what I have argued ever since *Technics and Time, 3*, positing that it constitutes the *question of invention* – as a *decisive counterpart, literally speaking, of convention and of its provention*, and we shall read this once again tomorrow, in *Meno* itself.

Hence an attentive reading of Socrates's response would be decisive for an understanding of the origin of the question of being, that is, for the history of its inaugural moment, for an understanding of the *history* of being, and of the *question* of being, and of the *meaning* of being – precisely inasmuch as it would also be the meaning of the *history of history*, of the birth of history qua *polis*. And we must explore it, this response, scrutinize it, as a response, in its necessity, *and* in terms of justice *and* shame that are as such the inventiveness of thinking – which presupposes a primordial 'conventuality', this being the very thing to which Aristotle would later return, under the name of *axioma*.

Around the interpretation of the aporia of Meno, the sceptical power of which is immense, incommensurable, containing both the motive of every humility and the cause of every excess, all renunciations, all effacements of difference, in the understanding of this passage where for the first time Socrates launches what will become the already-there of the entire Platonic construction of his character – become metaphysical – there plays out a *war of spirits*, through which the *tragic spirit is lost* qua unity *of* the spirits inherited from the already-there, and where the *metaphysical spirit is forged* as the unity of what is always already dividing itself.

What is at stake, here, is the question of invention as *exhumation, in the already-there, of what remains there as retention that is yet to be protentionalized towards its meaning*, namely, its meaning of being, its meaning as suddenly marking, but in *another way*, the horizon within which it has already been given, and has always done so, or almost always: as that tradition inherited in the conglomerate. This is what, in *Meno*, Socrates calls a *reminiscence*. But it is also what breaks the hermeneutic circle within which appears what Heidegger called (the forgetting of) being.

> But in fact there is no circle at all in the formulation of our question. Beings can be determined in their being without the explicit concept of the meaning of being having to be already available.[176]

The question of provenance, *Geschichte*, would then be that of invention. But:

- this presupposes *thinking provention as doubly epokhal redoubling*, where *ruptures* in the retentional apparatus, either indirectly, via rupture of the *technical* system, or directly, via *mnemo-technical* rupture, pre-cede and necessitate a process of adoption that is a quantum leap in the process of psychic and collective individuation;
- the question of provenance as question of invention is precisely *what Plato will efface, in that, for him, invention is confounded with the fiction* that *tekhnē*, in all its forms (logography, poetry, theatre and so on), will always generate, and where, for Plato, fiction is literally *the opposite of truth*.

Against what in *Technics and Time, 3* we have called the 'desire for stories', therefore, for Plato it would be a matter of *no longer telling stories*: this is what he argues for against the pre-Socratics, from whom, for Plato, it is a matter of breaking. 'No longer telling stories' means, here, *eliminating the interpretability of the text, effacing the textuality of the law* – which is also to efface, and to efface before anything else, the *law of textuality*.

When at the end of *Being and Time*, however, Heidegger chooses to expel *Weltgeschichtlichkeit* from originary temporality, he is himself opting for the same, typically metaphysical gesture. And when, at the beginning of his book, Heidegger mobilizes the *Sophist*, he is also giving his blessing to Plato's position that it is now a question of putting an end to these stories told by the old pre-Socratics: it is no longer a question of 'telling stories' because it is now a question of staring being in the face – *at the risk of finding oneself blinded.*

After the *Kehre*, Heidegger will return to a history of being, a history of being older than an existential analytic. But in doing so, he will still fail to re-evaluate the weight of the question of this *historiality* insofar as it consists above all in telling *stories*, recounting *histories* (*logoi*), rather than *a story, one history* (*muthos*).

SEVENTH LECTURE

Against the Current

Going against the current that is the Platonic oeuvre – periodization

I remind you that what we are attempting to do, here, is go against the current. The 'current', in this case, is that of a history, the history of philosophy, which is to a large extent also simply the History of the West, what we mean when, beholding the figure of Napoleon, we see in this figure, as Hegel or Beethoven did, the 'march of history', but which itself falls within what Heidegger called the history of truth.

What place does China hold in this history? Of course, this is not something I can really talk about here. But it is a discussion that Yuk Hui begins to open up in his recent book, *The Question Concerning Technology in China*,[177] and so I recommend that you read it.

We are going against the current: against the so-called mainstream – a dominant current that has today become that of 'post-truth', within which we ourselves are immersed, and which seems bound to become more and more unpleasant. It stems from a regression, and from a fall – about which *Phaedrus* will propose an interpretation that I maintain breaks with what until then amounted to a tragic culture, itself stemming both from an archaic inheritance and from the Greek *Aufklärung* (borrowing this formula from Dodds) that emerged with alphabetical writing, and which led to the formation not just of the city but of geometry, positive law, history in the sense of Herodotus, and so on. Hence we are trying, *here*, to go back upstream against this fall into the fall, not just by trying to get out of the water, but by pushing against it, so to speak, and even by wiggling the tail – like a salmon.

Luc Brisson has proposed to classify and date the Platonic dialogues: I do not totally accept Brisson's periodization (which is similar to Léon Robin's), in particular because I situate *Phaedrus* before the *Republic*, but also because in my view *Apology* and *Crito* remain within the strictly Socratic register. *Ion, Protagoras* and *Apology* belong, according to the perspective I am defending here, to the 'Socratic' or 'youthful' period, during which Plato essentially gave an account of the teachings of Socrates through his words, as dialogues, but also, in *Apology*, as his defense during his trial (to which Xenophon bears witness through another testimony), where he addresses the body of citizens in replying to his accuser.

Following this is another series of dialogues, in which the Platonic questions properly speaking are formulated, and within which an increasingly specific interpretation of how we *should* understand Socrates's words takes shape. This coincides with the appearance of *Platonism* properly speaking. This involves those dialogues that we can group around *Meno* and *Symposium*, *Gorgias* being a kind of intermediary dialogue.

Meno
Cratylus
Symposium

Then came a new series, extending from *Phaedo* to *Sophist*, a sequence in which Plato becomes dogmatic, referred to as his 'mature' period, but in which he begins to literally *contradict*, on certain key points, the fundamental teachings of Socrates. This period includes, in particular:

Republic
Phaedrus
Theaetetus
Sophist

Again, *Phaedo* can, perhaps, be considered an intermediate dialogue, but nevertheless an important one. Finally, with old age, there are the texts that I consider to be aporetic, especially *Timaeus*, texts that complicate and salvage this dogmatism – saving it in the sense that they save Plato himself from this dogmatism, that is, they save that *Plato who puts into question much of what may have seemed for him to have been acquired in the preceding texts*. This includes, notably:

Timaeus
Philebus
Laws

As these periods unfold, in their relations and through the evolutions through which they can be characterized, contradictions or *countercurrents* form, which require detailed analysis, but which we don't have time to do now.

It could be shown, through Heidegger's readings, how all this falls within a history of truth that is also a history of the individuation of Plato himself as he individuates himself *to the letter*, and how Heidegger himself individuates himself *to the letter* between 1925, the year of the course on the *Sophist*, and 1942, the year he publishes his analysis of Book VII of the *Republic* (and of *Theaetetus*), which he had begun in 1931.

I would like now to draw your attention to *what links the following three dialogues,*

Meno
Symposium
Phaedrus

and to what links them in terms of questions that never cease haunting and even harassing Plato, which in a way obsess him, and, I believe, *perplex and embarrass him,* and keep *returning* to him – as revenants, ghosts, spirits and demons – across these three dialogues, and also others, of course, but not as clearly as in this trio, and not necessarily with respect to the themes that explicitly characterize these three dialogues. These characteristic themes are:

- Poetry
- Delirium
- Love
- Memory
- Mysteries and mystagogy

With respect to mystagogy and the *mysteries of Eleusis,* we may not have time to discuss these in this course. But in that case, I will try to come back to it next year.

The aporia of Meno

Everything begins, then – in what becomes the properly Platonic corpus, through which Plato interprets Socrates and tries to extend him – with the aporia of Meno, which is the matrix of philosophy. It is a *topos,* a common space for the objections made by the sophists to philosophy, and to a certain way of thinking that was inherited from, among others, Parmenides, and which is inscribed in a *thinking of being* claiming access to idealities such as the triangle – which *is* in an absolute way, which does not become, whose notion bears within it the intimate knowledge of its omnitemporal necessity – and, finally, access to what Plato describes as *essences* and *ideas,* hence providing access to what falls under ontology, to discourse on *that which is.*

The sophists, on the other hand, are inscribed in a tradition that, rightly or wrongly, is often referred to Heraclitus, who posits that everything becomes, and that the question of being is itself an illusion, or a *local eddy,* in this becoming – in the flow of this river that is *phusis.* In this context, the aporia of Meno consists in positing that it is not possible to know something that we do not *already* know. And since by *knowing*, here, we mean the fact of *learning* something, of transforming oneself, of dis-covering something that was previously unknown, then if we already know what we claim to learn, well indeed we are an impostor, as Meno says to Socrates, who himself treated as impostors those sophists who claim to know – to have knowledge:

> SOCRATES: I see what you're getting at, Meno. [...] The claim is that it's impossible for a man to search either for what he knows or for what he doesn't know:
>
> - he can't search for what he knows, since he knows it and so there's no need for the search;
> - nor can he search for what he doesn't know, since then he doesn't even know what to look for.[178]

It is through this response by Socrates to Meno's aporia that, for the first time, Plato's position is founded and formulated, a position we might be forgiven for thinking is also that of Socrates. (This is something we *might* think but about which we cannot be absolutely sure, and we must never forget that what we know of Socrates, we know only from what is said in Plato, Xenophon and the doxography – and we know of Jesus in this same kind of way. Let us, then, not take the statements that have been reported at face value.)

The aporia of Meno, and the response to it given by Socrates, which we are now going to examine, will eventually become the foundation of what will later be called *transcendental philosophy*, which posits that there is an *a priori* sphere of knowledge, a sphere that is constitutive of the possibility of knowing in the sense that it is not given by experience but is, on the contrary, that which gives access to experience. This is what Kant will argue in *Critique of Pure Reason*.

In the articulation of the nineteenth and twentieth centuries, this question will become, in a manner quite degraded from its initial formulation, the question of what is called the innate versus the acquired, and it will do so on the basis of a profound misunderstanding that one can already find in Descartes. This misinterpretation consists in believing that the ideas – which Descartes discusses, after Plato, and which Kant *will* discuss either as pure concepts (*a priori* synthetic judgments) or as what he calls the ideas of reason (which are its motives, aims, ends, as Kant says, ends that put it in movement, and that 'move' it in an e-motional sense, that stir it) – the error consists in believing that this belongs to the innate in the biological sense of the term, as psychobiology raises these questions. More specifically, it is an error committed by Noam Chomsky.

What is an aporia? An aporia means a dead-end, an impasse. An aporia is a question that arises, a true question, but one to which it is not possible to give an answer, or, more exactly, to which it is not possible to give an answer through *ordinary discourse*. To answer such a question, we cannot remain on the usual, habitual plane of discourse: a discourse expected to be rigorous, noetic, but which remains an ordinary discourse, which is to say that it remains on the plane of reason defined as common rationality, as non-contradictory, as respecting all the rules of what Kant called the understanding.

Faced with such an aporetic question, says Socrates, we can respond – and we must respond: it is a radical putting into question that calls for a radical answer, a radical *response* (as in antiphony) – only with an *extra-ordinary* answer, with a response that is necessarily *mystagogical*. I must get out of the ordinary in order to face up to it, being itself out of the ordinary. It is dangerous, extremely dangerous. It can lead me into *delirium*, in Plato's sense of this word, which he uses on several occasions, particularly in *Phaedrus*, but also in *Symposium*, and already in *Ion*.

In *Symposium*, and then in *Phaedrus*, it is said that amorous delirium is what grants access to wisdom. And it is, of course, very important and quite striking, not to say shocking, to see Plato – who is constantly pleading for rationality, reserve, *metron*, and against excess, passion, lies – here appealing to delirium and excess (which is the flip side of the *défaut*, and we must develop this point further by reading *Symposium*).

Finally, as we will see, Plato regularly makes a plea for excess, delirium, or for what he calls enthusiasm, possession if you will, that of the poet Ion in particular, an excess that is also the drinking to excess we see in *Symposium* – where everyone has a hangover, having already celebrated Agathon's victory at the poetry contest.

In *Symposium*, Plato makes his case for excess by saying that *it is only in this excess that love must be* that we can attain wisdom. Yet in *Meno*, when Socrates appeals to the priests, priestesses and poetesses who tell the story of Persephone, we see that it is already a question of excess, or, more precisely, of delirium, or of the extraordinary.

In *Meno*, the issue is this *collective delirium* that is *mythology* and *poetry*, which are recognized to be *timiotata*, that is, they are recognized as partaking in the highest values – which are, therefore, in Greek society, delirious. It may well be that Greek society is rationalist, but reason is sometimes summoned to attain a level where it must pass reason – to in some way go beyond itself, surpass itself, to lift itself up by the hair like Baron Munchausen, in order to pass onto the plane of the extra-ordinary and the mystagogical – for what is at stake, here, is what constitutes the foundation of what are called the mysteries of Eleusis.

Note that by surpassing itself in this way, and by returning to the mythological and poetic sources, one could say that Socrates and Plato are heading upstream, going back up against the current, like salmon, just as we, too, are trying to swim back upstream along the course of the Western history of truth.

What lies in the background of *Meno*, what goes unmentioned either by Socrates, or by Plato, but which would have been obvious to any Greek, is what stems from an experience that they would all have had: that of being initiated into the mysteries of Eleusis, into rituals – which were practised there, where, evidently, Socrates and Plato had gone (Plato talks about it in Letter VII), and which have an *essential link to the mythology of Persephone.*

In order to bring to a close this introduction into Plato's philosophy as that which engenders metaphysics, we can see that we have already entered the subject matter of *Symposium*, whose central and literally extra-ordinary character is named Diotima. Diotima, who speaks to Socrates as to a young man, almost as to a child, which is in itself highly extra-ordinary, Diotima is a priestess just like those to whom Socrates appeals in responding to the aporia of Meno:

> Socrates: I've heard both men and women who are skilled in divine things [...] priests and priestesses [...] Pindar and many other inspired poets [...] say that the human soul is immortal – that it periodically comes to an end (which is what is generally called 'death') and is born again, but that it never perishes. And that, they say, is why one should live as righteous a life as possible, because [...] for those who have, for their previous faults [*palaiou pentheos*: old wounds], paid ransom to Persephone, she will, to the sun above, in the ninth year, restore their souls anew, from which illustrious kings, mighty in strength and great in knowledge, will arise, who will for all time as sacred heroes be honoured among mortals.[179]

The myth of Persephone, evoked by Socrates in answer to the aporia of Meno, is evoked by default, from out of the inability to respond 'rationally', in what counts as *ordinary* for the rational: in such a case, we must respond *extra-ordinarily*, not *against* reason but *beyond* reason, not in contradiction with reason, but outside the limits of our own reason.

This may be an exit from the limits of our own reason, but that is not, of course, how Socrates refers to it: for him, it is a matter of *logos*, which we should avoid translating as reason. This exit from *logos* was carried out by Socrates, who is himself a mystagogical figure. This is something we must insist upon: the famous *daimōn* of Socrates shows up whenever there is something important at stake for Socrates, when he is *troubled* and *challenged*, profoundly *thrown into question*. Suddenly he stops, he gives the impression he's about to fall backwards, he's caught, possessed by his *daimōn*, by something that is no longer himself, which interrupts him, leaves him in suspense, which is in this way his *epokhē*, and which belongs to what Dodds calls the Inherited Conglomerate, that is, to that set of beliefs and ritual practices that are the mythological and political funds or ground of the traditional and archaic Greek culture within which Socrates and Plato still think, and which they regularly call upon whenever what Dodds calls the Greek *Aufklärung*, Greek rationality, the rationality of the philosophers, runs up against its own limits.

Here, in this limit that Socrates encounters via the aporia of Meno, Socrates responds by convoking the myth and mystagogy of Persephone. Through this convocation, he opens a completely new possibility that puts forth a highly unusual discourse that will, in the Platonic works that follow, take on strange, unexpected, complex forms, and that will deform it – this is the heart of my thesis on Plato, and it is also the heart of my interpretation of the history of philosophy – for a reason that will lead Plato to contradict, almost point by point, what he had said at the beginning of his work, because, when he began his work, what it said, this work, was *still* what Socrates said.

When he begins his work, Plato is the pupil who records his master's teachings, a master who did not himself write. In the beginning, Plato set out to preserve the memory of those dialogues in which he, along with so many others, participated. But in the work of recording that he carries out, he encounters difficulties with the internal coherence of the statements. And in order to try and resolve these difficulties, which are *apparent contradictions*, he adds interpretations of his own. This will eventually lead to the creation of something that is no longer Socratic – Platonism – of which we are the heirs, we, contemporary philosophers, who have ourselves inherited it from modern philosophers, and, before them, from medieval philosophers.

It is this tangled web that we will now try to disentangle. To do so will be complicated but crucial, because, if I may remind you of the thesis I presented at the beginning of this course: we are confronted, today, with these questions formulated by Plato, but we are confronted with them in a new way that is extreme, radical, violent and dangerous.

These questions were formulated in a situation of crisis that was also the situation of the birth of philosophy. And if I am doing this course of philosophy with you, it is not just for fun: doing so gives me immense pleasure, thanks to you who allow me the privilege and the pleasure of teaching you, and, indeed, I love to teach, but my reason for doing so stems firstly from necessity.

We find ourselves, today, in an extremely dangerous situation, one that forces us, all of us, to think outside our usual habits of thinking, and not just with the degree of philosophical exigency that philosophical conversions always require, where these conversions are already exits from the ordinary. What we are compelled to think about, today, is the question of the extraordinary as such, this question of the extraordinary being that of desire.

What lies on the horizon of the dialogue of Meno, and the reference it contains to Persephone, is the question of desire. But this *does not yet*, in that epoch, present itself as such. At that time, in that epoch, it presents itself as the question of death and rebirth, of resurrection, revival and of the return of spirits, of their *revenance*.

Technicity, history, salmon and pharmacology

Mortals are technicians, and, as such, they never stop inventing – and through that, inventing their destiny. But by inventing, they never stop finding themselves challenged once again, thrown into question in *eris*, confrontation and emulation. With ancient Greece appears a new dynamism of *anthropoi* or *thanatoi*, corresponding to the beginning of history and constituting a psychic and collective individuation process. It is from this dynamism that the specifically Greek way of posing questions arises.

Heidegger, too, says that the one who questions has an already-there, that is, a past that is not just his own, but that of a history that precedes him, and which he inherits. This inheritance must be turned into the object of an interpretation, which is to say of an individuation, by each of us insofar as we individuate ourselves, that is, insofar as we exist.

In ancient Greece, this is called questioning. To question is to go back in time, which is what, in *Meno*, Plato will call anamnesis. Anamnesis is what I have depicted with the image of the noetic salmon, who returns to the source to pose her questions, that is, to lay her eggs and fertilize the time that is history qua history of a default of origin, or history of technicity: which is a default of source, that is, of what remains always to be interpreted by going back to another source.

What makes it possible to go back into history, inasmuch as it leads to this anamnesis, is, precisely, writing. The writing I am referring to is in this case alphabetical. It enables a return to the default of origin that is different from that enabled by Chinese writing, which of course has its own anamnesic characteristics. Moreover, it is striking to speak here about characteristics, since through this word we can refer to what Leibniz called the *characteristica universalis*, and to reflect on the attention Leibniz gave to writing in Chinese characters.

Now, Leibniz's reflections on the *characteristica universalis* lie at the origin of computer science, and then of digital tertiary retention. This subject lies on the horizon of Yuk Hui's own reflections, and it is necessary to consider these Leibnizian questions once again for our own age, which is that of digital writing, where it is a question of knowing what new anamnesic possibilities and impossibilities are made possible by digital writing technologies.

Alphabetical writing is the noetic element characteristic of Greece. And alphabetical writing is also what the sophists taught, but they did so by practising it as that which prevents going back, as a barrier preventing the salmon or the trout from going back upstream… This is what it says in *Phaedrus*. So, when such barriers present themselves, it is necessary to build specific works, works that are artificial but that make it possible to go back to the source – that is, to the default of origin.

The status of truth in Greek psychic and collective individuation, *epokhē* and intermittence

Heidegger says that to translate *alētheia* as *veritas* is incorrect. Whatever the case may be in that regard, Greek society, *the polis, is what in principle makes the truth arising from public debate into the key criterion of its becoming*, which is to say, of its collective individuation, its becoming-together, that which forms a future.

The history of philosophy is a history of conversions, and it is from these conversions that the history of truth proceeds. Does it then follow that philosophy is the *cause* of the transformations of the truth? Not in any way, but, after literal tertiary retention, philosophy does establish the rules of processes of transindividuation inasmuch as they constitute epochs, and it does so as the second moment of the doubly epokhal redoubling.

I am trying here to give you a very condensed account of that process of transindividuation whose criteria is provided by philosophy, and I'm trying to do so specifically by following the thread of *ideality* – from Plato to Husserl, via Descartes and Kant, an ideality that also passes through the question of categorization. I myself argue for the *contemporary* need for a conversion on the basis of which I interpret the preceding conversions, given that the new conversions that make up the history of philosophy always reinterpret the path that precedes them, whether deliberately or otherwise. As for the conversion that *we* require, Heidegger opens up the question of such a conversion under the names of *Gestell, Ereignis* and *Geviert*. But let's leave that for now.

Let us interpret conversion in general from an exosomatic standpoint, and as a departure from the milieu of our existence, a deviation in relation to this milieu, a radical displacement, even a dislocation (*arrachement*, which means both wrenching away and abduction) from a milieu, but to which we always return. (To go deeper into these questions, we should read Canguilhem.)

This milieu is not stable: it is metastable. It is metastable not only in the sense that living things in general are composed of dynamic metastable systems, but in the sense that tertiary retention constantly disrupts the interior and exterior milieus that living things constitute, and does so by adding artificial organs that escape the laws of biology and more generally of what we sometimes call nature, or *phusis*. The exosomatic metastable milieu is always at the limit of equilibrium and disequilibrium, always in unstable equilibrium, in the sense that it is constantly destabilized by the artificiality that Heidegger also calls facticity. It is a milieu that is not just logical (as milieu of *logos*, of the symbolic, of language) but techno-logical.

The possibility of leaving this milieu lies in changing our relation to it: it lies in the passage to a reflexive relation, which the Greeks called dianoetic, and which they name *dianoia*, *dia-noia*, a hollow, a gap, a schize or a cleavage in the soul, as well as a *crack* or a *fissure*, and in that a kind of *defect*, a *default*, which also opens the possibility of distanciation, of suspension, of what the Greeks call '*epokhē*'. Being in time is not, for us, simply – as it is for the wind, stones, blades of grass or animals – to undergo becoming in its various animal, vegetable and mineral forms. Being in time means being capable of trans-*forming oneself*, and, by trans-forming oneself, trans-*forming* the world in which one lives – which is the milieu in which one lives, and in order to inscribe into becoming a bifurcation that grants a future.

The world is our milieu, but such that we can trans-form it as much as it can permanently trans-form us, because it is constituted by temporality and as temporality, which is therefore not just becoming [*devenir*] but future [*avenir*], itself founded in a *relation* to a past and a present that never stop trans-forming.

The relation of the Greeks to their past is very different to that of the Egyptians, and very different from the past of China, which is then that of Confucius, the relation of the past of the ancient Egyptians or ancient Chinese being itself very different from the peoples who existed before the rise of empires, and very different from our own. Such a temporality is founded on the possibility that it can be distinguished into epochs, and the latter are made possible by the epokhality that is temporality, itself made possible by the exo-somatic *epokhē* that is any ek-sistence.

What does *epokhē* mean? It means interruption, suspension. And it is in this sense that Husserl's phenomenological method takes up this term. But it also means epoch, that is, collective individuation. Individuation: this is what occurs in a noetic milieu, inasmuch as it is noetic only to the extent that we can tear ourselves away from it only intermittently, and, in so doing, trans-form it. Individuation means constant trans-formation.

EIGHTH LECTURE

Conclusion?

In *Logical Investigations*, Husserl posits that phenomenology – as a method for accessing the constituent sphere of phenomena, which cannot be found in experience, since, as Kant says, it gives access to this experience – Husserl posits that phenomenology conceived in these terms requires a conversion of the gaze.

What Socrates calls anamnesis is always of the order of such a conversion. And it is by convoking Persephone that he indicates that such a conversion is a passage beyond the ordinary and onto the plane of the extra-ordinary, access to which is granted by the priests, priestesses and poets. If we had time, we could at this point have read what Vernant has to say concerning the Homeric Greek poets, who are often blind and who 'see what is invisible'.[180]

True 'thinking for oneself' is always such an anamnesic conversion, which one does not access spontaneously: it requires a dialectical relationship, either in a dialogue with an other, or in a dialogue with oneself, which implies that one is always, oneself, at least two, as is said in *Phaedrus*, where the soul is a winged pair of horses driven by *logos*.

That the soul is split, as *Phaedrus* says, that it is two, means that:

- as *Phaedrus* says, it harbours contrary tendencies;
- as Freud says, these contrary tendencies are fields of the drives, one of which Freud ascribed to Eros, who is the hero of *Symposium*, and the other to Thanatos, which is also to say, to what Freud called the drive to destruction;
- what Aristotle described as the noetic soul, which passes into noetic actuality only intermittently (which is noetic only intermittently), is precisely this soul inasmuch as it is drawn both 'by the high' and 'by the low', its trans-formation being the result of this play of forces, a result that can turn negative, trans-formation then amounting to a regression.

We are constantly transforming, and there is no stable state: either we progress, or we regress. To not 'progress', to not learn, is always already to be regressing, because it is always to become less capable of progressing: it is to become old, sclerotic, ossified. One must constantly exercise, train oneself and struggle against one's own laziness, take care of oneself, and, in order to do so, develop an art of living, a *tekhnē tou biou* (as Foucault will say, when in particular he comments on the letters of Seneca), an *epimeleia*, a technique of the self, a way of life, such as philosophy (which I myself discuss in *Taking Care of Youth and the Generations*).

This is so because the soul is more than one, at least two, and Socrates is himself inhabited by such a 'spirit' – by what he calls his *daimōn*. This defender of reason always also speaks of what, for us, would rather be of the order of the irrational, as Dodds says in *The Greeks and the Irrational*.[181]

In any case, in the Plato still faithful to Socrates, or in other words in the young Plato, true thinking requires this conversion that he calls anamnesis. We have tried to see in what this anamnesis consists by reading *Meno*, a question to which Plato returns in *Phaedrus*, and which in *Meno* obliges him to make an appeal to mythology and to mystagogy, to the irrational, precisely, in order to justify its necessity. Then, in *Symposium*, he appeals – as he will do in *Phaedrus*, but in another way – to love, arguing that all this is a matter of desire, and that it is based on the *philo*-sophical capacity of our souls (insofar as they are noetic, that is, in a relation to the spirit, to *nous*, and, through that, to the intellect), and on the fact that our souls *love* knowledge, that they desire it. Plato will thereby posit that the question of truth is essentially tied to the question of desire.

We asked, what does truth mean? And we ask ourselves this question in the age of post-truth. We noted that Heidegger says that the Latin word, *veritas*, is not a correct translation of *a-lētheia*, and that in Greek society the *polis* is in principle what makes the truth arising from public debate the major criterion of its becoming, its collective individuation. Truth means, at one and the same time:

- that truth established deliberatively before a court;
- mathematical truth, that is, demonstrative truth;
- logical, non-contradictory reasoning, which is also to say cumulative reasoning;
- the historical relationship to the past, founded on non-mythological, non-legendary sources, and so on;
- public debates based on opposing arguments: a form of life founded on a law known by everyone and open to critique by everyone.

But this truth involves a history of truth.

At the beginning of this seminar, I tried to explain why I believe we must understand this history from the standpoint of tertiary retention and its history, which is based on the evolution of a process of grammatization, and where the latter is the hypomnesic dimension of a process of exosomatization. You will remember, I hope, that it is, in particular, *intuition*, *understanding* and *imagination* that are exosomatically reconfigured. In the seminar I have been giving in Hangzhou, I have tried to show that we must reflect on these questions with Freud – and we can understand why by recalling that, in *Symposium*, Plato argues that it is with respect to desire that we must think knowledge.

In *Phaedrus*, Plato further posits that the dialectic must be both analytic and synthetic. I argue that this perspective stems from the relationship that the Greeks had to their own language, inasmuch as written language makes necessary both analysis, that is, cutting and dividing it into elements, and synthesis, that is, interpretation in and through reading. It is on this basis that Book VII of the *Republic* will define truth as *orthotēs*, that is, exactitude, which in 1942 Heidegger will lament, and in which he saw the beginning of metaphysics. On this question I agree with him, but with this additional qualification: with this evolution, which is engendered by literal tertiary retention, Plato prepares the way for what will become, with Kant, the difference between analytical understanding and synthetic reason. To try and understand this, let us try to draw some conclusions on the history of truth more generally.

The history of philosophy is a history of conversions – from Plato to Husserl, via Descartes and Kant, and the question of ideality that passes, moreover, through the question of metacategorization, metacategories and metalanguage – about which I have said a few words through a quotation from Roland Barthes, but of course we would need to dwell on this much further. Perhaps I'll return to it next year.

As I have said, I myself argue for the contemporary need for a conversion, on the basis of which I interpret the preceding conversions, given that, in the history of conversions that make up the history of philosophy, each new conversion reinterprets the path that preceded it, whether deliberately or otherwise. And I interpret conversion in general as a departure from the milieu of our existence, where this milieu is not stable: it is metastable, always at the limit of equilibrium and disequilibrium, always in unstable equilibrium – and it is so because it is a milieu that is not just logical (as milieu of *logos*, of the symbolic, of language) but techno-logical, because it is exo-somatic.

We have seen that the possibility of escaping this milieu lies in changing our relation to it: it lies in the passage to a reflexive relation, which the Greeks considered to be dianoetic, and which they name *dianoia*, *dia-noia*, both a kind of hollow and a kind of defect, a default, which also opens the possibility of distanciation, of suspension, of '*epokhē*' – a term that covers scansions, stases and changes of epoch. The world is our milieu, but such that we can trans-form it just as much as it can permanently trans-form us, because it is constituted *by* temporality and *as* temporality, which is therefore not just becoming [*devenir*] but future [*avenir*]. Such a temporality is founded on the possibility of being able to distinguish different epochs, and what makes these epochs possible is the *epokhē*.

Epokhē and epokhality, which fall within what Heidegger calls *Geschichtlichkeit*, are at the same time constituted and destituted by the technicity of 'mortals', who are occasionally called *oi anthropoi*, humans, but are more generally called, especially in the poetic or pre-Socratic texts, *oi thanatoi*, mortals, that is, those who know they will die, and who, as Freud will also say, are constantly pushing death away, deferring it, and yet are also drawn to it, by Thanatos as the drive to destruction, including self-destruction.

In this dangerous knowledge of death – which is ceaselessly composing with the erotic drive in a play that is always somewhat perverse, knowledge of death being also a non-knowledge – mortals, these mortals who are both perverse and loving [*amoureux*], cultivate their knowledge of death, and they do so in a relation to immortals, to the gods – which is something animals do not do, being, in this regard, merely perishable.

Why do mortals cultivate such a relation? Because into their hands has been that fire of which Dionysos (represented in sculpture as an infant held in the arms of Hermes) is, I believe, an embodiment, as the embodiment of going over the edge [*débordement*], of *hubris*, of immoderation, and of excess as counterpart of the default that is the lot of mortals: mortals who *are* only by default, who do not fully exist, who live and ek-sist only in and through the default that is their mortality, and inasmuch as the latter trans-forms itself into a technicity. Mortals are technicians: this is what we learn from *Protagoras*.

▪ ▪ ▪

Technics is our milieu, but we have naturalized it: we do not see it as such, *as* technics. We are in technics like fish are in the water – except, however, that technical innovation never stops disrupting our milieu, and disrupting we who dwell within this milieu, which is therefore constantly changing, but this is something that has become truly perceptible only since the industrial revolution, which vastly accelerated the pace of this innovation, which at that time was called 'progress'.

The question that arises now is that of the Anthropocene. I have argued that this is what is at stake in Heidegger's text, *Die Kehre*, and that it is from this standpoint that we must reread the history of truth in the epoch of post-truth, from the perspective of what I call the Neganthropocene, which, as I see it, is a response to the Heideggerian question of *Ereignis*. Heidegger was unable to address the *Ereignis* as the question of neganthropology because he rejected the cybernetic conception of entropy and negentropy as defined, for example, by Norbert Wiener, and because he didn't see that the question was to *re*-address entropy as anthropy, and that is possible only from the standpoint of exosomatization, which is to say, the question of the *pharmakon*. From such a standpoint, the ontological difference turns into the intermittency of noesis as a leap above toxic *pharmaka* so as to produce a therapeutic point of view. It is for this reason, I maintain, that he ignored *Protagoras*, *Meno*, *Symposium* and *Phaedrus*, in his analysis of the work of Plato.

What do we find in *Protagoras*? What is said there is that the technical and tragic fate of mortals is also what requires them to interpret their pharmacological situation with Hermes, and with the feelings of *dikē* and *aidōs*, which they feel when they are not just and not quite themselves. In *Meno*, this becomes the question of the revenance of spirits from Hades, the realm of dead souls, some of whom are able to come back thanks to *pharmaka* that are also tertiary retentions. Now, Plato encounters here the difficulty opened up by the interpretation of the extra-ordinary language of figures such as Diotima the priestess and the poets: how should we explain that a mortal can be a quasi-immortal, like a hero?

In *Phaedrus*, this begins to be transformed into an *opposition* between the soul, which would be immortal, and the body, which would be mortal. And in this opposition, body and soul are opposed *as are logos* and *tekhnē*. *Tekhnē* and the body become attributes of mortality, while the soul is dogmatically declared to be immortal, rather than being considered *tragically* as the quasi-immortality of a hero who is *intermittently* noetic.

Such is the basis of metaphysics, as it will engender the history of truth, which becomes today's post-truth.

2018 Lectures

Organology of Platform Capitalism

FIRST LECTURE

Introduction: From Biopower to Neuropower

Michel Foucault developed the concepts of biopower and biopolitics during the 1970s. I have tried myself to show that, in these analyses that remain highly relevant, he nevertheless neglected to analyse marketing and the culture industries as psychopower. Now, the psychopower controlling the flux and flow of the time of consciousness leads to a reticulated neuropower that is still just getting underway – and this *year we* will try to introduce general considerations in order to identify the main and genuine questions at stake beyond that storytelling and strategic marketing that is called transhumanism. Before doing so, however, let us first remind ourselves of the theory of retentions and protentions, and how they are affected by the culture industries.

Right now, you are listening to me, and, as I speak to you, I am trying to make you pay attention to what I say. But to understand this, we must give and pay attention to what Husserl said in taking up Saint Augustine's analysis, which led him to distinguish, in the passage of time, two types of retentions: primary retentions and secondary retention. Retention in general is what is retained. And what is retained contains chains or concatenations of possible potentials, that is, *expectations* (in French, *attentes*, the same root as attention) contained in what is retained, which Husserl called protentions. The play of retentions and protentions, where the latter are the expectations contained within the former, constitutes attention. In this play of attention, we must distinguish between *primary* retentions and *secondary* retentions. Primary retentions are retained *in* the present and *by* the present, which presents itself only through those retentions through which it is maintained, and which thereby constitute a *now* (in French, *maintenant*). So, *you retain what I have just said in what now presents itself to you as what I am in the course of saying* – for otherwise, you could not com-prehend, or main-tain through this com-prehension, what I am saying.

This primary retention, Husserl says, is not something that belongs to the past: it constitutes *the present insofar as it passes presently and now*, insofar as it is *passing*. As for the *past*, it consists of secondary retentions, that is, retentions that once *were* primary, but which have since gone past, and therefore become secondary. If we now ask ourselves what each of us here in this room, on the basis of my discourse, understands, retains and maintains as the meaning of what I have said, we will undoubtedly discover that *not one of us* has heard or understood or maintained the *same* thing as anyone else, in what presented itself to each of you through my discourse.

This is so because each primary retention retained during listening is a primary *selection*. The latter operates according to the secondary retentions specific to each of the listeners. Secondary retentions in this way function as the *criteria* of selection, and thus of retention, and what this really means is that everyone hears what I am saying with a different ear. If, however, my discourse is sensible, or even necessary, and so, in one way or another, *true*, it will probably provoke, in the audience that you constitute through your attention, *a common and shared expectation* – a common protention, to speak with Husserl.

If this is what happens, *I will in some way have cultivated within you something necessary*, something that we call the *social*. This culture and this sculpture, however, are possible only in the artificial but hidden conditions that must be reconstituted and brought to the clarity of the circumspect gaze: these conditions are, besides the fact that we are listening in a language that is not necessarily our own, those of more or less sharing a fund or background of collective retentions and protentions, which has been bequeathed to us through what I call tertiary retentions, that is, through being inscribed in the exosomatic and spatialized fabric that constitutes our space, our time and our common memories.

Those tertiary retentions are things and objects in general. Now, some of them are what I call *hypomnesic* tertiary retentions. This means: things made to record and keep memory, mnemotechnical things, like characters or letters, but also audio recordings or visual recordings, and now computers and smartphones. The play of primary and secondary retentions and protentions can be changed by such hypomnesic tertiary retentions. This is already the issue at stake in Plato's *Phaedrus*, where Socrates says that writing is a *pharmakon*. I will not develop this further right now: I did so last year. I will just remind you that this *pharmakon* is what makes geometry possible, for example, or history, or philosophy, or grammar, but also sophistry, and hence the manipulation of retentions, protentions and the attention of souls submitted to these artefacts.

For centuries, tertiary retentions in general and hypomnesic tertiary retentions in particular have been objects of worship and *culture*, of social *sculpture* in this sense, for organizations and instruments of power and knowledge attempting to constitute in this way a common will, that is, a society, a social milieu composed of retentions and protentions that are more or less shared, through which what we call culture takes care of what, as the process of exosomatization, requires the contingencies and accidents produced by this process to be turned into necessity and truth.

For the fact is that our psychic, intimate and singular retentions and protentions are founded on and supported by *collective, shared retentions and protentions*, beginning with the words we speak and listen to, and which were coined before us. All knowledge and all works are such crafts, worships, sculptures and cultures of collective retentions and protentions bequeathed by a common past, more or less anonymous and ancestral, projecting a common future that is always indeterminate, inaccessible and improbable, but which insists and remains open through works.

Now, with the culture industries, a vast reticulated capture of attention gets underway, producing increasingly standardized retentions and protentions, which are placed under the control of marketing. And this profoundly modifies the process of transindividuation that is constituted by the sharing of collective retentions and protentions. This affects and, in a way, dis-affects (*dés-affecter* in French means *to close down*) the symbolic milieu in general and language in particular.

A symbolic milieu is based on the reciprocity of symbolic exchanges, such as, for example, in a dialogue. Even when reading a book, we read on the basis of our capacity to write, and, for example, to write from our own reading, that is, to interpret what we have read. With the culture industries, inasmuch as they are based on a separation between producers of symbols and consumers of symbols, this exchange is broken. Now, what is broken is the symbolic as such – if it is true that only what is shared is properly speaking sym-bolic, this symbolization being, moreover, a metabolization of collective individuation.

▪ ▪ ▪

For nearly one hundred years, with the introduction in America of civilian radio, cinema and then television, the advertising industry has had a significant impact on the collective individuation process that is language. This collective individuation process is materialized through processes of transindividuation. What Simondon called the transindividual, which is conditioned by the existence of objects and things bearing this transindividual, is another name for meaning, and it is what results from the co-individuation of psychic individuals who thus form collective individuals, social groups through which social systems metastabilize themselves, the same social system being common to numerous groups – hence the fact that a language may be spoken differently by different groups.

Metastabilization is a process of stabilization at the limit of instability, that is, the formation of a structure that is in movement but which maintains its form as it deforms – like a vortex or a tornado. This is the case, for instance, with language. Transindividuation is what results from processes of co-individuation, that is, co-ordinated processes of psychic individuation, such as the dialogues of Plato, these dialogical relations causing language to evolve – by giving, for example, a new definition to a word, therefore enabling it to be used in new ways. This new feature – which is at first local, as for instance when two speakers agree on something, for instance Socrates and Meno – can then be disseminated through time and to other speakers along various vectors, such as through books, Plato's academy, the trial of Socrates, and so on. This dissemination constitutes the process of transindividuation.

Now, it is possible to influence the transindividuation process in a rational and systematic way via vectors of this kind, which are always constituted on the basis of tertiary retentions. Through the culture industries, advertising and publicity today draw on every poetic, rhetorical, prosodic and pragmatic effect through which transindividuation processes are reinforced, that is, through which meanings are shared, and they do so by exploiting linguistic and semiological forms of knowledge. Thus in order to illustrate what in 1960 he referred to as the poetic function of language, Roman Jakobson took as his example the political slogan 'I like Ike', used in Eisenhower's 1956 presidential campaign.[182]

It seems to me that linguistics has yet to take full account of what is at stake in the *new relation to words* inaugurated by advertising. What advertising is doing to language is what Saussure had earlier suggested *could not up till then be done* because in his view language is too complex:

> A language constitutes a system. [...] The system is a complex mechanism that can be grasped only through reflection; the very ones who use it daily are ignorant of it. We can conceive of a change only through the intervention of specialists, grammarians, logicians, etc.; but experience shows us that all such meddlings have failed.[183]

Advertising is clearly incapable of *systematically* intervening in the *totality* of the system. It does, however, make it possible to introduce diachronic tendencies and to control their development, and this eventually results in changes at the synchronic level, that is, at the level of the system itself.

As such, advertising amounts to a psychotechnology of control of the linguistic transindividuation process, and more generally of the symbolic transindividuation process – and the process of transindividuation is one of the concepts absent from Saussure's structural linguistics:

this absence will block its development, to the great detriment of generative grammar.

Psychotechnologies change the development of language to the extent that language is

> a treasure deposited through the practice of speaking in subjects who belong to the same community, a grammatical system that exists virtually in each brain, or more exactly in the brains of a collection of individuals; for language does not exist in complete form in anyone, but exists perfectly only in the whole group.[184]

This means that language changes to the extent that the brains of speakers themselves change. The advertising and communications psychotechnologies founded on analogue tertiary retention, such as radio and television, are technologies that imprint 'messages' in brains, brains that must be made 'available'. As such, these psychotechnologies constitute technologies of transindividuation.

The critique of psychotechnologies – that is, the analysis of their effects and of their pharmacological potential, which is to say, of their toxic effects as well as their curative effects – should lead to a new critique of linguistics and of the sciences of the symbol in general, a critique itself based on an organology, that is, on a rational study of the organs of transindividuation.

Transindividuation is in fact made possible by tertiary retention, by those tertiary retentions constituted by artificial organs (technics and mnemotechnics) that, developing in the course of the individuation of the technical system, are the link between psychic individuals and collective individuals – that is, social systems. Social systems are those bodies of rules governing ways of life that are inevitable wherever one finds those artefacts and technics that are *pharmaka* (in Plato's sense of this word): a *pharmakon* is a remedy that always contains a poisonous element, and a poison that always holds a therapeutic virtue.

Social systems are organizations that implement bodies of rules defining therapeutic prescriptions with regard to these *pharmaka*. The totality of these social systems constitutes society, as the collective and integrated individuation of these social systems themselves, and, through them, of the *pharmaka* implemented by this society. Today, societies are subject to a veritable flood of new pharmacological apparatus that produces countless toxic processes – but also genuine therapeutic inventions.

Pharmacology (in the sense I use this term) is the study of the effects (both positive and negative, that is, individuating and disindividuating) resulting from the threefold individuation of: psychosomatic organs;

technical, technological and mnemotechnological organs; and social organizations – and where the totality constitutes *a transductive relation with three terms*. General organology is the study of the innumerable dimensions of this threefold transductive relation.

In other words, the *toxicity* of this or that technology, and in particular the toxicity of those psychotechnologies implemented by psychopower, is not inherent in the technology on its own, but derives from those social arrangements (or, in this case, anti-social arrangements) brought about by power operating *through* these technologies (for example, as psychopower). And it is for this very reason that any organology must also be a pharmacology: its task is not merely to describe the toxicity of this organology, but to prescribe other social arrangements that constitute therapies or therapeutics, that is, systems of care, of attentional forms, and of *knowledge*.

This task becomes all the more urgent once the psychotechnologies of the analogue communications industries, and the economic models of attention (or rather, of the destruction of attention) organized by marketing and founded on advertising, begin to combine linguistic engineering with the automated treatment of natural languages – and it is this combination that lies at the basis of the worldwide success of Google.

Frédéric Kaplan has shown that this combination leads to the development of a form of linguistic capitalism through which industrial society passes from an economy of attention to an economy of *expression*. Google is its worldwide model, and it operates by articulating two kinds of algorithms:

- one, which makes it possible to find pages corresponding to certain words, made it popular;
- the other, which provides these words with a market value, has made it wealthy.[185]

The first algorithm, PageRank, 'scans' the state of the transindividuation process as reflected in the relations between the sites of that symbolic milieu that is the Web: it is literally equivalent to a vast filing cabinet filled with Web pages that calculates, for someone who is navigating it, the level of penetration of such and such a phrase within the framework that constitutes the digital symbolic milieu.

The calculation involved here is that of a Markov chain, a probabilistic process. As a result of this calculation access is granted to pages in order of their ranking, thereby reinforcing these differences of rank: the performativity of search engines thereby tends to lead to the logic of the *audimat* (that is, of what, in the world of television advertising, is called the system of 'ratings'). It is, however, not *quite* the same logic: most web pages are not designed specifically in order to receive a top ranking – even if it is true that some pages *are* designed to increase their ranking, and even if it *is possible* to take advantage of the system by diverting it to this end. But that is why Google is constantly updating the algorithm in order to try and minimize such possibilities, because this kind of manipulation diminishes the use value to be gained from scanning search terms and increases the exchange value that accrues to advertisers as a result of such diversion.

The second algorithm is targeted at advertisers, and it works by auctioning words to those wanting to link to them – these are the famous 'sponsored links' (or AdWords, the operation of which is performed by a *linguistic robot*, Mediapartners or Mediabot, in the service of Google's advertising arm, AdSense):

> In order to choose which advertisements to display for a given request, the algorithm offers a three-stage bidding system:
>
> 1 Bid on a keyword. A company chooses an expression or a word, such as 'vacations', and defines the maximum price that it would be willing to pay if a web user came to them through it. To help buyers of words, Google supplies an estimate of the amount to bid in order to have a good chance of appearing on the first page of results. [...]
>
> 2 Calculation of the quality score for the advertisement. Google assigns a score, on a scale of one to ten, to each advertisement as a function of its text's relevance to the user's request, the quality of the page put forward (the interest of its content and download speed) and the average number of clicks on the ad. [...]
>
> 3 Calculation of the rank. The order in which the advertisements appear is determined by a relatively simple formula: the rank is the bid multiplied by the score. [...]
>
> This bidding procedure is recalculated with every search by every user – millions of times per second![186]

These sponsored connections between words are processes of the *industrial* creation of *circuits* of transindividuation, processes that are grafted onto the transindividuation processes produced on the web by navigation, and which are scanned and reinforced by the first algorithm – the entire thing constituting circuits of *automatic* transindividuation, that is, a planetary system that *automates transindividuation processes.*

Kaplan shows that this results in a 'stock exchange of words'. This 'gives a relatively accurate indication of important global semantic shifts'. In other words, it gives an indication – but from a very specific perspective, an obviously performative one, that is, one that trans-forms what it expresses through the very fact of expressing it – of what we are here calling linguistic transindividuation processes, whereby 'everything that can be named is an opportunity for a bid'. In other words:

> Google has succeeded in expanding the domain of capitalism to language itself, making words into a commodity and basing an incredibly profitable commercial model on linguistic speculation.[187]

Nevertheless, this system would be unable to function for long if the linguistic and orthographic competence of Web users completely collapsed. Certainly, we have all seen that Google itself automatically corrects typographical and spelling errors. But this automatic correction could contribute to such a decline in the attention paid to spelling that it could eventually threaten the viability of the calculations that can only be done on the basis of discrete and unambiguous units:

> What do the actors of linguistic capitalism fear? Language that eludes them, that breaks, is 'misspelled', that becomes impossible to put into equations. When the search engine corrects on the fly a word that you have spelled incorrectly, it does not do so only to help you: most often, it transforms something without any significant value (a misspelled word) into a directly profitable economic resource.[188]

According to Kaplan, with the advent of Google, capitalism passes from being an economy of attention to an economy of expression:

> The discovery of what has been up to now an unknown territory for capitalism opens a new field for economic competition. Google certainly benefits from a significant lead, but rivals, having understood the rules of this new competition, will emerge in the end. The rules are ultimately quite simple: we are leaving behind an economy of attention in order to enter an economy of expression. The stake is no longer so much to capture attention as to mediatize speaking and writing. The winners will be those who can develop close and lasting linguistic relationships with a large number of users in order to model and modify language, create a controlled linguistic market and organize speculation on words.

> The use of language will henceforth be an object of desire. Undoubtedly, it will only take a short time before language itself is transformed.

The economy of *expression* that is established with digital tertiary retention (which constitutes the digital stage of writing), however, does not require an economy of attention, which, precisely, it surpasses, but an *ecology* of this attention, for example of that attention to written language that is orthographic knowledge – that is, a training and formation of attention (and of the expressive capabilities it makes possible) based on a therapeutic practice of orthographic correction that protects the individual knowledge of orthography, failing which automatic spell-checkers will no longer work. This constitutes the question of the *contemporary organology of elementary knowledge* from the perspective of the relation between automatism and autonomy.

Spell-checkers were among the first systems experienced by the public through social practices of electronic language, introducing them into a new international symbolic milieu constituted by automated idioms. This milieu is then massively traversed by automated translation processes, or translations assisted by automated systems. More recently, rapid communication systems such as SMS and Twitter have appeared, which, with their 'social networking' aspect, are also amplifiers of transindividuation. These transformations of the conditions of transindividuation change writing and thereby also change speech and thought. The way we write overdetermines the way we speak and think, as Walter Ong explains in relation to the emergence of the alphabet in Antiquity:

> Without writing, the literate mind would not and could not think as it does, not only when engaged in writing but normally even when it is composing its thoughts in oral form. More than any other single invention, writing has transformed human consciousness.[189]

Digital writing nevertheless takes new forms that increasingly pass, at the speed of light, through automatic 'machine to machine' writing, deforming and transforming consciousness, that is, that general set of attentional forms that adds up to a human mind. This deformation brings new forms of consciousness and of the unconscious, that is, of desire and therefore of attention. We posit this not only as a principle but as an obligation and a duty – given that the current system has ruined attention, and therefore amounts to a planetary time bomb that must be defused as soon as possible: the current economic crisis, too, is a crisis of attention. If this shift is not negotiated and supported by a political project – for it is the role of politics or the political to produce projects through which the economy can develop without destroying society, and the economy along with it – it will lead to the worst: it will result in a catastrophe. For the interests of Google do not coincide with those of society any more than do those of any other sector of the language industries, or for that matter of any 'pharmacy' whatsoever: without therapists to prescribe and set the rules, pharmacists inevitably turn into 'dealers', that is, poisoners – because the shareholders who are their 'prescribers' (that is, who influence them) *ignore in principle* the use value produced by these pharmacists, seeing nothing except exchange value.

Here a singular question arises, however, which in a way constitutes the elevation of transindividuation at both a political and economic level in the epoch of digital tertiary retention: to what extent does the symbolic and transindividual milieu created by these technologies that alter (that is, make other) linguistic practices and knowledge deposited not only 'through the practice of speaking in subjects who belong to the same community', but also through the practice of digital reading and writing, that is, of the organology produced by the economy of expression of symbolic subjects connected by the same network; *to what extent does this milieu, these technologies, these new practices and the forms of knowledge that they create, to what extent does all this enable us to conceive contributory transindividuation technologies* that manage to produce a *reticular reflexivity* and that constitute *new therapeutic sources of knowledge and understanding* – that is, sources and resources for these new forms of attention about which we have been speaking? Such are the stakes of this lecture series, stakes that extend well beyond the field of linguistics.

A strictly Saussurian perspective is incapable of addressing these questions because, for methodological reasons that were very understandable (and Saussure founded the structuralist perspective firstly through the methodological rigour of his linguistics) but also very unfortunate, the *Course in General Linguistics*, as Derrida showed in his analysis of its metaphysical twists and turns, posits as an initial principle that 'language is independent of writing'.[190]

Such a view is, however, *completely illusory*. That the image of spoken language given by writing is deformed, if not false, is obvious. And that this de-formation of the image of language is a de-formation of attention and of the attentional form in which this language consists: this is what we are claiming here. But the notion that language and its development (and language is *only* its development, its becoming: it is *irreducibly* diachronic, as Saussure himself taught so well) are *independent* of writing is completely false. Furthermore, the very possibility of linguistics, of a science of language, is *conditioned* by the existence of writing insofar as it is a 'technology of the intellect' in Jack Goody's sense,[191] and by the play of tertiary retentions constituting grammatization in Sylvain Auroux's sense (who extensively documented these questions in the history of the sciences of language).[192]

This constitutes, precisely, a question of general organology and of negative and positive pharmacology. Language is what writing (and not only writing) grammatizes. This grammatization is, above all, a de-formation. But from this deformation – which is a kind of *perpetual teratogenesis*, a constant production of 'monsters' – new linguistic formations emerge, of which the most prominent and individuating are those emerging from *literature*. This relationship between language and writing is a specific case of the relationships between social systems (here, language) and technical systems (here, the mnemotechnics that is writing). The arrangement between the two takes place through speakers through whom are negotiated the turns deforming and forming the future of language and, more generally, every symbolic milieu and social system, woven as their motives.

To think the future of language, the symbolic and attentional forms, today, that is, the future properly speaking, and in particular inasmuch as it can strictly speaking be brought about only by youth, is to return to this *a priori* illusion of Saussurian linguistics. But it is to do so in order to re-launch its fundamental achievements on a new basis, and to escape the impasse that is the domination of generative grammar and Chomskyan naturalism spread through cognitivism – at the very moment when the digital stage of writing poses all these questions anew, as shown so clearly by Kaplan.

▪ ▪ ▪

In France, the relation to language has seriously deteriorated. I presume that this is equally true in China. This is a fact in relation to which four attitudes are possible:

- one can deny it;
- one can denounce it;
- one can exploit it, either industrially or politically;
- one can (and if one can, one must) decide to fight it positively, by analysing the pharmacological positivity of new tertiary retentions and, to this end, by organizing and reinforcing new social arrangements.

Digital technologies now effect calculations on transindividuation operating in light-time. In so doing, what is being played out, with industrial reading and the economy of expression as implemented by Google, changes the conditions of linguistic becoming at a planetary level.

Linguistic transindividuation is in general and in itself a process of transformations that operate through correlations established between transindividual units, which, in the case of language, are words and phrases. The transindividuality of each 'item', that is, its shared meaning, is the result of this dynamic process that more or less metastabilizes the relations of each unit with all the others (whether near or far, Simondon describing the process of collective individuation as the spreading out of an 'internal resonance'). This metastabilization constitutes what Wittgenstein referred to as 'use'.

The simplified, abstract description and unified ideal of a metastable state of global uses of a language constitutes what Saussure called its 'synchrony'. This synchrony is only an ideality: it does not exist. But the tendency towards synchronization, on the contrary, does indeed exist. And the power of linguistics is established by imposing criteria on this tendency towards synchronization, that is, on the establishment of that metastability which is the condition of formation of the transindividual – which is itself a metastable state.

We saw by reading Kaplan that with the technologies of light-time, *pre-locutionary* correlations (performed on such and such a speech act of such and such a speaker, whether as reading or as expression) operate *automatically*, both by adding up the links made between units by preceding internet users, and by promoting units on the linguistic market – on that market which symbolic exchange on the Web has become under the financial auspices of the Google business model. This automation is thus a dual algorithmic organization of metastability, combining and imposing new criteria on the tendency towards synchronization for a metastable linguistic situation: on the one hand, ranking the links forged on the Web, which produces an extremely refined ratings system; and on the other hand, evaluating links on the linguistic market where, sold at auction, they are transformed into exchange value.

Automated pre-locutionary correlations clearly lead to new kinds of diachronic phenomena, since they have an impact on every speech act – which is thus itself an individuation of the speaker, and, through this, an individuation of language, that is, a micro-event within its diachronic evolution. And it may become a macro-event if this discourse is taken up in one way or another, by some sphere of language or another, for example, poetry, politics, science or advertising, with the result that this psycho-linguistic individuation causes a series of co-individuations that are ultimately consolidated into a new stage of transindividuation.

Google's two-sided economy at the same time cultivates 'use value' through the automated operation of 'page ranking' and 'exchange value' through an automated system that creates a linguistic market. The power of this two-sided economy lies in the arrangement that operates automatically and stochastically between the diachronic and synchronic tendencies, guiding and facilitating expression and intra-linguistic reading, and establishing inter-linguistic transindividual correlations through automatic translation.

With the linguistic technologies of light-time, the conditions of linguistic transindividuation processes have substantially changed for about two billion speakers, those who are the most affluent and therefore the most active on Earth: most of the linguistic transindividual units practised by these speakers now travel in one way or another through circuits of transindividuation that are inscribed in the data centres of cloud computing, in the form of digital tertiary retentions that can be analysed, qualified, quantified, correlated, treated, evaluated, modified, indexed, annotated, channelled and sold. Automated correlations thus create massive transindividual relations that directly affect the transindividual as such, that is, meaning, and this new transindividuation process is imposed on the hundreds of languages that constitute our *global semantic heritage* at a moment when, in addition to and parallel to neuroscience, we are witnessing the development of neuroeconomics and neuromarketing.

Tomorrow, we will begin to examine the discourse of Nicholas Carr on the digital and memory, and we shall begin to work out an outline of neuropower that synthesizes what Foucault called 'biopower' and what I am trying to conceive as 'psychopower'.

SECOND LECTURE

From Psychopower to Neuropower

We saw yesterday with Frederic Kaplan that digital technologies make it possible to intervene into transindividuation through linguistic capitalism – but also, more generally, through the 'buzz' that has accompanied 'marketing 2.0'. Twenty-five years after the Web first appeared, a new process of transindividuation, assisted by networked computers that circulate information at near light speed and passing through exospheric infrastructures, continues to impose itself upon the hundreds of languages that constitute the semantic universe of humanity. Meanwhile, neuromarketing, by drawing on the neurosciences and by concretizing the ideology of neuroeconomics, tries to systematically and directly intervene on the *neuronal* layers of transindividuation – that is, *on the psychic internalization and externalization of transindividual units*, and, through that, on their *psychic individuation*.

In the years to come, we will see digital technologies and neuromarketing combine more tightly together. Neuromarketing is an extension of marketing 2.0 using neurosciences and cerebral imaging. This combination will increasingly overdetermine all other human realities. It will therefore constitute a neuropower that, through the intermediary of digital retentional technology, will conjoin biopower and psychopower at the core of the cerebral organ itself. To study this becoming, its toxic threats, its curative possibilities and the therapies and therapeutics that can and must be implemented, we must adopt an organological approach to the brain. And in order to do so, we must *distinguish what it is about the brain that relates to the organic, and what it is that relates to the organological*. I will explain what I mean by this as we advance through this lecture series.

Contemporary neuroscience has shown that *education* is literally a *culture of the brain* – in the sense that one cultivates a *garden*, where in this case the seeds, plants, fertilizers and tools would be the collective retentions through which knowledge is constituted, and the tertiary retentions that form the *organology* of this knowledge, that is, 'technologies of the intellect', in Jack Goody's sense.

Let's go back to what is meant by primary, secondary and tertiary retention. At this moment, you are listening to me speak. My discourse, which began at 2:00 p.m. and which will finish at 4:00 p.m., is what Edmund Husserl called a temporal object: my speech flows; it is evanescent; it is constituted by its temporality. And this is even more true for a melody, which for Husserl was the temporal object par excellence. You listen to me. But as for what I say, each and every one of you will hear something different: if, for example, I asked you ten minutes from now to write down what I said at the beginning of this lecture, *none* of the texts you produce would be identical to the others – and this goes to show that *you have understood something different and unique in what I told you.*

The consequence of what I am saying to you is that it is *you* who say what I am saying – not me. Each and every one of us – since this is true for me too – *interprets* what I say in terms of our past experience and expectations, which are concealed, and which enable us to understand and to attend to what is said: to attend (*attendre* in French) is to be attentive. To understand this, we referred yesterday to the Husserlian concepts of retention and protention. We saw that retention means that which is retained. We refer to *primary* retention if, having been present, and being retained into the present, it is essential to the constitution of an element of present *perception* without being itself present. Husserl's example is the musical note of a melody that, no longer being actually present, nevertheless forms with what is currently present an interval – the interval between two sounds that establishes that these sounds are musical notes, and not just sonic frequencies.

In the same way, the sentence I have just uttered cannot make sense without retaining the preceding sentence, just as the verb of this sentence cannot make sense without the subject of the sentence, or the object of the verb without the verb, and so on: these *units of meaning* are formed through aggregations of primary retentions. And these aggregations all aggregate with one another. This aggregation of aggregations forms the unity of a temporal object in Husserl's sense – for example, the unity of the discourse that I am addressing to you at this very moment, or the unity of a sonata.

Such a unity is produced as what Immanuel Kant, after Aristotle, will call a synthesis. Now, the process of grammatization, made possible by hypomnesic tertiary retentions because they make possible the spatialization of time, also make the analysis of such a synthesis possible. What we then see is that the primary aggregations in the case of speech are not musical intervals, but grammatical rules, such as, for example, the aggregation of the adjective to the noun, and of the noun to the verb, and so on.

We saw that Husserl distinguishes primary retention from secondary retention, and that secondary retentions are former primary retentions that now belong to the past, and that constitute the fabric of my *memory*. Now, through these secondary retentions, which are also associative filters – in Hume's sense of association, but also in Kant's sense, for whom associative processes are involved in the three syntheses of the transcendental imagination – a process of *primary aggregation* occurs, and this is why every occasion of this process is specific: it is why we do not retain everything and why we do not understand the same thing, for example, in what I am saying at this moment. The process of aggregating primary retentions is thus in fact a *primary selection of retentions* carried out on the basis of secondary retentions that form the fabric of my past experience.

Everyone hears something different in what I say because we are all aggregating primary retentions in different ways: this aggregation is a selection. This is not Husserl's point of view in *On the Phenomenology of the Consciousness of Internal Time*.[193] It is, however, a point of view that he comes to adopt later, in *Phantasy, Image Consciousness, and Memory*.[194] This selection is carried out on the basis of our secondary retentions, which themselves contain secondary *protentions* (expectations, and this is what David Hume, too, described with his concept of associative relations[195]). Secondary retentions are thus in a certain way charged with expectations, with protentions, which are energetic processes of attention in something like the way that neurons are charged with energy in Sigmund Freud's *Project for a Scientific Psychology*[196] – these secondary retentions, *charged thus in this way*, constitute the mnesic selection criteria for perception. And this relation between perception and memory is to some extent also what Henri Bergson tried to describe in *Matter and Memory*.[197]

So, then, the play of secondary retentions forming my memory, my accumulated past experience, in this way constitutes the filters forged by this experience through which primary retentions are then selected and collected in the present experience of perception. But to this we must add that this play between secondary retention and primary retention is then *conditioned* and *constituted* by tertiary retentions, that is, *organological mnesic processes*. These processes are artificial, mnemotechnical and sometimes 'hypomnesic' in Plato's sense, supporting what Plato called anamnesic memory, first in *Meno*, then in *Phaedrus*.

Tertiary retention conditions primary and secondary retention in two ways:

- on the one hand, it is the condition of conservation of past *collective* experience – through *things*, which are always also *traces of forms of life* on the basis of which we learn to live: in entering the world, we inherit things that constitute it, and which conserve the already-there, where the experience of preceding generations is accumulated – and through these things, words are formed, which are artefacts as well as tools, works of art, customary rules and so on;

- on the other hand, tertiary retention enables past experience to be objectively stabilized (forming what Hegel called *objective spirit*) so that it can then be *repeated* – this *repetition* can produce a *difference*, that is, a variation at the core of a temporal object having been spatialized as this tertiary retention. What I say to you orally is temporal, but you may write it down and turn it into a written thing, which we call a text, that is, a *spatial object*. Having been spatialized and textualized, this speech can be repeated, and deepened, and transformed through this repetition – and through this, *you* may be trans-formed.

Now, we could annotate a text, as I did with Husserl's *Phenomenology of the Consciousness of Internal Time*, and we could analyse the types of annotations used, and then transform them into digital functions – but we don't have time to discuss this in detail now. Such a transformation, produced by the repetition of a written speech that we can read and reread, alters the play of primary and secondary retentions, the former being what you select and accumulate in perception, and the latter being that through which you operate this selection. Consider again the example of this lecture. You write down what I say. Suppose that tonight or tomorrow you decide to reread what you have written of what I said. When you read what you have written (which is no longer a temporal object strictly speaking, since it has become a spatial, textual object, an object that you re-temporalize by rereading), you select new primary retentions, ones that you did not previously select: the repetition of the same therefore gives a difference – and this gift is the différance of Derrida. The same does not come back to the same: it gives the other – in this other, it is you who are altered.

And this begins with what Hegel, in the first chapter of the *Phenomenology of Spirit*, calls sense-certainty. Let's ask what is 'now', Hegel says. And let's write it down. Now, it is night time. So we write: now is the night. 'We write down this truth', he says. And he adds: 'a truth cannot be lost by being written down'. And then we reread what we wrote, but now it is midday…

This alteration of the same, which can become much more complex than the one involved in sense-certainty – for example, the reading, interpretation and repetition of the *Phenomenology of Spirit* itself is a modality of what Jacques Derrida called différance. Such a différance is produced, notably, because:

1 in the time between when I gave my speech and your rereading of that textualized speech, you have yourself changed;

2 you can repeat what is past through tertiary retention insofar as it is the *spatial* concretion of what was initially *temporal*.

It might be objected that when you wrote down my speech, not every single thing was taken down: all you can write down is, precisely, whatever it was that constituted your primary retentions and, looking a little closer, you are only able to write down a fraction of these retentions. This is the case, not just because you don't have time to get everything down: even if you did have the time, you would undoubtedly be unable to textualize everything that ultimately constitutes your listening. The latter *is*, in fact, in its becoming. And it is this becoming that constitutes what Derrida called différance.

Suppose that you were able to take down what I say in shorthand – as was done, incidentally, with Husserl's lectures – or again, suppose that you were able to record this lecture on tape or with a voice-recorder, with your smartphone, perhaps, and, via this recording, were able to listen again to the whole of the lecture. Such a recording would also be a spatial object – in another modality than for a textual object. Alphabetical text, shorthand and recording are types of tertiary retention. And each of these types generates a process of reading and a specific kind of différance, resulting in specific arrangements of primary and secondary retentions.

▪ ▪ ▪

Let us now return to the question of neuropower.

Education amounts to a culture of the brain in the same sense that one cultivates a piece of land. The brain is cultivated through the mediation of tertiary retention insofar as it enables:

- primary retentions to be selected;
- psychic secondary retentions to be maintained and developed from these primary retentions;
- *collective* secondary retentions to be maintained and developed – such as the words and groups of words that, as phrases and agreed-upon formulations, constitute language: all of these linguistic units, whether simple or complex, were, once upon a time, first produced by an individual.

Hence are constituted processes of transindividuation, on the basis of which *every kind of knowledge* is formed, connecting together the generations. If ethnographic collections from diverse cultures are preserved in museums, this is because they are evidence of forms of knowledge connecting the contemporary world to the ancient world, and, through this, to the archaic foundations of contemporary knowledge.

Now, these forms of knowledge, which derive from transindividuation processes the genesis of which I have briefly described, form ensembles of collective secondary retentions, which themselves constitute attentional forms – that is, collective formations of attention. The collective formation or training of attention, which means, for example, that in Asia one is not attentive to the world or to others in the same way as in Europe, and that the attention found in Great Britain differs from that of France, these differences forming what is referred to as culture – all this is formed on the basis of collective secondary retentions.

For example, the group of words 'collective secondary retention' was created by me – and you might circulate this phrase, that is, transindividuate it, within Nanjing University or beyond, and by so doing, you in fact create a collective secondary retention, that is, one that is shared by a group that is itself in movement because it is a process of collective individuation. By forming this expression, 'collective secondary retention', I have myself taken up the expression 'secondary retention' formed by Husserl. And in doing so, I have extended and individuated the legacy of what is called phenomenology.

Retentions generate protentions, that is, expectations. Collective secondary retentions produce collective secondary protentions. Primary retentions themselves generate primary protentions. Retentions and protentions bind together in attention, and the collective arrangements of retentions and protentions constitute the attentional forms that form knowledge of all kinds, but these may be placed into three categories: knowledge of how to do (*savoir faire*), knowledge of how to live (*savoir vivre*), and knowledge of how to think (*savoir penser*).

When the neurosciences make it possible to directly intervene in psychic and collective retentional and protentional processes *at the neurochemical level*, they enable the creation of *industrial* attentional processes, that is, they make it possible to control attention via the organology of industrial tertiary retention. And it is for this reason that, to the extent that *political* society is constituted by an attentional form elaborated according to the canon of reason, *the regulation of the neuropower of marketing* now constitutes a *primary mission for education*.

In the age of neuromarketing and neuroeconomics, which are clearly heading towards a *monoculture* of brains that are capable of being neurologically modified through neuronal psychotechnologies that, as we shall see, articulate *biopsychic automatisms (or compulsions) with technological automatisms* – in this age, a true politics must place neuroscientific research at the service of a *noopolitics*: at the service of what, with Ars Industrialis, I call *an industrial politics of the fructification of spirit value (valeur esprit).*

My thesis is that, contrary to such a politics, neuroeconomics is leading to the systematic organization of what the French poet and thinker Paul Valéry described as a *decline* in the value of *esprit.*[198] Neuroeconomics is a branch of the neurosciences that studies decision-making behaviour on the basis of the work of Paul Glimcher. Glimcher is himself continuing the enterprise of American neoliberalism promoted by Theodor Schultz, in whose work there appears, in the wake of work undertaken by Lionel Robbins in the 1930s, the analysis of 'human capital' that constitutes the economic subject such as it is conceived by Schultz and Gary Becker,[199] with all its variants (consumers and producers, designers, investors, and entrepreneurs) but in particular as an 'entrepreneur of himself'.[200] All of this concerning Robbins, Schultz and Becker was shown by Foucault.[201]

On this basis, Glimcher defends a monist point of view, which aims to overcome the Cartesian opposition between *reflexive* behaviour and *reflective* behaviour. In Glimcher's view, *reflective behaviours* are complex and highly elaborated forms of *biological behavioural bases* with which they do not break, and of which *reflexive behaviours, as reflex, that is, as reactions,* are elementary forms: *like* reflexive behaviours, reflective behaviours would be the result of probabilistic processes, of which there are varying levels of complexity – whereas for Descartes the *determinacy* of reflexive behaviour could be opposed to the *indeterminacy* of reflective behaviour, that is, voluntary and free behaviour.[202]

Here, as with Google's automated transindividuation technologies, which operate across the planet in light-time via the exospheric infrastructure, probabilities are at the heart of the cognitive models involved – and just like neuromarketing, which is currently being developed on the basis of the neurosciences and Glimcher's neuroeconomics, the founders of Google are professionals when it comes to influencing decision-making (as was Edward Bernays): this is what Nicholas Carr shows, but from a different angle than Frédéric Kaplan.

During these lectures, we will not study in detail what we can expect from neuroeconomics, or the practices of neuromarketing, or the bases formed by contemporary neuroscience: for this, we don't have time. Instead, we will address what seems to be the central question raised by all these theories, but also for example by the Neuralink project, launched by Elon Musk, by analysing Nicholas Carr's arguments against digital tertiary retention and its toxic effects. Carr seems to find inconceivable that the digital *pharmakon* could ever become curative and placed into the service of therapies that could heal such toxic effects, which are produced not simply by the digital *pharmakon* but by the way in which it has been implemented via an economic and industrial model that has itself become massively toxic.

In his critique of Internet technologies in general, and of Google in particular, denouncing what he describes as a sapping of human intelligence and memory by an artificial and digital intelligence and memory the toxicity of which derives from its speed, Nicholas Carr constantly refers to the results of neuroscientific research in order to oppose Google's position. In so doing, he seems unaware that the practices of Google raise new questions for the sciences and philosophy, questions that complicate the dominant cognitive model and that could cause it to mutate, including and perhaps especially in the neurosciences.

Carr first shows in the paper that when using the Internet or Google, we use a silicon memory that we are told is a perfect memory. But Carr claims that this perfection could in fact amount to a destruction of memory. This is interesting, of course, but I think that such an analysis is insufficient. Carr refers to Maryanne Wolf, who says that when we read online, we turn into mere decoders of information. And she shows that to learn how to read and write is to sculpt, cultivate and organologically transform the organic fabric of the brain. This is the reason for which your brains are not made like mine.

Now, Nicholas Carr – despite his numerous valuable references to the work of neurophysiology and neuropsychology that shows the extent to which the plasticity of the cerebral organ is permanently reconfigured as a result of the artefacts belonging to this or that form of technical life, which seems to me to be less a matter of *sculpting* the brain than of a kind of *gardening* – doesn't see the fundamental issue raised by the practices of neuromarketing, namely:

1. that the brain of the noetic soul, that is, the technical form of life (in Georges Canguilhem's sense), equipped with the capacity for reflective decision, is a dynamic system traversed by *contradictory and functional tendencies* that support different *sub-organs* and that rebound on the *contradictory and functional social tendencies* that constitute, in the social field, the *bipolar dynamics* of any transindividuation process;

2. that this cerebral organ of the noetic soul arranges these sub-organs with one another, through circuits of transindividuation that are *not only cerebral and social* but also *artificial*, that is, technical, because it is conditioned by the tertiary

> retentions that support it – Google being such an *arrangement*, one that is completely new, socializing a tertiary retention that is itself very new, traversing the cerebral organs of two billion Internet users at a speed close to that of light, and on a planetary scale, that is, throughout the entire ecosystem supporting the technical form of life and the cultures that have developed on the basis of a cerebral gardening that is currently *hardly ecological at all.*

An *ecology of neuronal gardening* should constitute the basis of a noopolitics: what Nicholas Carr describes is a genuine *disaster for the ecology of mind and spirit*, and many of the effects and facts that he writes about are real, and his analyses convincing. But his final conclusion, his general interpretation of these effects and these facts, is profoundly wrong. And it is also dangerous: he gives credence to the idea that it is impossible to struggle against the situation he is describing – he himself being in a state of shock – and, in concordance with the ideologues of the conservative revolution, he postulates that there is therefore 'no alternative'.

Carr's entire reasoning relies on close examination of his own experience and personal journey, in addition to his wide knowledge of scientific, technological and industrial literature. On this basis, he tries to demonstrate that *noetic* memory is *living* memory, and that there is *no way to exteriorize it* in the form of digital tertiary retention *without damaging it*. In a certain way, I am saying the same thing: noetic memory is pharmacological, and the *pharmakon always* involves some injury. But what I am *also* saying, contrary to Carr, is that this pharmacology is the *condition* of individuation, and it always requires the invention of therapies, that is, of *positive pharmacologies*: this is so because for technical and noetic life, primary and secondary retentions (and the protentions they form) are always arranged via tertiary retentions, and the latter are always *pharmaka* – which always create toxic processes, and which always require therapeutic prescriptions in order to struggle against their intrinsic toxicity.

Because he does not see that digital retention raises the question of positive pharmacology, Carr does not say *one word* about the *political* question this imposes: the invention of therapies and therapeutics – that is, of prescriptions materialized as *attentional forms*, and sometimes set into *law* – is precisely what we call 'politics'. And because he does not clearly pose the question in these terms – which would be those of a public power assuming its noopolitical responsibilities in the face of the emergence of neuropower, which is also a *generalized automation of behaviour, expression* and, as we shall see, *'decision'*, of which Google is one aspect – Carr finds himself entangled in a *contradiction*.

In order to explain what he means by 'deep attention', which appears, he says, with the practice of *deep reading*, that is, *with the alphabet*, Carr refers to the work of Maryanne Wolf, who shows that the *brain of deep attention* – for the protection of which Carr militates against Google and the Internet – is in fact a *literate brain*, a *literary cerebral organ*, or what Wolf calls a *reading brain*, and what Walter Ong calls a *literate mind*.[203] This literate noetic brain *literally accedes to* apodictic reasoning because by acceding to the letter *of* apodictic reasoning, it constitutes itself *by the neuronal internalization of the grammatization of language by the letter*, a process of literary gardening that totally transforms speech, as Carr writes, paraphrasing Ong and Wolf:

> The Greek alphabet became the model for most subsequent Western alphabets [...]. Its arrival marked the start of one of the most far-reaching revolutions in intellectual history [...]. It was a revolution that would eventually change the lives, and the brains, of nearly everyone on earth.[204]
>
> [T]he invention of a tool, the alphabet, [...] would have profound consequences for our language and our minds.[205]

Linguistic technology, therefore, literally changed the regimes of transindividuation. Today, through Google, the digital is *once again* transforming language and modifying regimes of transindividuation. What, however, *distinguishes* these two types of modification? One might expect that Carr would raise this question in his analysis. But nowhere does he do so.

During the epoch in which the alphabet appeared, the noetic brain individuated itself psychically and noetically by internalizing the stage of mnemotechnical individuation and grammatization constituted by alphabetical writing. And Maryanne Wolf, building on the work of Stanislas Dehaene, shows that this resulted in *cortical reorganization*, that is, in the establishment of synaptogenetic processes *literally* inscribing the letter *into* the cerebral organ.

The formation of such neuronal, internal circuits by the cerebral internalization of external and literal retentional circuits leads to the formation of circuits of transindividuation of a new type, which are those of knowledge of a new kind, as Carr highlights by quoting Walter Ong, for whom alphabetization

> 'is absolutely necessary for the development not only of science but also of history, philosophy, explicative understanding of literature and of any art, and indeed for the explanation

> of language (including oral speech) itself'. The ability to write is 'utterly invaluable and indeed essential for the realization of fuller, interior, human potentials', Ong concluded. 'Writing heightens consciousness'.[206]

Taking support from both Wolf's developmental neuropsychology and Ong's theory of literacy (which deserves to be reread today, in the neuroscientific age, as does the work of Lev Vygotsky, Jack Goody, Mary Carruthers, Jean-Pierre Vernant, Friedrich Kittler and many others), Carr refers to the fact that Socrates was opposed to the writing of the Sophists, and argues that digital technology again raises the Socratic question concerning writing as *pharmakon* – a question that lies at the origin of philosophy.

For Socrates, who retells and resumes his account of the response of King Thamus to Theuth, who presented him with his invention,

> the written word is 'a recipe not for memory, but for reminder [*hypomnesis*]. And it is no true wisdom that you offer your disciples, but only its semblance'. Those who rely on reading for their knowledge will 'seem to know much, while for the most part they know nothing'. They will be 'filled, not with wisdom, but with the conceit of wisdom'.[207]

Despite this, Carr nevertheless does not pose the pharmacological issue *in the strict sense*, namely: that philosophy, by prescribing an appropriation of writing, constitutes a therapeutics capable of turning poisons into remedies, and thus of nourishing the very principle of noetic individuation. Rather than taking on this ambiguity of writing, Carr turns to Eric Havelock's argument that Plato chose writing over the oral tradition, over an orality that was, on the other hand, the choice of Socrates. According to Socrates, Carr says, 'writing threatens to make us shallower thinkers, [...] preventing us from achieving the intellectual depth that leads to wisdom and true happiness'. But:

> unlike the orator Socrates, Plato was a writer [...]. In a famous and revealing passage at the end of *The Republic* [...], Plato has Socrates go out of his way to attack 'poetry', declaring that he would ban poets from his perfect state.[208]

To support this thesis, Carr quotes Havelock and Ong:

> The 'oral state of mind', wrote [Havelock], was Plato's 'main enemy'.
>
> Implicit in Plato's criticism of poetry was [...] a defense of the new technology of writing [...]. 'Plato's philosophically analytical thought', writes Ong, 'was possible only because

> of the effects that writing was beginning to have on mental processes'.[209]

Having thus shown, in relying especially on Havelock, Ong and Wolf, that reading and deep attention are *historical noetic conquests conditioned by mnemotechnical conquests*, which obviously means that the literate brain (that reading brain which is the noetic brain that founds the literate mind) is *constituted* by the technical internalization of the letter, which totally reconfigures cortical organization, as Maryanne Wolf shows (in passing through Dehaene and Vygotsky) – having shown all this, Carr nevertheless believes that, in the context of the Internet, Google and digital retention, we can and must *oppose* psychic memory and technical memory:

Governed by highly variable biological signals, chemical, electrical, and genetic, every aspect of human memory – the way it's formed, maintained, connected, recalled – has almost infinite gradations. Computer memory exists as simple binary bits – ones and zeros – that are processed through fixed circuits, which can be either open or closed but nothing in between.[210]

Such a point of view, however, completely contradicts his defence of the role of writing in the formation of rational noesis – as if writing inscribed on paper, papyrus, parchment or marble was not itself something entirely different from that living memory contained in the cerebral organ (which was precisely Thamus's objection to Theuth).

THIRD LECTURE

From Writing to Digital Writing: On the Brain and the Soul

Last week we began reading *The Shallows*, by Nicholas Carr, and we saw that in order to describe what he calls 'deep reading', Carr refers to the role of writing in the formation of Western thought and philosophy, and in doing so relies on the analyses of Eric Havelock and Walter Ong. Carr argues that deep reading is threatened by digital technology, the Internet and Google. To support this analysis, he claims that digital, artificial memory destroys living memory. And we saw that by making this claim, the end of his book radically contradicts the analyses on which he relied at the beginning.

This contradiction, in my view, arises from a superficial reading of Plato and from a simplification of the question of the *pharmakon* that writing is in Plato's eyes. This is particularly clear when Carr takes up the analyses by Havelock and Ong of the relation that Plato maintained with writing and with the 'oral tradition'. By asserting that 'implicit in Plato's criticism of poetry was [...] a defense of the new technology of writing', Carr massively simplifies the questions faced by the epoch confronted with the abuse of writing perpetrated, according to Plato, by the Sophists – the abuse of writing: that is, the harmful use made of writing, the toxic use.

Through Plato's discourse on writing as *pharmakon* (and more broadly, and through this, his discourse on technics in general), the very foundations of Western thought are constituted – and for this reason one should not be hasty, *nor afraid of conducting deep readings*, of the type practised for instance by philosophy. In my view, however, Carr neglects to conduct such a reading at the very moment he is condemning the superficiality of 'the shallows'.

Contrary to Carr's assertions, *in no case* did Plato choose writing over speech: in the context of what Gilbert Murray called the 'Inherited Conglomerate', and the conflicts it generated, Plato wished to break with the *tragic thought* embodied in the bards, who are the *tragic figures of anamnesis*, in order to enter into metaphysical thinking, which constitutes a *new conception of anamnesis* – which is also to say a new definition of dialectics, based on analysis and on synthesis as two different moments, or a transformation of dialogism into dialectics.

It was in this context that Plato wished to produce a *therapeutic writing* through such a *dialectic* – and he himself speaks of a 'medicine of the soul'. But by inaugurating this new way of thinking – called nowadays 'metaphysical thinking', that is, founded on the *oppositions* of body and soul, sensible and intelligible, heaven and earth – and through an interpretation of the life of Socrates that is a *rejection* of the *pharmakon*, that is, a denial of the *irreducibly duplicitous* character of writing, Plato *claimed to have found a way of escaping the pharmacological situation*, which for the tragic thinkers was the *very condition of mortals*: their lot, their *moira*.

It is because in Greek tragic society the pharmacological situation is *insurmountable* that mortals must practise sacrifice. This was shown by Jean-Pierre Vernant: it is as remembrance and commemoration of the crime of Prometheus, who is their 'origin', that mortals can and must sacrifice to Zeus, who, according to mythology, as told by Hesiod in *Theogony*, was hurt by the theft of fire that *therefore* becomes a *pharmakon*.

As we outlined last year, in *Republic* – thus after the *Symposium*, which was the last Platonic text still inspired by the tragic tradition – Plato's goal was to *eliminate* the uncontrollable pharmacological effects of writing and, beyond writing, his goal was to subject the *pharmakon* to the power of the dialectic. And his goal was to do so for *all forms* of the *pharmakon*, that is, for technics in its totality, including as the *tekhnē* of the musical and poetic arts, as well as the body, which would thereby be reduced to the status of an instrumental means of the soul, and even language, whose idiomatic and singular diachronicity would need to be totally dissolved, by submitting it to a *pure synchronization, based on a kind of metaphysical and ontological prefiguration of cybernetics*, and effected by philosopher-kings who would be the guardians of the *politeia*. This dialectical operation prepares the way for ontology, and tries to impose a *new regime of individuation* that is later materialized as onto-theology and *theocracy*.

For Plato, this organization of the *politeia* submitted to the dialectical power of philosophers was a way of reducing all this (language, the body, technics, the arts and the *pharmakon* in general) to the status of being a *means* of the philosophical soul, the latter itself expressing the power of the ideas that the philosopher was able to contemplate by leaving the cave of illusions, as described in the famous cave allegory that opens Book VII of the *Republic*.

The cave of illusions is the cave of *pharmaka* to which and by which the multitude is enchained – the *oi polloi*, the mass who are lured by the *theatre of shadows that constitutes the pharmacological milieu of the cave*. For the blind herd that have been led astray by *doxa*, the philosopher, having reduced the *pharmakon* to the rank of means controllable through the dialectical activity of the soul, must become the shepherd – as Heidegger too will say.

Plato's goal in the *Republic* is to eliminate the toxicity of the *pharmakon*, but this is also about enabling tragic society to escape *muthos*, of which the poets are the memory – those for whom pharmacological duplicity is irreducible, and must therefore *always be made the object of care*, of disciplines, *meletē*, *epimeleia*, and so on. For the Greek tragics, the toxicity of the *pharmakon* could never be eliminated, and it is via the *pharmakon* itself that the therapeutic must be thought (such a perspective can also be seen in Aby Warburg's analysis of the Hopi Indian snake ritual – and I guess in China, the 'serpent' in a way becomes the dragon). For Plato, on the other hand, this toxicity must be eliminated once and for all.

But Plato's desire to synchronize transindividuation (as we saw, this is what Google tries to do with linguistic technologies), Plato's desire to synchronize transindividuation is the complete opposite of his claim, following the teaching of Socrates, against the Sophists: instead of encouraging citizens to *think for themselves*, he now wants to utilize writing and, more generally, the techniques of language (rhetoric, poesy), as well as technics and the arts in general, in order to *impose* on the citizenry the way of thinking of philosophers. Plato claims that the latter, because they have left the cave, are the only ones who embody thinking for oneself, and he therefore claims they have the right and the duty to impose this upon others. Ultimately, therefore, Plato does exactly that for which he reproaches the Sophists.

Plato's *Republic*, then, is a political program founded on the analysis of writing presented in the *Phaedrus*, in which Plato has Socrates say that writing is good if it is subject to the therapeutic in which dialectic consists. In this sense, there is for Plato a positivity of the *pharmakon*. At the same time, this *pharmakon* no longer *is* a *pharmakon*: he claims that his dialectical mastery *eliminates* writing's poisonous aspect, and can do so, he claims, because this dialectical mastery was constituted *before* writing practices.

Writing, however, is the *condition* of such mastery: this is precisely what has been shown not only by Eric Havelock and Walter Ong, but also by Jean-Pierre Vernant, Maryanne Wolf, Jack Goody, Marcel Detienne and many others – and, more than anyone, by Jacques Derrida. This 'mastery' *cannot* be a mastery *of* writing, since it *depends* on writing. Derrida began his 'deconstruction of metaphysics' by showing that dialectical activity, which Plato and Socrates founded on *anamnesis* – a word that is often translated as 'reminiscence', and which appears in Plato as early as *Meno, at a time when he was still referring to the tragic tradition* through the myth of Persephone – is itself conditioned by a writing that constantly escapes it: it is constituted by *hypomnesis* and *hypomnēmata*, which, in a general way, like alphabetical or other forms of writing, constitute the *conditions* of noetic individuation, and which, therefore, cannot be its 'means'. This is also, by the way, the question that underlies Foucault's analysis of Stoicism in 'Self Writing'.[211]

We are recalling these analyses because they are critical for an understanding of Carr's own propositions on the subject of the effects of digital writing on…on what? On the brain? The soul? The psychic apparatus? The mind? What is it that *distinguishes* these notions and the functions they are expected to designate: brain, soul, psychic apparatus, *esprit* – the last of these itself needing to be distinguished in terms of *nous, spiritus, Geist, Witz* and so on? These are questions that Carr does not raise – yet they may be *preliminary* for any possible analysis of what results from this or that type of tertiary retention.

What Socrates and Plato in fact refer to is the *soul*, and what it would write. The soul, however, is *not* the brain. The soul, as Aristotle said later, may be either noetic, or sensitive, or vegetative. There is no vegetative brain. But noetic souls, like sensitive souls, have a brain. For example, monkeys and mice, to which Carr refers by quoting Eric Kandel, have a brain, as do London taxi drivers who, as Eleanor Maguire has shown (and this is cited by Carr), have an overdeveloped hippocampus, which is tied to the overdevelopment of their spatial representation of London. Does the overdevelopment of the hippocampus of these cab drivers in some way change their psychic apparatus – that is, the *psychic functions* that Freud described in terms of *unconscious, conscious, ego, id, repression, ego ideal, superego* and so on? Such a question presumes that the psychic apparatus, which undoubtedly takes root in the brain, is not reducible to the brain: it passes through a *symbolic apparatus* that is not situated *only* in the brain, but in *society*, that is, in those *other* brains with which *this* brain is in relation, these *relations between brains* forming an associated, dialogical and transindividual milieu at the core of which there lies a psychic apparatus, which means a psychic potential for individuation – and when we say *between* these brains, this also means here: *in or on the tertiary retentions* that constitute every technical life-form.

Psychic individuation is *also and immediately collective* individuation, as we learn from Simondon, above all because psychic individuation always *participates* in a process of *transindividuation* – directly or indirectly – which always passes through a process of co-individuation. This co-individuation is always the learning, the apprenticeship of what is inherited by the group of psychic individuals, who thus individuate themselves collectively, and do so supported by tertiary retention – the totality of which forms a *preindividual* milieu common to all psychic individuals.

The ego is constituted through the *internalization of the relations* that form through co-individuation processes that participate in trans-individuation. This is what Freud meant when, in *The Ego and the Id,* he spoke of a sedimentation of the ego: 'the character of the ego is a precipitate [or sedimentation] of abandoned object-cathexes and [...] it contains the history of those object-choices'.[212] These relations are themselves conditioned by artefacts that *support* the symbolic milieus on the basis of which psychic individuals form their associated milieu through these tertiary retentions that constitute the world *as* world. And the first of these artefacts – which is thus the primordial *pharmakon* – is the transitional object: the blanket, the toy or the teddy bear.

Carr poses *none* of these questions because he seems completely ignorant of anything written in Europe in the last fifty years. He is more at home referring to the cognitivist current, based on a bad interpretation of Turing's theorem, a cognitivism that itself meticulously and even methodically represses these questions, initially by relying on analytical philosophy, and more significantly because it takes as a founding principle that it would be possible to reduce all of the noetic soul's mental activity – what is more commonly called 'human intelligence' – to *computational* activity. Carr himself clearly militates against this notion. But he fails to see the true question. As we saw last week, he claims towards the end of his book that so-called 'biological' memory is organized completely differently to technical memory:

> Governed by highly variable biological signals, chemical, electrical, and genetic, every aspect of human memory – the way it's formed, maintained, connected, recalled – has almost infinite gradations. Computer memory exists as simple binary bits – ones and zeros – that are processed through fixed circuits, which can be either open or closed but nothing in between.[213]

But what he is saying here about digital memory must:

- either, also be true of alphabetical memory, but then his references to Walter Ong would no longer be valid;
- or else, he must admit, as Maryanne Wolf does by referring to the works of Stanislas Dehaene and through her own clinical analyses, that *organic* memory is *recoded* by *organological* memory, which means that circuits of transindividuation have formed through which alphabetical organological memory has *recoded* the cortical areas, in such a way that

> language, *organologically grammatized by alphabetical writing*, is internalized by *organic* memory but *under organological conditions*, thereby finding itself trans-formed – and, *through this transformation, it itself participates in the metalinguistic transindividuation of language that alphabetical writing made possible*, as Sylvain Auroux showed in *La révolution technologique de la grammatisation*.

Despite his reference to Wolf, not for a second does Carr seem to envisage that it might be possible for digital organology, too, to result in neuronal recoding that would be beneficial to deep attention. And this is inconceivable to Carr because he has an uncritical relation to cognitivism, which is shown clearly by the fact that:

1. he considers it *relevant* to ask whether hypomnesic memory could *replace* anamnesic memory (which is the project of artificial intelligence, including as this new artificial intelligence that, according to Carr, Google is implementing);
2. while nevertheless presuming that hypomnesic memory, that is, technical memory, and anamnesic memory, that is, biological memory, do not originally *have anything to do with each other*, that is, while posing *a priori* that there can be anamnesic memory without hypomnesic memory, which completely contradicts his use of Havelock and Ong.

This is *thus not at all* how these questions ought to be posed – and Carr himself already said this: the memory of deep attention and deep reading is *constituted* by writing itself, that is, by its *internalization. The digital, however, is a new form of writing, just as the age of the printing press totally reconfigured scriptural technology.*

A remark on cognitivism

Cognitivism, as it has developed in the field of neuroscience, is in its current forms certainly no longer based on this computationalist and informational model. But as a general rule, what has replaced it has been a neurocentric biological reductionism, which tends to dissolve the hypomnesic and organological dimensions into the laws of the organic, that is, of biology. Eric Kandel, extensively cited by Carr, is a particularly interesting representative of neuroscience because, on the basis of recent discoveries about the organization and life of the brain, he opens up perspectives from which to reread Freudian theory. I have in my own work tried to show that it is because Freud takes no account of hypomnesic memory that he eventually returns to a Lamarckian point of view.

More generally, nervous memory, distributed in the different regions of the brain and nervous system, is always also the *internalization of social memory insofar as it presupposes the cerebral internalization of both tertiary retentions* that *conserve* this social memory and the *internalization of language* (which is itself a form of this social memory, ex-pressed to the individual by their family) in the brain of this individual when they are young, that is, *in the course of their education, of being raised above themselves and above their biological and nervous automatisms (or compulsions)*, in trying to *become grown-up* and therefore *more* than a brain, and even *much* more: a psychic apparatus.

No psychic apparatus can be formed without interiorizing both:

- the *symbolic, technical and hypomnesic categories* (produced by intellectual technologies in Goody's sense) through which the cerebral organ is '*organologized*';
- the *social relations* that grant access to these categories through *social rules* that are internalized not as 'instruction manuals' for these categories but as *therapeutic prescriptions* for their own practices, and through the care that they can and must take of themselves and others, thereby constituting *savoir-vivre* and attentional forms of all kinds.

During this internalization, the psychic individual – formed by this psychic apparatus, which rests on the brain, which accesses mind and spirit by reindividuating tertiary retentions and, more generally, by reactivating the circuits of transindividuation that form, across all psychic individuals,[214] a collective individuation process – in the course of this interiorization, then, psychic individuals may, within themselves, reinforce *contradictory tendencies*: they may intensify the *contradiction of tendencies that they inhabit*. Or they may, on the contrary, try to *make one tendency submit to another*.

A psychic individual is in effect constituted by a *dynamic bipolarity* that traverses them like a cross in relation to which they are constantly confronted with the necessity of deciding their existence. In the language of Freudian psychoanalysis such as it was formulated in 1920, this means that the psychic individual is inhabited by *drives* that, through education and more generally through object investments, are diverted from their goals and towards the creation of a dynamic, social energy – whereas the raw drive is antisocial.

These questions, taught to us a century ago by psychoanalysis, must today be revisited with respect to the organology of the brain insofar as *education consists in inscription into 'grey matter', such that it supports automatisms or compulsions of biological origin, and others of social origin,* granting access to reflective thought, that is, thought that is not automatic but deliberate, and socially elaborated in dialogical relation with others – in passing through circuits of transindividuation that make possible the encounter with these others.

If social and symbolic milieus can be constituted by the dual synchronizing and diachronizing tendency that supports the dynamic of transindividuation in general, this is because the psychic apparatus is itself structured by a *bipolar dynamic of desires* (which invest in and protect their objects) *and drives* (which consume and destroy these objects if they are not diverted into investments of desire), these psychic polarities between themselves being supported by the functional and automatic polarities that form in the noetic brain and through its education. Education works through the elaboration of synaptic circuits that in no way reduce the bipolarity of these dynamic tendencies, but which dispose the psychic individual to manifest itself as a social individual through their commerce with others or with those representatives of others that are tertiary retentions. In this way, the *social* tendencies that the psychic individual internalizes and cultivates, through attentional forms that have contributed to the formation of his cortical equipment, can be reinforced through social commerce and can consolidate the *submission of organic automatisms or compulsions* that are the 'deeper layers' of the central nervous system, that is, the most basic and archaic behavioural motors that education helps to socialize and *transform into social investments.*

Nevertheless, and completely to the contrary, it is possible to exploit the toxic power of tertiary retention, and through that to take control of psychic apparatuses by taking control of cerebral and drive-based automatisms and compulsions. In that case, instead of inscribing the psychic apparatus onto the circuits of transindividuation that attentional forms constitute by enabling the energy of the drives to be diverted and 'economized', the internalization of tertiary retention short-circuits the cerebral elaborations emerging from the attentional forms acquired through education, and triggers archaic automatisms outside of any noetic channelling. This is, of course, the whole point of neuromarketing.

To recapitulate, we can say that today a vast organological transformation is underway. This transformation is of an exceptional magnitude for many reasons, but three of the main ones are:

1 tertiary retention has become, via digitalization, the object of industrial and global exploitation, affecting every economic, political and geopolitical issue;

2 this transformation operates at extreme speed, given the colossal acceleration of innovation resulting from both Moore's law (that is, the industrial exploitation of microelectronic potentials) and near light-speed transmission, of which we have seen how it radically changes the transindividuation process in general, and that of language in particular;

3 as the digital combines with emerging neurotechnologies, this will amount to a radical organological revolution, changing the very basis of the relation between the psycho-somatic, the technological and the social – leading some to speak of an 'anthropological rupture', and others of 'posthumanism'.

In addition, neurological analyses of what the analogical and digital media do to infantile synaptogenesis, and comparing this to the synaptic bases of what Maryanne Wolf calls the 'reading brain', bases that Walter Ong himself called the 'literate mind', suggests that the noetic brain, insofar as it is an organ that is not just organic but organological, is capable of being reorganized *according to the organological models produced by grammatization*, the latter itself constituting a process of individuation of tertiary retentions that Plato called hypomnesis. All this leads us to argue:

- that an indissociably bio-technological morphogenetic process is put in place with the advent of the noetic brain;
- that this process cannot be analysed in strictly Darwinian terms;
- that this is the reason for which we must study Lotka.

This is occurring at the moment when industrial transindividuation, founded on increasing automation, exploiting the unprecedented potential of the inorganic matter that is silicon when organized at the microelectronic level, is generating or provoking circuits of transindividuation at near light speed, thereby short-circuiting and through that destroying the transindividuation circuits that lie at the foundations of political society, all of which radically transforms the human world at the planetary level. Such a situation constitutes an exceptional case of what I call an epokhally double redoubling.

The doubly epokhal redoubling is the arrangement between what the ancient Greeks called *prometheia* and *epimetheia*. Prometheus is the god of technics and Epimetheus is his brother. Prometheus is the god of technical intelligence and anticipation and Epimetheus is the god of that wisdom that arises from reflection after the fact – in the aftermath of immediate experience, which is itself above all stupefaction and stupidity [*bêtise*]. Through this arrangement of *prometheia* and *epimetheia* that is always an *epokhally double redoubling*, Promethean pharmacology enables the constitution of an Epimethean therapeutic – of an *epimeleai* (a technique of the self, in Foucault's sense) founded on a *meletē* (on a discipline in the Stoic sense), which is itself empirical and technical, which is therefore always itself taken back to its pharmacological provenance, and which, as the life of the spirit, is the *patho-logy* of this spirit, as we can learn from Georges Canguilhem's concept of 'technical life'.

The first redoubling is the primary effect through which a new *pharmakon*, provoking what Canguilhem called an 'infidelity of the milieu',[215] opens an *epokhē*, that is, a suspension of the programs governing an epoch: the three organological levels that constitute general organology are psycho-somatic, technical and socio-ethnic *programs* the unity of which is constituted through the process of transindividuation. The *primary suspension* provoked by the new *pharmakon* short-circuits the programs that it suspends, and it constitutes a pathological state firstly in this sense: it is an injury, a wound, an impairment, a process of disindividuation that disrupts the entire social milieu.

The second redoubling, the *epokhē* constituting an epoch in the strict sense, acts as a therapy, a therapeutics, a technique of self and others, a normativity that is established through a process of adoption, which is a new sort of affection, and a pathology in this other sense: that which, through *pathos*, through feeling, generates a new meaning that forms itself *against* the models of adaptation – that is, of disindividuation – that the first redoubling tries to impose. This *secondary suspension* constitutes a new *pathos* that is a new kind of *philia* – which is also a new 'form of life' (in Wittgenstein's sense) and a 'new way of feeling' (in Nietzsche's sense) – by creating, from out of the initial pharmacological and hypomnesic shock, circuits of transindividuation that lead to a new organization of psychic and collective individuation.

▪ ▪ ▪

Tomorrow, we shall examine:

- why writing constitutes such a hypomnesic shock, *recoding neuronal circuits as well as social circuits*, and generating an anamnesic process of individuation – in the sense in which Socrates speaks of anamnesis in *Meno*;

- why Nicholas Carr apparently excludes the possibility that digital hypomnesis could generate a new form, if not of anamnesis, at least of psychic and collective individuation.

FOURTH LECTURE

The Pharmacology of Technological Memory

In his analysis of the destruction of attention and, consequently, of the capacity for deep reading – this destruction being caused by digital tertiary retention – Nicholas Carr does not see that the point is not to compare the respective virtues of 'biological memory' versus 'technical memory' or 'technological memory'. Even though he summarizes the effects of writing on the noetic brain as the 'reading brain' in Maryanne Wolf's sense, and as the 'literate mind' in Walter Ong's sense, Carr does not grasp that *noetic* biological memory is not *simply* biological.

Noetic biological memory is not *simply* biological, but *nervous*, that is, *plastic*, and it is *not simply nervous and organic*, but *organological*, that is, precisely, and uniquely in the case of a *noetic* nervous system, *capable of integrating, on the organic plane, these non-organic and yet organo-logical forms that are tertiary retentions* – which are themselves organized inorganic beings (a concept developed in *Technics and Time*).

Here it would be necessary to take the time to analyse in detail the neuroscientific perspective on noetic memory – by examining, for example, Joseph LeDoux's descriptions, in *Synaptic Self*, of the cerebral functioning of memory, and his analyses of the relations between working memory and long-term memory, between the prefrontal cortex and the hippocampus, and finally between the prefrontal cortex and the subcortical regions.[216] One could then show that:

- on the one hand, through the relations between working memory and long-term memory, LeDoux describes the *neuronal basis* of the relationship between primary retention and secondary retention;

- on the other hand, to the extent that none of this is thinkable outside the sensorimotor loop conceived by Jakob von Uexküll, who showed that all reception leads to an effection, and must therefore be inscribed on the *circuit* of a motor behaviour, then in the case of the noetic brain, the organology of *artificial organs* implemented by these motor organs, which is also to say, via what von Uexküll called 'motor cells', which are, precisely, what LeDoux calls 'motor neurons', must be immediately taken into account and originally inscribed on the circuit of organs and sub-organs as

> the condition of possibility of forming a psychic apparatus, and not merely a cerebral organ.

But in order to explore this path, it would also be necessary to examine the meaning of the *question of forgetting*, to see what LeDoux says about telephone numbers, and especially to see what he *forgets* to say *about forgetting*, namely, that while it is indeed true that working memory 'has its limits', and that this is 'why you forget a phone number if you are distracted while dialing',[217] he does not say that a *specific motor behaviour*, such as *writing down* this telephone number, enables it to be *not completely forgotten* – and supports cerebral organization in the context of an *hypomnesic organology that radically changes things* – this organology being constituted by what I call tertiary retention.

This radically changes things because it follows that the question of the *perception of time*, and of remembering the present as it passes by, which is, precisely, the process of primary retention – and that LeDoux describes very well and in a way quite close to my own presentation of retention when he writes that,

> [w]hen listening to a lecture, you have to hold the subject of each sentence in your mind until the verb appears, and sometimes you have to refer back to your memory of earlier sentences to figure out the referent of a pronoun,[218]

– cannot be reduced merely to a question of working memory, contrary to what his analysis suggests. This primary aggregation must in fact then be related back to what Kant described as a *synthesis*, that is, as the *production of the unity of an object* that itself *presupposes* the *production of the unity of a subject* (which constitutes the basis of what Kant called the *transcendental affinity*, and, in this instance, it does so as the product of what Kant called the synthesis of recognition, itself founded on a synthesis of apprehension and a synthesis of reproduction). That this synthesis has neuronal bases and conditions is incontestable. But this does not mean that it can be *reduced* to this neuronal basis: a description of the cerebral organ alone is not sufficient for an understanding of this synthesis.

When Husserl described the aggregation of primary retentions from which results the melodious character of a sonata or symphony, he was not referring to a simple working memory that 'can do one or at most a few things at a time',[219] as LeDoux says, and this is so:

- firstly, because here it may not necessarily be a matter of 'doing things' but, on the contrary, of *not* doing them, of *deferring* an *action* and *intensifying* an *attention*, the latter being a combination of retentions and protentions;

- secondly, because a symphony, for example, or a lecture like the one I am delivering right now, may last two hours, and during that period of two hours, the unification (that is, the synthesis) of what is said in the lecture by those listening to it is a complex task that involves not only 'working memory' and 'long-term memory', but *artificial and organological memory that itself constitutes an external workspace*, which operates much more successfully if a *prior internalization of its organological working conditions* has occurred, that is, if there has been a *recoding of the relevant cortical regions.*

In other words, *noetic* attention is not simply the living thing's vigilance or alertness, and it is not an innate capacity, but is rather the outcome of social formation or training, that is, technique – it is organological: technical objects are artificial *organs*. The submission of the organic to the organological in which the formation of the noetic soul consists, where this soul is irreducible to the brain and corresponds to what Freud called the psychic apparatus, is the outcome of *education*, which is itself the process of the socialization of the living operating through a succession of processes of identification and idealization. It is for this reason that I cannot agree with Catherine Malabou when she writes that:

> the structures and operations of the brain, far from being the glimmerless organic support of our light, are the only *reason* for processes of cognition and thought; and [...] there is absolutely no justification for separating mind and brain.[220]

Such a discourse completely ignores the fact that *knowledge* is not simply *cognitive*, but presupposes the formation of social circuits of transindividuation through which a form of knowledge is constituted. This can be compared with Stanislas Dehaene, for whom, as for Alain Berthoz, mathematical concepts are inscribed in the brain. Moreover, this discourse is a regression in relation to what Freud more than anyone helped us understand, namely, that the libido is *irreducible* to the drive. Malabou, on the contrary, declares that 'cerebral organization presides over a *libidinal economy* whose laws have just begun to be explored',[221] and she claims that it is the neurosciences that are undertaking this exploration.

The libidinal economy, however, which is precisely not sexuality, that is, the sexual drive, but rather the question of the drives in general insofar as they are themselves *not* instincts – this libidinal economy is what, precisely, neuroscience completely ignores. This has nothing to do, here, with whether neuroscience makes its case well or otherwise, nor is it a matter of its opposition to psychoanalysis: the latter, in fact, itself ignored the question of tertiary retention, that is, the organological question, despite what Freud had to say about the fetish and what Winnicott thought, through this, about the transitional object. (If I had the time, I would explain how a very different theory of art and, through art, of technics, can be conceived with the transitional object – and on the basis of the work of Alexander Calder.)

What Catherine Malabou ignores is that the brain harbours drive-based automatisms or compulsions that become object investments of desires and idealizations only because the non-organic recoding of the cerebral organ meant that the instincts were replaced with the drives, and that the latter thereby became (thanks to this recoding) educable.

When the living thing is not socialized well, it is said to be *asocial*, that is, dangerous for society. The socialization of the living is obviously not a domestication but rather an acculturation, that is, an endowment of new capabilities for individuation that the living thing is unable to access on its own. This acquisition of capabilities – and I take this word also in the sense developed by Amartya Sen – consists in *replacing biological automatisms or compulsions*, that is, behavioural schemes prescribed by genetic inheritance, with *social automatisms*, which fall within what Leroi-Gourhan called socio-ethnic programs, such as learning to read or basic cultural behaviour in all its forms (politeness, hygiene, culinary habits, table manners and so on), on the basis of which deliberate and psychically individuated behaviour becomes possible. This possibility is what constitutes the kernel of the '*and*' in what Simondon called *psychic and collective individuation*.

▪ ▪ ▪

This general context, whereby through the arrangement and reorganization of compulsive automatisms the organic becomes organological and the sensitive soul becomes a noetic soul, is what Nicholas Carr completely ignores. To be clear: my thesis in this regard is a way of calling into question a Darwinian definition of the noetic brain. The latter is in fact essentially incomplete – this is what Maryanne Wolf says when she writes of human beings that '[w]e were never born to read',[222] and that any capability of this sort is not preformed in the brain: it is only produced through profoundly recoding existing cerebral functions. This is the situation, in my view, for all couplings between psychosomatic organs, artificial organs and social organizations.

But more generally, what is at stake here is the whole economy of desire, sublimation, superegoization and idealization, which is at the heart of the noetic soul, and which conditions the formation of the psychic apparatus: from 1920, Freud described the psychic apparatus as a system for diverting the aims of the drives. The latter are obviously biological automatisms. And yet, they are not instincts, to the extent that the latter cannot be remodelled, whereas the drives are essentially open to being reoriented and differentiated/deferred in Derrida's sense of différance (and this différance governs what Simondon called processes of individuation, both psychic and collective).

If we had time, I would refer here to John Bowlby's theory of attachment, where he raises this question of the passage from the instinct to the drive, though in my opinion he does not succeed in conjoining this to an organological perspective. We shall see in the final lecture how Vygotsky provides openings to such a point of view.

Be that as it may, if what I have been arguing is true, then we can see that the challenges of the pharmacological situation that constitutes the organological condition of the noetic soul are:

1. to ensure that the *pharmakon* does not cause the regression of those social investments that enable the drives to be transformed into desires, a trans-formation that is the formation of attentional forms;

2. to ensure that the *pharmakon* does not return the noetic soul back to its sensitive stage – that is, such that it is subject to biological automatisms.

This is what, in *Taking Care of Youth and the Generations*, I call 'care'. Therefore, in relation to the epoch of digital retention that concerns Nicholas Carr, the genuine issues are:

- to understand the arrangement over time between *anamnesis*, which is deep attention, and *hypomnesis*, which is its condition, but which is also what can destroy it qua *pharmakon*, and to *identify the specificities of its digital arrangement*;

- to know in what conditions these arrangements can and must, in a general way, and more specifically in the case of digital *hypomnesis*, be put at the service of an individuation that is always *simultaneously psychic, social and technical*, an individuation that, as positive pharmacology, is the *bearer of negentropy and neganthropy*, that is, of *capabilities of both plastic neuronal matter and social circuits of transindividuation*, thereby constituting *attentional forms*, that is, ways of arranging primary and secondary psychic retentions and protentions on the basis of collective retentions and protentions, and via tertiary retentions;

- *with regard to our own epoch*, to see how this negentropy and neganthropy must itself be the bearer of an *alternative* to the contemporary economic, political, moral and intellectual crisis, and not something that *worsens* the entropy and anthropy in which this crisis consists, *resulting in the destruction of all forms of deep attention*: this is what Carr describes, and it is the reason he militates against Google and more generally against the Internet and digital technology – but this entropy and anthropy is *also* a problem *for* Google, for example, in terms of the risks of dysorthography, as highlighted by Frédéric Kaplan;
- to figure out how the *automation of the transindividuation process* can be put at the service of the formation of long circuits of transindividuation, and even circuits that are *infinitely* long, that is, *anamnesic*, which is possible only on the condition of *preventing the technology of light-time from serving the dictates of short-term investment returns* demanded by the increasingly speculative shareholders of the digital industry.

▪ ▪ ▪

Now, a brief clarification of the infinite character of the anamnesic circuit (anamnesic in Plato's sense). An example of such a circuit is geometry. It is infinite:

- firstly, because it rests on an idealization of its object, which constitutes so-called mathematical idealities – these do not literally exist, that is, they cannot be found in nature, but are produced through the process of idealization (the geometric point, for example, does not exist, but grants geometric consistence to Euclidean space);
- secondly, because this idealization stems from desire, which is what Diotima claimed in Plato's *Symposium*: what characterizes desire is the capacity to invest in an object by infinitizing it, that is, by making it *incomparable to everything that exists* – and by projecting it onto the *plane of consistence*;

- finally, because geometry is constituted, as Husserl said, by the community of geometers such that they know that geometry is *infinitely open*, that is, structurally unfinished and unfinishable, and such that they constitute, on the basis of this primordial knowledge of this infinity, what Husserl called 'the infinite we of geometers'.[223]

The future of education in the epoch of the digital organology of knowledge passes through the implementation of digital technologies of transindividuation at the service of a reconstitution of such anamneses, that is, forms of academic knowledge that would constitute noble objects for the digital epoch. This presupposes the engagement of an *industrial politics founded on a positive pharmacology driven by public power,* and *public investment in education, research and the constitution of new attentional forms* (which also pass through the arts), creating *long-term solvencies.*

This seems inconceivable to Carr. His discourse is that of a traumatized man, repentant, suffering from addiction…and *American* – that is, *virtually unwilling to give any credit to the possibility that a public power could act,* having internalized the ideological onslaught of 'American neoliberalism', as Foucault called it[224] – which led to the disastrous crisis of 2008 – even though American industrial policy has largely been guided by the federal government, especially in relation to the transition from analogue to digital, and under the impetus of Al Gore, which is the main reason that America still dominates this sector.

Like all those who have suffered the historic collapse that is this hyper-crisis, Carr is in a *dual state of shock.* The first shock is the one described by Naomi Klein in *The Shock Doctrine*, a shock systematically practised by the conservative revolution in Great Britain and the United States, and eventually throughout the entire world under the name of 'globalization'.[225] But what has equally shocked and disoriented Nicholas Carr, just like the rest of America and indeed the whole world, beyond the ideological manipulation and conceptual disarmament in which consists the ultraliberal ideology disseminated and implemented by the famous Chicago School and Milton Friedman, is not only the conservative revolution, which began there more than thirty years ago: it is also what began twenty-five years ago with the deployment of the Web, which has multiplied the deleterious effects of this epoch of *extremist* ideology. This shock was further exacerbated a little over a decade ago with the appearance of Google, which, reconfiguring the *space of publication*, produced a new public space, a new public thing that seemed to *worsen public impotence* (public powers as well as the public itself – all of us), given that this public space is that of an *ever-increasing public dependence on private investment* – which, however, puts into opposition the 'top down' logic of the public powers and the 'bottom up' logic of the collaborative networks of the Web 2.0. All this has been seized by libertarian ideology – without the left ever taking whatever might be the measure of this irreversible movement, nor proving itself capable of criticizing this ideology, which is that of the *opposition* between the top down and the bottom up.

Carr reproaches himself for, and is repentant about, having listened to the sirens of digital memory, and for having dived in with such enthusiasm and delight – giving in to mechanisms that dispossessed him of *his own* memory. This dispossession is above all the ordeal of an *addiction* that *disindividuates* psychic memory. His discourse is that of a man who has become dependent on digital retention. Carr suffers from addiction because his mnesic circuits now *need* to pass through artificial circuits – just like the drug addict who, having allowed artificial molecules to short-circuit his own ability to produce neurotransmitters, will do anything for his next fix: he is no longer *capable* on his own of producing the endorphins that are indispensable to his organism.

Now this is *typical of the consumerist economy*, for which Amartya Sen analysed the process of incapacitation in all its forms. And the question is that of the *consumerist anchoring* that continues to command the two-sided economy of Google through its algorithm for producing 'exchange value', even though the algorithm that produces 'use value' seems to open onto *another industrial model* – but the prerequisite for this would be a new public politics.

Having become dependent, Carr will remain dependent: he does not believe in his own disintoxication. Having explained that he tried to disintoxicate himself by disconnecting while he was writing his book, Carr admits that he is

> already backsliding. With the end of this book in sight, I've gone back to keeping my e-mail running all the time and I've jacked into my RSS feed again. I've been playing around with a few new social-networking services and have been posting some new entries to my blog. I recently broke down and bought a Blu-ray player with a built-in Wi-Fi connection. It lets me stream music from Pandora, movies from NetFlix, and videos from YouTube through my television and stereo. I have to confess: it's cool. I'm not sure I could live without it.[226]

I am sorry to confess myself that I find these two last sentences frankly stupid…

With this confession, Carr evinces a radical and disturbing pessimism. Even if there are a thousand reasons to be alarmed, as *we* are too, by the current situation, by the contemporary state of fact – by the state of shock from which it originates, leading as it does to the ruin of attentional forms – one cannot help but think that *Carr's radical negativity is just as excessive as was his initial enthusiasm,* and that something is wrong with his analysis, an analysis that, precisely for this reason, still comes across as *immature* (in the sense of 'maturity' used to translate Kant's term, '*Mündig*', in 'What is Enlightenment?' – in French it is translated as *majeur,* majority [as in, 'to achieve one's majority' – *trans.*]).

Computational cognitive science (which has been widely challenged by more recent cognitivist models) postulated that technics can and will duplicate and eventually replace the intellectual functions of the noetic brain. This was not a scientific program: it was a political program, utterly in line with neoconservative ideology insofar as it proposed the in principle *solubility* of any decision, that is, the *dissolution, disintegration* and *replacement of the power to decide* with the *power to calculate* – this power itself finding its fulfilment in the market, confronted with which there would no longer be any alternative: there would be nothing to be decided, and generalized disindividuation would be an unsurpassable horizon.

Such reasoning ignores that the noetic brain has *always* been constituted through its relation to a memory that is dead – that is, inorganic – and that this dead memory, which is an organological organ, has never replaced the noesis of the noetic organ that is the living brain through which this noesis is produced. By transgenerationally articulating the singularities that are psychic individuals, linking their brains together via tertiary retentions that are their organologically spatialized temporal expression, noesis constitutes, as a circuit *between* dead memory and a living memory that undergoes a *process,* a *psychic apparatus bipolarized* by *two tendencies* that are constantly active:

- a tendency to regression and to what Deleuze called 'baseness';[227]
- a tendency to elevation that Freud redefined as investment and that was already thought by Aristotle, then by Spinoza and Hegel, as desire.

The relation between the dead and the living, which is the *pharmacological* origin of this mental bipolarity – and which is translated into the moral and spiritual experiences of the psychic apparatus (which Simondon addressed in terms of the question of temptation[228]) – is *made possible by the neuronal plasticity* that enables living memory to internalize and to *individuate* this relation and its duplicity, that is, to *interpret, transform* and *express* it, in the form of a new impression in dead memory that living memory creates each time it expresses itself, thereby exteriorizing itself by externalizing that which it has internalized, and individuating it by individuating itself.

The issue in question is this *noetic loop*, a stitching where, exteriorization fulfilling itself in internalization, and vice versa, circuits of transindividuation are woven, enabling the psychic individuation of noetic brains and the collective individuation of societies to either be intensified, thereby augmenting their negentropic potential, or instead to liquidate their potentials for individuation, to become disconnected from one another, and to be used up *in the form of the drives* – in order to capture added value, that is, capital gains. It is this loop of exteriorization and interiorization that makes the dialogisms of Socrates and Bakhtin possible, and it is what Vygotsky studied. And it is what we shall examine more closely next week.

FIFTH LECTURE

Neuroscience, Neuroeconomics, Neuromarketing

Nicholas Carr argues, strangely (although his perspective conforms to the dominant perspective of today's cognitivist current, under the influence of Noam Chomsky), that language, but not writing, is based on an innate faculty:

> Language itself is not a technology. It's native to our species. Our brains and bodies have evolved to speak and to hear words. A child learns to talk without instruction, as a fledgling bird learns to fly.[229]

These statements are odd, hasty and vague: they are superficial, they remain mired in *the shallows*. Carr would probably point out that learning to speak does not require going to school, but simply being around older speakers. But would it be true to say that this occurs *without instruction*? Are not parents constantly correcting the way their children speak? Admittedly, this is not a 'metalinguistic' transmission of the kind referred to by Sylvain Auroux or Roland Barthes, but it already and originally contains the possibility of *speaking the language*, and thus of making it into a *self-referential object*, which Auroux calls 'epilinguistic knowledge'.[230] I argue that this is possible only because language is originally and irreducibly exteriorized, and because this exteriorization is what opens a primordial and irreducible dehiscence between *psychic* individuation and *collective* individuation.

Contrary to Carr, the Russian psychologist Lev Vygotsky, who is referred to by Maryanne Wolf in her own work, considered that social and therefore artefactual exteriorization and interiorization are already at work in oral language, so that it conditions interior language (what Husserl called soliloquy); Vygotsky thus argued that it should be understood as what he called a *psychological tool*:

> 3. Psychological tools are artificial formations. By their nature they are social and not organic or individual devices. They are directed toward the mastery of [mental] processes – one's own or someone else's – just as technical devices are directed toward the mastery of processes of nature.
>
> 4. The following may serve as examples of psychological tools and their complex systems: language, different forms

> of numeration and counting, mnemotechnic techniques, algebraic symbolism, works of art, writing, schemes, diagrams, maps, blueprints, all sorts of conventional signs, etc.
>
> 5. By being included in the process of behavior, the psychological tool modifies the entire course and structure of mental functions by determining the structure of the new instrumental act, just as the technical tool modifies the process of natural adaptation by determining the form of labor operations.[231]

Jean-Paul Bronckart comments on this as follows:

> Thought and consciousness are not an emanation of internal structural or functional characteristics. [...] They are on the contrary determined through the external and objective activities carried out with others, in a determined social environment. [...] The central concept of psychology is *activity.*[232]

Rather than determined, I would say conditioned. But in any case, this is in profound contrast to the perspective that has dominated since Chomsky and that was radicalized with the cognitivist theories of the origin of language, such as biolinguistic accounts, or those theories that appeared in the 1990s and were developed by Steven Pinker and Paul Bloom, two so-called evolutionary psychologists, who thus place themselves firmly within a Darwinian framework.

Today, Chomsky himself (that is, since 1986, in *Knowledge of Language*), distinguishes innate language, which he also calls private language, or I-language (for 'internalized language'), from cultural languages, E-language (for 'externalized language').[233] This kind of notion is what leads Jerry Fodor to refer to what he calls 'mentalese'.[234] And it is a catastrophe. It is worth noting that this distinction is in stark contrast to Wittgenstein, who is nevertheless claimed by cognitivism as one of its pillars.

I myself consider that language, just like writing, involves a recoding of prelinguistic cerebral functions (communicational and cognitive – for example, categorization functions), but that language nevertheless did not exist *prior* to this recoding. As for 'private language', it is an internalization by psychic individuation along a circuit of transindividuation that is originally social. Here we should obviously refer to the question of the preindividual in Simondon, but unfortunately we lack the time for that today.

The writing of which Wolf speaks is a more advanced form of that *placing into exteriority* that lies *at the origin of language* – an advanced form that changes language itself. But this is possible only because language is an *originally social* system founded on the *artificial organ* that the 'word' *already* is, as Vygotsky understood in the 1920s. Bronckart states:

> Cooperation in social activity occurs by means of *instruments*, among which *verbal signs* play a primary role; it is through the progressive internalization of these instruments of cooperation that conscious thought is constructed. [...] At the end of this process, consciousness becomes a 'social contract with oneself'.[235]

And it is because the word is *already* an artificial organ that the written word can come to *replace* the spoken word (this is what underlies Derrida's reasoning in 1967 in *Of Grammatology*).

Speakers *internalize* words and individuate themselves by *exteriorizing* this internationalization in what one calls *expression*, and thereby contribute to the formation of circuits of transindividuation. The study of such circuits falls within general organology, and what Vygotsky called the *instrumental method*, which studies *instrumental acts*, which in turn rest on what we call tertiary retention. The totality of tertiary retentions constitutes the field of what I have referred to in *Technics and Time* as 'epiphylogenesis', based on the fact and founding the fact that '[i]n the instrumental act man masters himself from the outside – via psychological tools'.[236] This constitutes what I call the organological space of work – without which what Joseph LeDoux described as working memory, located in the prefrontal cortex, could not function. This also relates to what Jack Goody called 'technologies of the intellect'. Vygotsky adds:

> The application of psychological tools enhances and immensely extends the possibilities of behavior by making the results of the work of geniuses available to everyone (cf. the history of mathematics and other sciences).[237]

Like all noetic organs, the cerebral memory of the psychic individual is constantly being *dis-organized* and *re-organized*, *de-functionalized* and *re-functionalized* – that is, *recoded* – in a tertiary retentional milieu that thus 'organologizes' somatic organic memory, which becomes *psycho*-somatic only on this condition. It therefore constitutes a psychic individual who individuates himself or herself only by being in dialogical relation to a social individual for which transindividuation presupposes those technical artefacts – for example, those of schooling – that are tertiary retentions.

There is therefore nothing unusual, contrary to Carr, about the fact that the digital *overwrites* itself into organic brain tissue, just as did alphabetical writing – even if the *automation of this new form of writing* that writes and reads at near light speed radically modifies social organology, most often by short-circuiting or bypassing it. That social organology is modified, however, does not imply that the *pharmakon* should be rejected: to do so would be utterly futile, and would simply be to create a scapegoat. But it does indicate the need to establish a therapeutics, which presupposes:

- on the one hand, a *new critique of political economy* that supports this new organology;
- on the other hand, and consequently, *new organological principles* for the design of artefacts – and I began to present this here.

What is in question here – namely, *autonomy* in relation to *automatisms* and therefore in relation to the *capacity* to *decide* – is not constituted in the brain, but in the circuits that *connect* brains, and it is of course possible that these circuits, *imprinting onto brains*, may lead to *brains that function like machines*, but they cannot lead to machines that function like brains.[238] This question revolves around what occurs socially: it is the question of the conditions in which psychic individuals and their brains can or cannot *participate in writing and in the critique of circuits of transindividuation* that, in the epoch of digital writing, are produced via intermediaries that operate automatically.

The *answers* to these questions revolve around a *new organological craftsmanship* – in the sense one refers to the crafting of musical instruments such as violins – and around a *therapeutic socialization* of this organology. This involves:

1. devising and implementing, as soon as possible, the industrial production of *organological alternatives*;
2. *implementing an educational policy completely rethought on the basis of new intellectual technologies* – but also on the basis of taking account of older intellectual technologies (which are forever being ignored) and their *constitutive* role in the formation and transmission of knowledge between students, researchers and teachers, as Husserl understood towards the end of his life, and as indicated in the quotation from Vygotsky cited earlier.

It is obviously not possible to abstract these questions from the emerging context of neuropower, a context that in the coming years will redistribute all these questions – and that must be understood as the transformation of neuropower into a noopolitics reconstituting public power, that is, as a *re-capacitating of public powers as well as of the public itself in the form of citizenship*, and therefore as the *reconstitution of the power to make decisions*. Such a noopolitics needs a new epistemology to analyse the new *epistēmē* – and this is the aim of what I call digital studies.

The goal of neuroeconomics, and of its secular arm, neuromarketing, is:

1. to *liquidate* the capacity to decide, that is, *to dissolve it into the calculation of probabilities* through a modelling theory that eliminates the bipolarity characteristic of psychic apparatuses;
2. to *control any behaviour that might escape the stochastic laws of calculability*.

Neuroeconomics and neuromarketing together amount to a technological and scientific ideology. The instruments of this ideology are: 1) those devices dedicated to the automation of behaviour; and 2) those devices through which it is possible to observe brain function. Together, these instruments lead to the formation of a new neurotechnological organology.

What this excludes *a priori* is any possibility of exiting the current hyper-crisis that erupted in 2008: neuroeconomics is with libertarian transhumanism the latest episode of the conservative revolution, which has been a matter of 'scientifically' grounding and performatively imposing the absence of any alternative. This closing off of alternatives is based on the obvious fallacy that consists in reducing all decision-making processes to psychic automatisms or compulsions that would be deeper than reflective decision, and in making the *act of consumption* the *model* of all *decision-making*. Neuroeconomics is an ideology that implants itself in the body by *conditioning* the relations between cerebral organs, psychic individuals and the market – the latter being intended to replace every type of social system, and to be imposed as the organizational model for all social relations, that is, to dilute collective individuation through the calculable automatization of behaviour, for which it is therefore necessary to eliminate all singularities.

Such is the program of neuromarketing, based on the systematic solicitation of psychic automatisms – and thus representing a new step in the reign of systemic stupidity – in a world itself dominated by the technological automatisms made possible by digital tertiary retention. That these impacts result directly from the work of Paul Glimcher is highlighted in a French report by the Parliamentary Office of Technology Assessment, the MPs Alain Claeys and Jean-Sébastien Vialatte noting that the Glimcher Lab is 'dedicated to the psychology of decision' and that its goal is to obtain a 'better understanding of consumer behaviour when faced with multiple choices or external data'. That this is also the goal and effective outcome of neuromarketing emerges from a series of interviews in Laurence Serfaty's documentary, *Neuromarketing: Citizens Under the Influence?* (2009).

In this documentary, having drawn attention to the fact that the consumer is exposed to two million television commercials over the course of a lifetime, and that this occurs in the context of a hyper-solicitation of attention, in an era of extreme competition where 'every dollar counts' and thus where marketing must constantly become more efficient, A. K. Pradeep, founder and director of a company called NeuroFocus, explains that thanks to neuromarketing, 'we can look directly into the brain [...] without human interpretation'. Gemma Calvert, from the company Neurosense, says that it is therefore a matter of 'knowing what the brain of the consumer *truly* wants'. It would be necessary here, however, to specify what is meant by the words 'want' and 'truly'.

What is it 'to want'? Is it the sequence of electro-chemical micro-processes that mechanically and automatically follow and respond to a stimulus, like, for example, the sensorimotor loop that Jakob von Uexküll described in the case of the tick? Or is it not rather, precisely, and *truly*, the subject of a *choice* that can be called such only because it presumes a *decision* through which a psychic individual is *divided between two choices* insofar as the individual is *not just a brain* – or insofar as their brain is *not just organic* but, precisely, *organological*, made of spirals, and not simple loops, and, as such, *social*, that is, having the *possibility* of being attentive and caring?

The psychic individual is not simply a brain, but a psychic apparatus that develops in the course of an education through which it is inscribed on circuits of transindividuation based on transitional spaces, circuits that are thus themselves inscribed on the brain and through which this organ is intrinsically social – this organ, insofar as it is a noetic brain, being *incomplete* outside of its socialization, a socialization that, moreover, itself *remains* incomplete, that is, *historic*.

A psychic apparatus, which is not reducible to 'what the brain wants', is divided between two possibilities situated on what Simondon called the 'indefinite dyad'[239] of a bipolarity that is constituted and internalized through education and through circuits of transindividuation (that is, through attentional forms), thereby *constituting* this psychic apparatus – which is as such *irreducible to the unity* of its brain (which is 'divided' [*dédoublé*], as Simondon puts it). As a *noetic* organ, the brain is, *precisely, not one*, since it passes through an *organological 'third'* that lies outside it, as culture *collectively* transindividuated and supported by those tertiary retentions of all kinds that haunt it and of which it is the therapeutic adoption.

To justify 'looking directly into the brain [...] without human interpretation' in order to 'know what the brain of the consumer truly wants', A. K. Pradeep, CEO of NeuroFocus, adds that 'from the moment you ask a question, you bias the response. *One must therefore avoid asking questions*'. This is post-truth as such.

Knowing what the brain 'truly wants' without needing to pose questions is possible only on the condition of positing in principle:

- either, that the brain would be one, rather than traversed, divided, thrown into movement and turmoil by *opposing tendencies* that may want to *respond in opposing ways*, and therefore *to pose questions*;

- or, that it is possible and desirable to *make* it a unity by *eliminating* whatever else there might be, and to do so by causing *short-circuits* (which, however, involves the risk of 'blowing a fuse') – that is, by eliminating education, the formation and training of attention insofar as it is the condition of a deliberative and reflective life, rather than a life guided by the automatisms and compulsions of the drives.

Here it is obviously a matter of the brain of the consumer – and of reducing decision itself to the act of buying: one of the neuromarketers interviewed by Laurence Serfaty speaks of 'buy-ology'. It is the behaviour of the consumer, insofar as he or she can be manipulated by the campaigns and techniques of marketing, which is here set up as a model for all decision-making:

> Consumers do not know themselves what they are doing because our choices are the result of our emotions more than of our reason. [...] When we make a decision, emotion always takes over. It helps to sort through all the information that the brain needs to process. But most of the time we do not realize this, and we look for an *a posteriori* rational justification of our choice.

But what is meant by 'emotion' here?

> no living thing is without affectivo-emotivity [...]. It is the oldest layers of the nervous system that form the centres of this *regulation*, and particularly the *midbrain*.[240]

It is striking how the question of 'regulation', which is now such an issue for the financial sector, is being associated here with the midbrain, that is, with archaic cerebral sub-organs.

Now, in the case of the *psychic* and *noetic* individual bipolarized through participation in the collective individual, emotion can resolve itself into *action*, and the latter is *precisely not reaction* (it is not a 'response' to a 'stimulus'), only because it passes through circuits of transindividuation (and this was precisely the question that Nietzsche raised through his discussion of *ressentiment*). Action is itself participation in collective individuation, that is, in the formation of the transindividual:

> Action and emotion arise when the collective individuates itself [...]. The world has meaning because it is oriented, and it is oriented because the subject orients themselves according to their emotion. Emotion [...] is [...] a certain momentum through a universe that makes sense; it is the meaning of action. [...] Emotion extends itself into the world in the form of action, just as action extends itself into the subject in the form of emotion: a transductive series running from pure action to pure emotion. [...] Spirituality is the meeting point of these two slopes, action and emotion, that face each other as they rise to a single pinnacle.[241]

These two aspects, these 'slopes', also produce both faith and knowledge, and spirituality is what projects the motive of these tensions *as their pinnacle*, where, far from emotion and reason being opposed, they are transductively divided: *as participation in the processes of transindividuation*, the slope of action

> expresses spirituality insofar as it escapes the subject and institutes itself in an objective eternity, a monument more lasting than bronze, in language, institution, art, work. [The slope] of emotion expresses spirituality insofar as it penetrates the subject, floods back into the subject and fills him in an instant, making the symbolic relate back to itself, understanding itself in relation to what floods into it.[242]

It would obviously be necessary to relate all of this to Winnicott's 'transitional object' (and here it would be necessary to look as well at the work of Calder).

This *duel* between action and emotion can decompose into 'science and faith [which] are the debris of a spirituality that has failed and that divides the subject, opposing it to itself instead of leading it to discover meaning in the collective'.[243] Noetic emotion, as it affects the brain of a psychic individual, who is not merely a living thing, is an affect situated on a dyad where it circulates and moves itself as e-motion – traversing the psychic individual insofar as it is bipolarizing, precisely insofar as it is not merely a vital, living individual, and insofar as its organism is not merely organic but organological, and projecting into the collective individual where the tension that divides it is resolved through transindividual formation: work, language, remains, trace, or any tertiary retention whatsoever.

In this way, attentional forms are established, of which reason is the pinnacle. And I am not sure that Antonio Damasio poses this question correctly in his readings of Spinoza. This is also the problem with the claims made by Catherine Malabou, which on this point remain in *the shallows* of the question.

If all attention is of the order of an expectation (an *attente*), it is also of the order of an affect, and reason is a kind of affect running through all noetic affects and which they always aim at – positively or negatively, and as that which connects the dyads. Via criteria that provide a *libido sciendi* that elaborates, socially, rules enabling the idealizing of an object, and, as such, the creation of a sublime object attachment, reason produces itself at the summit – just like an actor produces himself onstage – through attentional forms that project and constitute processes of transindividuation founded on disciplines (on askeses), whereby the objects of reason can present themselves only by passing through a transindividual social formation, that is, a formation that is not merely cerebral.

Hence are produced *reason-able* beings. Now, a reasonable being is a very bad consumer – including that exceptional consumer, the 'trader', 'hooked' on the 'adrenaline rush' and as often as not on cocaine as well – if not including the head of the U.S. Federal Reserve himself. This is why the goal of Glimcher, as of neuromarketing, is to eliminate the différance that operates in the noetic brain as *dianoia*, through the fact that organic memory may become organological, and does so through differentiating and deferring those drive-based mechanisms that neuromarketing wants to understand as the 'emotions' lying behind consumer 'choices'.

And indeed, this is a point of view that does not concern only consumers: it is a matter, too, for neuroeconomics, of applying it to stock-market traders – where the goal is then to align the automatisms of financial robots with those of brains, *against* reason, which is also an emotion, but an emotion formed as attention, that is, cultivated, and that as such responds to a culture that it is a matter of short-circuiting and bypassing, so as to be able to install an automated society in which there is no longer any place for decision – a *perfectly rationalized* system, that is, one that is *totally irrational*, given that nothing is *less rational* than 'perfection'.

SIXTH LECTURE

On Automatisms and Posthumanism

We saw yesterday that for A. K. Pradeep, "from the moment you ask a question, you bias the response. *One must therefore avoid asking questions"*. This could be understood as a pharmacology of the question, and as a question of what pharmacology means. But for Pradeep, on the contrary, it suggests the futility of any question, the end of the question of the question, so to speak. Now, the question of the question is the first question for any philosophy, and philosophizing is first and foremost a matter of being able to distinguish between real questions and fake questions. In *What Makes Life Worth Living*, I tried to show why the 'question' of posthumanism *is not a question* – or at least, not a consistent philosophical question.

During the previous sessions, we tried to identify some new prospects and possibilities opened up by the neurosciences, and today this leads me to the question of the relationship between *autonomy, psycho-biological automatisms, technological automatisms and regression*. Ours is an age of widespread and general automation and automatization that is also a new step in the history of the noetic brain insofar as it is an organological brain, and hence, a pharmacological brain – for example, a brain capable of completely forgetting how to question. This context leads some to believe that we should refer to 'posthumanism': at the horizon of automatation we find projections of the figures of the Cyborg, the Golem, the Superman as an enhanced being, as instantiations of a transhumanist future – where biological automatisms and psychic automatisms are rearranged by and with technological automata in a completely new way.

These rearrangements indeed make it seem that the process of hominization that has taken place over the last two million years or so, and which we can understand as a process of exteriorization, has, if not turned *against* itself, at least turned *in* on itself: technology is less and less what exteriorizes itself; technology is, increasingly, that which is *interiorized*. Today, when we refer to 'enhancement', it is less a matter of adding supplementary organs to the human body than it is a question of modifying and transforming the organs that constitute the psychosomatic body, by techno-logically redesigning them from the inside, so as to make this 'interior' (formerly referred to as the soul) *compatible with control by robotic 'peripheral' devices*. This is currently being done, for example, to assist those suffering from hemiplegia, or Parkinson's disease, but here we are also talking about creating forms of *compatibility with systems designed to automatically control these souls themselves* – by submitting them to the kinds of *sociotechnical systems devoted to tracking and tracing* that are presently being installed everywhere via generalized digitalization.

All of this may be true. Nevertheless, to refer this to posthumanism or even transhumanism is to pass far too quickly over a prior question, which is that of the relation between autonomy and automatism, which is also to say, between autonomy and heteronomy. It is to dispense, in the name of humanism, with any reconsideration of the *heteronomic conditions* (the technical conditions) of autonomy. In fact, all this must be comprehensively revisited. And it is also to ignore the *questions, both economic and political,* that these heteronomic conditions insistently raise, at the very moment when generalized automation is clearly giving rise to a new age of heteronomy.

The relationship between autonomy and heteronomy should be understood, in general terms, not as an opposition but as a *composition* (in saying this, I am raising a theme that I discussed in terms of political economy in *The Decadence of Industrial Democracies*[244]). To fail to do so would be to posit the *inevitability* of a 'posthuman' fate, a fate in which autonomy, conceived thus as pure interiority, would be lost in the heteronomization in which the internalization of artificial organs, now becoming automata, would consist. In fact, however, *autonomy is always constituted specifically as the internalization of heteronomic artefactuality.*

The question of the posthuman attempts to raise the possibility that any possibility of questioning might be closed off forever. But aside from the fact that this question was already posed by Plato as the question of the *pharmakon,* and by Marx as the question of the proletariat, such a possibility is a possibility only insofar as it composes with *another* possibility, failing which it would not be a possibility at all but rather the *end* of *any* possibility – the result of which would be a *determinism* where nothing is possible other than its own auto-fulfilment.

There is another possibility, another alternative, which is that the age of generalized automation could constitute a *new age of autonomy,* the conception of which would derive from a redefinition of past, present and future autonomy, and as a *relation to heteronomy that composes with it in a therapeutic manner,* rather than in a toxic manner. If autonomy must be understood as the capacity to intensify the possibilities of individuation, and if, as I have long argued by relying on Simondon, psychic individuation is possible only on the condition that it contributes to and participates in collective individuation and technical individuation, then *technical heteronomy, far from being the opposite of individuating autonomy, on the contrary contributes to its development* (this constitutes the horizon of the 'free software' movement, the thought behind the work of André Gorz and the possibility of an economy of contribution).

Before arguing these points in more detail, I must return to the question of *post*humanism: the latter could be posited by, or impose itself upon, a way of thinking that can be called philosophical *only* if we accept that the question of *humanism* has been correctly posed. But I have myself always rejected the humanist way of questioning (which means: the *way of questioning* that posits that the question of philosophy is above all the question of man, of the human). My rejection is not quite the same as Heidegger's, who rejects it in the name of the *question of being*, so that the question of man becomes radically *secondary*; I reject it because it is an *obstacle* (for reasons that clearly intersect with those invoked by Heidegger from the side of the 'question of being') *to thinking the question of technics*, and more particularly, technics as the *inhuman* that continually, always and forever, *puts the human into question* (and puts in question the *question of man* itself).

Kant, to whom I always try to stay as close as possible – but there comes a point at which this is no longer possible, and this is the point at which I try to do my own philosophy – erected the question, 'What is man?', to the rank of philosophy. If he did so, it was because he was not himself able to pose the question of the schematism in the way required to provide what Derrida called a logic and a history of the *supplement*, that is, a thinking of iterability and *therefore of repetition* that *can grant* a difference, namely: as the projective possibility of a pharmacological field (and a schema is a projective apparatus) that brings the *best and the worst* (not the best or worst of human beings, it should be noted in passing).

Whatever may be the case for Kant, in *Sein und Zeit*, what Dasein poses is not the question of man, but rather the question of being through the existence of this being who can question being. And this being, this who, is Dasein rather than the human (and not just 'rather than the human', but 'before the human', 'earlier than the human'). The question of being: which is to say, the question of this privilege of Dasein insofar as, *in being the being who questions*, it can *inscribe a difference* between being and beings *in* being and *in* beings, a difference that is the time of being and the being of time as epokhality, that is, *Geschichtlichkeit*.

It is not because Heidegger rejects the question of the human (despite what the existential analytic seems to suggest – which will fool Sartre) that I myself dispute its philosophical necessity, but because, contrary to what Heidegger says, what makes this question *possible* (which is, furthermore, always also the question of the possible and of its 'conditions of impossibility', as Derrida liked to say), and what *puts in question* the human itself, and does so by showing that the question is *never just* that of the human, is *technics*. What I am talking about here, however, is no longer just the 'question concerning technology': it is technics, *not as a question that comes to the being who questions*, but *that puts this being into question* – it is the *condition* of *any* question, and in this respect I do not believe that Heidegger truly grasped the 'question concerning technology' in terms of the radicality of its 'questioning', even if what he called 'unconcealment' holds only on this condition. Heidegger was incapable of thinking this because he rejected the question of what I have proposed calling 'tertiary retention' in order to rethink what he himself called *Weltgeschichtlichkeit*.

I apologise for having to recall these questions that I raised at the end of *Technics and Time, 1*: I feel compelled to do so because they constitute the grounds on the basis of which I want to investigate our own age insofar as its automatic condition puts us into question – at the risk of interrupting all possibility of questioning.

What posthumanism lacks is the *primordial* question of proletarianization, that is, the question of a *primordial proletarianization* which is that of the *pharmakon*, and which is first formulated by Plato as the question of *hypomnesis*. *Hypomnesis* puts into question 'the being that we ourselves are' insofar as we are the being who questions: it is that which can always come to interrupt *anamnesis*, which is the name Socrates gives to what Heidegger calls questioning. I have argued that this interruption is a techno-logical *epokhē*, and that this *epokhē* always has two stages: the stage of *putting* into question, and the stage of the *formation* (*paideia, Bildung*) of this question as the constitution and transmission of a circuit of transindividuation through which is established the 'understanding that there-being (*Dasein*) has of its being', and which is the *perpetually forgotten condition of all positively constituted knowledge*.

Positively constituted knowledge is anamnesic, that is, autonomous: it finds its own law within itself, and does so as the *inaugural possibility of 'thinking for oneself'*. But if it arises from out of the heteronomic interruption by *hypomnesis*, and more generally from an artefactuality that puts it into question, then this anamnesic and autonomous knowledge finds its power in the ability to *turn a moment of disindividuation* (of interruption, of putting into question, of challenge) *into a promise of individuation*, a 'quantum leap in individuation', as Simondon said, and of doing so through the *adoption* of *techno-logical epokhal power* and its trans-formation into *psycho-social and socio-technical epokhal power*. We are challenged by technics, and technics is itself a process of individuation that both *supports and threatens* psychic and collective individuation, and that *supports it through that which threatens it*: technical individuation requires the psychic and social individuals that it threatens, and such is the primordial pharmacological situation.

Simondon taught us that the psychic individual can individuate itself only by contributing to a collective individuation. But the passage from the psychic to the collective, which engenders the transindividual, is possible only with the support of that hypomnesic milieu that is the *technical milieu associated with psychic and social individuals*. This associated milieu is composed of artificial organs, and the threefold process of individuation that constitutes the becoming of the pharmacological beings that we try to be by becoming what we are (by individuating ourselves) must be conceived on the basis of a *general organology* – where the three strands of the individuation of technical life (always simultaneously arranging the three processes of psychic, collective and technical individuation) are its *three inseparable organological modalities*: psycho-somatic organs, artificial organs and social organizations.

▪ ▪ ▪

These days it is tempting to get caught up in the question of 'posthumanism' because the artefactual sphere that is constituted by technical individuation does tend to operate as a *process of total automation*, reflected in the figure of the robot. The stage of total automation is the most recent stage of the ongoing process of grammatization, that is, of the discretization and technical reproduction of human fluxes and flows – of which writing (Plato's *pharmakon*) is one stage, the machine tool is another stage (one founded on Vaucanson's automata), and where the digital extends this to every sphere of existence, in all human societies that currently subsist – the question being to know if societies in the sense of collective individuation processes can survive such a process of automation.

The question that the 'question' of posthumanism avoids is that of the politico-economic *choices* that are opened up in the epoch of automated man, that is, in the age where the human being lives in an *automatically administered society*. Such a question, which presupposes a new critique of political economy, for which I have previously argued at both Cambridge and Goldsmiths, must firstly and profoundly revisit the question of the relation of life to automatism in all its dimensions, and in particular in the so-called 'human' field insofar as this is inclusive of technological automatisms, psychic automatisms and biological automatisms – whereas in the animal field automatism presents itself spontaneously as instinct.

Automatism repeats. And if it is true that technical life is no longer governed by instincts but by drives, then to think automatic repetition we must refer to Freud's discoveries in 1920, discoveries which, passing through Kierkegaard and Nietzsche, constituted the ground of Deleuze's meditation on the relationship between difference and repetition, where the automatism of repetition (or repetition as the condition of possibility of all automatism) is presented essentially as a pharmacological question (Deleuze would prefer to say 'problem'), for

> if *we die of repetition we are also saved and healed by it* – healed, above all, by the other repetition. *The whole mystical game of loss and salvation* is therefore contained in repetition, along with the whole *theatrical game of life and death* and the whole *positive game of illness and health*.[245]

That what Deleuze sees as repetition is capable of producing a difference (that is, an individuation) but also a baseness (which occurs when we disindividuate), however, means that this repetition *presupposes technical exteriorization*, that is, grammatization as the *possibility of a repetition that is neither biological nor psychic, via the hypomnesic and pharmacological support* of repetition that grants a difference, that is, an individuation (and a différance) as well as a baseness, that is, an indifference and a disindividuation (in what Simondon and Deleuze also describe as an 'interindividuality', whereby the transindividual *loses meaning*, being no longer a *preindividual potential for individuation* but merely a formal signification through which the group *regresses* and falls into baseness).

In the nineteenth century, grammatization, which is the *technical history of the repetition of discretized mental and behavioural flows* (flows that are in this sense grammatized), or in other words the history of the *technical power of repetition*, leads to automation, as it was described by Marx in the *Grundrisse*, and this constitutes a *turning point in the history of repetition* – given that today, *in industrial capitalism, economic development will occur only on the condition of putting 'bad repetition' to work* – by implementing the kinds of repetition *that result in baseness and indifference*.

This is the historical background, constituted by man qua technician, that leads him to produce robots, manmade creatures ('beings' created by man and *endowed with autonomy*), creations of the human technician who might therefore produce what in *Blade Runner* were called replicants – but which were already suggested to thinking by the Golem of the Talmud, Sefer Yetzirah and Yehudah Leib. The robot, as the *industrial realization of the Golem*, amounts to an exit from the human being of the history of hominization. That is, it is an exit from life insofar as it is characterized by its technicization as a process of exteriorization enabling the putting in question of the questioned and questioning being thanks to the very fact that it *exteriorizes itself – to be put outside oneself either makes you furious* (in English, as in French, to be 'beside oneself' is above all to be furious, to lose composure, *to lose control,* to *give in,* if not to the instincts, then at least *to the drives*) *or makes you dependent,* alienated, subjected and disindividuated.

In our own epoch, this exteriorization leads to what proves to be a process of *internalization* rather than *externalization,* a process sometimes described as the convergence of nanotechnology, biotechnology, information technology and cognitive science (NBIC). It is justifiable to argue that if this situation does not insert us into the question of posthumanism, then we are nevertheless indeed confronted with the question of a turning point, of a *radical change of trajectory* in that process which, across two million years, will have constituted 'technical life' in Canguilhem's sense – a turn the result of which will be a *new epoch of life.*

Life has had many epochs: the epoch of bacteria, of archaea, of protists and other single-celled eukaryotes, right up to the aggregations of cells and organs that we are ourselves – ourselves, that is, these multicellular beings who cannot do without non-living organs, artefacts, prostheses and eventually, today, automata. As I prepared for this lecture, for example, I searched among the masses of tertiary retentions (which are mnemotechnical traces) that we (living technicians) have produced for two million years (and organized in the form of knowledge), in order to find out about archaea, using Google and then Wikipedia, the latter being a collaborative site, although what we usually forget is that this is also highly reliant on so-called 'bots', which is an abbreviation for 'robots' when by the latter we mean logical and algorithmic automatons that are 'mainly used to perform repetitive tasks that automation allows to be performed at high speed' (French Wikipedia).

The *differentiation of the living* unfolds from the parthenogenesis of single-celled organisms right up to the higher vertebrates such as ourselves, endowed with both an endoskeleton *and* an exoskeleton, and surrounded by the exo-organisms and organizations that are human societies producing a collective individuation founded on artificial organs, and passing along the way through the sexuation of multicellular bodies lacking a nervous system such as plants, through invertebrate animals protected by an exoskeleton such as the snail, the crab, the insect and so on. *Today,* long after technical organs first appeared, this differentiation of the living has led to the *automatic differentiation of the nonliving,* the production of organs and organizations where the difference between organic and inorganic is blurred in becoming industrial – at the cost of an indifferentiation of life (that is, its decline), a loss of biodiversity as much as of 'cultural diversity'.

At each step of this history of the *struggle of negentropy against the entropy that results from its becoming technical* – and it is perhaps precisely this that defines the 'pharmacological', in other words, to have, in a Janus-like way, one face that is negentropic and another that is entropic – *each epoch of life implements new conditions of automatic repetition in which differences are produced,* differences that we generally relate to forms of autonomy, of the *psukhē* defined by Aristotle as having three types, and as self-movement in autopoiesis in the theory of enaction, and passing through thinking as dialogue with oneself according to Plato, or the conquest of majority (maturity, *Mündigkeit*) in the Kantian sense.[246]

But in order to understand what we are, and on the way to which we will have been underway for at least two million years, or four million if we believe Leroi-Gourhan, and to understand it *correctly,* all this must be thought with the concepts of mineral, vital and psychosocial individuation.

Psychosocial individuation is the *second epoch of automatism* (there is no mineral automatism, and this is why Canguilhem can claim that there are no mineral monsters: when life reproduces itself, it repeats life in an automatic way, but within vital reproduction there can be deviations that we can call monstrous insofar as they do not automatically repeat the schema of the organic form that is reproducing itself – and this is what cannot happen to a crystal). The advent of psychosocial individuation, however, will in turn eventually lead to a generalized industrial automatization founded on automation such as it began in the nineteenth century with that fact described by Andrew Ure (and cited by Marx) as a 'vast automaton'.[247]

A *new epoch of psychic and collective individuation* thus emerges, which would which would take us into a process that would perhaps not be posthuman – because humanism, as the question of knowing what humanity is, is not a true question, if it is true that man is the one who individuates himself with technics such that he constantly *becomes other* and such that the human adopts the inhuman or else *becomes inhuman from not adopting the inhuman* and from *adapting himself instead of individuating himself,* that is, from a failure to think the inhuman and to 'concretize' this thought – but rather an *inversion of exteriorization, where it becomes interiorization* such that this technical internalization seems to induce a psychic dis-interiorization.

There is no exteriorization without interiorization – except in the case of proletarianization, the precise goal of which is to submit the proletarianized to an exteriorization of its knowledge without the need for re-internalizing what has been exteriorized. Today the evidence of neuroscience opens new vistas in relation to these questions. When we see how neuroeconomics 'applies' this evidence, we can better grasp how significant are the stakes of what I believe we should describe as the age of generalized automatization.

SEVENTH LECTURE

Automation and Automatisms

Generalized automatization is what leads to the industrial development of a kind of robotics that constitutes, through 'ambient computing', a *robotized living space*, which means that there is gradually *less and less left for me to do* (I no longer need to open doors, order groceries and so on), and means that I gradually lose all my *savoir faire* and *savoir vivre*, my knowledge of how to do things and how to live. Such an ambient computing, which then also involves the question of smart cities, domotics, private and public spaces, and so on, and, ultimately, total automation, amounts to a new stage of exosomatization, which becomes exospheric, and concretizes Heidegger's understanding of *Gestell*. Here, our question becomes: how should we deal and compose with these new automata – in order to be able to reach something like this *Ereignis* about which Heidegger tells us?

In order to introduce these issues – which are also addressed in my seminar at the China Academy of Arts in Hangzhou with my friends Lu Xinghua, Yuk Hui and Dan Ross – today I would like to look at those 'bots' to which I referred earlier by citing the Wikipedia entry devoted to them, and where on Wikipedia itself, for example, such bots format the work of contributors – contributors like you and I who, when we do not content ourselves with reading entries, sometimes correct them, or even create them. Here, a certain amount of individual and collective autonomy is made possible by a technological and automatic heteronomy: I'll come back to this.

Wikipedia is a *space of transindividuation assisted by logical and linguistic automata*, a space that shows how an *automated transindividuation can serve an autonomized transindividuation*, if I may put it like that – autonomized transindividuation designating, then, what used to be called sovereignty. Bots, however, presuppose an ensemble of apparatus to track and produce metadata, also involving RFID systems and an infrastructure of generalized automatization that should be described in detail, all this amounting to what Christian Fauré entitled the 'transfer industry', which is on the way to changing the face of the human world.

All this, which also involves the so-called Internet of Things, machine-to-machine or device-to-device communication, all this, which is still little known and largely underestimated, constitutes the industrial infrastructure of a new apparatus of reading and writing, not only between human beings but also between, on the one hand, robots and automated apparatus, and, on the other, humans, which communicate between one another via these bots and automata. This is what makes it possible to 'scan' groups with these data-analysis technologies, along with deep learning and machine learning, which together form these automata, and through which it becomes possible to anticipate and create behaviour – for example, with those user-profiling systems that everyone now knows about, with performative effects in real time as big data processes billions of simultaneous and correlated feedback loops all across the Earth.

One of the issues here is to know how all this is articulated with psychic automatisms via the technologies emerging from neuromarketing.

Without bots, Wikipedia would not work properly, and these bots in turn can themselves function only via the contribution of psychic individuals and collective individuals who through this process develop (or at least some of them do) forms of knowledge, that is, perspectives on the autonomous world. Perhaps this foreshadows *new forms of knowledge* – those that should form the heart of digital studies, that is, of the organological study of the knowledge and thought of man in the *epoch of digital tertiary retention*, studies that should not ignore scholars and contributors who come from a much wider sphere than just those connected to so-called 'ubiquitous human computing', the latter consisting in making people do *computer-based piece work and exploiting them through a process of decentralized proletarianization in what amount to networked factories*, where they perform tasks that are highly automated, and which require *psychic*, and not just technological, automatisms.

Here the outlines of an *alternative* begin to appear. In automatic society, technological automatisms can be made to serve:

- either, an elevation and a transformation of psychic automatisms in a new age of the *libido sciendi* and more generally of the idealization and sublimation processes that are always potentially entailed by any process of formalization;

- or, a regressive exploitation of those psychic automatisms that are the drives and archaic behaviours concealed within the so-called 'reptilian brain', which technological automatisms, under the guidance of neuromarketing and neuroeconomics, are able to solicit by bypassing and short-circuiting the cortical zones dedicated to the internalization of knowledge, that is, to the constitution of capacities founded on anamnesic processes of adoption of the hypomnesic possibilities proper to any particular stage of grammatization.

Such would be the stakes of what we could call a philosophy of light-time, of its shadows [*ombres*] and its numbers [*nombres*], where automatization is on the dark side of the numerical inasmuch as it is a new 'age of Enlightenment' – where automation, as a social and scholarly project as much as an industrial project, would lead to a complete renegotiation of the question of work, and where the delegation to automata of those tasks hitherto constituting 'employment' (or jobs) is completely rethought. Within such a project, those automatisms that are realized concretely by robots would still make possible the delegation of functions that were previously performed by human beings, but only on the basis of a complete rethinking of the social project – and where the acquisition and formation of new forms of knowledge and new capabilities (in Amartya Sen's sense of this term) becomes the main way that work is 'remunerated', such work being no longer just a job. Here we would need to devote time to examining the proposals of André Gorz and Oskar Negt, but unfortunately there isn't time to do so now.

We cannot investigate any deeper into these questions without asking what it is *in* these various automatisms – and there are *automatisms of exteriorization* (technological automatisms) and *automatisms of interiorization* (psychic automatisms) – that means that *processes of internalizing technological automatisms (deriving from exteriorization) can produce psychic and technical automatisms of a singular type in relation to purely machine-based or drive-based automatisms.*

Automatism or automata in Vaucanson's sense, automata as a technical object endowed with relatively autonomous movement (we may refer, in temporal terms, to the autonomy that the battery, for example, gives to the computer: my own device, for instance, has twelve hours of battery life), allow the reproduction of one or more operational sequences, that is, one or many movements, and it is this that can take the place of a temporal sequence of human movements. In addition to the techno-logical automatism that currently pervades the world in all its dimensions, there is an *automatism of the drives*. In this case, automatism presents itself as symptomatic automatic behaviour and more generally as psycho-somatic phenomena. Something moves me, affects me, and I blush, or I blanch, I turn red or I turn white: these are automatisms of my body; or again, anxiety causes obsessional automatic behaviour (which in the id forms a compromise between consciousness and the unconscious, the id being a space of automatisms deriving from both consciousness and the unconscious, the whole issue of the id lying here, according to Freud himself). My obsessional and as such automatic behaviour indicates to everyone who sees it – except to myself – that something is not right: such behaviour allows me to hide *from myself* that something is wrong, to repress it, preventing me from expressing it to myself while still letting me express myself, but in the form of automatisms, that is, by default and without seeing it, 'unconsciously'.

Such automatisms of the unconscious and the id, which are not those of the drives but defence mechanisms against drive-based automatisms, are pathological in the sense that they produce a *pathos*, an emotion, an alteration that represses what I call a traumatype, and that engenders very specific stereotypes – memory being constituted from retentions that are themselves organized by *synchronizing* stereotypes that contain *diachronizing* traumatypes: the stereotypes of neurotics do in certain situations mean that they constantly repeat the same behaviours – and here we are brought back to Deleuze, who explored beyond the pleasure principle – because they contain a traumatype that they thus prevent from manifesting itself, that is, in an autonomous way.

To develop this point, it would be necessary to pass through Derrida's *Archive Fever* (*Mal d'archive*), where he refers to an *'archive drive'*,[248] that is, a drive to exteriorize: a *hypomnesic drive* producing what I call tertiary retentions. I believe that this Derridian discourse on the relations between the drive and the archive (relations that constitute the crux of both technological and psychological automatisms) is, however, ill-founded: *Mal d'archive* interprets badly, gives a *mal*-interpretation, of those archives that are the Freudian oeuvre. Derrida's *Archive Fever* is in many ways an extraordinary book, reopening the question first opened in 1962 with Derrida's introduction to Husserl's 'The Origin of Geometry', and continued in 1966 with 'Freud and the Scene of Writing', in 1967 with *Speech and Phenomena* and then with *Of Grammatology*. *Archive Fever* reopens the whole question of *hypomnesis* that is not formulated as such, under this name, and as the question of the *pharmakon*, until 1972, in 'Plato's Pharmacy' (in *Dissemination*). *Archive Fever* is the first true Derridian product of the history of the supplement that he promised in *Of Grammatology*. In a way, this work constitutes the psychoanalytic and Freudian prolegomena to a true history of the supplement, where Derrida asks in a long preface what would have become of Freud in an epoch where mail circulates at the speed of light, and what would have become of psychoanalysis.

By questioning along these lines, Derrida gives great weight to tertiary retention – and this is what I myself am trying to do: this leads him to say that the *psychic apparatus is trans-formed by tertiary retention*. In saying this, Derrida, who, twenty-five years ago, is already writing about the consequences of *digital and industrial tertiary retention*, is extremely clear-sighted. He sees in the distance the coming of those elements that will put us in question, will challenge and confront us in the pharmacology of the question presupposed by this challenge – by the *technology of the question* – and in relation to which he tries to create an anamnesic return of this putting in question through the hypomnesic return begun in 1962, and formulated as such in 1972, this return being a kind of anamnesis in 1995 of his own journey (which also happens to be the year that Deleuze committed suicide).

Here we should consider two points that due to time constraints I will simply mention and leave them aside for another time:

- on the one hand, the pharmacological question and challenge of and by the archive drive, that is, the drive to exteriorize, necessarily passes through Nietzsche and through his *will to power*;
- on the other hand, the archive *as exteriorization* is what puts into question Derrida's way of posing the question of this archive drive, that is, the way in which he *relates it to the death drive* – not that I disagree that we should relate the archive drive (if we want to keep this formulation) to the death drive (in fact, I agree that we must relate it to the death drive), but because *Derrida does not conceive the death drive correctly*: he posits that the death drive is *opposed to the pleasure principle*, which is an astonishing *counter-reading of the Freudian archive* and of the Freudian question of the archive such as it constitutes *noetic life as archivization*, that is, as *technical life*.

Whatever its forms, life, which is defined by its reproductive capacity, in some way auto-archives itself, either under the pressure of Darwinian biological evolution, or from an evolution of techno-logical forms of the archive itself as what is exteriorized, deposited or sedimented, forming a technical milieu that is the condition of noetic life. The relation of archivization to technical life is an essential effect of the technicization of the life that is the noetic soul. To think in this way is to think the *birth of desire as the capacity for projection and exteriorization, for the ex-pression and im-pression of the soul* as the *arrangement of automatisms and autonomies, desire being what transforms drive-based automatisms*, themselves being *trans-formations of instincts into drives via the technical exteriorization of life* founded on these *detachable organs* that are the *technical objects that archivize this life* and that are the *condition of constitution of what Freud understood as the fetish.*

Derrida opposes the death drive to the pleasure principle even though Freud says specifically that the repetition compulsion means that the question of *libido* is displaced from being just a question of pleasure (of discharge): the drive is anarchic, and as such an-archivistic, and the question of libido is that of the transformation of the drive as automatic into the autonomy of desire founded on the *composition* of the death drive with the drive-based, automatic counter-tendency that is the life drive, as the *drive of vital reproduction. Desire* is thus *what arranges technical reproduction and vital reproduction* as *two automatisms the composition of which is autonomous.*

The automatic process that is life and, in particular, sexuated life endowed with a nervous system and a neocortex – unlike snails or slugs – leads through a transformation of these automatisms into a conquest of autonomy. It leads, in other words, to a leap into what Simondon called psychic and collective individuation. In the context in which I am attempting to rethink the question of autonomy, which is also the question of automatization characteristic of contemporary society, what hangs over the whole thing is the hypertoxic reality of the *automated superego*, that is, the *dis-internalization of the law* as a foundation itself automatic (a law applies itself as a necessity and to everyone, even if it is also true that, interpreted by a judge or jury of citizens, it continuously *puts back into question* and trans-forms its automaticity through jurisprudence, which is a process of dis-automatization).

Today, automatization has reached very deep levels where neuronal automatisms – that is, the biological foundations of the drives – are arranged with the industrial automatisms that emerge from the process of grammatization, of (technical and mechanical) reproducibility, of formalization and of the digital treatment in which archivization in light-time consists, short-circuiting the anamnesic circuits acquired through *paideia* and *situated* in the neocortex. These industrial automatisms systematically solicit the archaic neuronal automatisms of the 'reptilian brain', and establish, as a permanent threat, an automatization in the service of the autonomization *of technics*, such as Friedrich Kittler has long anticipated, rather than in the service of noetic autonomy. Such an automatization attempts to subject noetic souls to an adaptive process short-circuiting the process of adoption in which the internalization of the superego consists. This is what, taking up an expression from Marcuse, I call the automatization of the superego.

In *Beyond the Pleasure Principle*, Freud attempted to think, from 1920 onwards, both the automatic status of the drives insofar as they contradict each other, and the way in which this contradiction elevates them and synthesizes them into a dialogic of desire and libido that causes them to move from the *an-archive of the drives* to the *archive of libido* by *propping themselves up* not just on the drives, but on this *constitutive crutch of the psychic apparatus* that is the archive insofar as *tertiary retention enables a transformation of the drive into an object investment*. This archive that is tertiary retention, however, as the possibility of transforming the drive into object investment, appears in Freud long before he thinks the drive as such: first in 1895, and then in his theory of sexuality, at the point when he becomes interested in fetishism. The question of the fetish is that of tertiary retention which, as a *proto-thinking of what will later be called the transitional object*, is an *exteriorization of the drive* such that, finding itself between two beings who are themselves drive-based, it enables them to *share the exteriorization of their drives*, which, since they are shared, means that this is also a *diversion* of the *aim* of these drives – and this diversion (this différance) *constitutes* the desire of those who share this object, which is then no longer merely a fetish, but, precisely, a transitional object. What plays out between the mother and her child in Winnicott also plays out, in Freud, between the Jews in the epoch of *Moses and Monotheism*, but Freud does not himself explicitly think this play.

Autonomy in relation to the drives does not mean ridding oneself of the drives, but rather transforming them into an energy that submits to a master that is also a 'metre', a *metron*, a measure that is desire, but the subject of desire is not master of its desire: its measure [*mesure*] is its excess [*démesure*]. This is the figure of an *amour fou* that becomes *social* and that, through a drive *of archivizing and of death*, will subdue its impulses and so tame them that it results in a submission (or even a destruction by the return of the repressed), when the moment occurs that a psychic automatism can be sublimated into an investment in a technical, hypomnesic, technological automatism – for example, in the form of science. This process of *binding through archivization* produces a *heteronomic autonomy*, dependence, as investment in a singular object on the basis of which and around which there occurs a process of psychic and collective individuation – and through which the amorous kernel produced by co-individuation becomes transindividuation.

I took this long detour so as finally to arrive at the question of whether there is a *politics of automation* capable of creating a new age of autonomy. This is possible only on the condition of revisiting the question of the *libido sciendi* that constitutes the foundation of what is not just an archive drive, but a *care* taken of this drive, a maintenance of this archive and of that which, in this drive, which is therefore archived and has thus become knowledge, exceeds the drive while containing it.

▪ ▪ ▪

What is the digital, if not a form of writing? The digital is writing that can be inscribed and 'read' by automata – 'scanned', as one says – at close to the speed of light: it is an *essentially automatic* writing (and reading), in relation to which we should ask what it would have meant not just for psychoanalysis, but also for surrealism, if the soul of André Breton (his psychic apparatus) had been supported by a *digital brain*: by a digitalized cerebral organ. I pose this question in order to state in conclusion the heart of my argument, namely that the *noetic brain*, the central organ of the psychosomatic noetic body, is essentially the *organ capable of acquiring automatisms and of gaining something like autonomy*, which in Plato is called *anamnesis*, the latter constituting the capacity to think for oneself, not in the sense that I would know the origin of knowledge, but in the sense that *I only ever know by going back over, each time, the origin of all the knowledge that has always already preceded me* – just as Dasein is always already preceded by its past.

These techno-logical automatisms are acquired only through a *paideia* that can itself become a conquest of autonomy *only through the automatization of mind or spirit that operates through being literalized* (in Plato's case) or digitalized (in our case) and (if we can say this) analog-ized (in Freud's case, by the telephone, the phonograph, cinema, by a whole spread of psychic trans-formations, and I am close here to the sense of spiritualism, in the sense according to which to be *psychic*, in English, means to be affected by a *spirit*: without all this, all these revenances, could the Viennese neurotic *and his or her guilt* have arisen?). But all these automatisms that are the *pharmacological condition of autonomy* can equally become that which inter-dicts all autonomy. They can be what interferes with autonomy, or intrudes into it, speaking through an automatism and saying what might have been said by an alleged autonomy, which then seems to be only the ventriloquism of and by this psycho-social automatism that Heidegger clearly tried to think as *das Man* – before himself descending into it just five years later, in his fascination with the neo-pseudo-Germano-Romantic marionettes of this cave that *Mittel Europa* becomes – passing through Babelsberg, Leni Riefenstahl and the damned wife of Fritz Lang, staying behind when he was forced to leave his country in order to keep animating these marionettes, these automated hopes that are movie characters, but on another stage, and in the service of a new consciousness (that of the thousand eyes of Doctor Mabuse), while Marcuse, like Adorno and Horkheimer before him, will find a new automated horror in the culture industries and television, discovering that they produce an automatic superego, that is, action without the necessity of being internalized by the psychic apparatus.

These questions, which are still not grasped well and little explored as such, and for which neuropsychology supplies new concepts, are the great questions of the twenty-first century. I have tried to provide a kind of image of them in what in the first volume of *Symbolic Misery* I referred to as the digital anthill. Examining this anthill requires new research methods and cooperation between the disciplines of general organology, which is also a pharmacology, and what I now call an exorganology – which studies the evolution of simple, complex and hyper-complex exorganisms.

EIGHTH LECTURE

The Future of Neurotechnology

Let's try to conclude this course. The augmentation and enhancement of the human brain – undertaken by arranging so-called neurotechnological prosthetic pathways, such as cerebral implants, in combination with neurochemical pathways, so as to optimize neural performance and conceived in direct relation to these additional units – is a *new stage* in the history of human life and of the *organological augmentation and transformation* that has, ever since the beginning of hominization, occurred *continuously.*

Hominization is the pursuit of the organogenesis that is life in general. It is organogenesis at the ontogenetic level as well as at the phylogenetic level – these two levels together constituting the endosomatic. Hominization is the continuation of organogenesis but in an exosomatic way. As with many human organs, the brain has always organologically 'augmented' and transformed itself: this self-transformation is precisely what characterizes human life inasmuch as it is also and immediately technical life, that is, a form of life that realizes its dreams. Leonardo da Vinci, for example, had a dream in the fifteenth century that Clément Ader realized in the late nineteenth century.[249] But unlike other organs, the brain can be enhanced through internal processes of disorganization (that is, defunctionalizations) and reorganization (refunctionalizations) that occur in accordance with external organs. This is what Maryanne Wolf claims in *Proust and the Squid,* where she shows that the reading brain is transformed by learning how to read and write. These disorganizations and reorganizations correspond to what Freud described as defunctionalizations and refunctionalizations of the sensorimotor system. And we now know that these transformations are based on what Stanislas Dehaene has described as neuronal recycling.

What is really new about this organological transformation, this *endosomatization of the exosomatic* – which consists in this addition of units, that is, prostheses conceived and fabricated *exosomatically* but endosomatically *implanted,* just as are those prostheses added to the heart or to the ears – lies in the fact that *it is now tertiary memory,* that is, technical artefacts (which shape and materialize *knowledge,* that is, *memory and spatialized time,* produced in an industrial and standardized way), that are beginning to be *introduced into the organ of psychic memory that is the brain.*

Hence is heralded the arrival and the realization of the neuroindustry – some of whose issues were anticipated in *The Final Cut* (2004), as Patricia Pisters has shown in her analysis of the film.[250] The neuroindustry opens up the more general question of the *management of exosomatization according to the selection criteria of the market*, where exosomatization is in general terms what characterizes the technical form of life that appears with and as hominization.

Transhumanist 'storytelling'[251] is the attempt to legitimate the subordination of such a selection to the criteria of the market. This necessarily and exclusively computational criteriology, however, is absolutely illegitimate, for reasons that are not ethical but systemic: it leads inevitably to an increase of entropy. Entropy as irreversible dissipation of energy is the law of the universe that Rudolf Clausius exposed to view in 1865. Now, life is that which defers entropy, as was shown by Schrödinger in 1944 in *What is Life?* With that in mind, a critique of the transhumanist project as subordinating exosomatic becoming to market criteria, and as radicalizing what we are now calling disruption, must start from an analysis of the process of exosomatization such as that undertaken by Nicholas Georgescu-Roegen from the point of view of bio-economics, which is more relevant today than ever before. And what Georgescu-Roegen shows is that bio-economics must take account of the exosomatic situation of the human, as a being producing an increase of both entropic and negentropic potentials for life.

No serious reflection on the stakes of transhumanism, of which cerebral rearrangement is obviously one highly specific and exemplary aspect, and on the pharmacology that all this constitutes, can be conducted without investigating organogenesis. Organogenesis characterizes the history of life in general, but, later, with the appearance of the technical form of life, that is, of what Aristotle called the noetic soul, it becomes above all exosomatic. The noetic soul is the soul that is capable of thinking. Thinking is noesis. The exosomatic soul is noetic because it must perpetually decide how to play with and use the exosomatic organs it produces insofar as they are always pharmacological, artificial organs that are always both remedies and poisons. The exosomatic soul raises the question of the organo-logical and pharmaco-logical condition of noesis, and of the form of life to which it corresponds, but also of the *function of noesis* in life, and, faced with the disruptive transformations currently underway, the question of the future of noesis itself.

Noesis is a specific case of the negentropic process that is life in general, and it is so inasmuch as it constitutes, in its inseparable relation to exosomatization, a neganthropology that is constantly confronting the ambiguous character of exosomatic artificial organs, the latter being, as *pharmaka*, organs that make possible both the production of new neganthropic forms and a massive increase in the rate of entropy. At the moment, it is this second alternative that predominates, specifically in terms of the threat to biodiversity, but where, today, another issue looms equally large, in particular with respect to neurotechnology: the question of the threat to noodiversity.

It is firstly by asking how neganthropology has unfolded since the beginning of exosomatization, about how it has been able to struggle against the 'entropology' evoked by Lévi-Strauss at the end of *Tristes Tropiques,*[252] and by inquiring about its stages – from the purely epiphylogenetic stage that I attempted to described in *Technics and Time, 1,* passing through the primary hypomnesic stage that begins in the Upper Palaeolithic, then the various epochs of hypomnesis, up until the most recent stage of grammatization referred to as NBIC (nano-bio-info-cogno) – it is by asking how all this has either allowed or prevented neganthropological production (that is, inscription) within the entropic becoming of the cosmos, a sequence of bifurcations constituting and opening a neganthropological future, that we can rationally and reasonably investigate the issues, politics and economics of the neuroindustry.

The question of neuroindustrial reason is also and firstly that of the justice of cerebral becoming, and *in* cerebral becoming – where justice is never a question of human rights in the degraded sense in which this phrase has become entangled in the twentieth century, but, rather, the stakes and the challenge of the *coherence of reason*.

This coherence of reason, moreover, conditions *economic rationality*, and, therefore, the reason of the new critique of political economy required by the *highly entropic state installed in the Anthropocene qua process of generalized proletarianziation*, which has led to the entropic explosion that now threatens biodiversity in general, including the human species, but therefore also threatens noodiversity, as the condition of noesis that is in turn the condition of any neganthropological bifurcation.

From other perspectives – linked to the process of full and generalized automation that I describe in *Automatic Society* – I have tried to show why and how we must now enter into an economy that systematically and systemically values negentropy, which amounts to the prospect of what I call the Neganthropocene, wherein the future lies in de-proletarianization as that which is made possible by a contributory economy.

It is starting from these general reflections that I will make the preliminary assertion that any neuropolitics and neuroindustry must be dedicated to *maximally enhancing the conditions of rationality* inasmuch as they are evidently conditioned to a fundamental degree by a *widely distributed* cerebral organology – that is, inasmuch as they are conditioned *by the relations between noetic brains* and the exosomatic systems that support them, therein forming social organizations, which govern the relations between psycho-somatic organs and artificial organs – all these transductive supports constituting the objects of general organology inasmuch as the latter names an approach to transdisciplinary research.

Behind such questions, there of course lies an astonishing renovation of the political question as such, in relation to which:

1. we must intensify the neganthropological potentials of each noetic individual so as to enrich noodiversity;
2. we must cultivate this noodiversity through social diversity, that is, a sociodiversity that takes care of its noetic heritage – its languages, archives, works, knowledge and noetic exteriorities in general;
3. we must therefore struggle against the extreme violence within which the massively entropic becoming provoked by the Anthropocene – that is, by generalized proletarianization – encloses us, and which, in the short term, can only explode, unless there is a resolute bifurcation in the direction of the Neganthropocene, these being the real stakes involved in what Heidegger referred to as the *Kehre, Gestell* and *Ereignis.*

All these analyses, which I am introducing here in view of a *global geopolitical alternative to transhumanist marketing,* build upon the work of Maryanne Wolf, as well as on the questions that I have addressed to Jean-Pierre Changeux about his book, *Neuronal Man,*[253] in my preface to the French edition of *Proust and the Squid,*[254] and upon my critique of Allen Buchanan's theory of the augmented human in *Better than Human,*[255] which I presented six years ago at Berkeley.[256]

▪ ▪ ▪

What is quite sure is that a new process of psychic and collective individuation (in the sense given to this expression by Gilbert Simondon) will be constituted through this new stage of exosomatization, characterized as it is by *a second endosomatization.*

This amounts to the industrial production of new forms of technical life, organological and pharmacological forms whose unprecedented character resides in the fact that they are *bio-computational* and therefore *secondarily endosomatized* – a standardized endosomatization that can *replace* the noetic interiorization of exteriorized knowledge with mnemotechniques like reading and writing or mental calculation, mnemotechniques and artificial forms of memory which are that in which all exosomatic organology consists, forming what archaeologists call material cultures.

It is a question of knowing if, behind this process or these processes of psychic and collective individuation, as they have arisen through the successive and parallel eras and epochs of humanity – diversely localized and temporalized through the noetic process of what Derrida called différance, and as the 'history of the supplement' – it is strictly speaking a new *regime* of individuation that is appearing, or merely one or more new *processes* of psychic and collective individuation.

If the former were to prove the case, if the new process or processes of psychic and collective individuation made possible by neuroindustry do contain the seeds of a new regime of individuation, then, by concretizing itself as a *mega-bifurcation* over and above the bifurcations through which new processes of psychic and collective individuation become possible, this would add a *fourth possibility* to the three regimes of individuation described by Simondon: the physical individuation of entropic becoming, embodied in the crystal; the vital individuation of the living operating through negentropic organogenesis; and the psychic and social individuation that occurs in anthropological exosomatization.

If that were the case, and it *probably is* the case, this would raise the question of the *wide diversity* of arrangements that can be imagined and that constitute *diverse new types of noo-organisms*, and of *mega-noo-organsisms*, which might take on a wide variety of forms, from the digital anthill I described in 2004 in *Symbolic Misery*[257] (three years before the appearance of the digital network that would concretize this hypothesis[258]) to new types of aggregations, more organically and organologically integrated (of which technological monsters in the style of *The Terminator* style (1984) the 'cyborgian' hypotheses), proliferating meta-noo-organisms of limited size: one can imagine anything.

Such imagination must always be the result of a noetic dream, that is, a dream that is realizable according to the conditions of sufficient rationality, but also according to relations of force that are political, economic and ecological, thanks to which it may always turn into a nightmare, which we understand now more clearly than ever before.

This must be imagined, precisely so that the new stage of exosomatization, leading to a second, industrial endosomatization, may also lead to the diverse proliferation of new territorialized forms, diversifications not just linguistic, religious, architectural, culinary, anthropophysical and so on, but locally reticulated and organized via new organological arrangements. All these will fall within a *fourth regime of individuation*, which will constitute *new forms of the noetic social body*, widely territorialized but not necessarily in a sedentary mode, given that there are also nomadic forms of territorial organization, which may proliferate within larger territorialized organisms, often to their benefit – such is the case, for example, within our intestines, which play host to more than a kilogram of bacteria, and without which we could not assimilate the food necessary for survival.

It is therefore necessary to constitute an eco-neuro-geopolitics focused on the emergence of a new noesis, and to do so from the perspective *not* of the struggle for life, that is, for subsistence, which characterizes vital individuation, *nor* just the struggle for existence, which characterizes psychic and collective individuation, but, rather, from the perspective of the *struggle for consistence after the exhaustion of existences deprived, precisely, of consistence, by the fulfilment of nihilism*, as Nietzsche foreshadowed and of which what we are calling disruption is the concretization, as the final stage of the Anthropocene before the great 'shift'[259] that must lead either to the Neganthropocene or to the disappearance of noesis – along with the sixth mass extinction.

To struggle against this is precisely a matter of *not* delivering the new stage of exosomatization over to the market and its selection criteria, which are essentially entropic, and which constitute the transhumanist project. It is instead a matter of struggling *for* the generalized enhancement of noetic potential at all organic and organological levels for new noetic organisms: such are the stakes of neganthropology, which posits that *noodiversity will be the key issue over the next few decades*, and that this will require a *noopolitics* to operate *above and below the emerging neuroindustry.*

It is not a question, for me, of proposing some kind of assessment of the blessings or curses to be expected or feared from the endosomatization of technics itself, in particular at the cerebral level: the possibility of such an assessment requires the elaboration of its practical and theoretical conditions of possibility and impossibility, which have yet to be identified. But it is in order to begin such an identification that I would like here to sketch some outlines, which must *not fail to do justice to the excessiveness of what it is a question of thinking* – we must not, in other words, fold this thinking back into commonly agreed wisdom that avoids the issue, or, as we say in French, *noient le poisson*, drowns the fish.

For in fact, the new stage of the process of exosomatization accomplished as a second, industrially-effected endosomatization raises the *question of the future of knowledge in all its forms* – knowledge of how to live, do, conceptualize, spiritualize, that is, interpret, and so on – in such a way that the 'well-known' (in Hegel's sense) forms of knowledge find themselves *destroyed, annihilated, devalued* and having to be *transvalued in totality.*

To recapitulate, our questions are the following. It is a matter of knowing:

1 if we are entering a new stage of psychic and collective individuation, or if, rather, we are coming out of this regime of psychic and collective individuation and entering into another *regime* of individuation, after the physical individuation of the crystal, the vital individuation of the living and the psychic and collective individuation of 'technical life';

2 if a *new political regime* can be conceived that will preserve in this new regime of highly pharmacological individuation the care and concern to protect neganthropy against computational entropy;

3 what conception of education is required, in the context of this second endosomatization, where education is understood as the noetic interiorization of new forms of knowledge, themselves inherently exteriorized;

4 what macroeconomic revolution is needed to make this new regime of individuation solvent, a regime that is clearly also a new form of economy – and a general economy in Bataille's sense as well as a bio-economy in Georgescu-Roegen's sense.

▪ ▪ ▪

For we who live in the twenty-first century, in the age of 11 September, 2001, of 13 November 2015, of the COP21 climate summit, which was a dismal failure disguised as success, and of what we should describe as a disruption in exosomatization, the *question* is the future [*avenir*] insofar as it is not reducible to becoming [*becoming*] and cannot count on being – which has 'become' *Gestell* in the sense it was referred to by Heidegger in 'Time and Being'[260] and *Identity and Difference.*[261]

What I have called the future is what, as singularity, is capable of inscribing into becoming a *bifurcation*. Such a bifurcation is what reason – or what the Greeks called *logos* – has as its *function*, in the sense of Whitehead.[262]

Since the nineteenth century, the conception of the universe as a whole has been radically altered by the thermodynamic account of the dissipation of energy. This state of fact did not just theoretically or philosophically transform the understanding we have of the world in which we live: it changed the 'understanding that there-being has of its being' *in its very banality* – particularly given that this banality, when it corresponds to what we call the Anthropocene, continuously increases the rate of entropy in the biosphere, and to a very significant extent – which amounts to a new form of the 'banality of evil'.

The (co)production of phenomena by intuition and the understanding, as Kant described this cooperation in order to specify the characteristics of noetic experience, is nevertheless conditioned by a hetero-condition, that is, a hetero-poiesis, and this is what Kant remained unable to think. It is, however, something of which Herder had a presentiment, and it involves an exosomatization that prescribes the 'function of reason' in Whitehead's sense, as a speculative faculty that *operates* bifurcations. This is what follows from my argument about the role of tertiary retention in the *genesis of apodictic reason* – an idea that is taken up from Husserl's 'The Origin of Geometry'.

The question of tertiary retention is not anthropological but organo-genetic: it is the stage of organogenesis in which it becomes organological and pharmacological exosomatization, which poses not just a question but a neganthropological problem. This problem is that of the *pharmakon* in which any pursuit of exosomatization consists.

The true question is that of noesis – which is accessible only intermittently [*par intermittences*]. And noesis must always and in principle confront the possibility of its non-human – if not inhuman – constitution. This is why Plato and Aristotle always relate this to the question of a god. In addition, noesis must always be capable of imagining, of fearing and of struggling against an inhumanized and de-noetized humanity, which is always imminent, and today more than ever.

The possibility of *de-noetization* is *constitutive* of noesis: it is the very ground upon which all noesis must be thought, and it is in this that it *first confronts itself* – in this *affront*. And hence it is that philosophy was born in struggling against sophistic stupidity – or against the sophistical exploitation of a certain stupidity inherent to badly cultivated *logos*. This is why Deleuze can and must pose the question of stupidity, which he takes up from Nietzsche.

As an expression of the fulfilment of nihilism, transhumanism is a project of de-noetization, that is, of noetic dis-interiorization (of proletarianization, loss of knowledge – of the knowledge of how to live, do and conceive), and this dis-interiorization is founded on the delegation of noetic services to analytical artefacts and to interfaces designed to optimize interactive reaction speeds – as in the case of implants designed to optimize the reaction speed of fighter pilots via optical fibres operating almost four million times faster than nerves.

From this perspective, transhumanism is the *anti-economic*, because *entropic*, culmination of proletarianization carried to its final extreme – which then, too, is entropic to the ultimate degree.

▪ ▪ ▪

The noetization of the living is its exteriorization. The latter does not begin with man, and it may not end with him. Nevertheless, noesis seems indeed to begin with the *promise* of man, and it seems it may go out with him insofar as humankind cannot think *itself other than as promise*, and as the promise of *Neganthropos*, builder of the Neganthropocene.

'Man', in becoming anthropocenic, becomes not a wolf to man,[263] but the enemy of 'humanity' and life in general. As the 'last man', he is no longer able to think the *non*-inhuman being that he can be only as noetic – which he can be only insofar as he is in-existent: only insofar as he *does not yet exist*, only insofar as he exists *only as 'not yet'*, always *already* having become anthropic, *all too* anthropic.

Noesis is what should provide the *criteria* for a noetic exosomatization that we also call the human, but where the human is not what is given but what must be *produced* (as Marx and Engels show in *The German Ideology*), re-produced and repro-duced (as I have argued elsewhere through a commentary on Kant's transcendental deduction,[264] and as is at stake in Walter Benjamin's work on the work of art in the age of technical reproducibility[265]).

The question of the promise is the question of the positive collective protention (this meaning anticipation, desire and will in Husserl's vocabulary) that alone allows the constitution of an epoch. The question of transhumanism is the question of an *absence of epoch*, in relation to which transhumanist 'storytelling' functions to conceal that this is the result of de-noetization, a de-noetization that transhumanism claims fills in for, or makes up for, a defect, a fault, a default, but where in fact the latter is precisely the origin of any noesis insofar as it participates in the neganthropic future that is non-inhumanity. The claim of transhumanism, that it makes up for a noetic flaw, resembles a discourse on the *perfect* human, that is, a project to *eliminate that flaw, that default, that is* noesis. Completely to the contrary, the Japanese artist Masaki Fujihata shows that noetic evolution is the conquest of imperfection.[266]

To start from the human, even as a 'transhumanist', is to always be on the verge of designating sub-humans, and of doing so by rejecting the improper, that is, the default. To posit that the human does not exist *yet*, or barely exists, on the other hand, as Derrida reiterated after Jean Jaurès in 'My Sunday "Humanities"',[267] is to confront *everything that we are* in our *daily inhumanities*, in our cowardice, our pettiness, our envy, our ambitions, our betrayals – everything that makes us other than gods, *we who think only by intermittences*, and we who *live worthily* only by intermittences.

▪ ▪ ▪

In Heidegger's final period, if we read it through the lens of Rudolf Boehm's analysis,[268] which I unfortunately do not have time to discuss here, technics, an issue that runs through Heidegger's entire oeuvre, eventually resurfaces in the 1960s as his final *word*. In this last word, which is *Ereignis* (the Event or the Advent), a fundamental step is lacking, a leap into 'co-propriation', *inasmuch as what this amounts to is the question of entropy and of its negentropic reversal*, such that it therefore implies the need for a neganthropology, and such that it replays in their entirety all the questions of philosophy since its point of departure – which therefore demands that reason be rethought after Whitehead, reason that Whitehead himself calls a function beyond being, the latter having itself become *Gestell*.

This struggle is another name for *Sorge*, which must be understood in relation to the following statement by Georges Canguilhem:

> Life tries to gain, to win out over death, in all senses of the word win [*gagner*], and firstly in the sense that a win is what is acquired by playing. Life is a play [or a gamble] against increasing entropy.[269]

Like Nietzsche, Marx and Engels never knew the problematic of negative entropy, and hence this problematic leads today to taking a step beyond dialectics, including the dialectic of nature and beyond dialectics in general.

Faced with Lévi-Strauss's assertion that the history of humanity amounts to an entropology, there is a tendency:

- either, to sink into metaphysical anti-humanism, that is, to ignore the play of entropy and negentropy such that one cannot overcome the other, which requires a new form of tragic thinking;
- or else, to project ourselves towards the appallingly naïve (and nihilistic) temptation of proclaiming the necessity of overcoming the human, and of doing so from, precisely, a transhumanist perspective, and in particular from a so-called 'extropian' perspective.

To confront the absolute need for a new age of negentropy, it is necessary to surpass anthropology, which, indeed, necessarily leads to entropy; and this surpassing of anthropology must pass through what Canguilhem called play (in a way that is close to Bataille), as the win gained from this *form of différance* that is play (but where Derrida himself always defined différance as the play of différance).

Transhumanism is an industrial strategy, and the most astounding, stupefying consequence of what we are calling *disruption*, a disruption that commenced in 1993. The *situation* of disruption and *strategy* of transhumanism together constitute the new stage of exosomatization in which noetic organogenesis consists. Exosomatization is now generated according to the development strategies of the *lords of economic war without limit*, that war in which this disruption precisely consists and whose result has already been intense *de-noetization*. Only a neganthropology can constitute a *rational* critique of this situation and of the stakes of this war – with a view to *an indispensable and sustainable noetic peace*. The question is the *revaluation criteria* that must, therefore, be actively extracted from this nihilism, in order to leap not towards the overman, but towards *Neganthropos*.

Stanislas Dehaene, in *Reading in the Brain*, describes the neuronal recycling that was shown by Maryanne Wolf to be the condition of possibility of learning to read.[270] The consequence of this recycling, which programs the possibility of a deprogramming (and of what Paul Ricoeur called the 'collapsed zones' of genetic coding[271]), is that the *noetic* cerebral organ, that is, the brain *capable of questioning the truth and in return of transforming the world*, is perpetually in dialogue with the artificial organs that it creates – from flint tools to smartphones, passing of course through writing, and in particular the alphabetical writing that we ourselves have learned to read, and that allows us to be trans-formed by Proust during the passage to the act of reading.

The exploration of these vertiginous questions opened by Maryanne Wolf calls for the mobilization of new resources that have been provided by palaeo-anthropology, especially through the problems posed by Merlin Donald, Kim Sterelny and Michael Tomasello, which must be brought together with the way Jean-Pierre Changeux introduces the question of reading as taught by Stanislas Dehaene.

In the case of human beings, Changeux points out, 'the cultural cannot be thought without the biological and [...] the cerebral does not exist without a powerful impregnation from the environment'.[272] Could we not, here, invert the perspective while modifying the trajectory? Ought we not, more accurately, speak *firstly* of technics, and of its organs, and of the relationship between technical organs and biological organs, before investigating culture itself?

This would make it possible to establish the conditions in which culture may appear, namely: on the foundation of a *transformation of organogenesis*, which, with the appearance of tools, becomes an exosomatization. And this would in turn make it possible to better situate cultural technologies themselves within a broader becoming. As Changeux himself highlights, reading and therefore writing belong to a field of cultural techniques or technologies that amount to 'mental intermediaries', a subject to which Ignace Meyerson, a founder of social psychology, was dedicated:

> Culture should not be confused with writing [...]. People without writing still produced [...] mental intermediaries, or signs, to put it in the terms of Ignace Meyerson: works of art, whether visual or musical, ritual and symbolic systems, codes of conduct, essential [...] to the community life of the social group.[273]

These mental intermediaries, in the reflection upon them that Lev Vygotsky, too, pursued throughout his whole psychology, enable the formation of what Gilbert Simondon called the transindividual, that is, meaning insofar as it is shared by noetic individuals belonging to the same group. And Simondon emphasizes that the condition of possibility of the transindividual is the existence of technical objects that support it and revive social sharing.

I have argued that these technical supports of the transindividual are tertiary retentions, that is, material exteriorizations of motor behaviours and mental contents that amount to an inorganic memory, external to the cerebral organ and the nervous system, but essential to its functioning from the moment it becomes noetic. I say tertiary retention because psychic memory is composed of secondary retentions and perception is the production of primary retentions, which are the time of perception. To put it more precisely, tertiary retentions condition the play of primary and secondary retentions. What Maryanne Wolf shows, on the basis of an example taken from Proust's *On Reading*, is the way in which these tertiary retentions are arranged and organized during the act of reading.[274] Among these tertiary retentions, there emerges indeed a particular class, which I call hypomnesic, and which are specifically dedicated to the conservation and the transmission of mental contents. Such is the case for writing.

Tertiary retentions in general are 'inscriptions in material that is more stable than nervous tissue: mineral pigments, earth, wood, stone, ivory, [...] "there is no sign without matter", as Meyerson wrote'.[275] Changeux stresses here that artificial retentions last beyond the fleeting impressions that traverse the nervous system and that are metastabilized in the form of neuronal connections in the brain, so long as the individual to whom the organ belongs remains alive.

Maryanne Wolf shows that the written text, which is the foundation of Western culture, presupposes a long work of transformation of the cerebral organ in order that it can be read and interpreted. This work consists in arranging the primary and secondary retentions of the reader with the play of tertiary retentions that compose the book that is read – or written. Here, *nothing* is reducible to biology: *everything* must be thought in terms of the composition of the organic and the organized inorganic, that is, of the tertiary retentional materials that form the organological milieu conditioning the survival of the organic-become-noetic.

This is also why Changeux urges us not to perpetuate the kind of confusion he sees in Steven Pinker:

> Genetic disorders of spoken language [...] reveal the importance of genes like FoxP2, which some people, like Steven Pinker, rush to call 'language genes'. Yet we find these genes in the animal [...], which doesn't speak![276]

Changeux concludes that there are

> processes of another type, of an 'epigenetic' nature, that make possible a strong alliance of genes and experience in the construction of cerebral complexity.[277]

This alliance forms what I have called the epiphylogenetic,[278] that is, what André Leroi-Gourhan called the third memory,[279] and this radically changes the conditions of organogenesis, that is, of life itself qua evolution.

> The margin of variability offered by an expanded genetic envelope [expanded by the '*cognitive games* of the newborn'] allow [...] an 'appropriation' of developing neuronal networks and their amplification in the form of 'cultural circuits'. Novelty enters into the incompletely specified human brain through its genetic equipment, and so it is that reading is inscribed in the brain.[280]

These considerations call for a new conception of pharmacopeia and pharmacology – which should be expanded to include *pharmaka* as understood by Socrates in *Phaedrus*, but where *Protagoras* showed that we must extend this notion to artifices and expedients of every kind, that is, to the whole of technics (and this is also what we learn from Canguilhem) – in the framework of a 'pharmacology of processes of selection, amplification and reafferentation of interneuronal connections, both during development and in the adult'.[281]

▪ ▪ ▪

In his great work, *Gesture and Speech*, Leroi-Gourhan posits that human memory and its development cannot be studied independently of the evolution of its techniques. The genesis of the latter falls under what Leroi-Gourhan called a 'process of exteriorization', through which is formed an artificial memory essential to the functioning of the nervous memory of human beings. The prehistorian stressed that human nervous memory is not self-sufficient, and is, from the outset (more than two million years ago), augmented and conditioned by a social memory that is not organic but organological, and with which it co-evolves.

If flint tools (and other tools that accompanied them, but which we remain unaware of because they have disappeared) are not made *for* the conservation of memory, they nevertheless *do* keep the trace of the gestures through which they were fashioned, and, in this way, they already constitute supports of memory: the cut tool in fact preserves the memory of the techniques of cutting, and this is why archaeologists can reconstruct them (through the methods of experimental archaeology). But the memory that is conserved in this way is gestural, not mental. It was only during the most recent periods of prehistory that mental contents began to be exteriorized.

The co-evolution of nervous memory and technical memory involved, according to Leroi-Gourhan, a series of stages, during which:

1. It is first and foremost the cerebral organ and its cortical organization that is transformed, the pace of the expansion of the cortical fan (that is, the formation of the cerebral cortex and its organization in the cortical regions) being directly correlated with the evolution of lithic tools.

2. The physiological evolution of the cortex was stabilized at the time of the appearance of the Neanderthal, some 300,000 years ago, while the use of tools diversified considerably, as if biological organogenesis had been replaced by exosomatic organogenesis.

3. In the Upper Palaeolithic, that is, in the epoch of cave painting, there appear the first forms of the exteriorization of mental contents, both as paintings and as inscriptions that anticipate what, after the Neolithic, will constitute the first

> forms of writing, ideogrammatic writing, until the appearance of the alphabet as we still know it today.

We ourselves care very much, in our day, about what will become of educational institutions, and about the difficulties they face in undertaking the formation of the younger generations for which they are responsible. We have cause to be concerned. If education is so fundamental for us and for our children, it is because for each new generation, everything that has been learned by the preceding generations must, as much as possible, be appropriated by the new generation, and this is possible only on the condition that they first prepare their cerebral organ by submitting to that process of learning we call 'elementary', that is, that enables them to enter into the basic *element* of knowledge, which is, in this case, in the West, and for almost three thousand years, alphabetical writing – first handwritten, then printed.

Maryanne Wolf shows how this occurs: first the acquisition of elements, followed by the acquisition of the knowledge derived from the reading that these elements make possible. And Wolf stresses that the 'reading brain' that was formed in this way was in no way originally configured for learning to read: 'we were never born to read', she writes.[282] Neuronal recycling, which makes the noetic brain capable of profoundly disorganizing and reorganizing itself in order to interiorize the possibilities afforded by the artificial memorization that I call organology, is the condition of this exosomatic organogenesis in which consists the individuation of the technical organs that constitute an artificial milieu, and where the pursuit of evolution no longer occurs by submitting to biological constraints but through the individuation of social organizations.

This is why, beyond the scientific and epistemological stakes of her work, the research of Maryanne Wolf greatly opens up the question of a politics of the organology of the brain in the context of what we are calling the age of disruption, that is, an epoch of innovation in which exosomatization is now completely controlled by economic powers and subject to the constraints of short-term profitability. Hence we must hear the alarm sounded by *Proust and the Squid*, even if we must not unduly dramatize it: the 'digital brain', which is being organologically transformed at a dizzying rate, raises the question of the preservation of a capacity for deep reading and therefore for deep attention. What is being referred to here as 'deep attention', however, is nothing other than the ability to reason by inheriting the experience of our ancestors and by making a worthwhile contribution to the fruitful growth of this heritage.

It is clear that nanotechnology multiplies these questions almost to infinity. Will we take care of the reading brain that is becoming the digital brain and ultimately the *endosomatically enhanced brain*, and will we do so without *losing* our reason, and our minds?

ANNIVERSARY LECTURE

On the Need for a Hyper-Materialist Epistemology

Address on the Occasion of the 200th Anniversary of the Birth of Karl Marx, 3 May 2018, Nanjing

At the very beginning of *Technics and Time*, I pointed out that when Marx posits in *Capital* that we require a theory of technical evolution, which would be an extension of Darwinian theory, he at the same time raises the question of a kind of *matter* that would be *neither simply the inorganic matter of physics, nor the organic matter of biology*. This is the question of what I have myself called *organized inorganic matter*.

Matter can be organized: this is what Aristotle described in terms of what he called *poiēsis*. This dimension of matter – of which technology, understood here as science, would be the theory of its evolution – is what is at stake in production inasmuch as the latter is inscribed in material forms that amount to the fabricated organs of that form of life which is specific to humankind, a form that Georges Canguilhem will call 'technical life'. This conception of production as the genesis of artificial organs that are themselves inorganic and yet vital is outlined in *The German Ideology*, and it extends the considerations set out in the *Economic and Philosophical Manuscripts of 1844* concerning human sensibility, such that the latter is understood to be social through and through, that is, formed by the practice of artificial organs, as for example by the practice of musical instruments, as Marx says – this practice being the formation of meaning [*sens*] by education in all its forms, from the most elementary to the most elaborate.

More recently, I have tried to show that this conception of human life as *exceeding* its *purely* biological dimensions – a question that was opened up by Darwin himself in *The Descent of Man* (1871) – was expressed in other terms by Alfred Lotka in 1945. In 'The Law of Evolution as a Maximal Principle',[283] Lotka posited that:

1 Life in general (both endosomatic and exosomatic) – which in 1922 he understands (as will Vernadsky[284] in 1925) in terms of an *organic mass* composed of biochemical transformations, and such that it amounts to a dynamic system[285] that must be understood in its totality as a competition between species *mobilizing and maximizing the transformation of the available energy resulting from solar combustion*[286] – life in

general, in the framework of this *process of selection* that is the struggle for life, *tends in a functional way to transform all energy and all inorganic matter into organic matter, and hence into vital movement, and to do so in an* endosomatic *manner, up until the appearance of man, who produces exosomatic organs.*

2 *In exosomatic life,* which appears in the biosphere some three million years ago, *bio-chemical trans-formation becomes techno-chemical,* and it is henceforth accomplished not according to the rules of organic matter, namely biology, but according to the socio-economic prescriptions made both possible and necessary by inorganic organized matter, but where this also leads to *conflicts between exosomatic groups* – that is, between what we should consequently refer to no longer as organisms or species, but as *exorganisms.*

These exorganisms have forms that themselves continually evolve, but where this occurs according to the evolutionary dynamic of exosomatic organs: hordes, tribes, ethnic groups, cities, communities, nations, but also, today, brands and conglomerates.[287]

With exosomatization, the process of selection becomes artificial, and it takes place through conflicts that range from economic competition to war – where war may itself become commercial and economic – and passing through class struggle. War means destruction, and Lotka outlines his theory in the aftermath of the process of *massive destruction* in which the two world wars of the twentieth century will have consisted: he writes ‘The Law of Evolution as a Maximal Principle’ at the very end of the Second World War, in 1945, and he quotes from an international report on the effects of the conflict on civil populations,[288] referring at the same time to the work he himself published in 1922 at the end of the First World War – three years after ‘The Crisis of the Mind’[289] [*crise de l’esprit*], where Paul Valéry laid out the question of the mortality of civilizations in terms of a pharmacology of spirit.[290]

I refer to ‘pharmacology’ to the extent that the exosomatic organs are what Socrates, referring to writing and to technics in general, called *pharmaka*: remedies that are also poisons. What is peculiar to exosomatic organs is that the rules governing their mutual functioning are not prescribed by any biology. Instead, they must be made the subject of a political economy – the latter must, as far as possible, minimize their toxicity and maximize their beneficial character. But such a political economy itself requires the constitution of forms of knowledge (knowledge of how to live together, knowledge of how to make and do things, conceptual knowledge) that make it possible to differentiate between the beneficial possibilities and the harmful possibilities afforded by *pharmaka*.

Now, on this issue Marx and Engels raise a fundamentally new point: the *pharmakon* that is the industrial machine leads the worker to lose his or her knowledge, so that he or she becomes a member of what they call the proletariat. In *For a New Critique of Political Economy*, I argue that, in *The Communist Manifesto*, Marx and Engels in this way rediscover the same conclusion already reached by Socrates when he spoke about writing and against sophism, namely that, in the hands of the sophists, writing destroys knowledge, and that it must therefore become the subject of therapeutic prescriptions capable of making it beneficial. As for Marx and Engels, they refer to 'the icy water of egotistical calculation'[291] to denounce the criteriology that capital imposes in order to define what is beneficial in the industrial political economy, namely, calculation, and more precisely calculation of the rate of profit. What Marx fights against, and what we must critique, therefore, is the reduction of life, production and work to pure calculation – just as Heidegger describes *Gestell* as the absolute reign of calculation via cybernetics.

Let's now go back to the theory of exosomatic evolution. What I call general organology tries, from a pharmacological perspective, to address the question of what Lotka described as exosomatic orthogenesis (in biology, the orthogenetic perspective disputes the notion that *natural selection* is the *sole* criterion involved in the evolution of life):

> Whether physiologically speaking orthogenesis is [in the case of endosomatic species] fact or fiction is a matter of dispute, but the *exosomatic* evolution of the human species is indisputably subject to orthogenesis.[292]

In any case, *exosomatic* evolution is according to Lotka *clearly* orthogenetic, and this means that it utilizes evolutionary criteria that constitute a process of *artificial selection* endogenous to the system formed by the psycho-somatic organs, the exosomatic organs and collective organizations, where the *whole* constitutes a *social group* in which the challenge lies in the *local adjustment of humankind to organs that are constantly transforming through its own production*:

> Knowledge breeds knowledge, and with present-day methods of recording, this means unceasing accumulation of knowledge and of the technical skills based upon it. But [...] 'knowledge comes, but wisdom lingers', if by wisdom we understand that adjustment of action to ends which is for the

> good of the species. It is precisely this that has gone awry in the schemes of men: The receptors and effectors have been perfected to a nicety; but the development of the adjustors has lagged so far behind, that the resultant of our efforts has actually been reversed.[293]

Once again, we must stress that these lines were written in 1945, and in clear sight of the misery inflicted upon civil populations by all the sufferings of war. It is in such an *extreme* moment that there arises the fear of seeing exosomatic beings succumb to the same fate that Freud ascribes to 'infusoria', Freud writing of the infusorian that,

> if it is left to itself, [it] dies a natural death owing to its incomplete voidance of the products of its own metabolism,[294]

just as Lévi-Strauss will declare 75 years later that:

> The human race lives under a regime of a kind that poisons itself from within.[295]

In other words, this *extreme 'perfecting'*[296] has the potential to turn into a *fatal flaw* – an astonishing limit the question of which Freud encountered in 1929, and by considering exosomatization itself from another angle: that of the drives. It is also such a fate that Lévi-Strauss will evoke at the end of his *Tristes Tropiques*, in which he states that anthropology turns out to be an *entropology*.

It is indeed a question of the survival of the human species, in that, being exosomatic, it *lags further and further behind* this incessant and constantly accelerating perfecting of its artificial organs, to the point of reaching a limit that is extreme and therefore eschatological. It is in the proximity of this limit that Heidegger raises the questions of *Gestell* and *Ereignis* while reflecting on Norbert Wiener's cybernetic discourse. At the very same moment, Lotka posits that the human species is no longer capable of forming the 'adjustors' that it needs, and that its knowledge lags so far behind that it fails to provide the orthogenetic constraint that exosomatic evolution requires. All this stems from what I have analysed in *Technics and Time* and in more recent works[297] in terms of what I call the doubly epokhal redoubling.

At this point, two questions arise:

- On the one hand, the question of knowing *exactly* what Lotka actually means when he refers to the orthogenetic character of exosomatic organogenesis, that is, such that it requires exorganic organizations, themselves founded on knowledge capable of taking care of these organizations in terms of their inorganic organs, and such that they support those social relations that organizations constitute: it is a question of an organology in which, despite his warnings about the perennial lateness of knowledge, *it seems that what Lotka fails to see clearly is that the exosomatic organs in general have an irreducibly pharmacological character* (not just in 1945 and not just in the context of war) – and this will be the case also for Nicholas Georgescu-Roegen.

- On the other hand, we must ask: to what extent are morphogenetic and orthogenetic evolutions *determined* or *conditioned* by specifically technical systemic functional constraints? This question is simultaneously that of:

  1. the relations between *technical tendencies* and *technical facts* in Leroi-Gourhan's sense;
  2. the *dynamics internal to technical systems* in Bertrand Gille's sense;
  3. the *processes of concretization of industrial technical objects* in Simondon's sense, as these appear with machines, that is, *within industrial exorganisms*, where they form technical ensembles and technogeographical associated milieus.

Advance and delay thus lie at the very heart of the exosomatic condition, which simultaneously and perpetually *constitutes and destitutes* noetic souls – which makes noesis an *incessant intermittence* – technics and time *weaving* together as the accumulation of tertiary retentions that, in the preceding quotation, Lotka calls recordings.

The inability of the 'adjustors' to think or to take care of [*à penser et à panser*] exosomatization, and hence to produce an economically solvent and ecologically sustainable orthogenesis, amounts to what we should refer to as an *absolute non-knowledge.* And this is so because the technologies that Lotka refers to as 'methods of recording' have now become algorithmic computing technologies operating at the speed of light and at the scale of the biosphere – and on information that deprives these adjustors of all knowledge. Such is the age of total proletarianization, which was foreshadowed in *The Communist Manifesto* of 1848, a perspective that returns in 1857 in the *Grundrisse* as the question of *automated fixed capital* that *absorbs scientific knowledge* as a function of production in the broad sense – involving design, manufacturing and distribution.

In the absolute non-knowledge of this totalizing 'smart capitalism', however, there remains a concealed opportunity for 'another thinking', that is, for a new power to dis-automatize conferred by automation itself, and as a new function of reason. This is the meaning of Heidegger's statements concerning *Gestell* and *Ereignis*, provided that we interpret them on the basis of the position laid out by Marx in his 'fragment on machines' – where he quotes Andrew Ure. To conceive this possibility and opportunity as *praxis*, that is, as knowledge of how to do [*savoir faire*] that comes neither before nor after conceptual knowledge, and so to arrange *theoria* and *praxis* in order to generate new forms of the knowledge of how to live [*savoir vivre*], as ways and means of *re-viving ourselves noetically*, that is, as techniques of the self and others – for all this, it is necessary to interpret the *Grundrisse* from the perspective of *Gestell* and vice versa, and to do so from the exosomatic perspective outlined by Lotka.

It is as a vanishing point and a turning point – or a 'turn' – in exosomatization that *Gestell* appears as the Entropocene, and as the *ordeal* of a total de-noetization provoked by generalized proletarianization, referred to nowadays as 'post-truth', the politics of denial having reached the very top of the most powerful of the 'Great Powers', the United States of America – while these Great Powers in general, or what remains of them, and inasmuch as they encounter New Powers, might well prove, in the encounter with their own limits, to be nothing more than Great Impotences, simply the local and conflictual expression of the *functional impasses* of the *fully anthropized* biosphere.

These considerations demand a complete rereading of the trajectory pursued by Marx and Engels – from the *Contribution to the Critique of Hegel's Philosophy of Right* and the *1844 Manuscripts* to the *Dialectic of Nature*. Marx, in the *Manuscripts*, and later Marx and Engels in *The German Ideology*, pose the question of a general organology capable of thinking exosomatization, which they are the first to describe, and where they describe it definitively in terms of the production of psychosocial individuation, and as a continuation of evolution, which will be reaffirmed when Book 1 of *Capital* asserts the need for a theory of technical evolution.

It is on the basis of these considerations, along with the additional notion of the class struggle where each class aims to take hold of the exosomatic organs according to their own interests, that proletarianization comes to be defined as a loss of knowledge. Here, the struggle against German idealism in general and Hegelian idealism in particular consists in positing that exteriorization – of which the *Phenomenology of Spirit* had posited that it was the condition of this 'Spirit' – is not soluble into 'Spirit', and hence neither is it reducible to the absolute knowledge of this 'Spirit' as the total assimilation and interiorization of the moments of its exteriority: there is a primordial and irreducible materiality as the materialization of a time of evolution beyond biology and zoology, and as techno-logy.

These epistemological perspectives, however, which are fundamental in the struggle against the hegemony of calculation imposed by capitalism, remain incomplete and in want of reconstruction, in particular on the basis of the theory of entropy, which Engels did not know how to think, as he showed in his *Dialectic of Nature*, but which is in fact the fundamental question of the Anthropocene.

I would like to conclude by recalling my fundamental position with respect to German idealism and by opening up a perspective by referring to Alfred Sohn-Rethel.

I argued in 2001, and on the basis of a reading of the *Critique of Pure Reason*, for the need for a new critique: for a critique passing through the question of tertiary retention, that is, through the question of *exosomatized memory* – and, more generally, of technics inasmuch as, as the *materialization of experience*, it always constitutes a *spatialization of the time of consciousness beyond consciousness*, and, in that, an unconsciousness.

In *For a New Critique of Political Economy*, I argued that, from such a point of view, *logos* appears to result from a discretization by writing of the continuous flow of language, which, spatialized, may then be considered analytically, and which then enters into its diacritical age, from which, in a fundamental and specific way, logic stems. But this discretization of flows is something that also affects gestures. This is what, after the technology of Vaucanson's automaton was transplanted into Jacquard's loom, comes to be concretized and generalized as the industrial revolution of machinism.

Like speech, gesture must here be considered as a retentional flow, that is, as a *sequence* of gestures, and the apprenticeship in a trade or a craft consists in learning to produce gestural secondary retentions, while the discretization and spatialized reproduction of the time of gestures constitutes the technical automatism through which it is no longer just the *logos* of the *soul* but also the gesture of the body that becomes *analytically reproducible* as tertiary retention. This reproducibility is what produces retentional grains that we can call *grammēs*, and this is why the evolution of tertiary retention amounts to a process of grammatization.

During the nineteenth century, we see the rise of technologies that grammatize *audio-visual perception*, in which it is the flows associated with the sense organs that find themselves rendered discrete and reproducible. It is henceforth every noetic, psychomotor and aesthetic function that is transformed by the process of grammatization. From the perspective of political economy, this means that all the functions of conception, production and consumption find themselves grammatized – and thereby integrated into an apparatus that produces tertiary retentions controlled by *retentional systems and devices*.[298]

On the basis of these analyses, I have tried to show that the three syntheses of the transcendental imagination expounded in the first edition of the *Critique of Pure Reason*, as well as the schematism of concepts provided to the understanding by this transcendental imagination in order to seize the data or the givens or the data of intuition, must be reinterpreted from the perspective of tertiary retention as the concretization of the exosomatization of noesis itself inasmuch as it is founded on exteriorized memory, that is, spatialized memory, supporting what Lotka called recordings, that is, knowledge in all its forms.

Here, it would be necessary to read in detail the proposition put forward by Sohn-Rethel concerning the birth of the concepts of pre-Socratic Greek thought, which he sees in direct connection with the invention of money, where the latter is a tertiary retention of a specific kind that enables calculation to be generalized, as Clarisse Herrenschmidt has shown.[299] I do not have time now to explain why I share this analysis and yet find it completely insufficient – just as we must reread Lefèbvre and his statements concerning space and the city as a work, but also those of Meyerson on works, understanding the latter in a sense that is concomitant with Lefèbvre, yet distinct. In the absence of such analyses, it will not be possible to take a step beyond Marx's analysis when he states in *Capital* that

> what distinguishes the worst architect from the best of bees is that the architect builds the cell in his head before he constructs it in wax.[300]

Such a statement is in complete contradiction with what is said in *The German Ideology*: the architect's knowledge resides not in his head, but in his instruments, on his plans, and in the buildings he has inhabited, traversed and conceived as processes of exosomatization of complex exorganisms. Such a question is fundamental in the epoch in which we refer to 'smart cities'.

Let us posit that an epistemology that I will call hyper-materialist – which must become a neganthropology overcoming the Lévi-Straussian paradox and impasse of 'entropology', and which is hyper-materialist because, confronted with the fundamental achievements of quantum mechanics, it exceeds the opposition of form and matter, while incorporating the question of the organization of the inorganic – is the condition upon which we can revive and relaunch a knowledge of exosomatization that would realize the prospects and perspectives opened up in Book 1 of *Capital* in terms of the theory of technical evolution.

2019 Lectures

Elements of a Hyper-Materialist Epistemology

FIRST LECTURE

Introduction

The seminar I'm offering this year is the continuation of those given in the previous three years – during which we examined:

- the necessity of a new reading of Marx and Heidegger in the context of the Anthropocene era;
- the meaning of the current post-truth ordeal and its anchoring in the idealist metaphysics of Plato;
- the formation in the twentieth century of psychopower, and, in the early twenty-first century, of neuropower.

This year's seminar aims to outline the main characteristics of what I will call a hyper-materialist epistemology.

I put forward the concept of hyper-matter on the basis of the work of Gilbert Simondon. Simondon shows that, in the framework of quantum mechanics, physics can no longer think in terms of what he called the hylemorphic schema that separates matter from form. At the quantum scale, form and matter can no longer be distinguished. I myself have proposed the term hyper-matter, not only in order to take account of the need to overcome this hylemorphic schema inherited from Aristotle, but also to take account of the fact that, as it operates in human life, matter essentially presents itself through materialized technics and such that it always amounts to what in *Technics and Time, 1* I call organized inorganic matter, which is to say, matter that has been shaped into a form. This hyper-matter (as organized inorganic matter) makes possible the constitution and accumulation of a hyper-material memory, which I have also called epiphylogenetic memory in that it is the result of both an autonomized epigenetic activity of genetic memory (biological memory) and a phylogenetic accumulation of shared individual experience, constituting what we call 'knowledge'.

We will see in the second part of this seminar that Lev Vygotsky, Ignace Meyerson and Alfred Lotka provide key concepts to take these perspectives further within the meaning of a hyper-materialist epistemology. And we will see how this allows us to take account of the questions raised by the Frankfurt School and more particularly by Alfred Sohn-Rethel concerning the need to elaborate a true materialist epistemology, something missing in both Marx and Engels.

(In addition to organized inorganic matter, there is also disorganized and reorganized organic matter, as is massively the case in contemporary biotechnology, but also in agricultural production, which for the moment I'll leave to one side – but I should specify that the cerebral organic matter of the human brain has the precise characteristic of being constantly disorganized and reorganized by the practice of artificial organs composed of the organization of inorganic matter. We approached this issue during last year's seminar.)

Furthermore, I added that organized inorganic matter such as tools are an exteriorized memory, which is also to say that they are objectified knowledge, and that this is what allows Hegel to refer to 'objective spirit'. This objectified knowledge is the consequence of the epiphylogenetic formation that arose in life with the practical activity of human beings. What Marx called fixed capital is an example of such objectified knowledge, at the moment it reaches an advanced stage of industrialization, and so what Hegel called objective spirit becomes, in Marx, the general intellect – and we are now immersed in this stage of the inscription of objectified knowledge in fixed capital to a degree that Marx could never have anticipated, this knowledge being now transformed into information, which is also to say into non-knowledge, amounting to what Heidegger called *Gestell*, and that we will also call the absolute non-knowledge engendered by generalized proletarianization. It is to specifying this stage that our seminar this year will also be devoted.

▪ ▪ ▪

This year, I would like to show that what we know as historical materialism is one way of considering what I am talking about here, but also that this theory of the historical character of matter has not yet reached the stage of being able to constitute a new epistemology capable of taking account of what makes the material constitution of knowledge in general possible, whether this materiality is organic (brain, hands, body) or inorganic (tools, technics, language). All this knowledge presupposes noetic activity, that is, the faculty of thinking in all its forms – thinking, *pensée*, always also being a practice, that is, a *pansée*, a care, in this sense a *Sorge*.

In previous years, I pointed out that in *The German Ideology* Marx and Engels lay out the beginnings of what will become historical materialism by positing that man is a living thing characterized by the fact that he produces the organs of work essential to him (the organs and the work), and that this production, which results from social relations, posits technics as the basis of noetic life, quite the reverse of what philosophy had affirmed insofar as it was founded with Plato on ideas, which are then defined as apodictic knowledge of transcendental origin, which, for Plato, is opposed precisely to technical knowledge that is merely empirical. Technical knowledge, as it is posited for example in *Gorgias*, is for Plato a pseudo-knowledge, an illusory knowledge. For Plato, true knowledge is demonstrative knowledge of which the canon is geometry, which is considered to be the matrix and canon of all truth – even if, as Heidegger points out, in pre-Socratic thought *alētheia* does not mean *orthōtes* (exactitude) or *omoiosis* (adequation of the concept to its object), so much as it means coming out of the latent (*lēthe*), which is to say, out of oblivion, out of forgetting: *anamnesis*. That this is also true of geometry is that to which the dialogue *Meno* attests.

Last year, I pointed out that the thesis advanced in *The German Ideology* is a first formulation of what the mathematician and biologist Alfred Lotka called exosomatic evolution. This year, I will return in detail to the consequences of this standpoint, as Lotka examines them with respect to the nature of knowledge.

For the moment, I would like to remind you that:

- On the one hand, Marx's position on these matters is neither stabilized nor elaborated as such, that is, theorized for itself – as Sohn-Rethel, too, points out. Although it takes on primary importance in the *Grundrisse*, it appears rather fragile in Book 1 of *Capital*, when Marx compares the conditions of the constructions of the architect and the bee, positing that unlike the bee, the architect has 'in his head'[301] the conception of what it is that he wants to build. As I pointed out last year, such a statement completely contradicts the position put in *The German Ideology*, according to which it is because the knowledge of humans is outside their body that they are noetic, that is, capable of thinking, conceiving and realizing what they conceive.
- On the other hand, unlike Lotka, Marx and Engels do not take the theory of entropy into account, inasmuch as it completely redefines what constitutes the universe, so that it is no longer a unity eternally identical to itself, but an expanding process oriented by the arrow of time that is itself induced by the dissipation of energy.

As I pointed out last year at the colloquium organized in Nanjing University as part of the commemoration of the bicentennial of the birth of Karl Marx, the latter, in *Capital*, and in the chapter devoted to 'large-scale industry', posits the need to elaborate a theory of technical evolution just as Darwin proposed a theory of organic evolution.[302] In the history of Marxism, however, this theory has never been elaborated, despite the fact that it would remain essential to the completion of the theory of historical materialism, and instead, by going completely outside the analysis of Marx himself, it proposes a dialectical materialism of which Engels's *Dialectic of Nature* is the starting point, and which will lead, precisely, to the rejection of the theory of entropy.

Having recalled these elements that we have discussed in previous years, I would like now to specify the nature of the debate that I would like to open by taking up and giving a critique of the hypotheses advanced by Sohn-Rethel against German Idealism and especially against Kant and the transcendental deduction of the categories, but also against pre-Socratic Greek thinkers, including Parmenides. Through these hypotheses, Sohn-Rethel argues that what leads to the formation of an idealist perspective that opposes manual work and intellectual work, while claiming to ground intellectual work on eternal idealities and *a priori* forms, that is, on what Kant called the transcendental, is in reality an effect of the emergence of money – and for this, Sohn-Rethel builds on the arguments of George Thomson. We will read Sohn-Rethel's arguments in detail, and we will see that he quite surprisingly ignores the work of Lev Vygotsky, despite the fact that during the 1920s and 1930s Vygotsky undertook a fundamental analysis of psychogenesis and thus also of noogenesis, in a way that builds upon historical materialism as Marx conceived it.

We will study these texts only after having undertaken a long sojourn through the industrial, technological and scientific actuality of the twenty-first century, inasmuch as it makes obvious the need to go much further in the elaboration of historical materialism, which, in being projected into the twenty-first century, becomes what I am calling hyper-materialism.

. . .

Within universities and within technology companies, there is (and has been for a long time) much talk about Turing's thesis, and this is the case now more than ever, because of the current expansion of so-called artificial intelligence. And after Turing, but also after information theory, information is talked about as something inherently calculable, and as if it were a reality that exists *independently* of its supports. But when we talk about information in this way, we continue to ignore the totally unprecedented fact that, as Gordon Moore showed in the 1960s, binary grammatization, that is, grammatization based on Boolean algebra, encounters the physical structures of matter at the microelectronic scale. (I remind you that I use the term 'grammatization' for everything that consists in discretizing the continuous flows produced by humans, or by what humans perceive, and this has been so since the Upper Palaeolithic, when animal movements were discretized by reproducing them in the form of drawings and paintings, and up until the discretization, today, of 'sequenced' DNA, via all the forms of writing and through the automated mechanization of industrial production.) When binary grammatization encounters the microelectronic structures of matter, it amounts to a concretization in Simondon's sense, that is, an inscription of grammatizing abstraction into exosomatized matter, which in this way re-concretizes what has been abstracted, and this inscription is itself inscribed in what Whitehead calls concrescence, which describes the fundamental character of the universe.

This hyper-material concretization of the abstract constitutes the current stage of capitalism, which must therefore be viewed on the basis of a new materialist epistemology, involving what I have called tertiary retention, a concept that Husserl made it necessary to think. Tertiary retention is what makes materially stable and solid – which is to say spatial – that which is first of all temporal, fluid and unstable: time. It is the spatialization of what Husserl calls primary retentions, which are what we retain temporally from a perceptual flow, for example, the flow of my speech at this moment, and secondary retentions, which are the memories of primary retentions of perception as these are kept in memory when this perception has become past and no longer produces new primary retentions, but presents itself, therefore, as what I have retained of what was present, and which thus becomes past. If you take notes of what I say, however, you 'tertiarize' in advance, in the form of hypomnesic tertiary retentions, your secondary retentions, which become objective retentions, bases of objectified knowledge and 'objective spirit'. I will come back to all of this, which we have already studied in past years.

Tertiary retention refers, more generally, to all the forms of organized inorganic matter. It is the fruit of the process of exosomatization and of what Lotka calls exosomatic evolution. When it becomes hypomnesic, tertiary retention sets off the process of grammatization – that is, of abstraction, in a sense that conditions the process of what Marx himself calls abstraction, and of what Sohn-Rethel refers to with the same name.

What is known as 'Moore's law' will, then, constitute the starting point for my seminar this year in Nanjing. From the standpoint of hyper-materialist epistemology, we must make the following hypothesis: capital, by inscribing its interests in matter in the form of informational (that is, digital) hypomnesic tertiary retentions, performatively realizes and concretizes its *epistēmē* by controlling it as a 'smartified' asocial relation – and here I'm using the vocabulary of Evgeny Morozov.[303] A hyper-materialist epistemology must elaborate a critique of this state of fact, which is in fact an absolute non-knowledge, and not the absolute knowledge heralded by Hegel. Such a critique is a new critique, that is, a critique of the *Critique of Pure Reason*, amounting in the end to a hyper-critique.

This hyper-critique involves a reinterpretation of the *Critique of Pure Reason* starting from the position that the schematism, which connects the understanding and intuition through what the first edition of the *Critique of Pure Reason* calls the transcendental imagination, is the result of exosmatization in its various stages. This activity of the so-called transcendental imagination, but which I will call exosomatic (and 'transcendent' in this sense), is what, through a faculty of dreaming, accomplishes what in *Technics and Time, 1* I called the doubly epokhal redoubling. This occurs when:

1. Exosomatic production generates a new technical system that, during an epoch of the history of technics, is metastabilized around a dominant technique, and this new technical system emerges both from the situation established in a previous technical system and from an inventive realization of the 'faculty of dreaming'.

2. The new technical system causes social systems to enter into crisis, and leads to their reconfiguration – where this reconfiguration generates new circuits of transindividuation (that is, meanings and rules binding together those who thus form a society); new circuits of transindividuation in turn generate many new categories (new concepts of the understanding emerging from experience) and retentional supports for these categories, through which schemas (in Kant's sense) form.

For Kant, these new concepts of the understanding emerging from experience are based on *a priori* synthetic judgments and *a priori* forms of intuition that form what he considers to be the transcendental sphere. For us, this sphere is not transcendental: it is constituted by the singularity of the tertiary retentions produced by exosomatization, and in particular inasmuch as they are shaped and combined as hypomnesic tertiary retentions, that is, as a function of advances in grammatization. This *constitution*, which is not transcendental, is nevertheless also not empirical. It is constitutive in Husserl's sense in 'The Origin of Geometry'. And this means that it is 'metempirical', as Derrida sometimes says:[304] it *maintains itself* over the course of historical empiricity, and as a techno-transcendent (that is, exo-transcendent) condition of singular experiences becoming common and shared experiences, in this way forming social forms of knowledge – knowledge of how to live, do and conceptualize.

I thus distinguish here, among tertiary retentions *in general, hypomnesic* tertiary retentions. Tertiary retentions such as manual tools or instruments for observation shape sense perception in an exo-transcendent way. Hence Simondon posits that the tool handled by the worker constitutes a technical sensorimotor schema that is shaped not by the *a priori* forms of space and time, but by the exo-transcendence of the tool or the instrument. Or again, Galileo's telescope trans-forms the space and time of perception. And this is also what lies on the horizon of sensibility as understood by Marx in the *1844 Manuscripts*.

The grammatization that emerges with hypomnesic tertiary retention affects the analytical processes of discretization that condition the formation of concepts of the understanding – this condition being also the condition of bringing to light the synthetic judgments that are *a priori* only after the metempiricity that grammatization has made possible. It is equally the condition of abstraction in all senses of this word in Marx and in Sohn-Rethel: abstraction of labour, abstraction of exchange, theoretical abstraction and so on. And it is starting from this capacity for abstraction on the basis of the tertiary schematization that the architect conceives what he will build, whereas the bee realizes a structural coupling with its environment (in the sense of Maturana and Varela) that passes through an adjustment that is genetic and not social, and hence not historical.

When exosomatization reaches the stage of the Upper Palaeolithic, whose Lascaux cave paintings were admired by Georges Bataille, the imagination that is supposedly 'transcendental', and in truth exo-transcendent, is then the result of the exosomatization that occurs through the generation of tertiary retentions of a kind that we should call hypomnesic, in the sense that:

- on the one hand, their primary function is to preserve memory, whether imaginary or perceived (which is not the function of those tertiary retentions that are tools);
- on the other hand, this mnemo-technical retention is what, in *Phaedrus*, takes on the hypomnesic function of writing as an aid to memory that Socrates called, precisely, *hypomnesis*, giving rise to diverse forms of what the Greeks called *hypomnēmata* – books, supports of calculation and accounting, notebooks, ephemerides, calendars, maps and so on – where we see that the forms of space and time are reshaped each time that new forms of *hypomnēmata* appear.

The hypomnesic tertiary retentions that appear in the Upper Palaeolithic set off the process of grammatization, in which these diverse forms of writing make possible forms of knowledge based on the *analytical* intellect – and this is something I'll come back to during the seminar.

I first put forward this point of view when I tried to show why Adorno and Horkheimer, Marxist philosophers, failed to question the Kantian and idealist theory of the schematism when they undertook their critique of American cinema and the culture industries in general, even though they posited that the latter leads to an exteriorization of the faculty of schematizing, the secret of which, for Kant, was the transcendental imagination (in the first edition of the *Critique of Pure Reason*). The key thinkers of the Frankfurt School, therefore, tried to constitute a materialist epistemology by the paradoxical gesture of taking as their starting point the idealist perspective of Kant – and, before them, Engels too recognized in Kant the basis of all epistemology. At the end of this seminar, we will see how Sohn-Rethel breaks with this Kantian reference and yet fails in his attempt to critique the *Critique of Pure Reason.*

Before entering into these questions, however, we must redefine the techno-industrial context within which they arise in completely new terms, simultaneously in relation to the young Marx of 1844, the Engels of 1880, the Adorno of 1944 and Sohn-Rethel in 1970. This is what we will do in the second session.

SECOND LECTURE

Specification of the Context in which there Arises the Need for a Hyper-Materialist Epistemology: The Reign of the 'Notion of Information'

What is the origin of microelectronics, from out of which the microelectronics company Intel, founded by a chemist and physicist from Caltech, will forge America's power today, a microelectronics whose techno-logical dynamic constitutes a specific form of performativity, as we will see, one that is now reaching its limits, as it moves towards nanotechnology in a way that is itself opening onto what has been called NBIC convergence – the convergence of nanotechnology, biotechnology, information technology and cognitive technology?

The origin of microelectronics is the vacuum tube, which was studied in *On the Mode of Existence of Technical Objects* (specifically, the triode and pentode), and which will eventually lead to semiconductors, but first to diodes, these silicon components being called transistors, in combination with resistors and capacitors. At that time, in the industry that would become 'consumer electronics', these components were still soldered onto *printed* circuits, that is, pre-wired circuits.

This silicon semiconductor technology would lead to 'chips', that is, to microprocessors and to the microelectronics of our time: semiconductor components are now miniaturized to the scale of millionths of a metre, and the production of electronic circuits, which has become inaccessible to human gestures, is now fully automated. In becoming microelectronic, semiconductors have been combined on the scale of millionths of a metre on circuits that are no longer simply *printed*, but *integrated* – through the use of Complementary Metal Oxide Semiconductor technology (CMOS).

My father, who was an electrical worker before becoming an electronics technician, lived through this change of scale during his career: from the transistor, which was between about one and ten millimetres across, to the *microphysically concretized*[305] microprocessor, invisible to the naked eye. During his retirement, he was aware of the shift to billionths of a metre: the scale of the *infinitely small*, accessible only through a scanning tunnelling microscope (STM) of the kind first conceived by IBM in 1981. The nanometric distances involved with so-called nanostructures are those of the quantum scale, meaning that these nanostructures remain invisible *even to the instrument-equipped* eye, that is, the exosomatized eye, except by visually *simulating* it with the STM, this simulation being a kind of techno-logical schematization, and here exosomatization crosses a threshold whose implications are still very unclear.

A billionth of a metre is infra-luminous, that is, 'beneath' the field of luminous frequencies, and therefore it is indeed *invisible*. With nanoscience, and the nanotechnologies on which it is based, exosomatization operates where the laws of matter known on the macroscopic scale simply no longer apply: it operates by feeling its way along, as no doubt has occurred throughout the history of exosomatization, but here, in some way, this groping is carried out *with thoroughly digital fingers, digital digits* that lie outside all sensible intuition (and we rediscover here the questions that Gaston Bachelard had already raised in the 1930s, but which have now arrived at a far more radical point).

This means that images of nanostructures are at the same time what a researcher sees and what he does not see, strictly speaking, because the image is only a *simulation* of what *cannot* be seen. The scientific gaze of the researcher is instrumentally equipped by this simulacrum, which conditions it – and which brings to a highly specific stage the process of exosomatization involved in any noetic gaze, beginning with that of the humans whom Georges Bataille discovers by seeing them in the Lascaux cave.[306]

What, then, does *seeing* mean here – and there? I add '*and there*' because we might equally say that Bataille *himself does not see what he sees*. This at least is what Plato says at the beginning of Book VII of the *Republic*, when he recounts the cave allegory. What does Bataille see? He sees 'animals' that have been seen, or imagined, or dreamed of, starting from the visible, by humans who disappeared thousands of years ago. But Bataille does not see 'animals': he sees only phantasms, in the first sense of the word, fantasies of animals – as do the prisoners in the cave.

These phantasms, which are thus only images of them, are made visible by the ability of the noetic soul to exo-somatize its *impressions*, which is also to say, as Marc Azéma says, to *realize* its dreams.[307] Unlike the tick studied by Jakob von Uexküll,[308] the *noetic impression* does not remain within an endosomatic circuit between the receptors and effectors that are the sensorimotor organs of the insect but also of the endosomatic higher living thing. This noetic *impression* gives an expression, and this expression is exteriorized via fabricated objects – of which words and all transindividual ex-pressions are layers – and *it is noetic only on this condition*.

What Bataille sees is what amounts to the *hypomnesic turn of exosomatization* – through which *hypomnēmata* emerge, that is, those mnemotechnical supports that Socrates posits as *pharmaka*: at the same time making noesis possible and permanently and irreducibly threatening it, these *hypomnēmata* being also what Seneca maintains are the condition of techniques of the self – of that *tekhnē tou biou* that Michel Foucault studied at the end of his life. This is very important insofar as Pierre Hadot has shown that ancient philosophy is above all what aims to constitute, disseminate and stabilize techniques of the self,[309] which Foucault has in turn shown amount to techniques of the government of others – and this is undoubtedly true of the pre-Socratics of whom we shall see how Sohn-Rethel, building upon Thomson, attempts to identify the material and historical conditions of their advent in Ionia (situated in what is today called Anatolia, that is, the Asiatic part of Turkey, located in the immediate vicinity of what was then called Lydia, where the first forms of currency appeared).

Techniques of the self are required by exosomatization given that what it produces, exosomatic organs, are *pharmaka*, that is, remedies that are also poisons. We will see that this is also what Lotka says when he describes the function of knowledge in exosomatic evolution.

Exosomatization, which began some three million years before the Upper Palaeolithic, is described by Alfred Lotka in 1945[310] as a major transformation of the organogenesis of living things: endosomatic organogenesis engenders organic organs, whereas exosomatic organogenesis produces inorganic (but organized) organs, constituting organized inorganic matter, which I have called *hyper-matter*. Hypermatter, which is thus inorganic matter organized by exosomatization during exosomatic evolution, presents itself in the form of technical objects that accumulate by forming what Leroi-Gourhan calls technical milieus and what Bertrand Gille calls technical systems.

Materialism must then consider four completely different types of matter:

- inert or inorganic matter;
- organic matter;
- organized inorganic matter;
- disorganized and reorganized organic matter.

The last of these (reorganized organic matter) includes the human brain and body educated and thus trans-formed by social artefacts, along with those plants and animals that have been created through agricultural selection since the Neolithic. In another seminar, given in Hangzhou, I showed how Sigmund Freud sometimes tried to conceive this as a process of organic defunctionalization and refunctionalization characteristic of the formation of what he called the libidinal economy. And I myself argue that this libidinal economy is the condition of all noesis – which is something we should explore further with Spinoza, but we won't have time to do so now.

The technical milieus that transform inorganic matter via organs that are themselves inorganic but organized, that is, hyper-material, allow organic but exosomatic beings to *constitute worlds* by doubling up on these technical milieus with ethnic milieus. We call these beings humans and these worlds human worlds. These redoublings, which constitute the doubly epokhal redoubling already mentioned, form circuits of transindividuation that engender layers of what Simondon called the transindividual, that is, significance [*signification*], whose inorganic but organized substrates (hypomnesic media or supports) constitute *hyper-materiality*. We will see how these hyper-material formations of technical milieus constitute hyper-material formations of social systems, where the latter themselves govern what Marx and Engels describe in *The German Ideology* as social relations. And we will see why these social systems depend on the types of knowledge that are generated by the redoubling of exosomatization.

From a hyper-materialist perspective, itself composed from the exosomatic standpoint developed by Alfred Lotka, we must, then, very carefully consider and distinguish four types of matter (inorganic matter, organic matter, organized inorganic matter, disorganized and reorganized organic matter). The last two of these types of matter require the formation of social systems governing social relations, and the last, insofar as it consists in disorganizing and reorganizing living hyper-matter, from the Neolithic forms a process both of raising and cultivating vegetative souls (of plants) and sensitive souls (of animals), and of the education of noetic souls (human beings). Let's now examine how these social forms are presented and engendered in the course of history.

To the extent that the noetic forms of life embodied in human groups spread out into the *oikumenē*, the milieus that Leroi-Gourhan calls ethnic become imperial milieus, then politico-religious, until they find themselves dissolved by the great transformation resulting from the disembedding of the market.[311] Along with Karl Polanyi, Arnold Toynbee will try to describe this becoming as that of what he calls civilizations (he rejects the idea that the nation is the relevant level for taking account of this dynamic[312]), civilizations that, he argues, are always inhabited by a suicidal tendency.[313]

In 1944, Erwin Schrödinger described nutrition as a function by which the organism maintains itself in a state of negative entropy, enabling it to locally struggle (in the locality of its organic body) against the loss of energy that is the mineral law of the universe.[314] Building on Lotka's concept of exosomatization, Nicholas Georgescu-Roegen[315] shows that the artificial organs that constitute hominization, that is, exosomatization – which are already at stake in man's production of his own organs as this is described in 1846 by Marx and Engels in *The German Ideology* – are the operators of the transformation, assimilation and metabolization of organic and inorganic matter, through which humankind itself struggles against entropy.

Marxian materialism begins in this way: by taking account, early on, of exosomatization, which is not an accidental or temporary situation imposed on prisoners in a cave, but the condition of all noesis. The definition of man as *producer* and of his ideas as *results* of this production, which idealism would rather prefer to put at the origin of the world through the 'realism of ideas', which Marx and Engels call ideology – this definition, however, which is anticipated and prepared in the *1844 Manuscripts*, remains incomplete and inadequate insofar as it is not reintegrated into the becoming of endosomatic and exosomatic organs considered from the standpoint of entropy, negentropy and what Francis Bailly, Giuseppe Longo and Maël Montévil call anti-entropy.

Here, however, there is a difficulty: the second half of the twentieth century gets bogged down in its attempt to think différance (in Derrida's sense), which ties entropy and negentropy to the concept of information – and we will see why and how Simondon fails to escape this noetic trap. In fact, it is impossible to utilize a concept such as negentropy – or negative entropy – to describe human activity: as we have already seen when we specified the function of knowledge in exosomatization, the artificial organs that are mobilized in its struggle against entropy are *pharmaka* (in the sense of this term used by Socrates in *Protagoras* and *Phaedrus*). If an *economy* is needed in order to metabolize what is no longer strictly biological, but technological, it is because technology is pharmacological – and this means that it can as easily limit entropy as increase it.

We are therefore no longer able to conceive the possibility of struggling against entropy solely on the basis of negative entropy as defined by Schrödinger in his analysis of endosomatization. On the contrary, we must posit that exosomatization produces a new regime of différance, which is the name that negative entropy takes in Derrida. This exosomatic différance, inasmuch as it generates exosomatic organs that are *pharmaka*, sets up a pharmacological relation that is an irreducible tension, within which there occurs a simultaneous opposing and combining of what we should call anthropy and neganthropy. We refer to 'anthropy', here, in the sense implied when in 2014 the IPCC referred to 'anthropogenic forcings'[316] as what has produced that *biospheric disorder* known as 'climate change'.

Anthropy is what humanity discovers at the beginning of the twenty-first century under the name of the Anthropocene era, which is an Entropocene, as climate change slowly but surely emerges into public debate – and as its primary concern, even if in the mode of deafness, because massively *denied*, despite this change, and everything that (consequently) it accompanies, or that accompanies it (of which it is the cause), constituting a threat greater than any other, and this is what seems to be dawning on the youth of Europe in a powerful way.

This situation, however, remains denied by many politicians, business leaders and academics – even though it is increasingly documented and described by scientists around the world. Post-truth is the experience of these forms of resignation, denial, cowardice, compromise and complicity, and of the anxieties that all this causes. These miserable and impoverished aspects of contemporary morale, however, are merely effects of what noesis discovers today: that it is unable to redouble the techno-logical epokhal redoubling that is the digital stage of exosomatization, because the latter generates the kind of noetic short-circuits described in *Automatic Society*.

In this *post-truth* age, a new hyper-materialist epistemology is required in order to exorganogenetically redefine the *faculties and functions of noesis*, which must itself be conceived as work in all its forms ('manual' and 'intellectual'), but by distinguishing it from labour (muscular or nervous): the catastrophic situation that has been imposed on the biosphere as a whole stems from this new stage of the exosomatization of noesis itself, inasmuch as it does not succeed in redoubling itself. And this stage is now turning into the generalization of artificial intelligence – of which libertarian ideology tries to impose a transhumanist interpretation.

Noesis itself has been unfolding since the Upper Palaeolithic, when the process of grammatization contemplated by Bataille in Lascaux first began to unfold, and its evolutions since the Neolithic lie at the origin of the great empires, then of the monotheisms (among which we should include Buddhism, in the sense argued by Jean-Luc Nancy[317]), and then of the Greek *polis* – that is, at the origin of politics. It is by appropriating and directing this exosomatization through what will become universities that the West (starting from Islam, which is a *major internal border*) undertakes the territorial and economic conquest that will lead to the Anthropocene era, accomplished as globalization – that is, as the imposition of a unified technical system across the biosphere as a whole.

But this is possible only because, in the eighteenth century, the process of grammatization mutates, giving rise to industrial capitalism as machinism, but also, over the last two centuries, as the adoption of accounting rules that today are still called *ratios*. It is in this world increasingly dominated by monetary systems, account-keeping and the calculation of everything via *mathesis universalis* that Vaucanson's automaton and all its consequences will lead to the grammatization of gesture and of the sensorimotor circuits of the labouring bodies set in motion by the nervous-muscular system. After that, it is perception that will be grammatized (via phonographic and then photo-cinematographic recording), and then the understanding, already grammatized by writing, will be recoded by digital information transformed into calculable binary numbers on the basis of automated logical functions.

Exosomatization thus finds itself going through an acceleration that is *literally* incommensurable: without measure, out of all proportion. After the death of God, the standard that would provide such a measure is lacking. In the early twenty-first century, this reaches a limit whose eschatological character was inconceivable for Kant, as well as for Hegel and Marx. There are thus stages and a history of exosomatization, which is equally the history of the faculties and functions in the sense that Kant[318] and then Whitehead would give to these terms, which constitute noesis. Throughout these stages – prehistorical, protohistorical and historical – the doubly epokhal redoubling continues to occur, but *today*, the second, noetic moment, referred to with the term '*doubly*', is failing to occur.

The current stage of exosomatization is in this regard utterly singular: in the age of disruption, and as the most advanced and probably the ultimate stage of the Anthropocene, exosomatization no longer succeeds in redoubling – and it is in this way that the Anthropocene amounts to an Entropocene. To shift from this state of fact to a new state of law, constituting *a new era of noesis*, requiring what Nietzsche describes as a sur-human (*übermenschlich*) effort, is to establish a right to the Neganthropocene defined as the noetic therapeutics of the Anthropocene and a new age of knowledge (of how to live, do and conceive), these forms of knowledge being themselves conceived as the therapies and therapeutics of all forms of *pharmaka*.

To undertake such an enterprise, a new hyper-materialist and hypercritical epistemology is required, one that builds on Simondon's fundamental advances. Nevertheless, it is possible to rely on Simondon only on the condition of identifying its weaknesses and less solid zones, on which it is not possible to build without the risk of collapse: it is possible to build on this major work only if we set out its limits, inasmuch as they are tied to his way of invoking the 'notion of information'. As he uses it, this 'notion', as he himself calls it, in fact allows Simondon to completely bypass the colossal problem of the pharmacology of industrial exosomatization. It is for this reason that the first part of this seminar is subtitled *The Notion of Information*.

▪ ▪ ▪

Georges Canguilhem writes:

> though there are good works on technology, the very notion and methods of an 'organology' remain vague. Thus, paradoxically, far from coming in belatedly to occupy an abandoned viewpoint, philosophy points science toward a position to take.[319]

Hyper-materialist epistemology is such an organology. And the latter, which is also an exorganology, systematically examines the evolution of states of matter put into forms by the process of exosomatization. In the current stage of this becoming, which reaches a limit, and which requires a new critique that is a hyper-materialist hyper-critique, microelectronics gives way to nanotechnologies. It is in the context of the nano-initiative launched by Bill Clinton in 1999[320] that '*moderne Technik*'-cum-'*Gestell*' enters the era of nanotechnologies, which are miniaturized a thousandfold compared with microelectronic components that were themselves invisible to the naked eye, but on a scale of invisibility of another order of magnitude.

These *scales of invisibility* pose immense scientific, economic and political 'black box' problems: they inscribe the conditions for an absolute proletarianization in the atomic and molecular structure of microphysically then nanophysically concretized digital tertiary retentions. 'Absolute' means here: inasmuch as it leads to a *total and generalized denoetization*. Such is the backdrop of the post-truth age. This obviously does not mean that we should conceive the truth as being constituted by visibility: on the contrary, we posit with Heidegger that the truth, *a-lētheia*, is essentially part of the hidden, the latent and the invisible. But this does mean that we must continue to 'deconstruct' what has attached, to the notion of truth (and at the *moment of the e-vidence of its salience*), those of light and visibility, at least since Plato.[321] We must pursue this 'deconstruction' at a moment when invisibility has become in some way *patent*, and in a way *palpable*, as for example with a scanning tunnelling microscope – yet not visible: less visible than ever.

This is only the beginning of an im-mense transformation: the quantum nano-scale makes it possible to combine electronics, bionics and algorithmics, opening the age of what Jean-Pierre Dupuy and

Françoise Roure have called 'transformational technologies'.[322] It is on this techno-logical foundation, still being built, that transhumanist *storytelling* (to which we will return) relies. Confronted with this, 'metaphysics' – sedimented in diverse but inevitable forms of academic careerism and its associated cowardice – is lamentably helpless when disruption allows the functional integration of short-circuits that lead systemically to noetic forms of regression and resignation via 'functional stupidity' itself implemented by *functional sovereignty.*

(A note about what has been called 'speculative realism', which, too, claims to be the foundation of an epistemology, one that would be realist, if not materialist in our sense: it is striking to see Quentin Meillassoux highlight the absolute self-evidence of what he calls 'ancestrality'[323] without saying a word about the opacity so characteristic of what constitutes the age of phenomeno-technics, as theorized by Bachelard almost a century ago.[324] This blindness, which *apparently* has nothing technological about it, unless we happen to recall what is written in *The German Ideology,* is due to the silence that speculative realism maintains about the technical conditions of access to this ancestrality, conditions that we will try to show must lead us to critique criticism in a sense quite opposed to this restoration – which begins with Alain Badiou's rehabilitation of Plato's idealism in a manner that is the complete opposite of Marx's historical materialism.)

Microelectronics, whose conditions of possibility are established in the late 1950s with the technology of semiconductors and printed circuit boards, is the *physico-industrial reality* of what is known as 'Moore's law', which is itself the physico-industrial *strategy* pursued by Intel, of which Gordon Moore is the chairman emeritus.[325] It is 'Moore's law' that, in combination with the World Wide Web, has caused what is now called disruption. The latter builds upon the physico-industry in order to produce a *psychoindustry* that has now become a *neuroindustry* (which we studied last year) – one that disintegrates social and intergenerational relations, replacing them with algorithmic relations, that is, calculated relations, which no longer have anything to enact: *annihilating action* by taking control of the dopaminergic system, as Gerald Moore has shown at Durham University.

THIRD LECTURE

On Technological Performativity and Its Consequences for the 'Notion of Information'

What we call 'Moore's law' (of Gordon Moore, not Gerald Moore) is not a scientific law. And Sacha Loève shows that Gordon Earle Moore himself knows it:

> Intel, by marketing the first microprocessor in 1971, was literally created *in order to apply* the propositions [of an] article [by Moore] from 1965 ['Cramming More Components onto Integrated Circuits', in *Electronics*]. Moore's law would then be a program drawn up by Moore and his collaborators, and Intel the organization charged with applying it. In his own words, 'Moore's law has become a self-fulfilling prophecy. [Chipmakers] know they have to stay on that curve to remain competitive, so they put in the effort to make it happen'.[326]

This scientific-non-law that creates a state of fact by concretizing – that is, by *exosomatizing* – a microelectronic and hence 'informed' organization of matter,[327] this non-law will nevertheless *function performatively* as a physico-economic law on the basis of it being a self-fulfilling utterance, an utterance that will thus have been *functional*. A self-fulfilling prophecy is also what, after John Austin, has become known as a performative utterance.[328] Such a technological performativity is made possible by what we call *complex exorganisms*[329] of a specific type that appeared in the nineteenth century: industrial enterprises.

As a reminder: a simple exorganism is an organism equipped with exosomatic organs – as all of us are here. A complex exorganism is a collection of simple exorganisms sharing common exosomatic organs, such as a family, a workshop, a city or a country. We must distinguish between lower complex exorganisms, subject to a higher law, and higher complex exorganisms, which elaborate their own laws, to which they subject lower complex exorganisms, and, through them, the simple exorganisms that we are. The specific feature of what has been called modernity is that juridical laws approach closer to scientific laws, even if, as Alain Supiot shows, they should not be confused with and cannot be reduced to one another.

The convergence between law in the juridical sense and law in the geometrical sense is, moreover, constitutive of politics inasmuch as its origin is constituted in the Greek *polis*. And the gap between law in the legal and scientific senses is, in Christian Western Europe, the challenge of theology and of its philosophical translation as onto-theology. From the moment that Descartes and Leibniz set calculation at the heart of knowledge in the form of *mathesis universalis* that leads via *characteristica universalis* to digital tertiary retention, passing along the way through the machinic grammatization of the body and the analogue grammatization of perception, theological incalculability and the gap between juridical law and scientific law will be liquidated.

This liquidation is what Heidegger names *Gestell*. And this *Gestell* already refers to what we now call the Anthropocene. The *Ereignis* awaited by Heidegger is a bifurcation, which can occur only on the condition that an incalculability that is neither divine nor theological but systemic and functional (in the sense of Whitehead, who, however, himself keeps the function of God), reorganizes a planetary political economy in the biosphere-cum-technosphere. Having now posited this as the archi-protention of the hyper-critical *epistēmē* and its hyper-materialist epistemology, let us return to 'Moore's so-called law' and its performativity.

The way in which this proclaimed 'Moore's law' functions outside law (in the scientific sense of the term: without theory, that is, without *criteria* of truth in the strict sense, and so without *critique*) – where this 'law' is merely a particularly striking case of a much more general situation, generated by the submission of research to development (and we should mention another case, less striking but more disturbing, that of what Cathy O'Neil calls *weapons of math destruction*[330]), and which, among other things, explodes the frames of reference for primary, secondary and tertiary education – is the condition of possibility of the generalized feeling of the discredit of truth and of the installation of that scientifico-academic and politico-economic misery and poverty referred to as 'post-truth'. Hence is established the post-truth age. And in so doing, the difference between higher and lower complex exorganisms is erased.

This *techno-logical performativity* is not soluble into performativity in John Austin's sense: it is based on the *return effect of exosomatization on its own operation*.[331] Exosomatization is the producer of tertiary retentions generating new schematizations,[332] which are therefore performative[333] in that, in the post-truth age, and as the techno-logical performativity of physico-industry-cum-psycho-industry-and-neuro-industry, *they outstrip and overtake the categories and procedures of academic verification and certification enabled by the faculties* (of

Letters, Sciences, Law, Medicine, and previously Philosophy and Theology and so on). Hence is established what is no longer what Foucault called a regime of truth, but *a regime of non-truth* installed by *a state of fact that rejects the criteriology of truth* that theory is supposed to provide.

Moore, who received his PhD in chemistry in 1954, founded Intel in 1968, by attracting, through the *narrative* of opportunities and investments *conceivable on the basis of microphysics*, the capital necessary for investments in the *exosomatic reorganization of matter at the microelectronic scale*. He thereby induced a specific regime of what Simondon called concretization. This *pseudo-law*, which may be true *in fact*, is not so *in law*. This means that it is not true according to the scientific gaze, or, more exactly, that *it is not a law* but a *series of facts* whose *unity* remains to be described, that is, to be *theorized*. This is so because *to this day, science has no complete theory of exosomatization*, that is, of the *process by which noetic life constantly augments its power to act* through artifices that are always *also*, however, what *diminish* its power to act, even to disintegrate it, annihilate it and, ultimately, completely destroy it.

To characterize this kind of series, it is necessary to reinterpret the Platonic dialogue *Meno* and its reference to Persephone from an exosomatic standpoint. The goal of hyper-materialist epistemology is to produce the hyper-critical theory of the function of truth in exosomatization and of the series of facts presenting themselves as quasi-laws that are not, that is: that are not neganthropic, but on the contrary anthropic and thus toxic. In other words, it is a matter of identifying and différantiating exo-transcendent illusions and of transforming them into exo-transcendent knowledge.

Neither science nor 'interscience'[334] have a theory of the conditions within which a *techno-logical utterance* such as 'Moore's law' *can* massively structure – in a specific dimension of the *Umwelt* become *Welt* and then *Gestell*,[335] that is, by concretizing itself techno-logically via cybernetics – a scale of matter that is also the microphysical support, invisible to the naked eye, of what has become the dominant tertiary retention,[336] this being a possibility that is specific to a *new stage of exosomatization*.

Becoming microelectronic, on the way to becoming nanometric, when artificial *memory develops in tertiary retentional space at the microelectronic scale of wafers*,[337] it doubles every eighteen months – which means that, every eighteen months, it is possible to put twice as many microelectronic semiconductor components onto the surface of a wafer. This is what 'Moore's law' says – in the context of what Sacha Loève calls a 'technology without object' (a nanophysics where molecules are considered to have become machines). This law, however, is not one in the eyes of science: on the basis of its techno-logical performativity, it *provokes* this state of fact, whereas a law sets forth a state of law – which always remains pending, thus requiring a new *attention*, which is also to say a new discernment: a *new critique*, which is therefore a *hyper-critique*.

In other words, the performativity of this state of fact that still awaits its state of law – and the performativity that goes along with the law, as described by John Austin in his speech act theory – passes through the *analysis and synthesis*:

1 of the consequences of miniaturization inasmuch as it allows an astounding increase in the *performance speeds* of microelectronic machines, which tomorrow will become nanoquantum, and then bionic;

2 of the *fact* – to be trans-*formed* into law – that this is possible only because it is the continuation, *according to completely new modalities that were hitherto unknown and inconceivable*, of a process of exosomatization that metastabilized itself as the process of hominization some three million years ago.

These transformations of exosomatization (of which transhumanism is the global marketing strategy aiming to legitimize the hegemony of platforms), which have made it possible to generalize digital tertiary retention and the calculable functions that accompany it by setting up an algorithmic governmentality now founded on reticulated artificial intelligence – these transformations have, at the beginning of the twenty-first century, engendered a *conflict* between the noetic *faculties* in the era of digital tertiary retention. This conflict occurs between the *psychic faculties* of psychic individuals, and within these individuals themselves, which constitutes a noetic and psychic ill-being of hitherto unknown magnitude, especially among students, leading to addiction, drive-based behaviour and sometimes suicide, and is in turn reflected in a conflict between the *academic faculties*, that is, between the processes of collective individuation that are the communities of knowledge, which lose their knowledge and find themselves proletarianized by 'black boxes' as well as by the industrial hyper-division of 'intellectual' labour. This conflict of the faculties – in the two senses of this word in Kant – is itself induced by a conflict between the noetic *functions* provoked by the exosomatization of these functions (or 'lower faculties') that are for Kant intuition, imagination and the understanding (the higher faculties being the faculty of knowing, the faculty of desiring and the faculty of judging[338]), which we will now examine.

In automated society, automated understanding becomes purely computational and in so doing short-circuits the function of reason. This short-circuit also operates at the level of the academic faculties when, for example, data science departments develop to the detriment of the faculties that emerged from Kantian or related modernity, computer science imposing here its *efficiency in fact* upon the scientific *formalisms* and *finalities* of law – through its techno-logical performativity exercised on microphysical matter. In all this, what remains unthought is hyper-materiality, and reference is instead made to the 'immaterial' – this is done, for example, by those who along with Toni Negri fantasize about 'cognitive capitalism'.

Now, none of this would be possible without exosomatized matter inasmuch as it constitutes a *hyper-matter* irreducible to the hylemorphic schema. It is Simondon who makes it possible and necessary to go beyond the concept of matter that remains entangled either in substantialism or in the oppositional pairs that accompany the division between form and matter arising from Aristotelian ontology. Simondon's advance, however, remains 'caught midstream', because it takes up the concept of information emerging from information theory combined with the fiction of the 'abstract machine' (whose misuse is denounced by Turing himself): this concept of information is utterly confused, especially through its neutralization of matter that is evidently still hyper-matter. It is this reduction, eliminating matter, that allows everything to be dissolved into the abstraction of calculation, and we will see how Bailly, Longo and Montévil contrast this with the concept of anti-entropy that takes account of the geometrical dimension of matter.

Hyper-matter is the organized inorganic matter that Leroi-Gourhan described in the early 1940s in *L'homme et la matière* and *Milieu et technique*.[339] In *Gesture and Speech* (and more precisely in note 14, page 413), he shows that all hyper-matter (all inorganic matter organized through technical fashioning) factually constitutes a support of memory, that is, of what we are here calling tertiary retention. This technical materiality of memory, bearer of forms, cannot be reduced to its physical materiality alone, its form constituting what we will also call its organization – the question of which was outlined by Kant in his *Critique of Judgment*.

This is what leads Simondon to highlight the constitutive role of technics in the formation of the transindividual. Hyper-matter, understood as tertiary retention (and as the pharmacological exosomatization of the mnesic function) is the condition of possibility and impossibility of the schemas arising from the transcendental imagination in the first edition of the *Critique of Pure Reason*. And we have seen in previous sessions why we should refer to metempirical exo-transcendence rather than to *a priori* and transcendental forms and judgments.

Today, in the twenty-first century of purely computational capitalism, digital tertiary retention overturns the schematism inherited from previous epochs, a schematism formed by literary, ideographic and alphabetical grammatization, as well as the monetary grammatization founded on currency. This results in a new conflict of the faculties[340] and functions – which find themselves de-composed by electronic, cybernetic, informational and 'transformational' exosomatization – thereby constituting an age of post-truth that brings with it not just intergenerational conflict but intergenerational *disintegration,*[341] while the critique of political economy coming from Smith, Ricardo and Marx is left disarmed. Yet this conflict should and could be – albeit highly *improbably,* like the *anelpiston* of Heraclitus, and where this is conditional upon taking a *pharmacological* approach – the matrix of a change of era establishing a new age of noesis via the *Ereignis* whose advent lies in *Gestell.*

The situation established by the new conflict of the faculties and functions in the digital stage of exosomatization is insolvent, unsustainable and unbearable. Such a situation, leading to the disruptive stage of the Entropocene and thereby accomplishing what Nietzsche thought in terms of nihilism, cannot *last,* except in becoming the *end of everything*: in this way, it demands a change of era. Such a change is not a dialectical *Aufhebung*: it is a *quasi-causal* (in Deleuze's sense) and thus therapeutic *reversal* of the toxic pharmacological condition, a condition that exosomatization sets up but that is here brought to its *final* extremity (*eskhaton*). I will not have time now to develop this theme of quasi-causality, which will be expounded in detail in *La technique et le temps 4. L'ère post-véridique.*

This disintegrating conflict was itself made inevitable – if not necessary – by the contemporary stage of exosomatization: the latter is the effective, *material, efficient and formal,* but *not final,* and therefore *insufficient*[342] reality of this history of noesis that is the history of truth. It is this hyper-critical necessity that constitutes the finality of hyper-materialist epistemology, calling for an architectonics in a new completely new sense, which it would be tempting but erroneous to conceive as an *anarchitectonics*: this architectonics of metempirical and exo-transcendent *impure reason* must investigate data and network architectures as the engineering of computational, cybernetic and logistical tertiary retentions, amounting to a new schematism and the new condition of any process of categorization. Yuk Hui is working on this task through his research.

It would be erroneous to refer to anarchitectonics because the hyper-material schematization in general, and the digital in particular, insofar as it is rational, does not leave the notion of *arkhē* meaningless or futile. On the contrary: it requires it more than ever, but in a way that must be rethought and cared about from a pharmacological standpoint[343] – that is, an exosomatic and thus functional (in Whitehead's sense) standpoint. This new architectonics is what must arise from a critique of data formats and structures, and from the principles of calculability implemented in the field of permanent connectivity that is becoming an effective reality at the scale of the biosphere. This requires a trans-formation of the current stage of exosomatization – a trans-formation stemming from a *neganthropology* that has already been discussed in previous years.

In the absence of epoch[344] that is 'post-truth', newly embodied by the American president elected in 2016, an absence of epoch that amounts to *the intergenerational disintegration engendered by the new conflict of the faculties and functions* caused by digital tertiary retention, monopolized and hegemonically implemented by the industry of what is now referred to as 'platform capitalism', *the history of truth is what must be reconstituted from an exosomatic standpoint.*[345] It is from this standpoint that, at the end of this seminar, we will try to approach the work of Lev Vygotsky, Ignace Meyerson and Alfred Sohn-Rethel, which should be undertaken in dialogue with the research of Zhang Yibing.

▪ ▪ ▪

Man is a technical being, that is, unfinished. To survive, he *must produce* artificial organs, *learn to practise* these artificial organs, and, for this, *institute* social organizations that articulate the relations between generations, and between producers and practitioners of existing and future exosomatic organs. Urban commerce in all its forms – and as intelligence in the sense this word has in eighteenth-century Europe – is firstly this circulation of exosomatic production. To make it possible to learn how to practise the artificial organs bequeathed by the ascendants of this exosomatic being who is the human being is the role of education in general. Through this legacy, and by adding the new exosomatic organs always required by the dysfunctions that exosomatization inevitably produces, and as the *phase shifts* between

1 the endosomatic organs of the psychic individual,

2 the exosomatic organs of the technical system,

3 preceptive and prescriptive social organizations,

this exosomatic being must find its way towards what remains always yet to come – that is, improbable: not deducible from the previous states of the system. Truth is the criterion of such a search.

What is exosomatically inscribed and written in this way is the 'history of truth', in the sense that Martin Heidegger tried to conceive as the history of being – but philosophy, including Heidegger's, has until now denied this exosomatic soil, from Plato onwards, but not including Marx and Bergson: these two thinkers are thus exceptions, though in this respect completely misunderstood, except by Georges Canguilhem.

The future [*avenir*] that seeks itself in becoming [*devenir*] is the *truth* of this destiny, and if we must read Heidegger, it is because it is here that his fundamental teaching lies: truth means the truth of time, and this time is always what remains to come, including and firstly as the past. The truth of this possible destiny *in becoming*, which thus comes to it from a *possible future*, and as a promise, is nevertheless also what is *concealed* [*celée*] in its past, the latter being constituted by the exosomatic and epiphylogenetic accumulation of the facts, gestures and precepts of ascendants: this accumulation contains [*recèle*] – like the *receiving of the fire stolen*[346] *from Zeus and Hephaestus by Prometheus* – a truth that remains always and improbably still to come for the descendants, inasmuch as, from the precepts of those who are deceased, extra-ordinary ex-ceptions can still occur.

Without drawing out all the consequences, Simondon names this concealment the 'preindividual' – and the reason he fails to draw out all the consequences is that he does not manage to clarify the relationship between the preindividual and the transindividual. The Simondonian preindividual is 'supersaturated', that is, it contains opportunities for bifurcations in the process from which it stems and which stems from it, and it is recursive. This recursivity is that of which cybernetic feedback loops are the computational grammatization, now effected through three billion smartphones spread across all continents of the biosphere, which has thus become a technosphere and an exosphere.

It is from this supersaturated preindividual potential that, in Simondonian theory, the 'quantum leaps' of psychosocial individuation occur as processes in which events happen in a sense that can in this way be understood by a historical hyper-materialism. Such potentials are incalculable precisely because they change the rules of calculation that always govern any individuation (by synchronizing it in its metastability). This is why they are the sources of all singularities.

Truth is the *challenge and the issue* of *continuing* exosomatization *in these conditions that are always pharmacological, and that are therefore metempirical and exo-transcendent conditions of impossibility as well as of possibility.* So conceived, truth is at stake *in all knowledge*

– of how to live, do, interpret and conceive.[347] Forms of knowledge are the primordial functions of exosomatic life, and they are governed by the *contest* [*épreuve*] of truth – whether it is between football teams or between Albert Einstein and Niels Bohr, and as the struggle for the better.[348] Knowledge, conceived in this way – in the wake of Georges Canguilhem – is what, over time, effects *bifurcations* that fall within what, in what follows, we will call the neganthropy of a being who can just as easily be anthropic, the examination of this dual possibility being the subject of neganthropology as consideration of history, proto-history and prehistory understood from the exosomatic and hyper-materialist standpoint.

Neganthropy accomplishes, in an exosomatic and thus artificial mode, what Erwin Schrödinger called negative entropy (later abbreviated to it negentropy), which is *characteristic* of that life that is endosomatic organogenesis. The study of neganthropy and the anthropic forcings[349] that always threaten it is the subject of neganthropology. Today, we live in the Anthropocene. But the Anthropocene is *unliveable*: it leads to an immense increase in entropy. This is why hyper-materialist epistemology is political and economic through and through.

FOURTH LECTURE

The Noetic Faculties and Functions in Exosomatization

As the Entropocene reaches the disruptive stage, it radically affects the conditions of education, which are the conditions of what Kant called the higher faculties – of knowing, desiring and judging – but also of theology, law, medicine and philosophy. How do such *institutional* faculties relate to the subjective faculties of transcendental critical reason – as transcendental aesthetics, transcendental logic, transcendental imagination – subjective faculties that we would today call psychic? This is the question of the relationships between psychogenesis and noogenesis that we rediscover with Vygotsky and Sohn-Rethel.

The faculties such as Kant theorized them, both in the three *Critiques* and in *The Conflict of the Faculties*, are noetic in Aristotle's sense. We argue, however, that they are also historical, because they are hyper-material, and thus exo-transcendent, and that there is a history of noesis, not simply in Hegel's sense (for whom this history leads to the absolute, and was therefore only a detour), but in the sense outlined in *The German Ideology*, an outline to which Lotka brings decisive elements.

The noetic faculties and functions are exosomatically *conditioned*. Their exosomatic condition is established by constantly transforming themselves on the basis of schemas provided by the play of tertiary retentions with the primary and secondary retentions and protentions arising from the three syntheses of the imagination set out in the 'Transcendental Deduction of Categories' of the first edition of the *Critique of Pure Reason*. The noetic faculties are *constituted* by the *relations* between functions, in a sense of the word 'function' that we borrow from Alfred Whitehead (and which we relate to what Kant called the lower faculties of intuition, imagination, understanding and reason, as we have already indicated). If the Entropocene is the era of what has been called post-truth, it is because a new conflict of the faculties and functions is being played out, one that destroys the conditions of *temporalization*.

Always already conditioned by the techno-logical schemas emerging from exosomatization, and emerging as tertiary retentions, post-truth is an absence of epoch, that is, the absence of a time constituted by the common protention of an open future on the basis of its past, beyond entropic becoming, and capable of inscribing a bifurcation granting neganthropic time. Post-truth is the ordeal of an absence of epoch inasmuch as digital tertiary retention can, as calculation, overwhelm any neganthropic opportunity to bifurcate, that is, any possibility of exercising the faculties of knowing, desiring and judging in the sense of a decision. This is what leads to the *techno-logical collapse of neganthropic time.*

Does this mean that every possible will and every responsibility – if not all truth – are collapsing forever? Or does it mean that will and responsibility are still required, but in a wholly other way, after their deconstruction by, in particular, Nietzsche, Foucault, Deleuze and Derrida?

The deconstruction of metaphysics by Jacques Derrida has been widely interpreted as the admission, by what seems to arrive after philosophy – itself arriving always too late – of a powerlessness of thought to care [*panser*], that is, to decide, and therefore to want. Nothing could be more false, and nothing exasperated Derrida more than this notion. Deconstruction is what posits that at the origin, there is no origin other than a default of origin, which Derrida tried to think under the names of arche-writing, différance and supplement. Accordingly, neither the will, nor the potential for a subject or an autonomous being to decide, is any longer capable of being the *starting point* of the philosophical enterprise. Nevertheless, Derrida would never have accepted that the questions of will and decision no longer arise, or that there is no subject, and hence no responsibility. On the contrary, he posited that it is *necessary* to decide within the undecidable, that is, *in what could never have given itself otherwise than in the mode of the improbable.* In this way, Derrida tried to *think responsibility otherwise.*

To rethink and care about all this in the Anthropocene, after deconstruction, and as a new critique of impure reason, that is, irreducibly and originarily pharmacological (because exosomatic) reason, implies care-fully rethinking the faculties in their confrontation with the extreme and still inconceivable threat to which the current state of the biosphere amounts, dominated as it is by thoroughly computational 'smart capitalism'. It is because it is necessary to deal with the *pharmakon* – that is, take care of it, treat it, care for it – that we must think it.

In the aftermath of the French Revolution, and after the death of Frederick II, Kant investigated, through the conflict of the faculties, the *limits* of reason through the conflict within the *institution* of these noetic faculties that is the *university* in the epoch of Newtonian mechanics and in the Republic of Letters, that is, among books: in what he calls Writing. At every level, the Enlightenment develops the *new power* of the noetic faculties characteristic of modernity (which already passes through the express consideration of writing by Descartes in *Rules for the Direction of the Mind*). In so doing, the Enlightenment opens up the possibility of the industrial revolution, that is, of the *onset of the Anthropocene*, while, after Kant's publication of *Religion within the Bounds of Bare Reason*, Frederick William II of Prussia reprimanded that public scholar [*savant corporatif, Zünftigen Gelehrte*] who is Kant, his 'loyal subject' [*féal, Getreuer*], who in turn answers him with *The Conflict of the Faculties*.

We refer, here, to the faculties (from *facere*, to do) in a contradictory way, as both what is *acquired as knowledge* by the exosomatic being, who *thereby causes to pass into actuality* his potential of being 'endowed with reason', his noetic predisposition, *and* as what we still call today the *Faculty of Letters*, the *Faculty of Science*, the *Faculty of Medicine*, the *Faculty of Law*, but the Faculty of Theology has mostly disappeared and the Faculty of Philosophy threatens to disappear – the human and social sciences having engendered other faculties, although departments of data science would like to make them disappear too.

This tendency of data science departments, provoked both by the metaphysics underpinning their development and by the limitation of academic budgets – which inevitably sets the scene for conflict between faculties and departments – is highly immature, just as it would be fatal for the faculties in general to refuse to think and care about [*panser*] the emergence of a still unthought [*insciente*], that is, uncritiqued, data science. It is the goal of what I call 'digital studies' to take responsibility for this fact, which must begin by thoughtfully caring about exosomatization *in general*.

The *faculty* (of Letters, Science and so on) refers to the institutionally and socially exosomatized exercise of those disciplinary bodies [*organismes*] for the certification and transmission of truth that are academic forms of knowledge resting on institutions of truth. These institutions institute regimes of truth and constitute retentional systems.[350] Noesis is thus the *circulation* and the *process of transindividuation* of what Simondon called the *transindividual*, this circulation and this process operating in, by and between *simple and complex exosomatic beings*.

■ ■ ■

Kant's epoch paved the way for the advent of what Heidegger called 'modern technology' (*moderne Technik*). A new conflict of the faculties and functions is now arising again, a conflict occurring *between the functions of the faculties*, insofar as they have been exosomatized completely differently, by setting up the absence of epoch (the challenge of disruption) as the ordeal of post-truth (just the opposite of the

Age of Enlightenment) and as the approaching possibility of *crossing an irreversible threshold*: it is in this sense an *eschatological* conflict – if not apocalyptic. Every conflict of the noetic faculties is always, *in truth*, somehow related to the apocalyptic question – thereby inevitably reactivating schemas stemming from the faculty of theology.[351]

In order to reconstitute the possibility of a neganthropic bifurcation, we must *create a fresh epoch* – and in an absolutely urgent situation. *In truth*, however, this requires *a change of era*. This new era is the Neganthropocene, and it is also a new area: the planetary-scale region of the *biosphere, functionally and computationally unified* ('connected') by the networks of 'light-time'.[352]

In the *new biospheric locality*, which is *local* in that it is characterized by its *more or less anti-entropic activity*, the future more improbably than ever depends on the capacity that earthlings do or do not have to *regulate* (which does not mean to solve) the new conflict of the faculties and their functions, a conflict that is being played out at this very moment through the industrial, planetary and disruptive implementation of digital tertiary retention completely subject to 'smart capitalism' – engendering a 'soft totalitarianism' inevitably condemned to a brief existence. Such a regulation of conflict requires *new regulatory ideas*. Such ideas are not idealist: they are the epokhal redoubling of the state of fact established by digital exo-transcendence.

That this computational becoming is condemned to a brief existence is the conclusion that follows from the 2014 IPCC report: generalized reticulation as it is implemented at the biospheric scale aggravates anthropic forcing in a disastrous way, even though it alone would enable the very opposite – *on the condition of carefully rethinking architectonics through a hyper-materialist hyper-critique* – initially by containing such forcings, then by reducing them.

That this eschatological conflict requires *new regulatory ideas* stems from a mutation of physics that is *more* than 'historial' (*geschichtlich*) (and this is the meaning of 'Time and Being'[353]), as the astrophysical has to again become cosmo-logical, having to conceive orders of magnitude from microcosmic and macrocosmic points of view, that is, in terms of those localities found in the biosphere (life, noesis), in an expanding universe processually ordered by the thermodynamic arrow of time, *which can in no way be thought in ontological terms*.

By accomplishing a transition to the microelectronic scale and by developing an industrial microphysics (now on the way to the nanophysics of 'transformational technologies'), techno-logical performativity and what Simondon would call its allagmatics (its field of *operations*) have overturned human relations in all their dimensions. This overturning

1. can become truly comprehensible, that is, *accessible to a new critical understanding*, and,
2. beyond a mere comprehension, this overturning can become *surprehensible*, that is, *synthesizable by the function of reason as bifurcation*,

only under the following conditions:

- *First condition*: that we inscribe this overturning into much broader relations of scale, relations that now enable intensive computing to treat data derived from scales ranging from the nanophysical and microphysical levels to the macrophysical scales of human perception and the macrocosmic scales of the biosphere, now reticulated by platforms capable of integrating these different levels via algorithms operating at near light speed;
- *Second condition*: that we give consideration to the excess (that is, the *hubris* beyond measure, including in the sense of Brillouin and experimental science in general) of technological performativity this involves, as relations of scale and changes of orders of magnitude;
- *Third condition*: that we establish new certification institutions and procedures, opening onto a new era beyond the (metaphysical) history of truth.

We must have the new reticular realities set up by the digital exosomatization of psychic individuals and collective individuals in mind when, in 2019, we read these lines by Simondon:

> We can refer to mere technique when the mediation (use of a tool, fertilization) is set up only between two terms, which implies that they are of the same order of magnitude (the lever between the miner and the block of stone) or of the same kingdom, sometimes the same species. When the chain of mediations lengthens, it can set up effective action between different types of reality, kingdoms and orders of magnitude. Of all the aspects of the transductive character of technology, the one that makes it possible to change the order of magnitude, and consequently mobilization, intemporalization, potentialization, is undoubtedly the most important.[354]

Digital tertiary retention thus penetrates individual and collective activities at all scales. Given this, the faculties of knowing, desiring and judging – with which psychic individuals are endowed in potential, and which can pass into actuality only provided that they can be developed within these collective individuals that are the faculties (as institutions of knowledge and retentional systems) – must be rethought and taken care of *starting from their functions*, precisely as *faculties of care* [*panser*], and in terms of the question of exosomatization as formulated by Alfred Lotka in 1945, that is, by raising the question of the reconstitution and re-foundation of knowledge.

To think the faculties of care [*panser*] in terms of the question of exosomatization above all requires, so I claim, a *redefinition of the schematism*, and hence of the relations between intuition, understanding, imagination and reason, which are the noetic functions of these faculties – these functions being *noetic* only by their submission to the function of reason as the power to bifurcate *in law* beyond the *ordinary* play of these functions, and hence as the *faculty of dreaming*,[355] which is to say, of ex-cepting.

The noetic faculty of dreaming is the function of exosomatization that enables the realizing of dreams, which are potential bifurcations. And it is what enables these dreams to be concretized as a function of production passing through invention, discovery, creation and, more generally, care, and in particular education. *Care*: of which these various categories are instances. Freud and Binswanger must in this respect be reread with the anthropology of 'dreaming' – of the 'dreamtime' – and with the young Foucault, in order to elaborate an oneirology of the faculty of dreaming that would be thought and cared about with the concept of tertiary retention.[356]

At present, the faculty of dreaming, which can realize itself only between the psychic faculties and the academic faculties, has been placed into the service of the realization of the greatest nightmare humankind can imagine: its self-destruction, accomplished in having failed to heed Valéry, Husserl, Freud, Vernadsky, Lotka, Georgescu-Roegen, Toynbee and the IPCC – notably – where what the last of these called anthropic forcing relates to what the first described in terms of a pharmacology of spirit in the service of a destruction of spirit (Valéry observed this fundamental tendency of the twentieth century on two occasions: just after the First World War,[357] and just before the Second World War[358]).

This is so because the theory of the faculties did not conceive that the schematism escapes both the psychic individual and the collective individual: it participates in *technical* individuation. Consequently, the noetic faculties and functions are disintegrated through this collapse of time that the 'blank generation' announced in Liverpool in

1977, and that 'presents itself' as the absence of epoch thereby enunciated: No future.

The *fundamental and functional lateness of institutions* – which makes possible the play of what Simondon called *phase-shifting* [*déphasage*], which inhabits psychic individuals in themselves as well as the faculties in themselves, and that stems from what Derrida called différance – this lateness that is also the time of the après-coup is what, through disruption, 'smart capitalism' short-circuits, overtaking and eliminating it. This means that in many ways the new play of the faculties and functions becomes indifférant – oddly resembling a game of 'Russian roulette', or, in the Middle Ages, in the Christian West, ordalic behaviour understood as God's judgment.[359]

Accomplishing in totality the joint obliteration of the theory of four causes and the theory of places that began with modern physics, the 'correlationism' of intensive computing and deep learning, which claims to replace theoretical models and causal consecutiveness, plays with chance in a fundamentally suicidal way.[360]

The exosomatization demonstrated by Lotka is the organogenetic process by which the organism noetizes itself by equipping itself with inorganic organs. If vegetative and sensitive life is what constantly evolves through the *endosomatic* organogenesis of species, so that the latter can be characterized by the burgeoning and discriminating diversification of their organs – prokaryotes and acaryotes, then eukaryote cellular organelles forming multicellular organisms – through cotyledon, root, stem, leaves – then vertebrae, gills, teats, teeth, defences, noetic life is characterized by an *exosomatic* organogenesis, that is, by the production of artificial organs without which it could not live.

In 1944, Erwin Schrödinger described the endosomatic organogenesis that is life as producing what he called negative entropy – that is, locally limiting, deferring and differentiating the effects of entropy as the irreversible dissipation of energy. Exosomatic organogenesis, however, makes it necessary to complete the theory of negative entropy – or of what Giuseppe Longo calls (as did Norbert Wiener in 1948, but in a very different sense) anti-entropy: exosomatic organogenesis makes it necessary to conceive a neganthropology beyond anthropology and beyond negentropy (or negative entropy, or anti-entropy) – beyond what we will call vital différance, and beyond what, in anthropology, which for the most part ignores exosomatization, leads to the impasse of what Lévi-Strauss called entropology.[361]

Whether endosomatic or exosomatic, vital or noetic, organogenesis forms anti-entropic localities that temporarily defer the fulfilment of the universal entropic tendency. In the case of endosomatic beings, these temporarily animated localities form *simple or complex organisms* (unicellular or multicellular), where localities can be encased in other localities, or, in the case of exosomatic beings, these localities form *simple or complex exorganisms*. Psychic individuation is what occurs in the course of the development of a simple exorganism, which always exists in relation to complex exorganisms: the simple exorganism individuates itself by contributing to the collective individuation of complex exorganisms. In so doing, it individuates itself psychically on various planes, and at various scales – including the unconscious – thereby shifting phase, dephasing itself, always within and beyond itself, and always *intermittently*.

FIFTH LECTURE

Entropy, Negentropy and Anti-Entropy in Thermodynamics, Biology and Information Theory

Since negentropy is a temporal deferral and a spatial differentiation of entropy, it is a *différance* in the sense in which Derrida defines it in 'Différance':

> *Différer* [...] is to temporize, to take recourse, consciously or unconsciously, in the temporal and temporizing mediation of a detour that suspends the accomplishment or fulfillment of 'desire' or 'will', and equally effects this suspension in a mode that annuls or tempers its own effect. [T]his temporization is also temporalization and spacing, the becoming-time of space and the becoming-space of time [...]. The other sense of *différer* is [...] to be not identical, to be other, discernible, etc.[362]

This deferral that is accomplished differentially refers firstly to life in all its forms, and, despite the reference to desire or will, this is what Derrida explains in *Of Grammatology*, where the trace (or the archi-trace...*of* différance, and that *is* différance) designates retention in all its forms, and firstly as memory, from the most elementary life forms

> of the amoeba or the annelid up to the passage beyond alphabetic writing to the orders of the logos and of a certain *homo sapiens*.[363]

And in fact, the negentropic organogenesis of organisms *is* the *spatialization* of organs – *which may be either endosomatic or exosomatic*, and this dual possibility denotes two *functionally différant* registers, *that is, differently différant* from one to the other, and where one of the two – the exosomatic register of différance – defers differently what Derrida calls the *supplement*.

As *spatialization*, negentropic organogenesis, whether endosomatic or exosomatic, is a *localization* that *limits* the entropic tendency only *by itself limiting itself*, and through a *local economy* of its différance. This locality, however, is *open*: it is formed through *exchanges* with an 'exterior' milieu, which feeds an 'interior' milieu, of which it is the *supplement*, and it is so via flows of matter and energy – and in the first place of solar energy: this is what Vernadsky brings to light in a striking way, understanding life above all as the *becoming biochemical of a photochemical phenomenon*, and describing the biosphere firstly as a local production (within the universe) of molecules of a new kind, *supplementing* it.

That différance can be and is first and foremost a 'detour that suspends the accomplishment or fulfillment of "desire"' must therefore be understood:

- with Aristotle, who posits that life is the auto-mobility of a desire of the 'first unmoving mover', also called *theos*, showing that the different types of souls (vegetative, sensitive and noetic) are all auto-mobile (animated) relationships to this primordial immobility – and it is starting from this thought of life that we should read Spinoza;
- by taking note of the *intermittency* of the *passage to the act* of the noetic soul (which we are here calling the exosomatic soul), and of this soul's inevitable *regressions and latencies*;
- with Freud, who after the First World War reconsiders the whole of the *economy* he calls libidinal, and does so *beyond* the pleasure principle, from the perspective of the most elementary forms of life, and as the *play of two contradictory tendencies*, constantly negotiating *detours* along the way to the return to the *same*, namely, to death as the decomposition of organic matter into inert matter – these tendencies being here entropic and negentropic.

▪ ▪ ▪

Emerging from the works of Sadi Carnot in 1824, Rudolf Clausius in 1865 and Ludwig Boltzmann in 1877, the concept of entropy – which is a crucial element of Freud's context when in 1920 he writes *Beyond the Pleasure Principle* – describes the thermodynamic process, which then takes on a cosmic dimension with the theory of the expanding universe formulated by Georges Lemaître and confirmed by Edwin Hubble's observations in 1929.[364] The question of knowing to what extent it is possible to transfer the astrophysical scale of the universe to the microphysical and statistical theory of the second law of thermodynamics, however, remains open.

We have seen that with Schrödinger – in 1944 – the theory of entropy knows, so to speak, a *negative extension* that enables the physicist to *delimit* the field of biology as that which temporarily and locally defers the entropy that is nevertheless an *irreducible* tendency of matter, this tendency being a law of physics – 'the most important', Einstein would say.[365]

The expression '*negative entropy*' – or *negentropy* – is sometimes disputed by the scientific community: there can be no such thing as *negative* entropy to the extent that entropy, as the dissipation of energy, is irreversible. In the strict sense, 'negative entropy' would mean going backwards in time: only then would entropy be reversible. There may be, however, a *local limitation*, a *temporary deferral* of the entropic 'penchant' of inert matter, through a vital process of the accumulation of energy.

The concept of negentropy having been generalized in order to describe ordered structures, including those beyond the realm of life, and notably informational systems (in particular by Shannon, Wiener and Brillouin, to whom we shall return), Francis Bailly and Giuseppe Longo[366] refer instead to *anti-entropy*, which is not just negative entropy or negentropy, and which is quite different from what Wiener himself called anti-entropy in *The Human Use of Human Beings*:

> When I compare the living organism with [...] a machine, I do not for a moment mean that the specific physical, chemical, and spiritual processes of life as we ordinarily know it are the same as those of life-imitating machines. I mean simply that they both can exemplify locally anti-entropic processes, which perhaps may also be exemplified in many other ways which we should naturally term neither biological nor mechanical.[367]

Contrary to what Wiener says here, for Bailly and Longo anti-entropy occurs only in the context of what they call the *extended critical situation* that characterizes 'the state of life and the processes within it'.[368] In other words, anti-entropy is not the same thing, for them, as negentropy, whereas in Wiener it seems to be an *extension to machines* of the negentropy of life postulated by Schrödinger.

In a short programmatic note, Longo explains that he is endeavouring to produce 'mathematizable propositions' capable of describing life, and that it is from consideration of the *extended critical situation* in which it consists that life is *singular with regard to physics*, and constitutes in relation to mathematical physics a situation that *differs from the critical transitions described by physical theories*:

> In physical theories, [...] critical transitions [...] are in general defined by precise values of control parameters [...] representable by a point for each relevant parameter. [...] The

> critical situation that we are considering [extending and characteristic of life] remains as long as the living thing in question (an organism, for example) lasts; [...] no parameter can be reduced to a point.[369]

This is another way of saying what Simondon already said when he compared the crystal to the living thing – and hence, where Simondon refers to internal resonance, Longo refers to bio-resonance.

Locality then becomes a primordial functional element in the proper sense (wherein forms what those who think and care about immunitary systems sometimes call a self): as extended critical situation, a living state of matter always belongs to the locality *of a whole* in which 'the local [that is, the part, is] strongly correlated to the global [that is, the whole]'.[370] One might be tempted to say that for Wiener, this is also the case with the machine, notably by virtue of his concept of feedback. *But*: *correlation* in the organism is not the same as in the machine. *Critical organic locality*, forming a *whole that is constantly in crisis*, is constituted and maintained by an anti-entropy that, insofar as it defines here a mathematical descriptor in order to constitute a biomathematics, 'quantifies the production or permanent reconstruction of organization'.[371] This is why anti-entropy, conceived in this way as an activity in the extended critical situation of self-healing living matter (as seen, for example, in scar-formation),

> is not to be confused with the decrease in entropy that occurs in a physical movement from disorder to order in inert matter. [...] This anti-entropy [...] exists only in the extension of the extended critical zone.[372]

And, in contrast to Wiener, this is not 'exemplified in many other ways which we should naturally term neither biological nor mechanical', where this would be, as we have seen, a basic principle of cybernetics. This is why the *complexity* that results from the anti-entropy characteristic of the extended critical situation proper to the living

> should not be confused with algorithmic complexity, nor with the usual physical complexity involved, notably, in the constitution of levels of organization and functional relations of integration, and in the physiological regulation between these levels.[373]

Longo explains in an interview that

> in all its parts, to take up a fundamental chapter of Darwin's *Origin of Species*, 'correlated variations' make up the organism, but also the ecosystem, a conceptual challenge that

> cannot be envisaged as a 'piling up' of the elementary. Every machine is obtained by piling up elementary and simple components one upon the other: we construct by association, assembling components, screws and bolts, chips and bits [...] simple and elementary.
>
> Also, computers and computer networks are a superposition and a very complicated intermingling of simple and elementary components. In the natural sciences, on the other hand, it is not a given that the fundamental is elementary, or that the elementary is simple.[374]

We can see here how the starting point of modernity, namely Descartes's analytical method, is no longer useful as a way of characterizing living matter. This, along with organized inorganic matter, irreversibly complicates the form/matter oppositional pair. As we saw last week, various layers of hyper-matter must therefore be distinguished, from quantum mechanics to technological materials and passing through living matter – and where it is necessary to distinguish entropy, negentropy and anti-entropy, but also, as we will see, anthropy and neganthropy.

What this means is that here, there can be no question of separating form from matter, contrary to what is assumed by the notion of information, which

> has been dealt with by at least two rigorous and important scientific theories: the elaboration of information, starting from Turing, and the transmission of information (Shannon). [...] In both cases, the characteristics are dependent neither on code (apart from the negligible costs of coding: by 0s and 1s, or 0-9, or any other sequence of signs), nor, above all, on the material support.[375]

In the extended critical situation, on the other hand, living matter is radically material:

> a *radical materiality* [...] for which we cannot in any case distinguish *software* [*logiciel*] from *hardare* [*matériel*]: life is made *only* from this DNA, RNA, *only* from these membranes, with their physico-chemistry and nothing else.[376]

In *La Société automatique 2*, and perhaps, next year, here in Nanjing, I will try to elucidate the question of *knowing*:

- *what type of complex exorganism is generated by the automated correlationism* of intensive computing, machine learning and deep learning;

- what all this does to life in general, and noetic life in particular;
- under what conditions all this allows or prevents *performatively* anticipating a neganthropic bifurcation through a positive pharmacology of contemporary exosomatization, in such a way that it *affects* noesis in a completely new sense.

It is this that is at stake in what Heidegger called *Gestell*, which we translate, from the standpoint of Marx, who was the first to think and care about exosomatization, as the question of a *total proletarianization* generating a *total denoetization* in the service of a computational 'soft totalitarianism'.

But to confront such questions, we must *reconsider noetic différance in totality from the standpoint of exosomatization as exorganogenesis*, that is, as supplementary différance in a specific sense not analysed by Derrida, whereby noesis is itself *what is formed materially* in the course of exosomatization, beyond the hylemorphic oppositional schema and starting from a process of grammatization that in the Upper Palaeolithic gives rise to a specific type of tertiary retention that we call hypomnesic (in reference to the words of Socrates in *Phaedrus*).

For Bailly and Longo, anti-entropy refers to organogenesis insofar as it is the co-generation and re-generation of cells and their organelles, organic tissues, organs and the organism *inasmuch as all of these are strongly correlated*: it is in *this* way, by these *correlations* of the parts within the whole, that it locally defers the fulfilment of the entropic tendency, and that this temporarily animated locality *forms* an organism. The condition for such anti-entropic singularity within universal entropy is the bio-energetic trans-formation of solar radiation in the biosphere, as Vladimir Vernadsky understood in 1926.[377]

In the biosphere, and as the arrangement of its local interior milieu with its equally local exterior milieu (in the sense of Claude Bernard in 1850[378]), the organism forms a *niche*, delimited by its characteristic gradients, which is, in Derrida's sense, the supplement of the organism, which is also to say what Simondon called its associated milieu, inasmuch as its preindividual fund or background is constituted as the 'coupling of the individual and the milieu'. The milieu *associated* with this individual, insofar as it amounts to an extended critical situation, in Simondon's language constitutes the process of vital individuation insofar as it depends upon such a preindividual fund.

The 'associated milieu' – of the vital individual, then the psychic individual – is not just the 'exterior milieu' in Bernard's sense: it is this milieu inasmuch as through it – through sexual and intermittent relations – the *genetic milieu* is encountered that constitutes the *species* to which the individual belongs with other conspecific individuals. It is from these exchanges that vital organogenesis is produced and reproduced.

With psychic and collective individuation, what is reproduced are forms of knowledge and social structures, and, in this case, the associated milieu becomes the preindividual funds of the transindividual. These conspecific individuals thus in turn become co-tribalists, co-religionists, co-citizens, compatriots or collaborators within complex exorganisms that are more or less (de)territorialized in the biosphere – up to and including what we have elsewhere called contributors.[379] What these contributors contribute *to* is the struggle against anthropy, a struggle we call neganthropy, but which we will see should also be distinguished from anti-anthropy, which is intermittent, whereas neganthropy can become the empty form of what thus turns against itself: it is irreducibly pharmacological (as *institution*), while anti-anthropy is the intermittent act through which it *effectively* operates against anthropy.

The associated milieu in psychic and collective individuation produces psychic (that is, simple) exorganisms and collective (that is, complex) exorganisms, on the basis of sets of artificial organs of highly variable types and sizes, which are aggregated in various ways, and which are no longer governed just by vital individuation, nor by the form of anti-entropy characteristic of vital individuation. It is because this milieu is composed of artefacts – which, in the eighteenth century, become thermodynamic machines and industrial automatons, and then, in the twentieth century, cybernetic machines, that is, computational and informational machines – that great confusion can arise as to what, within this milieu, counts as entropy, negentropy (or anti-entropy in Wiener's sense) or *information*, these notions being what then supposedly enables all this to be *calculated* according to *probabilities*.

▪ ▪ ▪

The concept of entropy and its local and différant correlate, negentropy, or more precisely anti-entropy, lead to *countless attempts to transfer it* to other fields – to information theory (Shannon, 1948[380]), cybernetics (Wiener, 1948[381]), systems theory (Ludwig von Bertalanffy, 1937, 1968[382]), complexity theory (Henri Atlan, 1971,[383] Edgar Morin, 1977[384]), and, through all this, various attempts to formalize the human and social sciences, all more or less disastrous, albeit occasionally fruitful (Simondon).

To these confusing conceptual transfers – a confusion itself engendered by almost diametrically opposed transdisciplinary uses of these words in information theory (Shannon), cybernetics (Wiener) and physics (Brillouin) – has been added a mixture that with popularization becomes a real mess, with the addition of theories of order and disorder, 'noise' and self-organization. It is in this way that Ilya Prigogine's 'dissipative structures' came to be mixed up with anti-entropic localities, and that 'order out of noise' was confused with anti-entropic open systems, whether organic or exorganic. It is on this plane that the concept of anti-entropy put forward by Bailly, Longo and Montévil affords a salutary clarification.

A provocative article published by René Thom in 1980 in the journal *Le Debat*[385] curbed these heuristic ventures, and the theme of the relationship between statistical physics and forms of life has since declined to almost nothing, abandoning entropy to thermodynamics.[386] This abandonment, however, is a regression and a denial. This denial amounts to a denial of entropy itself insofar as, after 1824, thermodynamics demands a *wholly other thinking and caring about* that which had hitherto constituted the framework of ontology in *all* spheres, posing *in wholly other terms* the question of an *unfinished and différant whole*.

One could try to justify this retreat by the fact that the reference to the thermodynamic theory of entropy in information theory has led in return – due to the *techno-logical performativity of the computational theory of information* extended to life, itself thereby becoming an object of considerable bio-industrial investment – to significant theoretical shortcomings, to applying highly doubtful noetic patchworks [*bricolages*] to life, and to greatly accelerating the increase in the rate of entropy in the Anthropocene.

In reality, these patchworks operate under pressure from the transformation of knowledge into three functions, which, as they are currently divided, have been disintegrated, installing a situation of absolute proletarianization. These functions are those of design/conception, production and distribution of commodities, themselves functionally integrated within associated milieus reticulated by tertiary retention,[387] in the name of a pseudo-scientific unification that in reality is technological and industrial (and a rationalization in Adorno's sense), and *that disintegrates knowledge because it performatively disintegrates all forms of locality and singularity*: hence it is not just psychosocial localities and singularities that are disintegrated – as highlighted in the *Disbelief and Discredit* series and the *Symbolic Misery* series – but mathematical, physical and scientific forms in general.

This was possible only because the artefacts implemented by the communication and information industries neither thought nor cared from an exosomatic standpoint. Irrespective of whether they are theoreticians of information and cybernetics, or those who have continued their work from a cognitivist perspective (and by forgetting or effacing their most interesting propositions[388]), or theoreticians of systems and complexity: none have grasped that exosomatic artefacts in general and communicational and informational artefacts in particular are tertiary retentions constituting a new form of life whose earliest traces we can see on decorated cave walls (and looking at which we recognize ourselves), tertiary retentions that, in being grammatized, *exosomatically* generate the conditions of what we recognize *as a noetic life* – in Whitehead's sense when he defines the function of this form of life as being 'to promote the art of living'.[389]

As we will see in detail in the next session, Simondon himself gets bogged down in the question of information – which he conceives as the 'formula of individuation'[390] on the basis of the Theory of Form, and by positing, in complete contradiction with his own assertions[391] but in full conformity with dominant idea of his time, that information must be understood *independently of its supports*:

> the notion of information must never be reduced to signals or to the supports or carriers of information in a message, as the technological theory of information tends to do, a theory that was initially abstracted from transmission technologies.[392]

It is striking to note that when Simondon evokes the question of entropy and negentropy,[393] he ignores Schrödinger's hypotheses in *What is Life?*, while conversely, and as the cognitivists will do, he posits that the notion of form, whether it comes from Greek philosophy or from the Theory of Form, must be replaced by that of information:

> The notion of form must be replaced with that of information, which presupposes the existence of a system in a metastable state of equilibrium that can individuate itself. Information, unlike form, is never a unique term, but the significance [*signification*] that arises from a disparation.[394]

Such a substitution is obviously necessary and legitimate, at least as an initial step: it is a question of reconsidering form from a systemic, dynamic and processual standpoint, and not from the idealist tradition that originates in Plato, continues until phenomenology, and to which Gestalt psychology remains fundamentally tied.

But the convoking of information theory, which underlies this whole undertaking, comes at the cost of a fundamental negligence concerning the question of *probability* calculations that constitute the *limit* of the notion of information – a negligence that corresponds to Simondon's ignorance of the primordial question of the *pharmakon*, of its play between what we are here calling anthropy and neganthropy, and of what emerges from this: namely, the question of the *improbable*.

SIXTH LECTURE

Critique of Simondon's 'Notion of Information'

The impasses encountered in Simondon's use of the 'notion of information' derive from his debate with Wiener and cybernetics – which I partially reconstructed in *Technics and Time, 1*.[395] Specifying the contours of what he calls his mechanology, which is an *organology of machines inasmuch as they produce functional integrations*, Simondon posits that, like 'natural spontaneously produced objects',[396] and in particular living things, technical beings must become the subject of an inductive study within a

> 'science of correlations and transformations that would be a general technology or mechanology' more akin to biology than to physics.[397]

But in mechanology, contrary to the cybernetics of Wiener, who undertakes an

> abusive assimilation of the technical object to the natural and especially the living object […], it can only be said that technical objects tend toward concretization, whereas natural objects such as living beings are concrete from the start.[398]

What ultimately constitutes the technical dynamic, such that *with industrial machines, that is, with the Anthropocene*, it tends towards concretization, is thus for Simondon, and unlike (according to him) Wiener, the *protentional capacities of the noetic and fabricating being, that is, its ends, its finalities*, without which 'physical causality could never […] produce a positive and efficient concretization'.[399]

The question of the technical dynamic – which we are here calling exosomatization – is thus ultimately, for Simondon, the question of the relations between *noetic organic matter* and what *Technics and Time, 1* called *organized inorganic matter*, inasmuch as these relations pro-duce an epiphylogenesis, which raises the question of the *primordial coupling* (the 'correlation') between these *two inseparable dimensions of exosomatic organization*. This would form the primordial principle of a hyper-materialist epistemology, especially because access to inorganic hyper-matter (in physics), as well as to organic matter (in biology), would always presuppose such an arrangement between *organized inorganic matter* and *noetic organic matter*. Contrary to the claims of 'strong artificial intelligence' and transhumanist 'storytelling', therefore, the *living human being* can, in principle [*en droit*], never be eliminated from this organization.

And yet, is this elimination not *in fact* the very thing to which cybernetics has led via computational and absolute proletarianization – and which thereby amounts to an absolute non-knowledge? Is this not *strikingly clear*, sixty years after Simondon wrote *On the Mode of Existence of Technical Objects*, and twenty-five years after the World Wide Web was opened to the global 'public' (I put 'public' in quotation marks because public space has been transformed *in fact* into privatized audiences)? Such is the question of contemporary pharmacology, which, approaching *the extreme limit of the Anthropocene*, confronts us with this *irrational state of fact* in which the algorithmic *automaton* made possible by Moore's pseudo-law, and borne along by its techno-logical performativity, 'disrupts' *all* theoretical models – which, faced with this state of fact, then seem *powerless*.

My own claim is that, on the one hand, this is why we need a hyper-materialist epistemology, and a political economy that draws the consequences of the extremely short amount of time that the IPCC gives us to make a turn, the whole issue of which is to negotiate its worldwide direction. On the other hand, both transhumanism and post-humanism afford neither, in the first case, a future, nor, in the latter case, a question:

- the first, transhumanism – which ignores the questions of entropy and anthropy, reduces life itself to calculation and totally ignores the neganthropic challenge of the Anthropocene and more generally of reason as a therapeutic and pharmacological function, and not just a calculable function – is a terrifying scam perpetrated by technospheric marketing that tries in this way to seize power over every form of terrestrial life;
- the second, posthumanism, ignores that man has never been man, that the human has always been both an artificial production and a promise of the future that does not exist anymore than does justice on Earth, which also implies the following:

1. The human does not exist, it consists as an idea that always presents itself through another idea: belonging to a totem, creature of God, free citizen, communist man ('new man'), 'overman', and so on;

2 If we then object that noetic life has been fabricated and artificialized and thus augmented for millennia, and that we will continue to be able to do this in all kinds of ways, to this there can in principle be no objection. But here we must impose the condition, and we must impose this condition in principle [*de droit*] and as a new foundation of law: we must prevent augmentation from continuing the pursuit of systemic proletarianization, and we must be willing and able to pursue augmentation only on the condition that it serves deproletarianization. On this point, I refer to *The Neganthropocene*.[400]

Admittedly, in relation to this last point, one might object, on the one hand, that it is impossible to prevent proletarianization, including self-proletarianization, that is, voluntary toxico-addictive behaviour, and, on the other hand, that there is a division between those who will and those who will not be able to access deproletarianization. My response to these objections is that it is perhaps indeed here and in this way that a class struggle might play out, and that a new social hierarchy could be constructed, based on a new stage of exosomatization, characterized in particular by the re-interiorization of exosomatic organs, such as for example via the neuroindustry that is currently being put in place, and which could clearly lead to bionic forms that are in this respect highly disruptive.

We will, however, leave these questions aside for the moment: we will be ready to confront them, if we can ever be ready, only when we have first undertaken a critique of the 'notion of information', especially as it appears in Simondon.

Simondon's failure to consider the pharmacological question contained within mechanology (organology) inasmuch as it stems from exosomatization means that he cannot conceive or anticipate the *more than tragic* situation in which *thoroughly computational information capitalism* has entangled the entire biosphere.

It is in this absence of epoch (as the inability to project collective protentions unifying an epoch), and in the deranged ordeal of denial referred to as 'post-truth', that the *effective reality of the post-truth age* unfolds. Heidegger alone saw this coming – though he was never able to think this in the way we are doing here: by analysing in depth how causality passes through the questions of entropy and what we call neganthropy, and how this entails, with respect to calculation, neither a rejection nor a condemnation, but a *refunctionalization*.

A similar inability is also what makes the arguments of 'speculative realism' more than a little doubtful. This is why, if, *on the one hand*,

- we are bound to affirm without reservation and with Simondon that:

> One mustn't confuse the tendency toward concretization with the status of entirely concrete existence. To a certain extent, every technical object has residual aspects of abstraction; one mustn't go right to the limit and speak of technical objects as if they were natural objects. Technical objects must be studied in their evolution in order to discern the process of concretization as a tendency; but one mustn't isolate the last product of technical evolution in order to declare it entirely concrete; it is more concrete than the preceding ones, yet it is still artificial,[401]

then, *on the other hand*, we must still refine Simondon's analysis by adding that:

- In industrial concretization, noetic life is no longer in *command* – even if, as was said in *Technics and Time, 1*, it *operates*. But this *operator* is no longer the Operator discussed by Deleuze with respect to quasi-causality,[402] and next I will try to show that this is the reply we must give if we want to go beyond Heidegger's critique of the *causa efficiens* in his interpretation of the Aristotelian theory of the four causes that lies at the heart of 'The Question Concerning Technology': the Operator has been proletarianized; it has become what operates only on the basis of what is indicated to it by a system that has taken away its knowledge by reducing it to the status of an information system, an 'operating system'.

In this way, *every operator* is proletarianized, just as are 'designers' and consumers, as well as those producers who are also called 'manual labourers', but so too, now, are mothers and drivers. What is a proletarianized 'designer' [*concepteur*]? He or she is a *manipulator of concepts derived from automated understanding*, from an understanding devoid of the syntheses that emerge from dis-automatizing reason, or, in other words, devoid of capacities for synthesizing protentions converging towards a kingdom of ends – which become *non-dialectical* auxiliary services of a *system of information*, and where the *server learns nothing* (unlike the servant, *Knecht*, of the famous dialectic).

It is on the basis of Simondon (reader of the *Grundrisse*) that we have been able to say this, yet Simondon's own account remains *limited*, giving it a transitional and epiphenomenal character, if not purely accidental: the point of *On the Mode of Existence of Technical Objects* is to dispel what Simondon regards as a misunderstanding. What he describes in reference to Marx amounts to a process of disindividuation, but from this he draws no consequences whatsoever with regard to the inherently pharmacological character of exosomatization. He cannot conceive exosomatization as an exteriorization that generates a state of fact that dissolves knowledge – to the point of becoming absolute non-knowledge ('finishing off' knowledge, in the sense of *achever* in French that means both to finish and to kill, for example in the phrase, *'on achève bien les chevaux'*, the French translation of the film title, *They Shoot Horses, Don't They?*: in other words, indifférance).

The protentional capacities of the operator, then, are caught within a proletarianization of what is now called 'brainwork' [*cerveau d'oeuvre*] – which replaces 'manual labour' [*main d'oeuvre*] and which is the 'effective reality' of 'cognitive capitalism'. This capturing of psycho-noetic protentions, replaced by automatically-produced protentions that are generated by 'smart marketing' on the basis of mimetic and pseudo-personalized models, liquidates what, in the first edition of the *Critique of Pure Reason*, Kant described as the synthesis of recognition. This third synthesis of the transcendental imagination is the condition of the convergence of the experiences of the knowing subject in a rational unity constituting a transcendental affinity (with the physical world, but also with the human world – a theme taken up only in the *Critique of Judgment*) and thus forming the *horizon of truth*.

▪ ▪ ▪

When in the first volume of *Technics and Time* I discussed *On the Mode of Existence of Technical Objects*, I tried to show that the concretization of the industrial machine is effected (as the combustion engine, the electric locomotive or the turbine of the tidal power plant) when the latter must leave the purely technical milieu in order to form, with the natural milieu, a 'techno-geographical associated milieu', generated by the object itself, in the course of what Simondon calls its 'naturalization'. In *Automatic Society, Volume 1*, however, I argue that it is precisely in becoming a *human* (and not only *physical*) techno-geographical associated milieu – via the digital exosomatic devices of that half of the world's population who are now equipped with smartphones, that is, personal portable computers, perpetually eliciting and capturing 'data', which is to say digital tertiary retentions – it is precisely in becoming a human techno-geographical associated milieu that this *commodified retentional milieu*, perpetually provoking, activating and calculating arrangements of retentions and protentions, leads to the psychic and social disintegration of retentions and protentions.

This becoming results from the fact that the technical functions integrated by this *concretization* are based exclusively on statistical calculations dictated by the business models of these platforms, these calculations being perfectly homogeneous with the principles of a market where use value must be able to be turned into exchange value – but where automatic protentions now replace any noetic protention, that is, they replace any synthesis not calculable by the analytical understanding, and hence replace any end: whether Aristotle's final causality or Kant's kingdom of ends. It is for this reason that such a process of becoming functionally and systemically installs an absence of epoch devoid of protentions, as described in *The Age of Disruption*. Yet this is possible only because information, as defined in the information theory that Simondon mobilizes to replace the Theory of Form, is intrinsically calculable – by the probabilistic statistics that implement the 'H factor' that is identical to the Boltzmann constant. But Simondon does not see how this causes a problem.

If the analysis proposed here and in *Automatic Society, Volume 1* is well-founded, then it is crucial to understand how Simondon – perfectly in line with the context of the period, which was still locked in the dogmatic progressivism characteristic of eighteenth- and nineteenth-century metaphysics (as we will see), ignoring all the problems that characterize the Anthropocene – could come to neglect the extreme probability of an entropic becoming that Wiener, however, *does* imagine in terms of the 'fascist ant-state'[403] and as what is provoked by a purely probabilistic concept of information.

To understand this, we must return to Simondon's concept of information, which he confines to the status of a 'notion', and through which he forms the concept of 'disparation' – borrowing it from physiology.

What is disparation? It is the process by which the brain can produce a unified image with relief (with depth of field) on the basis of the dual source of nerve impulses coming from the eyes via the optic nerves. In *Automatic Society*, I tried to show that the way digital hypomnesic tertiary retention is exploited by 'platform capitalism' leads to the elimination of noetic relief, the elimination of noetic depth of field, that is, to the elimination of thinking as such.

That the Simondonian notion of information is directly tied to the concept of disparation[404] is shown by Thomas Berns and Antoinette Rouvroy in their analysis of 'algorithmic governmentality'. In 'Gouvernementalité algorithmique et perspectives d'émancipation. Le disparate comme condition d'individuation par la relation?',[405] Berns and Rouvroy raise the question, firstly, of an *inverted recuperation* of the concepts of Deleuze and Guattari by 'platform capitalism' (which I also call 'smart capitalism', in reference to the process that Evgeny Morozov calls smartification[406]), and, secondly, of the machinic and disruptive concretization of what Simondon described as a process of transindividuation. This disruption of transindividuation then produces what Guattari called the 'dividual', through a process of 'dividualization' in which the unity of the individual is broken down into profile elements that are analytically decomposed and statistically recomposed and massified according to probability calculations.

What does not occur to Simondon is that the information industry based on information theory has a pharmacological dimension, even though it is precisely his work that alone makes it possible to describe this concretization, which occurs through an inversion that arises out of the rhizomatic horizontality (in Deleuze and Guattari's sense) of the networks deployed by algorithmic governmentality, and

> in favour of an immanent and eminently plastic normativity (Deleuze and Guattari, 1980) [that] is not necessarily favourable to the emergence of new forms of life in the sense of an emancipation described by Deleuze and Guattari in the form of an overcoming of the organizational plane by the plane of immanence.[407]

(We should, however, refine and qualify this remark, since Deleuze and Guattari reject the question of emancipation, and their neglect of this point, which is by no means peripheral, is wholly symptomatic of a repression of the aporias of 'French theory', a repression that has been *avoided* by its heirs – aporias that, in our opinion, pass precisely through the notions of machine, information and entropy.)

The issue amounts, precisely, to ignorance of the question of tertiary retention, which requires a conception of *hyper-materiality* that Simondon made thinkable and necessary, but which, very paradoxically, he himself was incapable of thinking, despite being the one who made it thinkable. And this is so thanks to the way he conceives information.

Simondon does not question:

- either the *computational reductionism* involved in the application of probabilistic notions of entropy and negentropy to information, in particular by Shannon, Wiener and Brillouin, a computationalism that would subsequently be taken up by cognitivism;
- or the *singularity* of what, after vital negentropy, becomes, with exosomatization, *noetic singularity*, inasmuch

> as it always calls for the *invention of an art of living with* pharmaka.

Simondon's positions with respect to information are all the more strange and paradoxical in that they contradict both his analysis of technics qua process of individuation in *On the Mode of Existence of Technical Objects,*[408] and the assertion that the transindividual can be constituted only if it is *supported* by technical objects, as indicated by this passage from the conclusion of *On the Mode of Existence of Technical Objects*:

> The technical object taken according to its essence, which is to say the technical object insofar as it has been invented, thought and willed, and taken up [*assumé*] by a human subject, becomes the support and symbol of this relationship, which we would like to name *transindividual*.[409]

It is, then, the support, and it is so as tertiary retention. But it is also the symbol, and is so as the exosomatic organ that circulates, is detachable, exchangeable, charged with power – power that may be transitional, magical, religious, artistic, monumental, fetishized, economic and so on – constituting in this way, and in a thousand other ways, the functionalities of any kind of *noesis as such* (measurement, indication, datability, boundary-marking, etc.).

Given that, on the one hand, *L'individuation à la lumière des notions de forme et d'information* describes the transindividual in terms of significance [*signification*], which according to *On the Mode of Existence of Technical Objects* thus requires the support of technical objects, and given that, on the other hand, signification involves information, we can no longer understand how it is possible to separate information from its supports, nor how psychic and collective individuation could be considered *without inscribing into them the phase shifts of technical individuation that constitute the technical milieu that is exosomatization*.

Ultimately, these confusions are due:

- to Simondon's neglect of Schrödinger's conception of life, where negative entropy, as anti-entropy and not just negentropy, appears for what it is *in life*, namely: the struggle to defer entropy *through the differentiation of vital organs* (through their individuation), and as vital différance; not as information, nor as 'negentropy' in the sense of information theory, but as co-genesis and *concretization* of what thus constitutes an in-dividual, that is, an in-divisible; not just as that concretizing *tendency* that is machinic functional integration, but as an *organic* concretization that thereby constitutes an *organism*;

- to ignorance of the questions raised by Alfred Lotka when he showed that *exosomatic* organogenesis opens up a new form of life[410] – as Canguilhem said in other terms and by referring to *technical life*[411] – where this différance becomes noetic and constitutes what Simondon called psychic and collective individuation.

The fact that *machinic* functional integration is only a tendency has the following consequence: when it ignores the conditions of its sustainable accomplishment qua tendency – and as *exosomatic différance* generated by protentions that arise from psychic and collective individuals while in turn generating them transductively, these psychic and collective individuals coupling and co-individuating with machinic individuation within complex exorganisms – when it ignores these conditions, it disintegrates, because *it cannot last*, it becomes an indifférance, and it does so because it is irrational.

Machinic functional integration, ignoring the neganthropic conditions of its accomplishment, is irrational and therefore, *in principle* [*en droit*], cannot last. It remains the case, however, that very often, *being* irrational, it can *in fact* last – not sustainably, but on a timescale we call the short term, or the medium term. This occurs through what is known as 'speculation', but it causes time to crash in on itself, precisely because this process is utterly irrational. Such is the post-truth age that is our lot, and it brings the Anthropocene to a point of closure from which we have no hope of emerging other than by shattering this state of fact with a new state of law.

For the exosomatic form of life, knowledge and its supports are themselves always exosomatic – and thus can be *shared* by complex exorganisms that generate the transindividual, which from the eleventh century is, in the West, organized within *universities* and into *faculties*, and which takes other forms in other societies. For the exosomatic form of life, then, knowledge and its supports constitute *vital functions* in the sense of Canguilhem[412] and Whitehead. These functions, however, must no longer be thought within the framework of entropy or anti-entropy as they have been theorized from thermodynamics to cybernetics: they require a theory of anthropy and negathropy – and this is so because such exosomatic organs are *pharmaka*.

▪ ▪ ▪

Whatever may be the relevance, errors or limits of the conjunctions between information theory and entropy, they have very profoundly, performatively and techno-logically structured industrial fields and their markets – and, through them, every dimension of existence. Transhumanist 'storytelling' is perfectly in keeping with this performativity, and its effects have not been limited to the communication and information industries and the cognitive sciences: it has profoundly transformed the very notions of knowledge and truth, which means that this is also the performativity of a *materialized ideology*. This ideology is an anti-*epistēmē*: the negative *epistēmē* of an absolute non-knowledge in which all Hegelian and dialectical hypotheses are inverted in a non-dialectizable way – becoming inaccessible to the dialectical sublation of an *Aufhebung*.[413] The result is an immense overthrow of noetic faculties, *both psychic and institutional*, and a planetary, that is, biospheric, disarray – which in a more or less confused fashion we refer to as 'post-truth'.[414]

Vernadsky defined the biosphere first and foremost as a *bio-logical work transforming physical matter into geolocalized bio-chemical matter, produced by geochemical energy and geochemical work*:

> The diffusion of living matter [...] becomes apparent through the *ubiquity of life* [...]. [D]uring the entirety of geological history life has tended to take possession of, and utilize, all possible space. [...] The diffusion of life is a sign of internal energy – of the chemical work life performs [...] the transformation of chemical elements and the creation of new matter from them. We shall call this energy *the geochemical energy of life in the biosphere*. [...] This uninterrupted movement resulting from the multiplication of living organisms is executed with an *inexorable and astonishing mathematical regularity* [...]. Throughout myriads of years, it accomplishes a colossal geochemical labor.[415]

It is by starting from a similar hypothesis and by taking account of the theory of entropy that Lotka devised the hypothesis of exosomatization from the standpoint of applying mathematics to population genetics, and that he defined exosomatization firstly as an *astonishing acceleration* of organogenesis.

If it is true that in the nineteenth century the biosphere became massively anthropic through industrial exosomatization, and that the processes of biochemical transformation in which the biosphere consists are now conditioned by the selection of molecular combinations according to calculations undertaken by automated markets, then we should understand the biosphere itself as *a planetary-scale exorganism* that is functionally reticulated and integrated by platform capitalism. This integration, however, is also a disintegration: reticulation operates through a *purely computational technology that is therefore structurally entropic* because it hypertrophies the capacities of automated understanding, which are analytical but self-referential. This has the following consequences:

1. A new conflict arises between the noetic faculties and functions, both psychic and collective (subjective and institutional), as they are defunctionalized and refunctionalized by the new biospheric and hypercomplex exorganisms of 'smart capitalism', thereby installing the disorder of 'soft totalitarianism';
2. We must *resolve* this conflict by differentiating and deferring the runaway anthropy that is leading *Neganthropos* to its destruction – this is the practical, economic and political meaning of différance, which counters anthropy and its tendency towards indifférance;
3. The noetic faculties must regain their capacity to produce neganthropic prescriptions capable of providing new criteriologies for the selection of molecular combinations in terrestrial and now industrial geobiochemistry, as well as in the *vital and symbolic* retentional combinations that confer value upon geobiochemical combinations.

▪ ▪ ▪

John Pfaltz, at the University of Virginia, has undertaken a mathematical analysis of the morphogenetic processes that arise with social networking, very clearly highlighting how 'social networks' greatly reinforce entropic tendencies:

> [Through] the concepts of closed sets and closure operators [...] social networks [...] are represented by transformations. [...] [U]nder continuous change/transformation, all networks tend to 'break down' and become less complex. It is a kind of entropy.[416]

Here, the question is the status of information as a key concept in the digital reticular industry derived from information theory, along with the questions of its relationship to entropy in general, its anthropic effects in this sense, and the conditions for developing new neganthropic practices. The latter would need to be based on new data structures allowing the deferral of informational entropy – by rearming noetic différance on the basis of the present state of exosomatization.

The information technology of digital tertiary retention makes it possible to discretize linguistic data in binary form, in order to process it with probabilistic statistical calculations. This represents a fundamental change in the transindividuation processes in which the evolution of language consists – insofar as this is always a matter of languages, whose diversity is always delineated on two planes: the idiom (collective) and the idiolect (individual).

Based on automated synchronization processes that begin with the analysis of averages, the technology of 'linguistic capitalism' performatively and massively trans-forms linguistic performances, which are henceforth interactively controlled via interfaces that reformat all language transactions. And it does so on a planetary scale, involving a population of three and a half billion speakers, practitioners of several hundred idioms. In so doing, linguistic capitalism uniformly affects the elementary conditions of *semiosis*, drastically impoverishing the skills and competencies of speakers – and in turn impoverishing what we might call the dialogical semiodiversity that conditions semiosis.

The techno-logical performativity that places the noetic proliferation of meaning under the computational control of averages thereby massively proletarianizes linguistic competence. This is equally true of the decline of spelling ability due to the effect of auto-completion and auto-correct functions on writing activity, something that affects senior management just as it does all layers of the population. Hence is imposed a mass cretinism 'from kindergarten to the Collège de France' – to borrow an expression from Pierre Bourdieu.

Physiological cretinism is a pathology caused by iodine deficiency. *Noetic* cretinism results from the *generalization of functional noetic deficiencies,* caused by the proletarianization of all forms of knowledge – which is nothing other than their destruction. It is reflected in a massive reduction of idiomatic and idiolectical variability. These massive noetic deficiencies, combined with the effects of the proletarianization of production, essentially result from the combination of the 'language industries',[417] as Sylvain Auroux called them in the 1980s, and which are based on automating the analytical functions of the understanding, with the 'culture industries', as Adorno and Horkheimer understood them, along with the 'social networks' that create 'closed sets' and 'closure operators'.

Is it still possible to introduce a *noetic après-coup* into this stage of exosomatization, a stage that is the first moment of a doubly epokhal redoubling whose stakes are the relationship between noesis, language, hypomnesic tertiary retention and grammatization? Can grammatization still be made to serve an *idiomatic and idiolectical intensification* rather than a *planetary linguicide*?[418] If 'planetary linguicide' means a collapse of that noodiversity to which idiomatic and idiolectical diversity bear witness, it is because the exosomatization currently underway, which is not redoubled by those new circuits of transindividuation that alone could generate new epokhal capacities, affects the very structure of the noetic faculties and functions – in a way that goes right down to those very *roots* that are retentions and protentions. Does noesis then find itself left defenceless? And is exosomatization itself destined to lead to the general spread of entropy?

We posit that if there is an answer to this urgent and immense question, it presupposes:

1. a redefinition of anti-entropy from the standpoint of exosomatic organogenesis, which is not reducible to endosomatic organogenesis, the latter being the horizon of Schrödinger's analysis: hence it is also necessary to refer to neganthropy and anti-anthropy, and to do so in other terms;
2. a critique of information theory and its derivatives in cybernetics, cognitivism, theoretical computing and applied mathematics, inasmuch as they exhaust neganthropic milieus through anthropic forces of all kinds.

Over the past six sessions, I have presented you with theses and hypotheses on the basis of which I am attempting to elaborate a hyper-materialist epistemology and a hyper-critique of impure reason. During the final two sessions, I will propose parallel readings of works by Alfred Sohn-Rethel, Lev Vygotsky and Ignace Meyerson, in order to clarify these points in dialogue with this trio, that is, with two Marxists, one Russian and the other German, and a Polish social psychologist – who was also the great but unrecognized inspiration for the work of Jean-Pierre Vernant, whose work should be articulated with that of Maryanne Wolf, whom we discussed last year. But this last task is one for which we will not have time now: we'll save it for next year.

SEVENTH LECTURE

Critique of Sohn-Rethel and the Need for a Hyper-Materialist Epistemology

What has happened since the onset of exosomatization, which began some three or four million years ago? Man, who is what I call a simple exorganism, has altered landscapes and erected palaces. Then, starting from the constitution of these higher complex exorganisms that are civilizations, empires or kingdoms, he has engendered that industrial hyper-exosomatization characteristic of capitalism, which has led to an extraordinary acceleration, highlighted by Marx and Engels in 1848, who posit that the bourgeoisie is for this reason the revolutionary class, then highlighted in other terms by Lotka in 1945, and again in a film, *Welcome to the Anthropocene*, played at the 2012 Rio Summit.

As early as 1945, then, it seems that Lotka was aware, after Vernadsky (whose work he knew, and vice versa – Lotka is quoted by Vernadsky at the end of *The Biosphere*, as is Whitehead), and before Toynbee, of the fact that we have now entered into what we now call the Anthropocene era. The latter has, since the Second World War, undergone a constant and terrible acceleration. Terrible, because it seems to be leading to an inevitable loss of the planet, to a fatal situation for the human species and for all of the higher forms of life, a situation that led 15364 researchers to sign a second warning to humanity in December 2017,[419] followed by the IPCC revising its forecasts downwards in October 2018,[420] and then by the UN anticipating consequences on all kinds of levels in March 2019.[421] The catastrophic bifurcation that would thus be foreshadowed is described formally – as it was in 2012 in *Nature* – in terms of a 'state shift in Earth's biosphere'.[422] What could happen after this catastrophic bifurcation? Could this end of mankind be subsumed by a transhumanism that would itself leave Earth behind?

My intention is to show you that transhumanism is an ideological discourse aiming to establish total domination by calculation. What, however, is ideology? Ideology, if we follow Marx and Engels, is what stems from a causal inversion. This inversion consists in positing that social and historical reality descends from a 'heaven of ideas' that is itself atemporal, eternal in the theological sense, or *a priori* in the Kantian sense, constituting what since Plato have been called essences, which are the forms and laws of being.

Marx and Engels posit that, on the contrary, the ideas are generated by work, that is, by the production of exosomatic organs, and by the social relations to which they give rise. It by taking up this standpoint that Sohn-Rethel will be led to propose a materialist epistemology founded on the analysis of abstraction as resulting from the practice of commercial exchanges themselves based on that abstract 'general equivalent' which is money.

I will now try to show, in order to conclude this year's seminar – and in this way to open a dialogue with Zhang Yibing and Tang Zhendong – that this standpoint is not at all satisfactory, and how we can and must pass from this very *elementary* materialist epistemology to a hyper-materialist epistemology, which would also be, if I may so, a *supplementary* epistemology.

But let us first return to transhumanism as a post-apocalyptic narrative that paves the way for the apocalypse to come and its aftermath. What we say to counter this narrative, and against its absolute irrationality, which ruins in advance the hypothesis that we could flee the land of the earth by migrating either to the sea[423] or to another planet,[424] is that there is something beyond calculation, and that this is the condition of life, of the appearance of life as an open system, as well as of the pursuit of life as the struggle against entropy in which consists this opening of a system that is a living organism. This 'beyond' is what lies beyond the 'icy water of egotistical calculation',[425] as Marx and Engels put it in *The Communist Manifesto*, announcing that it is in such waters that the capitalists will drown.

Hyper-materialist epistemology turns this *moral* account of calculation (as 'egotistical') into a question of rationality founded on a new epistemology, by positing that the hegemony of calculation is utterly irrational: it is irrational because it leads to entropy, which destroys life. Reason is in this way always *beyond* calculation: it is the experience of the incalculable that requires, on each occasion, a decision, which means a neganthropic bifurcation.

As for our context – that of what could happen beyond the great catastrophic bifurcation that is well on its way – *it would be a matter of knowing how any kind of noesis would still be possible after this bifurcation*. In other words, it is not at all a question, here, of man. Man is a name given to this simple exorganism who lives within complex exorganisms, and this name, which this simple exorganism gives to itself, especially starting from the Renaissance and from so-called Humanism, refers to the noetic and technical form of life, which Aristotle called the noetic soul, and therefore to what, as noesis, is capable of accomplishing realizable dreams, which, however, can always turn into nightmares.

What we on occasion call 'man' does not stop changing its 'nature', and from this perspective, the questions of posthumanism or transhumanism are futile. To know what man 'is' is not the question. The question is to know what it means to think. For me, to think [*penser*] means to care [*panser*], that is, to take care of *pharmaka* so that exosomatization does not lead to anthropy. This is why we must fight the icy water of egotistical calculation, which is celebrated by Adam Smith, and which directs the bourgeoisie – which has moreover disappeared, replaced by the mafia of thoroughly computational capitalism, who are incapable of admiring anything, no longer able to know or do anything except envy and covet Ferraris, Maseratis and now Teslas, unlike the bourgeoisie of the nineteenth century.

It is not a question of knowing what man is. It is a question of knowing what *constitutes* what the Greeks called noesis. I have argued since I began these Nanjing seminars in 2016 that *noesis is the second moment of exosomatization qua doubly epokhal redoubling*. The *first* moment of exosomatization itself constitutes a first epokhal redoubling, which is technological – which is to say, precisely, exosomatic. It is this first redoubling that engenders, as the establishing of a *new stage of the individuation of the technical system formed by exosomatic organs*, an *overthrow of already constituted circuits of transindividuation* – constituted by previous exosomatic and epokhal redoublings – in favour of new circuits of transindividuation. These new circuits of transindividuation form a new epoch of noesis, that is, a *new epoch of the history of truth* in the sense referred to by Heidegger, and in particular in *The Essence of Truth*.[426]

Hence the great exosomatic transformations that characterize the Renaissance will give rise to Humanism, the Reformation and all its consequences, sometimes terrible, including consequences that according to Weber are constitutive of capitalism, and finally to the Republic of Letters and the classical age, which is to say, modern philosophy. But the constitution of new circuits of transindividuation, whose unity forms an epoch, also, in turn, always gives rise to a new exosomatization: hence, for example, what emerges from the classical age paves the way for the age of industrial capitalism.

In other words, it is not that exosomatization lies at the origin of noesis, nor is it that noesis lies at the origin of exosomatization: noesis *is* exosomatization and exosomatization *is* noesis. But this 'is' is something that phase-shifts, something that is out-of-phase – that is, a process.

This process is what occurs in the biosphere, on the Earth, and as a specific, noetic and zoological process, within the overarching process that is the universe itself. This processuality is reflected in what Marx and then Engels will say about the movement and the historicity of becoming beyond all onto-theology, and in particular about what leads to German idealism. But:

1 They do not see that this processuality is thermodynamic on the physical plane, that is, *entropic*, that it is *negentropic* on the biological plane, and both *anthropic and neganthropic* on the plane of what we should here call not anthropology but neganthropology, the question of which is opened up by Lévi-Strauss in *Tristes Tropiques*, but *by default*.

2 They do not produce a true epistemology of this processual and historical conception of becoming and future, in that they ultimately do not overcome the Kantian question of the imagination, and more generally the Kantian definition of the noetic faculties – and this is why Marx, in his comparison of the exosomatic faculties of the bee and the architect, will return to the idealist conception of noesis.

3 This is what Sohn-Rethel deplores, and yet, while deploring it, he nevertheless in some way repeats it, and this is what I will try to show you now.

▪ ▪ ▪

Each new doubly epokhal redoubling, on each occasion engendering a new epoch, and sometimes even a new era, itself constitutes a new interiorization of what has been exosomatized in the form of new knowledge, which in turn constitutes new circuits of transindividuation. These new circuits, taken as a whole, generate new kinds of exosomatization, which begin as noetic dreams, dreams that may not be fully realized until several generations later.[427]

Ideas do not precede their exosomatic realization, and exosomatic realities do not precede the ideas that result from interiorization, an interiorization that is noetic and endosomatic (within the brain) but also social (as the constitution of organization in the form of a complex exorganism): it is the *movement of the whole* that *constitutes* noesis *as* exosomatization, that is, as *exteriorization in the sense that Hegel gives to this term* in *Phenomenology of Spirit*, but by maintaining in his logic that the spirit can *absolve* and in this way *dissolve* this exteriorization by interiorizing it in totality, and as the *Science of Logic*, which is to say that this exteriorization would thus turn out to have been merely a 'moment' of the advent of Spirit that is accomplished as Absolute Knowledge. What Hegel could not understand, any more than did Simondon, is that *this exosomatization is pharmacological* and that this pharmacology is insurmountable. Marx provides a name for this pharmacology: he calls it proletarianization. And he interprets proletarianization as being the result of class domination, of an exploitation of man by man. This is what we will return to more closely, as we approach Sohn-Rethel.

Each new spiritual interiorization of what has been exosomatized by spirituality itself (as *intellectus* and *spiritus*) is reflected in a new social organization, which thus gives rise to a new higher complex exorganism. This is why *The German Ideology* posits that German idealism, and Platonic idealism in general, are in the service of class domination. From this it is also clear that Alain Badiou has understood nothing of Marx – and why his reading of Marx amounts to complete fantasy.

Sohn-Rethel aims to continue this Marxian critique of idealism from the perspective of a critique of political economy, and to do so in greater detail than Marx and Engels. He does so by focusing, after George Thomson, on what occurred between Lydia and Ionia around the seventh century BC, that is, with those whom we know as the pre-Socratic thinkers, and in particular Pythagoras, Heraclitus and Parmenides:

> The concept of 'knowledge', as it is understood by all theoretical philosophy and all theory of knowledge from its beginnings (with Pythagoras, Heraclitus and Parmenides), all the way to Wittgenstein and Bertrand Russell, etc., is a fetishistic concept that creates an ideal figure of 'knowledge in general', a knowledge deprived of any link to the historical and economic context.[428]

If the last clause is obviously not completely unfounded, the thesis as a whole is almost grotesque. And what Sohn-Rethel does not understand, here, is that this complex movement of exteriorizations, interiorizations and social organizations stems from the différantiation of exosomatization into ordinary tertiary retentions, then into extra-ordinary tertiary retentions – that is, hypomnesic tertiary retentions.

Sohn-Rethel does not see it because he does not see that *what is most revolutionary about the thinking of Marx and Engels is their consideration of exosomatization.* In other words, Sohn-Rethel does not see that the *challenge lies in the way they think technics, which is not a question for either Sohn-Rethel or Adorno,* but which *was* a question for Benjamin, for example, and which will (but only weakly) become a question for Habermas. For Adorno and Horkheimer, technics is simply the means by which capital dominates labour, and not the condition of any noesis whatsoever, as Marx and Engels say from the outset.

Last year, during the bicentennial of the birth of Marx, I recalled, here at Nanjing University, that Marx suggests in *Capital* that we must *create a theory of technical evolution, just as Darwin created a theory of the evolution of life*. This means that the initial movement outlined at the beginning of *The German Ideology* carries on into the 1860s. And it is towards the continuation of this movement that I am working here, by trying to develop a hyper-materialist epistemology from an exosomatic standpoint: contemporary exosomatization has in fact taught us that we can no longer be content with the Newtonian concept of matter, and that, furthermore, micro-electronic exosomatization and nano-electronic exosomatization, that is, quantum (and soon bionic) exosomatization, make informational and computational exosomatization possible in a way that leads to the necessity of adopting a hyper-materialist standpoint, that is, of going beyond the hylemorphic schema opposing form and matter, as Simondon understood as early as the 1950s.

As you also know, I have pointed out that in this same text, Book 1 of *Capital*, there is a 'post-idealist' regression (if I may put it like this), when Marx suggests that the architect is different from the bee because the former has the concept of what he will build 'in his head'. This is why I share Sohn-Rethel's point of view when he rightly emphasizes that there is no true Marxist epistemology, that is, materialist epistemology, which he expresses by taking up Adorno's thesis in *Negative Dialectics* that Marx did not elaborate a theory of knowledge because he was 'disgusted with the academic squabbles'.[429] Nevertheless, Sohn-Rethel himself fails to see the fundamental consequences of exosomatization, and in particular he profoundly ignores *the conditions of what I call the exorganogenesis of noesis*, that is, the conditions of the appearance and articulation of what Kant called the lower faculties.

To think this, we must adopt a hyper-materialist standpoint. The reason we must do so is not just because of the performativity of 'Moore's law', for example, and its hyper-material exploitation of the micro-electronic level of silicon while preparing the way for the nano-metric level of the bionic that in turn paves the way for the neurotechnological level of exosomatization as it shifts towards the cerebral re-endosomatization of the exosomatization of digital tertiary retentions. It is also because we must additionally posit that exosomatized materiality, insofar as it has formed tertiary retentions ever since the beginning of hominization, already counts as hyper-matter insofar as it is organized in a non-organic but organological way, which is to say that it forms artificial organs.

What I will try to show now is that, because Sohn-Rethel doesn't have the faintest idea of the questions I'm raising in this way, he introduces confusion between *money* and *writing*, and more generally between calculation and grammatization. For indeed he posits, taking up Marx's initial perspective, that capitalism is above all a process of *abstraction* from the social-as-*totality* and by the social-*divided*-into-dominant-and-dominated classes, on the one hand through labour, and on the other hand through exchange. And he argues that it is during exchange that this abstraction is accomplished as alienation:

> The form in which commodity-value takes on its concrete appearance as money – be it as coinage or bank-notes – is an abstract *thing* which, strictly speaking, is a contradiction in terms. In the form of money riches become abstract riches and, as owner of such riches, man himself becomes an abstract man, a private property-owner.[430]

But by proposing that money would be the origin of abstraction, and of alienation as Marx already described it in the *1844 Manuscripts*, he ignores the conditions in which the general equivalent appears, inasmuch as it itself stems from written numeration systems – such as Geneviève Guitel has described them, after the works of Charles Morazé – and *which themselves presuppose the appearance of writing as hypomnesic tertiary retention.*

The appearance of hypomnesic tertiary retention is, in my opinion, and I believe this is also the opinion of Leroi-Gourhan and to some extent of Vernant, as well as Meyerson, but also and especially of Vygotsky, the condition of what amounts to an *organogenetic history of noesis through which the lower faculties (in Kant's sense) are generated* – and which amounts to what in earlier sessions of this year's seminar I called *the exo-transcendence of tertiary retention in general and of exosomatic tertiary retention in particular.* This is why I argue that when Heidegger sees, in the transformation of *alētheia* to *orthōtes* that plays out in Book VII of the *Republic*, a forgetting of the primordial meaning of *alētheia*, he is right to see this transformation as marking the beginning of metaphysics as the 'forgetting of being'. But what he does not see is that, on the one hand, this transformation is caused by the analytical power of hypomnesic tertiary retention, and, on the other hand, that it at the same time prepares both what Descartes will establish in Rules 15 and 16 of his *Rules for the Direction of the Mind*, and what Kant, in offering a critique of the conclusions drawn from these Cartesian rules by Leibniz, will say concerning the difference between the analytical faculty of the understanding and the synthetic faculty of reason.

From this standpoint, it seems to me nothing short of *ridiculous* to suggest that Parmenides, for example, would be the expression of a class domination exercised by the Greek nobility against the slaves and foreigners who labour for them – this labour being here not *ergon*, that is, work [*oeuvre*], but *ponos*, that is, toil [*labour*]. But this is precisely what Sohn-Rethel does suggest, as we have already seen, on the basis of the following thesis:

> The possibility of theoretical knowledge of nature is not a capacity originating in the human mind, but is indeed the product (after having passed through complex mediations) of social developments determined by and based on specific forms of class domination.[431]

And again:

> Historically, we find metaphysical thought's way of conceptualizing to be specific to independent intellectual labour. The separate base-form of this intellectual labour is to be sought, according to our hypothesis, in market-related activities, namely, in functions on which is based the connection of private works in order to form overall social labour.[432]

For Sohn-Rethel, it is a matter of 'showing that the roots of the pure categories of the object appear as such in commodity exchange'.[433] According to Sohn-Rethel, the distinguishing of the categories that constitute both Aristotle's ontology-metaphysics and the logic that it grounds as *hermeneia* would therefore be nothing more than results of the various market practices involved in the valuation of commodities by, on the one hand, the conditions of exchange as defined by monetary abstraction, and, on the other hand, the abstraction of labour (which for him is the immediate background of this domination of exchange by money, and not the other way around as it is in Marx).

Such a conception of the stakes of Greek noesis is quite superficial, and consists in superimposing onto it the notion that the intellect and more generally reason and spirit are historically in the service of class domination, until that reversal which will be accomplished by Marx and historical materialism – a reversal that would in this way be noetically and socially revolutionary. What this fails to understand is that what is revolutionary in this historical materialism, which rightly posits that noesis itself has a history, is that this history begins with exosomatization – and that it is neither more nor less than the history of this exosomatization itself qua history of noesis itself and insofar as it always stems from psychic interiorizations and social organizations that are on each occasion original, as well as being constitutive of epochs that are also economies. These economies are both political and libidinal, that is, they on each occasion constitute new forms of what Aristotle called *philia*.

If this is how things stand with Sohn-Rethel, it can only be because, like Adorno – who was inspired by him – he ignores the question of the transcendental imagination raised by Heidegger on the basis of the first edition of the *Critique of Pure Reason*. With regard to this question, I have myself tried to show that, between intuition, understanding and reason, tertiary retention and hypomnesic tertiary retention constitute schemas, which are also and firstly themselves categories. Because Adorno fails to see that the Kantian notion of the schematism constitutes a problem for Kant himself, he unreflectively adopts the Kantian point of view without seeing that it is idealist: it is to this that the second chapter of the *Dialektik der Aufklärung* bears witness.

What I am now trying to show, here and in Hangzhou, is that this *exo-transcendent* (and non-transcendental) schematization is what lies at the origin of these *metastable* and thus *metempirical* forms that constitute the categories insofar as they condition, as the distribution of these metempirical metastabilizations interiorized by all forms of education (as we will see with Vygotsky), the synchronization and diachronization of ways of life within those higher complex exorganisms that have adopted them and that have done so as epochs in the history of truth.

EIGHTH LECTURE

Sohn-Rethel, Vygotsky, Meyerson

Yesterday I indicated that Kantian theory lacks a faculty of dreaming – which would arrive both upstream and downstream of the higher faculties of knowing, desiring and judging. In Hangzhou this year I have tried to outline – by referring to the work of Marc Azéma, but also to the young Michel Foucault and his engagement with the work of Ludwig Binswanger – the contours of such a faculty. This presupposes, at the level of the lower faculties, and in particular at the level of the imagination, the elaboration of a new theory of the schematization as well as the specification of what I have described in *Technics and Time, 3* as a 'fourth synthesis'.[434] I have called this fourth synthetic and functional dimension – which completes the syntheses of apprehension, reproduction and recognition – the synthesis of repro-duction – and not just of re-production.[435]

Re-production is the function of the synthesis of the understanding, which re-produces the concepts, that is, the categories, under which the various givens and data of intuition, furnished by the synthesis of apprehension, are gathered and unified. As for the synthesis of re-cognition, it inscribes what is thus provided by the understanding on the basis of the intuition into the unification of the flux (of retentions and protentions, but these are obviously not Kant's concepts) that constitutes the unity of the *I think* – thereby elaborating the *overall coherence of experience* from the perspective of both the transcendental apperception of the world, the unity of which *coincides* with that of the *I think*, and of what, as the *ideas of reason*, consists in what I call (in *Disbelief and Discredit*) the *'consistence' of ends* (themselves forming, for Kant, the *kingdom of ends*).

I conceive the synthesis of *repro-duction* – and not just of *re-production* – as being *what is produced by hypomnesic tertiary retention*. Walter Benjamin attempts to deal with this question in 'The Work of Art in the Age of Its Technological Reproducibility',[436] where he approaches (but without having time to fully explain the concept) the *question of the difference generated by the repetition* of what he thus calls reproducibility, but which I argue should be conceived as a *repro-ducibility*. Repro-ducibility is what stems from a *primordial repetition* that generates a *primordial difference*, which is the issue at stake in *Difference and Repetition*, and which also amounts to a *primordial différance* (which in French I call '*le défaut qu'il faut*', the necessary default).

I have tried to show that Kant was able to write the second edition of the *Critique of Pure Reason* only *because he was able to reread the first version to the letter.* Benjamin does something similar, as does Proust, in particular when he writes *On Reading*. We can understand, then, why libraries are rooms constituting a new faculty of dreaming, such as the library at the University of Bologna or the one that constitutes the empire of Alexander.

Going back to Kant, the first version of the *Critique of Pure Reason* amounts to *an exosomatized repro-duction of his own synthesis of recognition* (in the sense of the first edition), which has itself been *generated* by the *rereading* of what he wrote *to the extent that he wrote it by in this way stabilizing the unity of the flow of his reading-writing consciousness*: 'in this way', that is, *thanks to this literal (lettered) hypomnesic tertiary retention that is alphabetical writing as the fourth repro-ductive synthesis.*

It is necessary to reread Kant here, and it is necessary because Sohn-Rethel repeats Adorno's mistake, or the same neglect, in relation to Kant, which consists in not asking about the conditions of the syntheses of that imagination which Kant called transcendental, and which I myself argue stems from a metempirical exo-transcendence. Note, however, that here, unlike Adorno, Sohn-Rethel does put Kant himself into question.

Before elaborating upon these points, I would like to make a general preliminary assessment of our situation here and now, that is, in the biosphere in 2019, a biosphere that has become a technosphere, based not on libraries but on data centres, in which markets, along with universities, knowledge, technology and ways of life have all been globalized, and where proletarianization and denoetization, too, have become general and widespread.

At the end of the second decade of the twenty-first century – a century that began with the 11 September 2001 attacks in New York – we find ourselves in a position similar to that of Descartes in the seventeenth century with respect to scholasticism, which had been dismantled by humanism (but which was still taught at the Collège de La Flèche where Descartes studied), and, with scholastics, it is Thomist onto-theology and thus Christian-inspired Aristotelianism that will be 'epokhalized', suspended, making way for this new epoch that will be Renaissance humanism in Western Europe, largely brought about by 'great discoveries', as they are called in Europe, three of which, to be fair, to some extent at least come from China – the printing press, the compass and gun powder – while the other, America, opens up a new space to Europeans, all of this giving a very new meaning to what amounts to a rediscovery bequeathed by Islam: the reading of Plato.

With the Renaissance, which gives rise to capitalism in Max Weber's sense, things do not go well with ontotheology, and a 'reformation of the understanding' is required. The latter results from a techno-logical *epokhē* that generates a second *epokhē*, a second moment of the *epokhē*, which constitutes Humanism as well as the Reformed Church, capitalism in the Weberian sense, wars of religion, colonialism, and from which modern philosophy, too, emerges. And with this modern philosophy, it is the noetic dream of what Heidegger will call 'modern technology', then *Gestell*, that first takes shape – in the works of Descartes.

We ourselves, in the twenty-first century, and after the 'poststructuralist' attempt, which is an antihumanism (that of Foucault and Deleuze deriving from Nietzsche, that of Derrida stemming instead from Heidegger, and that of Lyotard, which will lead to consideration of a 'postmodern epoch'), we find ourselves living in an age of post-truth, that is, the epoch of the absence of epoch, in which it seems to us that the legacy of 'poststructuralist' thinking and of what has become 'postmodernity' (I put these words in quotation marks because those who are described and circumscribed by these terms did not themselves recognize them), it seems to us that this legacy will have led us into the *post-truth impasse of a total failure of thinking* – and in this situation *with no horizon*, that is, devoid of ends, of the kingdom of ends, of ideas of reason, or in other words of what I call collective secondary protentions, it seems that *this entire elaboration of what has been called 'French theory', with its key sources including Marx, Nietzsche and Freud, all this has now turned into a kind of scholastics* – and ultimately, along with all of this, *it is the modern that, considered in terms of the postmodern absence of epoch, presents itself as the scholastics from which 'poststructuralist' antihumanism would have emerged.*

(Here we should discuss the relationships between Lévi-Strauss, Lacan, Foucault and Derrida, but we no longer have time for that.)

▪ ▪ ▪

The difficulty of reading either Sohn-Rethel or Adorno in the twenty-first century, along with many others, lies in the scholastic opacification and sedimentation that occurred over the course of this 'history of truth' that 'modernity' and then 'postmodernity' will have been, and inasmuch as:

- on the one hand, it is always what stems from an occultation, the un-concealment of *a-lētheia* always re-concealing itself with the same gesture (an analysis that Adorno and Sohn-Rethel reject in the same gesture as rejecting Heidegger);

- on the other hand, it becomes accessible to us only through deconstruction and 'postmodern' detachment from this modernity, which is also a detachment in relation to Marx and to what Lyotard believed he could call the 'grand narratives of emancipation', while in so doing, he avoided truly rereading Marx, and notably in dialogue with the Frankfurt School.

I have tried to describe the reasons for these blockages in *States of Shock*, and what I am doing here continues this attempt.

The doubly epokhal redoubling is what an epigonal or scholastic reading of Derridian deconstruction, or for that matter Heideggerian deconstruction, has rendered inconceivable, invisible and impotent. This powerlessness consists in an *inability to generate the second moment of this double redoubling*, and this is what abandons us to an absence of epoch commonly known as 'post-truth'.

The doubly epokhal redoubling is a *double temporality*:

- that of the supports forming the memory composed of tertiary retentions;
- that of transindividuation, which, as the elaboration of new noetic dreams, that is, realizable dreams, installs a phase shift bearing new bifurcations within the whole, within which a struggle therefore ensues.

Today, this struggle has become that of the World [*Monde*] becoming Worldless and Befouled [*Immonde*], and of the Earth become the Globe, globalized by the technosphere that Heidegger called *Gestell* – the struggle being the bearer of the (im)possibility of the *Ereignis*. I refer to (im)possibility because, in view of the rationalization of the understanding that means the latter has become essentially probabilistic, there is *no* chance (no *probability*) that this *Ereignis* will occur.

'And yet it turns': so said Galileo. And yet the only path possible is that of this impossible: so I myself say in this Anthropocene era where I try to contribute to provoking the bifurcation of the Neganthropocene era – through a neganthropology. This neganthropology is what responds to Sohn-Rethel – and through him to the China that emerges from the Cultural Revolution, which was then his main interlocutor – by passing through both Vygotsky and Meyerson.

The doubly epokhal redoubling is, as I said, what results from the play of new tertiary retentions, arising from realized noetic dreams, forming a new stage of exosomatization, and generating new circuits of transindividuation and forming a new epoch, which in turn bears within it and then engenders a new stage of techno-logical epokhality – that is, a new stage of exosomatization. This is the whole point of *The German Ideology*, and this is what is forgotten by Sohn-Rethel, along with Adorno, Althusser, Badiou and so many others (but not Benjamin).

It is this *forgetting* that makes it possible for Sohn-Rethel to claim that the production of 'metaphysical' forms of consciousness can be described via the opposition between the manual and the intellectual. What Sohn-Rethel does not see here is that tertiary retention has, since the beginning of hominization, produced forms of what will lead to 'consciousness', which will later become a 'self-consciousness', and with industrial exosomatization a 'class consciousness', but that it could do so only *after* the advent in the Upper Palaeolithic of the first *hypomnesic* tertiary retentions, while the formation of the lower faculties, as I described them in deviating from Kant, occurs only with the advent of grammatization in the Great Empires, then in the Mediterranean Basin around Greece and Judea, and finally between Imperial China and Western Europe starting from the Renaissance, by way of the Jesuits and then the Marxists.

Before entering into the details of Sohn-Rethel's reasoning, I would like to clarify that we simply cannot say that, as he writes, 'it is men's social being that determines their consciousness'.[437] For in the doubly epokhal redoubling, which is what techno-logically constitutes the social, *it is not a question of determination, but of condition*. It is for this reason that we refer to the *exosomatic condition of noesis*, which conditions it both techno-logically and socially, but which, however, can and must always leave it *undetermined, that is, open*, and thus *neganthropic* – failing which exosomatization leads to denoetization.

What Sohn-Rethel does not understand is the schematization, and, first of all, he doesn't understand that it does not stem just from the submission of the intuition to the categories of the understanding, given that, for the Kant of the first edition of the *Critique of Pure Reason*, it also presupposes the threefold synthesis of the imagination, and in particular the synthesis of apprehension, and where the latter is itself conditioned (but this is what I say, not Kant) by the repro-duction of the faculty of dreaming upstream and downstream of the other three syntheses, and is so according to what the hypomnesic tertiary retention operating in the stage of exosomatization in which the noetic act of knowledge occurs makes possible in the form of *schemas that are simultaneously sensorimotor, conceptual and ideal*.

In other words, *the schematization is not just conceptual*, and this is what Sohn-Rethel cannot see: it is intuitive, in the sense that it falls within what Kant calls the synthesis of apprehension, that is, the synthesis of synoptic or synaudible or synesthetic acquisitions and gatherings of that lower faculty that is the intuition. Sohn-Rethel posits – having apparently undertaken no in-depth reading of the *1844 Manuscripts* – that a 'careful examination reveals that one cannot [...] separate the part played by the sense organs from the conceptual part'.[438] But in fact, it is *not firstly* the *conceptual* part that is involved (with the synthesis of apprehension that is intuition): it is the sensorimotor part, as Simondon has clearly shown. As for the 'conceptual part', it falls within the *synthesis of reproduction* as conceived in the first edition of the *Critique of Pure Reason*, and which constitutes the lower faculty that is the understanding.

In other words, the constitution of noetic *sensibility* does not *firstly* and fundamentally involve a conceptual apparatus: it involves a *set of sensorimotor schemas* that should be conceived as the exosomatization of the circuit of the tick,[439] and it is in this sense that Lotka refers to receptors and effectors.

We saw yesterday that from this starting point, which in my view is already quite compromised by a highly superficial reading of Kant, but also of Marx's *1844 Manuscripts*, Sohn-Rethel argues that:

> The possibility of theoretical knowledge of nature is not a capacity originating in the human mind, but is indeed the product (after having passed through complex mediations) of social developments determined by and based on specific forms of class domination.[440]

If I can but agree with the first thesis of this statement (knowledge is a historical product: of the faculty of dreaming noetic dreams, that is, realizable dreams), the second, which relates class domination to the abstraction effected by money, hypostasized into the categories and concepts of theoretical knowledge, is *extremely crude*. And to show this, we must return to what lies at the core of Sohn-Rethel's thesis, namely, what he calls *Abstraktheit*, which the French translator renders as '*abstractité*'.

Marx put the study of the abstraction of work by money, which turns it into an exchange value (in the form of wages) at the heart of his study of the proletarianization generated by what we are here calling grammatization, as what makes abstraction possible in this sense, but also in a much broader sense (for us), and at the same time before money and beyond money – through all forms of hypomnesic tertiary retention, including mechanical hypomnesic tertiary retention, which enables the grammatization of the gestures of manual workers, but also, eventually, *the grammatization of the gestures of 'intellectual' workers*, as

I maintained in *Technics and Time, 3* by building on the analysis of Geneviève Guitel, and starting firstly from the conditions necessary for the appearance of mental calculation.[441]

The result of what I have just suggested is that the oppositional and 'dialectical' pair that Sohn-Rethel claims to establish between the manual and the intellectual does not stand up to analysis. Abstraction, as the question of proletarianization, equally 'strikes' both the 'intellectual' worker and the 'manual' worker – and these are the stakes of *Phaedrus* and of the *pharmakon* that is this abstractive power.

For Sohn-Rethel, the abstraction of work (abstract work that becomes a commodity, which in the same movement proletarianizes it) is only one case of exchange in which the operator is money as the ab-straction of value. It is by starting from these considerations that, as I discussed yesterday, it is for Sohn-Rethel a question of 'showing that the roots of the pure categories of the object appear as such in commodity exchange'.[442] This is possible only because there is a *division of labour*: in exosomatization, it occurs that there are specialized producers of exosomatic organs, and they *must* specialize in order to become effective: a good hunter must practise a great deal, just like a good violinist or a good weaver, and this leads to a division of work, which then requires an exchange between producers, which in turn generates a market, and so on.

As a result, as Marx writes, and which Sohn-Rethel quotes:

> Objects of utility become commodities only because they are the products of the labour of private individuals who work independently of each other.[443]

These fruits of private labour become commodities through exchange, and it is to control these exchanges through the general equivalent that, according to Sohn-Rethel, 'metaphysical thought' comes to be constituted, and, more precisely, the domination made possible by the separation of intellectual labour from manual labour:

> Historically, we find metaphysical thought's way of conceptualizing to be specific to independent intellectual labour. The separate base-form of this intellectual labour is, according to our hypothesis, to be sought in market-related activities, namely, in functions on which is based the connection of private works in order to form overall social labour.[444]

From this, as we have already seen, Sohn-Rethel draws the conclusion that abstraction begins not with abstract work, but with the market's abstraction of value through the transformation of use value into exchange value, and where 'the categories of separate or "pure" intellectual labour [are] forms of social bonds where the latter are mediated by market-related activities'.[445]

For our own part, we say that these are indeed forms of social bonds, and that, in our societies, they are indeed mediated by the market, but we *also* say that they are *mediated by abstract work*, and that the latter is not of secondary importance in relation to commodity abstraction. On the contrary: it is the *grammatization of work* that is the primary issue. It is a question of asking, then, what *work* means and what abstraction means, in intellectual work as well as in manual work.

In this interpretation of what occurs with money as the condition of the abstraction of exchange value on a market that appears in Lydia, and that migrates to Ionia and Greece as a whole in the pre-Socratic epoch, *everything* in Sohn-Rethel's analysis is *predetermined* in terms of relations of class and domination, relations that, he believes, would form the basis of the opposition of the manual and the intellectual. But what is missing here is grammatization, which, being the essential condition of the exchange of abstractions that is the market, constitutes a bifurcation that begins as early as the Upper Palaeolithic, and which is transformed throughout prehistory, then proto-history, with the great hydraulic empires, as Karl Wittfogel calls them[446] – including China – then throughout history, in China, India, Japan, the Middle East, North Africa, Europe, and finally in America, other regions being inscribed into history, that is, into ideogrammatical and alphabetical grammatization, only through various types of colonization.

Here, we should read Kojin Karatani's *The Structure of World History*.[447] And we should take up Engels's *Dialectics of Nature* – where he tries to think hominization starting from Darwin and from prehistory, and this is something we might come back to next year – as well as *The Origin of the Family, Private Property and the State*.

Now, and in order to open a discussion, I would like to read and comment on a few quotations from, on the one hand, Lev Vygotsky, a Soviet psychologist and materialist who in my view opens up prospects for what I am trying to approach here under the name of hyper-materialist epistemology, and, on the other hand, Ignace Meyerson, also a psychologist, originally from Poland, of whom I have tried to propose a reading in the Hangzhou seminar, and where hyper-materialist epistemology requires a social psychology of exosomatization and of the faculty of noetic dreaming, the most illustrious representative of which I consider to be Jean-Pierre Vernant.

Since the beginning of this course, I have tried to demonstrate that in the twenty-first century we can no longer be satisfied with a materialist conception of the constitution of knowledge – which has become the primary function of the capitalist economy, as the *Grundrisse* anticipated. But to understand the conditions of such a genesis – which is also a destruction of knowledge and noesis that leads, pharmacologically and hyper-materially (via, for example, Moore's law), to total denoetization and absolute non-knowledge – we should read Vygotsky.

Thinking and consciousness are for Vygotsky *constituted* by *external activity,* and the latter is always *realized with one's contemporaries,* and therefore in a determined social environment. External activity means the ability to collectively realize noetic dreams. In Vygotsky, this determined social environment is characterized by tertiary retention and hypomnesic tertiary retention: he in a way prepares the ground for the question of grammatization. *Activity always also occurs through instruments, which may be 'psychological',* such as language and writing, and which are objects of interiorization, but starting from an initial exteriorization, that is, from an exosomatization.

Last year, I pointed out that the interiorization of a primordial exteriority is the issue at stake in the works of Maryanne Wolf, who herself often quotes Vygotsky. Consciousness is a 'social contract with oneself', according to Vygotsky.[448] No doubt it will not have escaped you that this statement very closely resembles what Socrates says in *Theaetetus*, when he posits that thinking is a dialogue with oneself.

A hyper-materialist and hyper-critical epistemology will thus have to take up all of those architectonic questions configured by Kant, who, if I may say so, planned them out like an urban planner of noesis. The transcendental dialectic, like the transcendental aesthetic and the transcendental deduction, must indeed be reconceived and reconsidered from the exosomatic standpoint – and it is a question of re-engineering it, so to speak, and of doing so for a new conception of artificial intelligence, and of what Yuk Hui calls artificial imagination (which I call noetic dreaming).

What would a dialectic be, or an aesthetic or a deduction of categories, considered in terms of the history of metempirical exo-transcendence? What would this metempiricity mean, insofar as it constitutes a metastability of the exo-transcendent conditions of experience (*empeiria*)?

To confront this question, everything that comes into play over the course of the Socratic dialogues, from *Ion* to *Timaeus* via *Protagoras, Meno, Symposium, Phaedrus, Republic, Theaetetus* and *Sophist*, all of this – analysed as a Platonic drift that moves from the still tragic experience of the dialogue as practised by Socrates to a dialectic that will be less and less dialogical, and more and more formal – all of this must be reconsidered from the exo-transcendent standpoint that the exosomatic standpoint imposes on noetic life. In so doing, we should also read two of Heidegger's lecture courses, *Plato's Sophist* (1924–25) and *The*

Essence of Truth (1931–32), in addition, of course, to the 1942 text on 'Plato's Doctrine of Truth' (written in 1940).

A reminder of what I said two years ago about this text: Heidegger is right, and yet he fails to see that Plato is preparing, by turning *alētheia* into *orthōtes*, the analysis of the lower faculties of noesis.

The exosomatic standpoint on noetic life and thus on truth and on its history is the *repressed* stake of what Heidegger says concerning the new understanding of *alētheia* imposed by Plato in Book VII of the *Republic* as *orthōtes* and *omoiosis*. And if it is repressed, it is because in 1927, at the end of *Being and Time*, Heidegger repressed the exosomatic question of *Weltgeschichtlichkeit*, after having wrongly characterized tertiary retention in general and hypomnesic tertiary retention in particular (including as sign or signal) as *determination*. On this point, see *Technics and Time, 1*, Part II, §3, 'The Disengagement of the *What*'. All of these questions will form the subject matter of *La technique et le temps 5. Symboles et diaboles*.

Here we should bring Bakhtin's dialogism into the picture. But for that, I have to read some more Bakhtin myself – I know him mainly through old books of Julia Kristeva and Tzvetan Todorov.

1 Vygotsky speaks of an *instrumental method* by positing that psychology is established and unified only with the study of instruments. This point of view is that of general organology, which I first developed by studying musical instruments, including software, concert halls and radio channels, during my time as head of Ircam. This hypothesis was previously introduced by Canguilhem.

For such an instrumental method, it is necessary to overcome what Heidegger called the 'instrumental conception' of technics, but where we should recall that he himself did not understand that an instrument is not just a means, but a matrix of ends:[449] an exo-somatic instrument instructs and potentially opens a world, and instrumental technics is that which knows how to take care of this instruction to the extent that, precisely, this instruction can become an intrusion, violence, that is, *hubris*, *Gewalt*, where what has been instructed (or taught) is destructed (destroyed).

2 Instruments, according to Vygotsky, are acquired through educational institutions, which are what I call retentional systems. These are of various natures and levels: the familial microcosm, the tribal mesocosm, the ethnic macrocosm located in the cosmos are all examples, and then there is the church, the school, the university, but also the media.

The problem is that the media are enslaved to the exclusive motive of value extraction, which impoverishes instruments that thus become instrumentalized – hence the smartphone that we think is serving us when we are the ones serving it.

3 The subject, according to Vygotsky, is constituted only through groups. This is also what Simondon says, and so too does Heidegger, in a way that is hard to pin down, but which is in any case clear after 1935.

Finally, a few quotations from Meyerson, *Les fonctions psychologiques et les oeuvres*:

> Man's actions lead to institutions and works. […] The spirit of man lies in works.[450]

> The mind […] is only, and can be known only, in its work. […] Mental states do not remain states, they project themselves, take shape, tend to consolidate, to become objects.[451]

> Man wants his creation to last and endure. He wants, he has always wanted, to create works that outlast him, that exceed him in solidity, dimension, value, intensity, force and productivity.[452]

And at the end of the book:

> When a generation finds beautiful and 'normal' some genre, some style of painting that astounded or shocked the previous one, […] can we not say that through the action of work, in an epoch when the work is spreading and becoming popular, perception has slightly changed?[453]

Notes

1 *Translator's note*: From this point, portions of the remainder of this lecture and the beginning of the next lecture more or less reproduce a lecture that was subsequently published as Bernard Stiegler, 'Automatic Society, Londres février 2015', trans. Daniel Ross, *Journal of Visual Art Practice* 15 (2016), pp. 192–203.

2 *Translator's note*: See Jacques Derrida, *Politics of Friendship*, trans. George Collins (London and New York: Verso, 1997), pp. 24–25.

3 *Translator's note*: See Paul Valéry, 'Freedom of the Mind', *The Collected Works of Paul Valéry, Volume 10: History and Politics*, trans. Denise Folliot and Jackson Mathews (New York: Bollingen, 1962), p. 190, translation modified: 'All these values that rise and fall constitute the great market of human affairs. Among them, the unfortunate value, *spirit*, continues to decline'.

4 Mats Alvesson and André Spicer, 'A Stupidity-Based Theory of Organizations', *Journal of Management Studies* 49 (2012), pp. 1194–220. See also Mats Alvesson and André Spicer, *The Stupidity Paradox: The Power and Pitfalls of Functional Stupidity at Work* (London: Profile, 2016).

5 Chris Anderson, 'The End of Theory: The Data Deluge Makes the Scientific Method Obsolete', *Wired* (23 June 2008), available at: <http://archive.wired.com/science/discoveries/magazine/16-07/pb_theory>.

6 Gilles Deleuze, 'Postscript on Control Societies', *Negotiations 1972–1990*, trans. Martin Joughin (New York: Columbia University Press, 1995).

7 Edmund Husserl, 'The Origin of Geometry', in Jacques Derrida, *Edmund Husserl's Origin of Geometry: An Introduction*, trans. John P. Leavey, Jr. (Lincoln and London: University of Nebraska Press, 1978).

8 Bernard Stiegler, *Technics and Time, 1: The Fault of Epimetheus*, trans. Richard Beardsworth and George Collins (Stanford: Stanford University Press, 1998).

9 Gilles Deleuze, *Difference and Repetition*, trans. Paul Patton (London: Althone, 1994).

10 Nicolas Fréret, *Réflexions sur les principes généraux de l'art d'écrire, et en pariculier sur les fondments de l'écriture chinoise* (1729), quoted in Peter Stephen Du Ponceau, *A Dissertation on the Nature and*

Character of the Chinese System of Writing (Philadelphia: McCarty and Davis, 1838), p. 9.

11 George Gheverghese Joseph, *The Crest of the Peacock: Non-European Roots of Mathematics*, third edition (Princeton and Oxford: Princeton University Press, 2011), p. 248.

12 *Translator's note*: On the notion of consistence in Stiegler's work, and its relationship to the notions of subsistence and existence, see Bernard Stiegler, *The Decadence of Industrial Democracies: Disbelief and Discredit, Volume 1*, trans. Daniel Ross and Suzanne Arnold (Cambridge: Polity Press, 2011), pp. 89–93.

13 Gustave Le Bon, *Psychologie des foules* (1895), quoted in Sigmund Freud, 'Group Psychology and the Analysis of the Ego', in Volume 18 of James Strachey (ed. and trans.), *The Standard Edition of the Complete Psychological Works of Sigmund Freud* (London: Hogarth, 1953–74), pp. 72–73, translation modified.

14 Thomas Berns and Antoinette Rouvroy, 'Gouvernementalité algorithmique et perspectives d'émancipation. Le disparate comme condition d'individuation par la relation?', *Réseaux* 177 (2013), pp. 163–96. See also Antoinette Rouvroy, 'The End(s) of Critique: Data-Behaviourism vs Due-Process', in Mireille Hildebrandt and Katja de Vries (eds), *Privacy, Due Process and the Computational Turn: The Philosophy of Law Meets the Philosophy of Technology* (Abingdon and New York: Routledge, 2013), pp. 143–68.

15 Gilles Deleuze, *Cinema 2: The Time-Image*, trans. Hugh Tomlinson and Robert Galeta (Minneapolis: University of Minnesota Press, 1991), pp. 171–73.

16 *Translator's note*: Portions of this lecture and of the next two lectures have been published in Bernard Stiegler, 'General Ecology, Economy, and Organology', in Erich Hörl and James Burton (eds), *General Ecology: The New Ecological Paradigm* (London and New York: Bloomsbury Academic, 2017).

17 Erich Hörl. 'A Thousand Ecologies: The Process of Cyberneticization and General Ecology', in Diedrich Diederichsen and Anselm Franke (eds), *The Whole Earth: California and the Disappearance of the Outside* (Berlin: Sternberg Press, 2013), pp. 121–130.

18 Ibid., p. 122: 'Contrary to all of the ecological preconceptions that bind ecology and nature together, ecology is increasingly proving to epitomize the un- or non-natural configuration that has been established over more than half a century by the extensive cyberneticization and computerization of life. The radical technological mediation that has been implemented since 1950 through the process

of cyberneticization – and which today operates within the sensory and intelligent environments that exist in microtemporal realms, in pervasive media and ubiquitous computing – causes the problem of mediation as such to come fully into focus, exposing it with a radicality never seen before. As such, it is both a problem and question of constitutive relationality; or, more precisely – to paraphrase Gilbert Simondon – the problem of an original relationship between the individual and its milieu, with which it has always already been coupled and which would not simply constitute a readymade, prior "natural" environment to which it would have had to adapt, but which must rather be conceived as the site of its originary and inescapable artifacticity, with which it is conjoined…'

19 Martin Heidegger, 'On Time and Being', *Time and Being*, trans. Joan Stambaugh (New York: Harper & Row, 1972), p. 7.

20 For example, in Gilbert Simondon, *Communication et information. Cours et conférences* (Chatou: Éditions de la transparence, 2010), p. 167.

21 Karl Marx, *Grundrisse: Foundations of the Critique of Political Economy (Rough Draft)*, trans. Martin Nicolaus (London: Penguin, 1973), pp. 693–94.

22 Ibid., p. 694.

23 The question of the generality of Bataille's general economy, which will be explored in depth in *La Société automatique 2. L'avenir du savoir* (forthcoming), has been introduced in *Automatic Society, Volume 1*, in order to counter the point of view developed by Claude Lévi-Strauss at the end of *Tristes Tropiques*, where he likens anthropology to an 'entropology', which I oppose by passing through Bataille and in terms of the question of a neganthropology that would also be an organology and a pharmacology.

24 But also with the concept of grammatization, that is, discretization, which is also to say, with respect to the question of categorization as *condition of concretization* – this reference to categorization pointing here towards a hypothesis formulated by IRI in relation to the Web: we posit that the Web must see its general architecture evolve in the direction of the constitution of a hermeneutic Web, itself founded on a graphic language of contributory annotation, a platform for sharing notes and a hermeneutic social network.

25 Gilbert Simondon, *On the Mode of Existence of Technical Objects*, trans. Cecile Malaspina and John Rogove (Minneapolis: Univocal, 2017), ch. 1.

26 Gilbert Simondon, 'The Position of the Problem of Ontogenesis', trans. Gregory Flanders, *Parrhesia* 7 (2009), p. 5, (extracted from

Gilbert Simondon, *L'individuation à la lumière des notions de forme et d'information* [Grenoble: Millon, 2013], pp. 24–25):

> We would like to show that the search for the principle of individuation must be reversed, by considering as primordial the operation of individuation from which the individual comes to exist and of which its characteristics reflect the development, the regime and finally the modalities. The individual would then be grasped as a relative reality, a certain phase of being that supposes a preindividual reality, and that, even after individuation, does not exist on its own, because individuation does not exhaust with one stroke the potentials of preindividual reality. Moreover, that which the individuation makes appear is not only the individual, but also the pair individual-environment. The individual is thus relative in two senses, both because it is not all of the being, and because it is the result of a state of the being in which it existed neither as individual, nor as principle of individuation.
>
> *Individuation is thus considered as the only ontogenesis, insofar as it is an operation of the complete being.* Individuation must therefore be considered as a partial and relative resolution that occurs in a system that contains potentials and encloses a certain incompatibility in relation to itself – an incompatibility made of forces of tension as well as of the impossibility of an interaction between the extreme terms of the dimension.

27 Sadi Carnot, *Reflections on the Motive Power of Fire*, trans. E. Mendoza (Mineola: Dover,1988), originally published in French in 1824.

28 As Nicholas Georgescu-Roegen recalls.

29 For in fact, if what reason produces is not concepts but rather ideas, which extend the pure concepts of the understanding beyond their regime of legality, which is experience given by intuition, and if these concepts are themselves conditioned by schemas conditioned by hypomnesic tertiary retention, as I argue in *Technics and Time, 3*, then the ideas of reason are themselves also conditioned by tertiary retention.

30 This order is that of the '*parure*' that is the *kosmos* as *that which appears*, according to a translation by Jean Beaufret, *Dialogue avec Heidegger* (Paris: Minuit, 1973), pp, 25–28.

31 Friedrich Engels, *Dialectics of Nature*, trans. Clemens Dutt, in Karl Marx and Friedrich Engels, *Collected Works, Volume 25* (London: Lawrence & Wishart, 1987), p. 334.

32 I have elsewhere argued, in *Automatic Society Volume 1*, that these conceptual mutations of physics and of cosmology-become-astrophysics also involve a mutation of the notion of work, which becomes force measured in watts (force being what Aristotelian metaphysics conceived as *dunamis*), and no longer conceived as *energeia*, that is, as *noetic act*, that is, as *individuation*. It is this transformation that also makes possible that proletarianization that occurs when the steam engine combines with the automatisms made possible by the mechanical tertiary retention characteristic of industrial mechanization.

33 Genesis 3:19, *The Holy Bible: Quatercentenary edition* (Oxford and New York: Oxford University Press, 2010), no page numbers: 'In the sweate of thy face shalt thou eate bread, till thou returne vnto the ground: for out of it wast thou taken for dust thou *art*, and vnto dust shalt thou returne'.

34 In the sense that I attempted to redefine this as a question, as creating a question, in Bernard Stiegler, *What Makes Life Worth Living: On Pharmacology*, trans. Daniel Ross (Cambridge: Polity Press, 2013).

35 See Bernard Stiegler (ed.), *Digital Studies: Organologie des savoirs et technologies de la connaissance* (Paris: FYP, 2014), esp. ch. 2 by David Bates, 'Penser l'automaticité au seuil du numérique'.

36 Ernst Kapp, *Elements of a Philosophy of Technology: On the Evolutionary History of Culture*, trans. Lauren K. Wolfe (Minneapolis and London: University of Minnesota Press, 2018), esp. ch. 2.

37 Martin Heidegger, *Being and Time*, trans. Joan Stambaugh, revised Dennis J. Schmidt (Albany: State University of New York Press, 2010), p. 7, German pagination, translation modified.

38 Maryanne Wolf, *Proust and the Squid: The Story and Science of the Reading Brain* (New York: Harper, 2007).

39 Wilhelm Dilthey, *The Formation of the Historical World in the Human Sciences*, trans. Rudolf A. Makkreel, John Scanlon and William H. Oman (Princeton: Princeton University Press, 2002).

40 This is the horizon of Arnold Gehlen's work in *Anthropologische und sozialpsychologische Untersuchungen* (Hamburg: Reinbek, 1994).

41 In the sense elaborated in Gilles Deleuze, *Logic of Sense*, trans. Mark Lester with Charles Stivale (New York: Columbia University Press, 1990).

42 Marx, *Grundrisse*, p. 706.

43 Karl Marx and Friedrich Engels, *The German Ideology*, trans. Clemens Dutt and C. P. Magill (London: Lawrence & Wishart, 1974), p. 42.

44 See Nicholas Georgescu-Roegen, 'De la science économique à la bioéconomie', available at: <https://books.openedition.org/enseditions/2302?lang=en>.

45 Bernard Stiegler, *States of Shock: Stupidity and Knowledge in the Twenty-First Century*, trans. Daniel Ross (Cambridge: Polity Press, 2015), p. 125, italics added.

46 Georg Wilhelm Friedrich Hegel, *Phenomenology of Spirit*, trans. A. V. Miller (Oxford: Oxford University Press, 1977), §195, translation modified.

47 Stiegler, *States of Shock*, p. 125.

48 Hegel, *Phenomenology of Spirit*, §196, translation modified.

49 Stiegler, *States of Shock*, p. 126.

50 Which cannot but radically affect ecological science, and not just political ecology. But it does so by inscribing the political event into the very heart of the science of the living in its negotiation with the organized non-living and the organizations in which it results.

51 René Passet, *L'Économique et le Vivant*, second edition (Paris: Economica, 1996).

52 Ibid., pp. x–xii.

53 Ibid.

54 Ibid.

55 Adam Smith, *An Inquiry into the Nature and Causes of the Wealth of Nations* (New York: Modern Library, 1937), pp. 734–35: 'In the progress of the division of labour, the employment of the far greater part of those who live by labour, that is, of the great body of the people, comes to be confined to a few very simple operations, frequently to one or two. But the understandings of the greater part of men are necessarily formed by their ordinary employments. The man whose whole life is spent in performing a few simple operations, of which the effects too are, perhaps, always the same, or very nearly the same, has no occasion to exert his understanding, or to exercise his invention in finding out expedients for removing difficulties which never occur. He naturally loses, therefore, the habit of such exertion, and generally becomes as stupid and ignorant as it is possible for a human creature to become. The torpor of his mind renders him, not only incapable of relishing or bearing a part in any rational conversation, but of conceiving any generous, noble, or tender sentiment, and consequently of forming any just judgment concerning many even of the ordinary duties of private life'.

56 Passet, *L'Économique et le Vivant*, pp. x–xii.

57 Ibid.

58 Ibid.

59 Alfred North Whitehead, *The Function of Reason* (Princeton: Princeton University Press, 1929), 'Introductory Summary', no page number.

60 Ludwig von Bertalanffy, *General System Theory: Foundations, Development, Applications* (New York: Braziller, 1968), pp. 3–29.

61 Whitehead, *The Function of Reason*, p. 2.

62 Ibid., p. 5.

63 Ibid.

64 Jean-Pierre Dupuy and Françoise Roure, *Les nanotechnologies: ethique et prospective industrielle*, public report (15 November 2004), available at: <https://www.ladocumentationfrancaise.fr/var/storage/rapports-publics/054000313.pdf>.

65 See Gilbert Simondon, *Communication et information. Cours et conferences* (Chatou: Éditions de la transparence, 2010).

66 See Kostas Axelos, *Alienation, Praxis, and Technē in the Thought of Karl Marx*, trans. Ronald Bruzina (Austin and London: University of Texas Press, 1976).

67 Karl Marx and Friedrich Engels, *The Communist Manifesto*, trans. Samuel Moore (London: Penguin, 1967), p. 88, translation modified.

68 Marx and Engels, *The German Ideology*, p. 42.

69 Ibid.

70 Marx, *Grundrisse*, p. 692.

71 Ibid., pp. 692–93.

72 Simondon, *On the Mode of Existence of Technical Objects*, p. 21, translation modified.

73 *Oxford Dictionaries*, 'Word of the Year 2016 is...', available at: <https://en.oxforddictionaries.com/word-of-the-year/word-of-the-year-2016>.

74 'The Curious Case of the Word POST TRUTH!!' (12 January 2017), available at: <http://swapsushias.blogspot.com/2017/01/the-curious-case-of-word-post-truth.html#.XMI6ny9L3jB>. *Translator's note*: The content of this blog post originally appeared in the article by Swapan Dasgupta, 'Don't Appropriate Post-Truth. India's Truth is Different', *The Time of India* (8 January 2017), available

at: <https://timesofindia.indiatimes.com/blogs/right-and-wrong/dont-appropriate-post-truth-indias-truth-is-different/>.

75 In a section of 'Word of the Year 2016 is…' entitled 'A brief history of *post-truth*', *Oxford Dictionaries* says the following:

> The compound word *post-truth* exemplifies an expansion in the meaning of the prefix post- that has become increasingly prominent in recent years. Rather than simply referring to the time after a specified situation or event – as in *post-war* or *post-match* – the prefix in *post-truth* has a meaning more like 'belonging to a time in which the specified concept has become unimportant or irrelevant'. This nuance seems to have originated in the mid-20th century, in formations such as *post-national* (1945) and *post-racial* (1971).
>
> *Post-truth* seems to have been first used in this meaning in a 1992 essay by the late Serbian-American playwright Steve Tesich in *The Nation* magazine. Reflecting on the Iran-Contra scandal and the Persian Gulf War, Tesich lamented that 'we, as a free people, have freely decided that we want to live in some post-truth world'. There is evidence of the phrase 'post-truth' being used before Tesich's article, but apparently with the transparent meaning 'after the truth was known', and not with the new implication that truth itself has become irrelevant.
>
> A book, *The Post-Truth Era*, by Ralph Keyes appeared in 2004, and in 2005 American comedian Stephen Colbert popularized an informal word relating to the same concept: *truthiness*, defined by Oxford Dictionaries as 'the quality of seeming or being felt to be true, even if not necessarily true'. *Post-truth* extends that notion from an isolated quality of particular assertions to a general characteristic of our age.

76 Bernard Stiegler, *The Age of Disruption: Technology and Madness in Computational Capitalism*, trans. Daniel Ross (Cambridge: Polity Press, 2019).

77 *Translator's note:* See, for example, Immanuel Kant, *Critique of Pure Reason*, trans. Paul Guyer and Allen W. Wood (Cambridge: Cambridge University Press, 1998), p. 157: 'Inner sense, by means of which the mind intuits itself, or its inner state, gives, to be sure, no intuition of the soul itself, as an object; yet it is still a determinate form [namely, time] under which the intuition of its inner state is alone possible, so that everything that belongs to the inner determinations is represented in relations of time'.

78 Martin Heidegger, *Being and Time*, trans. Joan Stambaugh, revised Dennis J. Schmidt (Albany: State University of New York Press, 2010), p. 5, German pagination.

79 André Leroi-Gourhan, *Gesture and Speech*, trans. Anna Bostock Berger (Cambridge, Massachusetts and London: MIT Press, 1993).

80 Georges Bataille, *Prehistoric Painting: Lascaux, or The Birth of Art*, trans. Austryn Wainhouse (Geneva: Skira, 1955).

81 Sylvain Auroux, *La révolution technologique de la grammatisation. Introduction à l'histoire des sciences du langage* (Liège: Mardaga, 1994).

82 *Translator's note*: Referring here to the post-war Heidegger's frequent use of the quotation from Hölderlin concerning the danger and the saving power.

83 *Translator's note*: Portions of the remainder of this lecture and the beginning of the next lecture were published as Bernard Stiegler, 'The New Conflict of the Faculties and Functions: Quasi-Causality and Serendipity in the Anthropocene', trans. Daniel Ross, *Qui Parle* 26 (2017), pp. 79–99.

84 Bernard Stiegler, *Automatic Society, Volume 1: The Future of Work*, trans. Daniel Ross (Cambridge: Polity Press, 2016).

85 See Stiegler, *The Age of Disruption*.

86 It is preceded by an exteriorization of the motor functions and fabricating functions during what Leroi-Gourhan called the period of the Archantropians, and it itself amounts to the period of the Palaeoanthropians.

87 See Martin Heidegger, 'Plato's Concept of Truth', trans. Thomas Sheehan, *Pathmarks* (Cambridge: Cambridge University Press, 1998); Martin Heidegger, *The Essence of Truth: On Plato's Cave Allegory and Theaetetus*, trans. Ted Sadler (London: Continuum, 2002).

88 'Functional integration' in the sense of Gilbert Simondon, which here means where humankind becomes a function of an associated techno-geographical milieu, and where humanity is the resource of this human-techno-geography. On this point, see Stiegler, *Automatic Society 1*, §42.

89 Ibid., §§21–22.

90 Karl Marx, *Grundrisse: Foundations of the Critique of Political Economy (Rough Draft)*, trans. Martin Nicolaus (London: Penguin, 1973), pp. 690–714.

91 On this topic, see Maryanne Wolf, *Proust and the Squid: The Story and Science of the Reading Brain* (New York: Harper, 2007); and my preface to the French translation published as *Proust et le calamar*, trans. Lisa Stupar (Angoulême: Abeille et Castor, 2015).

92 See Bernard Stiegler, *Technics and Time, 2: Disorientation*, trans. Stephen Barker (Stanford: Stanford University Press, 2009), pp. 134–37.

93 Immanuel Kant, 'An Answer to the Question: "What is Enlightenment?"', *Political Writings*, trans. H. B. Nisbet (Cambridge: Cambridge University Press, 1991); see also my interpretation in Bernard Stiegler, *Technics and Time, 3: Cinematic Time and the Question of Malaise*, trans. Stephen Barker (Stanford: Stanford University Press, 2011), pp. 157–62

94 In *Technics and Time, 2*, I tried to show that insider trading enables very precise calculation of the value of information with respect to a situation where someone who knows something that others do not know can buy and sell stocks, make transactions on the stock exchange, that ultimately enable him or her to make large profits – to add value, as they say. It was to prevent this, and after the scandal of the Bordeaux stock exchange, that the French government decreed a public monopoly on telecommunications in France.

95 It would be important to study the conditions of either the evaporation or the sustainability of the value of information – and to do so in the context of a history of difference and repetition, which is precisely the program of the organology and the pharmacology of hypomnesic tertiary retention.

96 Maurice Blanchot, *The Step Not Beyond*, trans. Lycette Nelson (Albany: State University of New York Press, 1992), p. 53. This was also used as a title by Roger Laporte for an article on Blanchot.

97 Humberto R. Maturana and Francisco J. Varela, *The Tree of Knowledge: The Biological Roots of Human Understanding*, trans. Robert Paolucci (Boston: Shambhala Publications, 1992).

98 Jakob von Uexküll, *A Foray into the Worlds of Animals and Humans, with A Theory of Meaning*, trans. Joseph D. O'Neil (Minneapolis: University of Minnesota Press, 2010).

99 Maurice Blanchot, 'The Beast of Lascaux', trans. Leslie Hill, *Oxford Literary Review* 22 (2000), p. 9, translation modified. This text, written in 1953, foreshadows the future work of Jacques Derrida.

100 Marcel Detienne and Georgio Camassa, *Les savoirs de l'écriture en Grèce ancienne* (Villeneuve d'Ascq: Presses universitaires de Lille, 1988).

101 Blanchot, 'The Beast of Lascaux', p. 9, translation modified, my italics.

102 Referring here to *The Infinite Conversation* and *Of Grammatology.*

103 Contrary to what Nietzsche argues.

104 Here, as elsewhere in this work, we must always understand invention in the sense defined in *Technics and Time, 3. Translator's note*: See, for example, *Technics and Time, 3*, p. 142: 'But in the most general way, the literary synthesis of the flux of consciousness also makes the invention of the principle of contradiction possible. I mean "invention" in the archaic sense of "exhumation" ("invention of the holy cross"). The principle of contradiction is neither discovered nor invented in its "fabrication"; from the very outset all consciousness accesses it, and in this sense it is not a discovery. But not all consciousness puts it to work successfully because of control mechanisms within its unity of flux and, in this sense, even though it is not fabricated, it is "invented"; that is, there exists a date from which it is formulated *as such* and somehow pro-duced just as one might "produce" a piece of evidence in a courtroom. And this "as such" requires a mechanism by which it can be projected'.

105 That is, as the very condition of the schematism in the Kantian sense, as implementation of the three syntheses constitutive of the transcendental flux and the unity of apperception, but where it proves to be the case that the *unification of the flux is not possible*, and that *time is always what betrays this process as that which cannot be completed* – even though, as we will see, *the death of Socrates is posited as a pure achievement or pure beginning*, which is also what, however, calls for interminable commentary.

106 Immanuel Kant, 'An Answer to the Question: "What is Enlightenment"', p. 55.

107 Plato, *Republic*, 514a–515a, trans. G. M. A. Grube, revised by C. D. C. Reeve, in Plato, *Complete Works*, ed. John M. Cooper (Indianapolis and Cambridge: Hackett, 1997), pp. 1132–33:

> Imagine human beings living in an underground, cavelike dwelling, with an entrance a long way up, which is both open to the light and as wide as the cave itself. They've been there since childhood, fixed in the same place, with their necks and legs fettered, able to see only in front of them, because their bonds prevent them from turning their heads around. Light is provided by a fire burning far above and behind them. Also behind them, but on higher ground, there is a path stretching between them and the fire. Imagine that along this

path a low wall has been built, like the screen in front of puppeteers above which they show their puppets.

I'm imagining it.

Then also imagine that there are people along the wall, carrying all kinds of artifacts that project above it – statues of people and other animals, made out of stone, wood, and every material. And, as you'd expect, some of the carriers are talking, and some are silent.

It's a strange image you're describing, and strange prisoners.

They're like us. Do you suppose, first of all, that these prisoners, see anything of themselves and one another besides the shadows that the fire casts on the wall in front of them?

108 See Jacques Derrida, 'Faith and Knowledge: The Two Sources of "Religion" at the Limits of Reason Alone', trans. Samuel Weber, *Acts of Religion* (New York and London: Routledge, 2002), pp. 50, 67, 79, 86 and 89. *Translator's note*: See also Samuel Weber's translator's note on p. 50, which draws attention to the problematic difference between 'world' and 'globe' involved in the translation of this Derridian neologism as 'globalatinization'. And see also Bernard Stiegler, *Symbolic Misery, Volume 1: The Hyper-Industrial Epoch*, trans. Barnaby Norman (Cambridge: Polity Press, 2014), p. 55, and Stiegler, *The Age of Disruption*, pp. 151–52.

109 Stiegler, *Technics and Time, 3*, p. 99.

110 Jorge Luis Borges, 'Funes, the Memorious', *Ficciones*, trans. Helen Temple and Ruthven Todd (New York: Grove, 1962).

111 Plato, *Phaedo* 59b.

112 Plato, *Apology* 41a.

113 Compare what *Ion* has to say about magnetism.

114 E. R. Dodds, *The Greeks and the Irrational* (Berkeley and London: University of California Press, 1951), p. 179.

115 Ibid., p. 180.

116 Ibid., p. 181.

117 Ibid., p. 189.

118 Ibid., p. 40.

119 Ibid., p. 5.

120 Ibid., p. 11.

121 Ibid., p. 10.

122 See Stiegler, *Technics and Time, 3*, ch. 5, 'Making (the) Difference'.

123 *Translator's note*: See Jean-Pierre Vernant, 'At Man's Table: Hesiod's Foundation Myth of Sacrifice', in Marcel Detienne and Jean-Pierre Vernant, *The Cuisine of Sacrifice among the Greeks*, trans. Paula Wissing (Chicago and London: University of Chicago Press, 1989); see also Marcel Detienne and Jean-Pierre Vernant, *Cunning Intelligence in Greek Culture and Society*, trans. Janet Lloyd (Chicago and London: University of Chicago Press, 1978), ch. 3, 'The Combats of Zeus', though this second (but earlier) text does not discuss Epimetheus.

124 André Leroi-Gourhan, *Gesture and Speech*, pp. 137–39.

125 Ibid., p. 413.

126 Plato, *Crito* 53e.

127 Bernard Stiegler, *Acting Out*, pp. 5–6.

128 Plato, *Meno* 71b–c, trans. G. M. A. Grube, in Plato, *Complete Works*, p. 871.

129 Plato, *Meno* 71c.

130 Plato, *Meno* 71d.

131 Roland Barthes, 'Zazie and Literature', *Critical Essays*, trans. Richard Howard (Evanston: Northwestern University Press, 1972), esp. pp. 120–21.

132 Ibid., p. 120.

133 Plato, *Meno* 71e.

134 Plato, *Meno* 72c.

135 Plato, *Meno* 80c, translation modified.

136 Plato, *Meno* 80d.

137 Plato, *Meno* 81b–c, translation modified.

138 Plato, *Meno* 81c–d, translation modified.

139 Jean-Pierre Vernant, *The Origins of Greek Thought*, no translator credited (Ithaca, New York: Cornell University Press, 1982), p. 9.

140 Ibid., p. 29.

141 Ibid, p. 35.

142 Ibid., p. 36: 'All this was destroyed by the Dorian invasion, which broke for centuries the ties between Greece and the East. [...] Isolated and turned in on itself, the Greek mainland reverted to a purely agricultural economy'.

143 Ibid., p. 37.

144 Ibid., p. 43: 'The emphasis was no longer on a single person who dominated social life, but on a multiplicity of functions that opposed each other and thus called for a reciprocal apportionment and delimitation'.

145 Ibid., p. 45, my italics.

146 This word, stricture, refers in Derrida to the articulation of the pleasure principle and the reality principle insofar as they can be opposed only by being composed, which does not, therefore, simply oppose them, since each needs the other. This relation of stricture is another name for what Simondon called transduction, even if in the latter case it more clearly concerns a dynamic relation. Stricture and transduction are thus two equivalent ways of designating the implication, co-implication and complication of the diachronic and the synchronic. And it is obvious that the structural homology between what defines desire and what defines the idiom owes nothing to chance. In the possible decomposition of idioms, that is, of the synchronic and the diachronic, it is the decomposition of desire that is at stake and in play. *Translator's note*: The notion of 'stricture' receives significant discussion in Derrida's *The Truth in Painting*, but for the elaboration of 'stricture' in relation to the 'binding' of the drives in the relationship between the pleasure principle and the reality principle, see Jacques Derrida, *The Post Card: From Socrates to Freud and Beyond*, trans. Alan Bass (Chicago and London: University of Chicago Press, 1987), esp. pp. 389–402.

147 Vernant, *The Origins of Greek Thought*, pp. 45–46.

148 Marcel Detienne, 'L'espace de la publicité, ses opérateurs intellectuels dans la cité', in Marcel Detienne (ed.), *Les savoirs de l'écriture en Grèce ancienne* (Lille: Presses universitaires de Lille, 1988), p. 46.

149 Stiegler, *Technics and Time, 2*, pp. 56–57.

150 Vernant, *The Origins of Greek Thought*, pp. 49–51.

151 Ibid., pp. 52–53.

152 Jean-Pierre Vernant, *Myth and Thought among the Greeks*, trans. Janet Lloyd with Jeff Fort (New York: Zone Books, 2006), p. 204.

153 Ibid.

154 Détienne, 'L'espace de la publicité, ses opérateurs intellectuels dans la cité', pp. 31–32.

155 Ibid., pp. 54–55.

156 Ibid., p. 75.

157 Nicole Loraux, 'Solon et la voix de l'écrit', in Detienne, *Les savoirs de l'écriture en Grèce ancienne*, p. 95.

158 Ibid., p. 125.

159 Pierre Lévêque and Pierre Vidal-Naquet, *Cleisthenes the Athenian: An Essay on the Representation of Space and Time in Greek Political Thought from the End of the Sixth Century to the Death of Plato*, trans. David Ames Curtis (New Jersey: Humanities Press, 1996), p. 52.

160 Vernant, *Myth and Thought among the Greeks*, p. 245.

161 Friedrich Nietzsche, *Philosophy in the Tragic Age of the Greeks*, trans. Marianne Cowan (Washington D.C.: Regnery Gateway, 1962), p. 45, translation modified.

162 Vernant, *Myth and Thought among the Greeks*, p. 205.

163 Vernant, *The Origins of Greek Thought*, pp. 70–71.

164 Ibid., p. 71.

165 Ibid., pp. 71–72.

166 Ibid., p. 72.

167 Ibid., p. 73.

168 Ibid., pp. 72–73.

169 Vernant, *Myth and Thought among the Greeks*, p. 380.

170 Vernant, *The Origins of Greek Thought*, p. 74.

171 Martin Heidegger, *An Introduction to Metaphysics*, trans. Gregory Fried and Richard Polt (New Haven and London: Yale University Press, 2000), p. 162, translation modified.

172 Ibid., pp. 17–18.

173 Let us recall from *Technics and Time, 2* that we call 'orthothetic' those syntheses composed of tertiary retentions when they are of the literal, analogical or digital type. Whenever such an orthothetic device or apparatus appears, in other words, a question of adoption is posed: in Greece with the alphabet, in the United States with cinema, and in the entire world, today, with digital networks.

174 Immanuel Kant, *Religion within the Bounds of Bare Reason*, trans. Werner S. Pluhar (Indiana and Cambridge: Hackett, 2009), pp. 29–30.

175 Heidegger, *Being and Time*, p. 7, German pagination.

176 Ibid., pp. 7–8.

177 Yuk Hui, *The Question Concerning Technology in China: An Essay in Cosmotechnics* (Falmouth: Urbanomic, 2016).

178 Plato, *Meno* 80e, translation modified.

179 Plato, *Meno* 81a–c, translation modified.

180 Vernant, *Myth and Thought among the Greeks*, p. 117.

181 Dodds, *The Greeks and the Irrational*, pp. 185 and 217.

182 Roman Jakobson, 'Closing Statement: Linguistics and Poetics', in Thomas A. Sebeok, *Style in Language* (Cambridge, Massachusetts: MIT Press, 1960), p. 357.

183 Ferdinand de Saussure, *Course in General Linguistics*, trans. Wade Baskin (New York: Philosophical Library, 1959), p. 73.

184 Ibid., p. 19, translation modified.

185 Frédéric Kaplan, 'Vers le capitalisme linguistique. Quand les mots valent de l'or', *Le Monde diplomatique* (November 2011), available at: <https://www.monde-diplomatique.fr/2011/11/KAPLAN/46925>.

186 Ibid.

187 Ibid.

188 Ibid.

189 Walter Ong, *Orality and Literacy: The Technologizing of the Word* (New York: Routledge, 2002), p. 78.

190 Saussure, *Course in General Linguistics*, p. 24.

191 Jack Goody, *The Domestication of the Savage Mind* (Cambridge: Cambridge University Press, 1977), pp. 10 and 81.

192 Sylvain Auroux, *La révolution technologique de la grammatisation. Introduction à l'histoire des sciences du langage* (Liège: Mardaga, 1994).

193 Edmund Husserl, *On the Phenomenology of the Consciousness of Internal Time (1893–1917)*, trans. James S. Churchill (Dordrecht: Kluwer, 1991).

194 Edmund Husserl, *Phantasy, Image Consciousness, and Memory (1898–1925)*, trans. John B. Brough (Dordrecht: Springer 2005).

195 *Translator's note*: Hume accounts for the connection between ideas (their 'association') through the 'gentle force' (neither too strict nor too loose) that leads them to coalesce along lines of 'resemblance', 'contiguity' and 'cause and effect'. See David Hume, *A Treatise of Human Nature: A Critical Edition* (Oxford: Clarendon Press, 2007), §1.1.4.

196 Sigmund Freud, *Beyond the Pleasure Principle*, in Volume 18 of James Strachey (ed. and trans.), *The Standard Edition of the Complete Psychological Works of Sigmund Freud* (London: Hogarth, 1953–74).

197 Henri Bergson, *Matter and Memory*, trans. N. M. Paul and W. S. Palmer (New York: Zone Books, 1991).

198 *Translator's note*: See Paul Valéry, 'Freedom of the Mind', *The Collected Works of Paul Valéry, Volume 10: History and Politics*, trans. Denise Folliot and Jackson Mathews (New York: Bollingen, 1962), p. 190.

199 *Translator's note*: Schultz and Becker published articles on 'human capital' with almost identical titles. See Theodore W. Schultz, 'Investment in Human Capital', *American Economic Review* 51 (1961), pp. 1–17, and Gary Becker, 'Investment in Human Capital: A Theoretical Analysis', *Journal of Political Economy* 50:5 (1962), pp. 9–49. Both would go on to publish books on this topic. This is discussed by Foucault: see Michel Foucault, *The Birth of Biopolitics*, trans. Graham Burchell (Houndmills, Basingstoke and New York: Palgrave Macmillan, 2008), p. 220.

200 See Foucault, *The Birth of Biopolitics*, p. 226.

201 Lionel Robbins describes economics as 'the science which studies human behaviour as a relationship between ends and scarce means which have mutually exclusive uses', in his 1932 work, *Essay on the Nature and Significance of Economic Science* (London: Macmillan, 1962), p. 16. This quotation from Robbins then appears quoted in Gary Becker's work, *The Economic Approach to Human Behavior* (Chicago and London: University of Chicago Press, 1976), p. 1, n. 3. Michel Foucault quotes Robbins via Becker in his account of neoliberalism and human capital in Foucault, *The Birth of Biopolitics*, p. 222.

202 See Paul W. Glimcher, *Decisions, Uncertainty, and the Brain: The Science of Neuroeconomics* (Cambridge, Massachusetts and London: MIT Press, 2003).

203 Nicholas Carr, *The Shallows: What the Internet is Doing to Our Brains* (New York: W. W. Norton & Co., 2009), p. 65: 'It was the technology of the book that made this "strange anomaly" in our psychological history possible. The brain of the book reader was more than a literate brain. It was a literary brain'.

204 Ibid., p. 53.

205 Ibid., p. 56.

206 Ibid., p. 57. The quotations are from Ong, *Orality and Literacy*, pp. 14 and 81.

207 Carr, *The Shallows*, p. 54.

208 Ibid., p. 55.

209 Ibid., pp. 55–56. The Havelock quotation is from Eric A. Havelock, *Preface to Plato* (Cambridge, Massachusetts and London: Harvard University Press, 1963), p. 41, and the Ong quotation is from *Orality and Literacy*, p. 79.

210 Carr, *The Shallows*, p. 190.

211 Michel Foucault, 'Self Writing', in Paul Rabinow (ed.), *The Essential Works of Michel Foucault, 1954–1984, Volume One. Ethics: Subjectivity and Truth*, trans. Robert Hurley et al. (London: Penguin, 1997).

212 Sigmund Freud, *The Ego and the Id*, in Volume 19 of James Strachey (ed. and trans.), *The Standard Edition of the Complete Psychological Works of Sigmund Freud* (London: Hogarth, 1953–74), p. 29.

213 Carr, *The Shallows*, p. 190.

214 Which are collected by *technical individuals* that tend to become a tertiary retentional apparatus.

215 Georges Canguilhem, *The Normal and the Pathological*, trans. Carolyn R. Fawcett with Robert S. Cohen (New York: Zone Books, 1991), p. 198, translation modified.

216 Joseph LeDoux, *Synaptic Self: How Our Brains Become Who We Are* (New York: Viking, 2002).

217 Ibid., p. 178.

218 Ibid., p. 176.

219 Ibid., p. 178.

220 Catherine Malabou, *The New Wounded*, trans. Steven Miller (New York: Fordham University Press, 2012), p. xiii.

221 Ibid., p. 3.

222 Maryanne Wolf, *Proust and the Squid: The Story and Science of the Reading Brain* (New York: Harper, 2007), p. 3.

223 See Edmund Husserl, 'The Origin of Geometry', in Jacques Derrida, *Edmund Husserl's Origin of Geometry: An Introduction*, trans. John P. Leavey (Lincoln: University of Nebraska Press, 1978).

224 See Foucault, *The Birth of Biopolitics*, lectures 9–10.

225 See Naomi Klein, *The Shock Doctrine: The Rise of Disaster Capitalism* (New York: Metropolitan Books, 2007).

226 Carr, *The Shallows*, p. 200.

227 Gilles Deleuze, *Nietzsche and Philosophy*, trans. Hugh Tomlinson (New York: Columbia University Press, 1983), p. 105.

228 This is itself founded on a primordial splitting of the personality. See, for example, Gilbert Simondon, *L'individuation psychique et collective* (Paris: Aubier, 2007), pp. 162–65 and p. 172, n. 3. This bipolarity is reflected in common space by elevations that Simondon calls key-points.

229 Carr, *The Shallows*, p. 51.

230 *Translator's note*: Auroux distinguishes between 'epilinguistic knowledge' and 'metalinguistic knowledge' (which he actually takes up from Antoine Culioli). The former refers to that linguistic *connaissance* possessed by speakers in non-literate societies who may, for example, know that a sentence sounds wrong (that is, ungrammatical) without being able to explain why, because they have a *consciousness* of language but lack concepts. The latter refers to that *savoir* required for a science of language. See Sylvain Auroux, *La révolution technologique de la grammatisation. Introduction à l'histoire des sciences du langage* (Liège: Mardaga, 1994), esp. pp. 23–24, and Auroux, *La philosophie du langage* (Paris: Presses universitaires de France, 1996), esp. pp. 60–62.

231 Lev Vygotsky, 'The Instrumental Method in Psychology', in *The Collected Works of L. S. Vygotsky. Volume 3: Problems of the Theory and History of Psychology*, trans. René van der Veer (New York: Plenum Press, 1997), p. 85.

232 Jean-Paul Bronckart, 'Vygotsky, une oeuvre en devenir', in Jean-Paul Bronckart and Bernard Schneuwly (eds), *Vygotsky aujourd'hui* (Lausanne: Delachaux & Nietstlé, 1985), p. 14.

233 Noam Chomsky, *Knowledge of Language: Its Nature, Origin, and Use* (New York: Praeger, 1986), pp. 19–24.

234 *Translator's note*: Fodor introduces these ideas in Jerry A. Fodor, *The Language of Thought* (New York: Thomas Y. Crowell, 1975), and the notion of 'mentalese' in particular is discussed in Fodor, *Psychosemantics: The Problem of Meaning in the Philosophy of Mind* (Cambridge, Massachusetts and London: MIT Press, 1987) and Fodor, *The Elm and the Expert: Mentalese and Its Semantics* (Cambridge, Massachusetts and London: MIT Press, 1994).

235 Bronckart, 'Vygotsky, une oeuvre en devenir', p. 14.

236 Vygotsky, 'The Instrumental Method in Psychology', p. 87.

237 Ibid.

238 And in this regard, it is quite ridiculous to say that 'computers have advanced at lightning speed, yet they remain, in human terms, as dumb as stumps. Our "thinking" machines still don't have the slightest idea what they're thinking' (Carr, *The Shallows*, p. 245): the mere fact of saying this gives credit to what is being opposed, and just shows that posing the question in these terms goes nowhere.

239 Simondon, *L'individuation psychique et collective*, pp. 21–22, 52 and 117.

240 Ibid., p. 100, my italics.

241 Ibid., p. 109.

242 Ibid., 110.

243 Ibid.

244 Bernard Stiegler, *The Decadence of Industrial Democracies: Disbelief and Discredit, Volume 1*, trans. Daniel Ross and Suzanne Arnold (Cambridge: Polity Press, 2011), pp. 58–61.

245 Gilles Deleuze, *Difference and Repetition*, trans. Paul Patton (London and New York: Continuum, 2011), pp. 6–7, my italics.

246 Immanuel Kant, 'An Answer to the Question: "What is Enlightenment?"', *Political Writings*, trans. H. B. Nisbet (Cambridge: Cambridge University Press, 1991), pp. 54–60.

247 Andrew Ure, quoted in Karl Marx, *Grundrisse: Foundations of the Critique of Political Economy (Rough Draft)*, trans. Martin Nicolaus (London: Penguin, 1973), p. 690.

248 Jacques Derrida, *Archive Fever: A Freudian Impression*, trans. Eric Prenowitz (Chicago and London: University of Chicago Press, 1996), p. 19: 'The model of this singular "*mystic pad*" also incorporates what may seem, in the form of a destruction drive, to contradict even the conservation drive, what we could call here the *archive drive*. It is what I called earlier, and in view of this internal contradiction, *archive fever*. There would indeed be no archive desire without the radical finitude, without the possibility of a forgetfulness which does not limit itself to repression. Above all, and this is the most serious, beyond or within this simple limit called finiteness or finitude, there is no archive fever without the threat of this death drive, this aggression and destruction drive'.

249 *Translator's note*: Compare da Vinci's drawings for a possible flying machine with, for example, Ader's *Avion III*, built precisely four hundred years later.

250 Patricia Pisters, 'Cutting and Folding the Borgesian Map: Film as Complex Temporal Object in the Industrialization of Memory, in

Ulrik Ekman et al. (eds), *Ubiquitous Computing, Complexity, and Culture* (New York and London: Routledge, 2016).

251 *Translator's note*: See Christian Salmon, *Storytelling: Bewitching the Modern Mind* (London and New York: Verso, 2010), esp. ch. 3.

252 Claude Lévi-Strauss, *Tristes Tropiques*, trans. John Weightman and Doreen Weightman (Harmondsworth, Middlesex: Penguin, 1976), p. 543.

253 Jean-Pierre Changeux, *Neuronal Man: The Biology of Mind*, trans. Laurence Garey (Princeton: Princeton University Press, 1997).

254 Bernard Stiegler, 'Préface', in Maryanne Wolf, *Proust et le calamar*, trans. Lisa Stupar (Angoulême: Abeille et Castor, 2015).

255 Allen Buchanan, *Better than Human: The Promise and Perils of Enhancing Ourselves* (New York: Oxford University Press, 2011).

256 Bernard Stiegler, 'Lights and Shadows in the Digital Age', keynote lecture at the Digital Inquiry Symposium, Berkeley Center for New Media, University of California Berkeley (27 April 2012).

257 Bernard Stiegler, *Symbolic Misery, Volume 1: The Hyper Industrial Epoch*, trans. Barnaby Norman (Cambridge: Polity Press, 2014), ch. 3.

258 *Translator's note*: Facebook.

259 Cf., Anthony D. Barnosky et al., 'Approaching a State Shift in Earth's Biosphere', *Nature* 486 (7 June 2012), pp. 52–58.

260 Martin Heidegger, 'Time and Being', *On Time and Being*, trans. Joan Stambaugh (New York: Harper & Row, 1972).

261 Martin Heidegger, *Identity and Difference*, trans. Joan Stambaugh (New York: Harper & Row, 1969).

262 Alfred North Whitehead, *The Function of Reason* (Princeton: Princeton University Press, 1929).

263 *Translator's note*: The reference here is to the Latin phrase, '*Homo homini lupus est*', 'Man is wolf to man', to which Hobbes and Freud, among others, refer.

264 *Translator's note*: On 'repro-duction', see Bernard Stiegler, *Technics and Time, 3: Cinematic Time and the Question of Malaise*, trans. Stephen Barker (Stanford: Stanford University Press, 2011), esp. pp. 213ff.

265 Walter Benjamin, *The Work of Art in the Age of Its Technological Reproducibility, and Other Writings on Media*, trans. Edmund

Jephcott et al. (Cambridge, Massachusetts and London: Harvard University Press, 2008).

266 See Masaki Fujihata, *Masaki Fujihata: The Conquest of Imperfection* (Manchester: Cornerhouse, 2008).

267 Jacques Derrida, 'My Sunday "Humanities"', *Paper Machine*, trans. Rachel Bowlby (Stanford: Stanford University Press, 2005), p. 100.

268 Rudolf Boehm, 'Pensée et technique. Notes préliminaires pour une question touchant la problématique heideggérienne', *Revue Internationale de Philosophie* 14 (1960), pp. 194–220.

269 Georges Canguilhem, *The Normal and the Pathological*, Carolyn R. Fawcett with Robert S. Cohen (New York: Zone Books, 1991), p. 236, translation modified.

270 Stanislas Dehaene, *Reading in the Brain: The New Science of How We Read* (New York: Penguin, 2009).

271 Paul Ricoeur, *Time and Narrative, Volume 1*, trans. Kathleen McLaughlin and David Pellauer (Chicago and London: University of Chicago Press, 1984), p. 58, translation modified.

272 Jean-Pierre Changeux, 'Préface', in Stanislas Dehaene, *Les Neurones de la lecture* (Paris: Odile Jacob, 2007), p. 14. *Translator's note*: This is the original French edition of *Reading in the Brain*, but Changeux's preface is not included in the English version.

273 Ibid.

274 Reading is a *temporalization* of the spatial object that is the book: it is in its temporality that we can and must observe the collection of alphabetical textual traces in which reading consists, through which we make *selections* from *possible semantic combinations*, while *limiting them*. It is this selection that Maryanne Wolf describes very precisely when, reading and interpreting Proust's *On Reading* (1905), she shows that each of us read something different in the same text. In Husserl's vocabulary, this means that it is on the basis of our secondary retentions, that is, of what we have already lived through, on the basis of our past, that we can project, in what we live through in a virtual way via reading, a material that, as a result, will be re-organized and re-combined by retaining, in the text read, traits that constitute what Husserl called primary retentions, which hence appear here to be primary selections.

275 Changeux, 'Préface', in Stanislas Dehaene, *Les Neurones de la lecture*, p. 14.

276 Ibid., p. 16.

277 Ibid.

278 In Bernard Stiegler, *Technics and Time, 1: The Fault of Epimetheus*, trans. Richard Beardsworth and George Collins (Stanford: Stanford University Press, 1998).

279 André Leroi-Gourhan, *Gesture and Speech*, trans. Anna Bostock Berger (Cambridge, Massachusetts and London: MIT Press, 1993).

280 Changeux, 'Préface', in Stanislas Dehaene, *Les Neurones de la lecture*, p. 17.

281 Ibid., p. 19.

282 Maryanne Wolf, *The Proust and the Squid* (New York: HarperCollins, 2007), p. 3.

283 Alfred J. Lotka, 'The Law of Evolution as a Maximal Principle', *Human Biology* 17 (1945), pp. 167–94.

284 Vladimir I. Vernadsky, *The Biosphere*, trans. D. B. Langmuir (New York: Copernicus, 1998).

285 A dynamic system that Vernadsky referred to as, precisely, the biosphere.

286 The residues of this biomass forming the necromass.

287 Georgescu-Roegen addresses this theme of the struggle of exosomatization, but without raising the question of exorganisms.

288 The quotation is from a report of the International Labour Office, *The Health of Children in Occupied Europe* (Montreal: November 1943), p. 28.

289 Paul Valéry, 'The Crisis of the Mind', in *The Collected Works of Paul Valéry, Volume 10: History and Politics*, trans. Denise Folliot and Jackson Mathews (New York: Bollingen, 1962).

290 This text is discussed in Bernard Stiegler, *What Makes Life Worth Living: On Pharmacology*, trans. Daniel Ross (Cambridge: Polity Press, 2013), §§1–2.

291 Karl Marx and Friedrich Engels, *The Communist Manifesto*, trans. Samuel Moore (London: Penguin, 1967), p. 82.

292 Lotka, 'The Law of Evolution as a Maximal Principle', p. 192.

293 Ibid.

294 Sigmund Freud, *Beyond the Pleasure Principle*, in Volume 18 of James Strachey (ed. and trans.), *The Standard Edition of the Complete Psychological Works of Sigmund Freud* (London: Hogarth, 1953–74), p. 48.

295 *Translator's note*: Claude Lévi-Strauss, interviewed by Laurent Lemire for the program *Campus* (broadcast on France 2 on 28 October 2004), and quoted in Bernard Stiegler, *Constituer l'Europe 1. Dans un monde sans vergogne* (Paris: Galilée, 2005), pp. 35–36. The complete quotation reads: 'The human race lives under a regime of a kind that poisons itself from within, and I think about the present and about the world in which my experience is coming to an end: it is not a world that I love'.

296 *Translator's note*: As mentioned, Lotka states that the 'receptors and effectors have been perfected to nicety', and Freud writes in identical terms: 'With every tool man is perfecting his own organs, whether motor or sensory, or is removing the limits to their functioning'. See Sigmund Freud, *Civilization and Its Discontents*, in Volume 21 of Strachey, *The Standard Edition of the Complete Psychological Works of Sigmund Freud*, p. 90. Freud goes on to say that, in this way, man becomes a kind of 'prosthetic God', but that we cannot forget that, nevertheless, 'present-day man does not feel happy in his Godlike character' (ibid., p. 92).

297 Bernard Stiegler, *Automatic Society, Volume 1: The Future of Work*, trans. Daniel Ross (Cambridge: Polity Press, 2016); Stiegler, *The Age of Disruption: Technology and Madness in Computational Capitalism*, trans. Daniel Ross (Cambridge: Polity Press, 2019).

298 Bernard Stiegler, *Technics and Time, 3: Cinematic Time and the Question of Malaise*, trans. Stephen Barker (Stanford: Stanford University Press, 2011).

299 Clarisse Herrenschmidt, *Les Trois Écritures: langue, nombre, code* (Paris: Gallimard, 2007).

300 Karl Marx, *Capital: A Critique of Political Economy, Volume One*, trans. Ben Fowkes (London: Penguin, 1990), p. 284, translation modified.

301 Karl Marx, *Capital: A Critique of Political Economy, Volume One*, trans. Ben Fowkes (London: Penguin, 1990), p. 284, translation modified.

302 Ibid., p. 493, n. 4.

303 *Translator's note*: On 'smartification', see Evgeny Morozov, 'The Rise of Data and the Death of Politics', *Guardian* (20 July 2014), available at: <https://www.theguardian.com/technology/2014/jul/20/rise-of-data-death-of-politics-evgeny-morozov-algorithmic-regulation>. And see Bernard Stiegler, *Automatic Society, Volume 1: The Future of Work*, trans. Daniel Ross (Cambridge: Polity Press, 2016), §8.

304 *Translator's note*: On the 'metempirical' in Derrida, see Jacques Derrida, *Edmund Husserl's Origin of Geometry: An Introduction*, trans. John P. Leavey, Jr. (Lincoln and London: University of Nebraska Press, 1989), p. 90. But more significant is Derrida's discussion of Kant's 'principle of subjective differentiation', within a broader reading of Heidegger's 1929–30 lectures on *The Fundamental Concepts of Metaphysics*, in Jacques Derrida, *The Beast and the Sovereign, Volume II*, trans. Geoffrey Bennington (Chicago and London: University of Chicago Press, 2011), p. 60, where, having outlined Kant's argument that 'orientation' in space depends on a 'feeling' that makes possible, for instance, awareness of the difference between left and right, and that for Kant the question is the extension of this necessity of an orientation and a feeling to *reason*, and hence to a '*need* of reason', Derrida describes what this implies as follows:

> The point, then, is to extend the always subjective, but sensory, principle of orientation to the right of reason, the right of the need proper to reason to orient itself in thought on the basis of a principle that is always subjective, of course, but this time carried beyond the sensory field and into the black night of the suprasensible, and thus the invisible, the metempirical. This leap into the night, the leap of right on the basis of need is an infinite leap, an infinite extension. And if you follow the huge consequences of this, the oceanic consequences [...], you will see why the need of *practical* reason is absolutely, unconditionally privileged with respect to the need of theoretical reason, for the need of reason in its practical use is, precisely unconditional [*unbedingt*].

305 'Concretized' in Simondon's sense.

306 Georges Bataille, *Prehistoric Painting: Lascaux, or The Birth of Art*, trans. Austryn Wainhouse (Geneva: Skira, 1955).

307 In Bernard Stiegler, *The Age of Disruption: Technology and Madness in Computational Capitalism*, trans. Daniel Ross (Cambridge: Polity Press, 2019), I argue that these are the hidden stakes of the conflict between Michel Foucault and Jacques Derrida concerning the dream and madness and their relationship in Descartes – as the realization of noetic dreams can always turn into a nightmare, and always assumes the possibility of madness. *Translator's note*: On our species as realizing its dreams starting from a 'prehistoric cinema', see Marc Azéma, *La Préhistoire du cinéma: Origines paléolithiques de la narration graphique et du cinématographe...* (Paris: Errance, 2011), and Marc Azéma and Florent Rivère, 'Animation in Palaeolithic Art: A Pre-Echo of Cinema', *Antiquity* 86 (2012), pp. 316–24.

308 Jakob von Uexküll, *A Foray into the World of Animals and Humans, with, A Theory of Meaning*, trans. Joseph D. O'Neil (Minneapolis and London: University of Minnesota Press, 2010).

309 See Pierre Hadot, *What is Ancient Philosophy?*, trans. Michael Chase (Cambridge, Massachusetts and London: Harvard University Press, 2002).

310 Alfred J. Lotka, 'The Law of Evolution as a Maximal Principle', *Human Biology* 17 (1945), pp. 167–94.

311 Karl Polanyi, *The Great Transformation: The Political and Economic Origins of Our Time* (Boston: Beacon Press, 2011).

312 *Translator's note*: See Arnold J. Toynbee, *A Study of History: The One-Volume Edition* (London: Oxford University Press, 1972), p. 14: 'I reject the present-day habit of studying history in terms of national states; these seem to be fragments of something larger: a civilisation. [...] I propose a composite model which seems to fit the histories of most of the civilisations we know'.

313 *Translator's note*: See Arnold J. Toynbee, *Mankind and Mother Earth* (Oxford: Oxford University Press, 1976), p. 21.

314 Erwin Schrödinger, *What is Life?*, in *What is Life?, with Mind and Matter and Autobiographical Sketches* (Cambridge: Cambridge University Press, 1992).

315 Nicholas Georgescu-Roegen, *The Entropy Law and the Economic Process* (Cambridge, Massachusetts: Harvard University Press, 1971), and Georgescu-Roegen, *Energy and Economic Myths: Institutional and Analytical Economic Essays* (New York: Pergamon, 1976).

316 IPCC, *Climate Change 2014: Synthesis Report. Contribution of Working Groups I, II and III to the Fifth Assessment Report of the Intergovernmental Panel on Climate Change* (Geneva: IPCC, 2015), p. 5.

317 *Translator's note*: See Jean-Luc Nancy, in 'A Conversation about Christianity with Alain Jugnon, Jean-Luc Nancy and Bernard Stiegler', in Stiegler, *The Age of Disruption*, p. 316.

318 Kant does not refer to functions but to 'lower faculties'. This is explained by Gilles Deleuze in *Kant's Critical Philosophy: The Doctrine of the Faculties*, trans. Hugh Tomlinson and Barbara Habberjam (Minneapolis: University of Minnesota Press, 1984), p. 7: 'In the first sense, "faculty" refers [in Kant] to the different relationships of a representation in general. But, in a second sense, "faculty" denotes a specific source of representations'. Whitehead, on the other hand, reinterprets the Kantian faculties from a functional

standpoint that we will here generalize *from an exosomatic standpoint* that emerges from the works of Alfred Lotka. See Bernard Stiegler, 'The New Conflict of the Faculties and Functions: Quasi-Causality and Serendipity in the Anthropocene', trans. Daniel Ross, *Qui Parle* 26 (2017), pp. 79–99.

319 Georges Canguilhem, *Knowledge of Life*, trans. Stefanos Geroulanos and Daniela Ginsburg (New York: Fordham University Press, 2008), p. 75.

320 See: <https://en.wikipedia.org/wiki/National_Nanotechnology_Initiative>.

321 In particular, in Books VI and VII of the *Republic.*

322 See Jean-Pierre Dupuy and Françoise Roure, *Les Nanotechnologies. Éthique et prospective industrielle* (Paris: La Documentation française, 2004).

323 Quentin Meillassoux, *After Finitude: An Essay on the Necessity of Contingency*, trans. Ray Brassier (London and New York: Continuum, 2008).

324 See Gaston Bachelard, 'Noumena and Microphysics', trans. David Reggio, *Angelaki* 10:2 (2005), pp. 73–78.

325 On this point, see Sacha Loève, *Le concept de technologie à l'échelle des molécules-machines. Philosophie des techniques à l'usage des citoyens du nanomonde*, doctoral thesis from the Université Paris X, p. 103.

326 Ibid. *Translator's note*: The full reference for the article by Moore is Gordon Moore, 'Cramming More Components onto Integrated Circuits', *Electronics* 38:8 (1965), pp. 114–17. The statement by Moore quoted by Loève is from W. Wayt Gibbs, 'The Law of More', *Scientific American* 8:1 (1997), p. 62, a special issue on *The Solid-State Century: The Past, Present and Future of the Transistor.*

327 Thus constituting hyper-matter, this having been introduced in Bernard Stiegler, *Économie de l'hypermatériel et psychopouvoir* (Paris: Mille et une nuits, 2008).

328 J. L. Austin, *How to Do Things with Words*, 2nd edition (Oxford: Oxford University Press, 1975).

329 Complex exorganisms were also one of the subjects of the 2017 pharmakon.fr seminars, accessible online.

330 Cathy O'Neil, *Weapons of Math Destruction: How Big Data Increases Inequality and Threatens Democracy* (New York: Crown, 2016).

331 As argued in Bernard Stiegler, *States of Shock: Stupidity and Knowledge in the Twenty-First Century*, trans. Daniel Ross (Cambridge: Polity Press, 2015), §42, such an effect in return is the condition of what Hegel called the speculative proposition.

332 On schematization conceived in this way, see Bernard Stiegler, *Technics and Time, 3: Cinematic Time and the Question of Malaise*, trans. Stephen Barker (Stanford: Stanford University Press, 2010.

333 Just as is *in fact* the case for the performativity of the speech acts analysed by Austin in *How To Do Things With Words*, but this is what Austin does not see, and, in the end, Derrida does not see it either. See Jacques Derrida, 'Signature, Event Context', *Margins of Philosophy*, trans. Alan Bass (Chicago: University of Chicago Press, 1982), where he tries to weaken if not to erase the opposition between the constative and the performative.

334 See Stiegler, *States of Shock*, pp. 185–88.

335 The conditions of such passages will be analysed in Bernard Stiegler, *La Société automatique 2. L'avenir du savoir*, forthcoming.

336 Digital tertiary retention, inasmuch as it dominates, *thereby* imposes a process of the transindividuation of reference, in the sense developed in Bernard Stiegler, *La Télécratie contre la démocratie* (Paris: Flammarion, 2006). But this process inevitably becomes a *dividuation*, that is, a *destruction of both psychic and collective individuation*, as this is analysed in Bernard Stiegler, *Automatic Society, Volume 1: The Future of Work*, trans. Daniel Ross (Cambridge: Polity Press, 2016). 'Thereby' means here: inasmuch as it is based on data architectures that 'are' *in fact*, but not *in law*.

337 Loève, *Le concept de technologie à l'échelle des molécules-machines*, p. 106: 'The wafer is a slice of purified silicon crystal containing all possible types of standard components for a given generation of the microelectronics market. All these are integrated into the different layers of the wafer: silicon, epoxy, oxide, doped regions, layers of interconnections. The wafer is what is ready for components intended to be implanted and combined in this or that computer for this or that function. Because it sums up the whole logic of the production system and embodies all the R&D efforts invested in its processes (agglomeration, crystallization, masks, epitaxy, oxidation, photolithography, plasma excavation, stripping, ion implantation, chemical vapour deposition, metallization, mechanical and chemical polishing, automatic characterization and testing, redundancy repair for memory parts, assembly and packaging), with each new generation of microprocessors, it is the wafer that is put on display'.

338 The denomination of intuition, understanding, imagination and reason makes these faculties incapable of being thought or cared about

as functions *of exosomatization*, and it naturalizes them in a dangerous way: the whole *uncritiqued* problem of Kantianism lies here. It is only by apprehending these faculties as functions of exosomatization that it is possible to read Kant from a standpoint that is no longer just 'materialist', but rather 'hyper-materialist'. It is equally from such a standpoint that it is possible to return to Lenin's theses on empiriocriticism, and thus to the relationship between matter, instrument and future. We will see in what follows why this necessitates bringing Léon Brillouin into this debate.

339 André Leroi-Gourhan, *L'homme et la matière* (Paris: Albin Michel, 1943), and Leroi-Gourhan, *Milieu et techniques* (Paris: Albin Michel, 1945).

340 New in the sense that it follows on from the conflict of the faculties studied by Kant in the late eighteenth century – in an eponymous work on which I have already commented in *States of Shock*.

341 It will be seen in Bernard Stiegler, *La technique et le temps 5. Symboles et diaboles*, inshallah, that philosophy was born in the fifth century BCE during a similar conflict. See also the 2010, 2011 and 2012 pharmakon.fr courses.

342 On the question of this insufficiency, and on its relations with Leibniz's principle of sufficient reason as well as the principle of insufficient reason in Robert Musil, see Bernard Stiegler, *Qu'appelle-t-on panser? 1. L'immense régression* (Paris: Les Liens qui Libèrent, 2018).

343 This is what Daniel Dennett, Claudine Tiercelin and Gayatri Chakravorty Spivak fail to understand in their 'dialogue of the deaf' about the post-truth situation and the works of Nietzsche, Foucault and Derrida. See 'La faute à Nietzsche, Foucault et Derrida?', *Philosophie Magazine* 113 (October 2017).

344 On the 'epoch of the absence of epoch', see Stiegler, *The Age of Disruption*.

345 This standpoint, which will be specified more precisely in what follows, will be more fully developed in forthcoming works.

346 *Translator's note*: '*Receler*' can mean 'to contain', 'to conceal', 'to receive' and, more specifically, 'to receive stolen goods'.

347 Such an *ex-perience* of truth is obviously not reducible to principles arising from misinterpretations of Aristotle and his categories, misinterpretations that will then engender the stage of metaphysics called *mathesis universalis*, which is the condition of the appearance and disappearance of the Anthropocene.

348 See Alfred North Whitehead, *The Function of Reason* (Princeton: Princeton University Press, 1929), p. 5.

349 We use the word 'anthropy' in the sense, for example, that the IPCC, in their *Climate Change 2014: Synthesis Report* (available at: <https://www.ipcc.ch/report/ar5/syr/>), refers to anthropic forcings and anthropogenic emissions that contribute to the destruction of the conditions of neganthropic life, that is, the conditions of the production of truth, and hence of bifurcations, and, in that, of a possible future within entropic becoming.

350 See Stiegler, *Technics and Time, 3*, ch. 4. Forms of knowledge are academic only if they are subject to the critique of peers, the community of whom constitutes a *disciplinary body* recognized as an academy (of science, French and so on) or an order (in France: of doctors, lawyers, architects and, later, corporations) certifying the certifiers and provided that this body practises the publications of its debates. That these faculties of knowing, desiring and judging are not faculties in the sense that there are faculties of theology, law and medicine – in relation to which the faculty of philosophy would, in Kant's epoch, effect a *critical bifurcation* opening up a new age of reason that thereby shows itself to be historical – is the entire question, precisely, of an exosomatic condition such that, ultimately, noesis (whose faculties and functions are arranged in 'reason') can be located *neither in the subject nor in the institution* of a discipline constituting a body through its organs, whether endosomatic or exosomatic.

351 Here we should turn to Carl Schmitt, and to the commentaries by David Bates in 'Catastrophe and Human Order: From Political Theology to Political Physiology', in Christopher Dole et al. (eds), *The Time of Catastrophe: Multidisciplinary Approaches to the Age of Catastrophe* (London and New York: Routledge, 2016).

352 On 'light-time', see Bernard Stiegler, Alain Giffard and Christian Fauré, *Pour en finir avec la mécroissance* (Paris: Flammarion, 2009).

353 Martin Heidegger, 'Time and Being', *On Time and Being*, trans. Joan Stambaugh (New York: Harper & Row, 1972).

354 Gilbert Simondon, quoted in Vincent Bontems, 'Quelques éléments pour une épistémologie des relations d'échelle chez Gilbert Simondon', *Appareil* 2 (2008), available at: <https://appareil.revues.org/595?lang=en>. *Translator's note*: According to Bontems, the quotation is from an as-yet unpublished lecture by Simondon given at the Sorbonne in 1970.

355 See Stiegler, *The Age of Disruption*, §§86–89.

356 This project, which was opened in *The Age of Disruption*, will be continued in *La Société automatique 2* and pursued more deeply in

La technique et le temps 6. La guerre des esprits. This will also be an opportunity to show why Simondon's *Invention et imagination* (Chatou: Éditions de la Transparence, 2008), and its concept of the *cycle of images*, promises much but does not keep its promises.

357 Paul Valéry, 'The Crisis of the Mind', in Paul Valéry, *History and Politics: The Collected Works of Paul Valéry, Volume 10*, trans. Denise Folliot and Jackson Mathews (New York: Bollingen, 1962).

358 Paul Valéry, 'Freedom of the Mind', in Valéry, *History and Politics*.

359 This will be elaborated in a forthcoming work.

360 I will return to this in Stiegler, *La Société automatique 2*.

361 Claude Lévi-Strauss, *Tristes Tropiques*, trans. John Weightman and Doreen Weightman (Harmondsworth, Middlesex: Penguin, 1976), pp. 542–43.

362 Jacques Derrida, 'Différance', *Margins of Philosophy*, trans. Alan Bass (Hemel Hempstead: Harvester, 1982), p. 8.

363 Jacques Derrida, *Of Grammatology*, corrected edition, trans. Gayatri Chakravorty Spivak (Baltimore and London: Johns Hopkins University Press, 1998), p. 84.

364 Thanks are here due to Dan Ross, who corrected a date error (in September 2017) adding: 'firstly because Lemaître's contribution needs to be understood in relation to Alexander Friedmann's, and secondly because Hubble's confirmation of the expanding universe occurred in 1929 (what Hubble discovered in 1924 was the existence of objects outside the Milky Way galaxy). My understanding of the timeline is as follows:

1922: Alexander Friedmann shows that the theory of general relativity means that the fabric of spacetime cannot be static, but must either be expanding or contracting (Einstein initially rejects this, but then changes his mind);

1924: Hubble shows that spiral nebulae (which were already known) are much further away than previously thought, and are actually other galaxies that exist beyond the Milky Way, thereby proving that our galaxy is only one among many in a much larger universe;

1927: Lemaître proposes that there is a relationship between the observed 'red shift' (Doppler effect) of other galaxies and the expanding universe, and notes what this implies – that there must have been a point in time at which everything coincided (that is, the Big Bang) (which, again, Einstein initially rejects, finding the notion distasteful to his preference for a static universe);

1929: Hubble observes that there is a linear relationship between the degree of the Doppler effect and the distance of a galaxy from Earth, thereby confirming the theory of the expanding universe.

365 *Translator's note*: One place where this statement can be found is in Damien de Failly, *Chemin de crêtes. Carnet de voyage d'Henri dit le Pèlerin* (Paris: Société des Écrivains, 2013), p. 111.

366 Francis Bailly and Giuseppe Longo, 'Extended Critical Situations: The Physical Singularity of Life Phenomena', *Journal of Biological Systems* 16 (2008), pp. 309–36, and Bailly and Longo, 'Biological Organization and Anti-Entropy', *Journal of Biological Systems* 17 (2009), pp, 63–96.

367 Norbert Wiener, *The Human Use of Human Beings: Cybernetics and Society* (London: Free Association Books, 1989), p. 32.

368 Giuseppe Longo, 'Quelques spécifications théorique de l'état vivant de la matière', available at: <http://www.di.ens.fr/users/longo/files/Abstracts/bio-model23-1-07.pdf>, p. 1.

369 Ibid.

370 Ibid.

371 Ibid., p. 2.

372 Ibid.

373 Ibid.

374 Giuseppe Longo, 'Complexité, science et démocratie (Entretien avec Giuseppe Longo)', *Glass Bead* (2016), available at: <http://www.glass-bead.org/wp-content/uploads/LongoEntretien.pdf>. An English translation will be included in Michael R. Doyle, Selena Savić and Vera Bühlmann (eds). *The Ghost of Transparency: An Architectonics of Communication* (Basel: Birkhäuser, forthcoming).

375 Ibid.

376 Ibid.

377 Vladimir I. Vernadsky, *The Biosphere*, trans. D. B. Langmuir (New York: Copernicus, 1998), pp. 60–61.

378 Claude Bernard, *Lectures on the Phenomena Common to Animals and Plants*, trans. H. E. Hoff, R. Guillermin and L. Guillermin (Springfield: Charles C. Thomas, 1974), p. 84.

379 Con-tributors are simple exorganisms within the complex and hyper-complex exorganisms that constitute the digital, biospheric, reterritorialized economy. They are studied and solicited within the framework of the research program of the Plaine Commune contributory learning territory (see recherchecontributive.org). The theory and practice of contribution conceived in exorganological terms has been the subject of the pharmakon.fr seminar since November 2016, dedicated to the study of exosomatization through what we

have called the principles of exorganology. On these questions, see pharmakon.fr.

380 Claude Shannon, 'A Mathematical Theory of Communication', *Bell System Technical Journal* 27 (1948), pp. 379–423, reprinted in N. J. A. Sloane and Aaron D. Wyner (eds), *Claude Elwood Shannon: Collected Papers* (New York: Institute of Electric and Electronics Engineers, 1993).

381 Norbert Wiener, *Cybernetics, or Control and Communication in the Animal and the Machine,* 2nd edition (Cambridge Massachusetts: MIT Press, 1961).

382 Ludwig von Bertalanffy, *Das Gefüge des Lebens* (Leipzig: Teubner, 1937); Bertalanffy, *General System Theory: Foundations, Development, Applications* (New York: Braziller, 1968).

383 Henri Atlan, *L'Organisation biologique et la Théorie de l'information* (Paris: Hermann, 1972). See also Henri Atlan, *Selected Writings: On Self-Organization, Philosophy, Bioethics, and Judaism* (New York: Fordham University Press, 2011).

384 Edgar Morin, *Method: Towards a Study of Humankind, Volume 1: The Nature of Nature,* trans. J. L. Roland Bélanger (New York: Peter Lang, 1992).

385 René Thom, 'Stop Chance! Silence Noise!', trans. Robert E. Chumbley, *SubStance* 12:3 (1983), pp. 11–21.

386 With the exception, precisely, of Bailly, Longo and Montévil.

387 See Bernard Stiegler, *Automatic Society, Volume 1: The Future of Work,* trans. Daniel Ross (Cambridge: Polity Press, 2016).

388 This is the issue in Mathieu Triclot, *Le Moment cybernetique: la constitution de la notion de l'information* (Paris: Champ Vallon, 2008).

389 Whitehead, *The Function of Reason,* p. 2.

390 Gilbert Simondon, 'Introduction', *L'Individuation à la lumière des notions de forme et d'information* (Grenoble: Jérôme Milon, 2013), p. 31.

391 In *On the Mode of Existence of Technical Objects,* and in relation to the transindividual, which is certainly not information, but about which one then wonders what information could possibly be if it is not the transindividual – which 'presupposes a phase-change of the system' and which 'supposes a first preindividual state that individuates itself according to the discovered organization. Information is the formula of individuation, a formula that cannot exist prior to this individuation' (Simondon, *L'Individuation à la lumière des notions de forme et d'information,* p. 31).

392 Simondon, *L'Individuation à la lumière des notions de forme et d'information*, p. 35.

393 For example, see ibid., p. 548.

394 Ibid., p. 35.

395 Bernard Stiegler, *Technics and Time, 1: The Fault of Epimetheus*, trans. Richard Beardsworth and George Collins (Stanford: Stanford University Press, 1998), pp. 76–78.

396 Gilbert Simondon, *On the Mode of Existence of Technical Objects*, trans. Cecile Malaspina and John Rogove (Minneapolis: Univocal, 2017), p. 50.

397 Stiegler, *Technics and Time, 1*, p. 78. The portion in quotation marks is from Simondon, *On the Mode of Existence of Technical Objects*, p. 50.

398 Simondon, *On the Mode of Existence of Technical Objects*, pp. 50–51, quoted in Stiegler, *Technics and Time, 1*, p. 78 (here we have followed the latter translation – *trans.*).

399 Simondon, *On the Mode of Existence of Technical Objects*, trans. Cecile Malaspina and John Rogove (Minneapolis: Univocal, 2017), p. 51, quoted in Stiegler, *Technics and Time, 1*, p. 78 (here we have followed the latter translation – *trans.*).

400 Bernard Stiegler, *The Neganthropocene*, trans. Daniel Ross (London: Open Humanities Press, 2018).

401 Simondon, *On the Mode of Existence of Technical Objects*, p. 51.

402 See Stiegler, *La technique et le temps 4*, forthcoming.

403 Norbert Wiener, *The Human Use of Human Beings: Cybernetics and Society* (London: Free Association Books, 1989), p. 52.

404 Simondon, *L'Individuation à la lumière des notions de forme et d'information*, p. 35.

405 Antoinette Rouvroy and Thomas Berns, 'Gouvernementalité algorithmique et perspectives d'émancipation. Le disparate comme condition d'individuation par la relation?', *Réseaux* 177 (2013), pp. 163–96.

406 See Stiegler, *Automatic Society, Volume 1*, §8.

407 Rouvroy and Berns, 'Gouvernementalité algorithmique et perspectives d'émancipation', p. 185.

408 Admittedly, Simondon never said that technics is a process of individuation. But we have highlighted – particularly in *Symbolic Misery* – that when he refers to the technical individuals that machines will

become, forming technical ensembles, and techno-geographical milieus, and to the fact that the individual is posited *in principle* as what stems from a process of individuation, then technics does indeed amount to a process of individuation as such – *associated* with psychosocial individuation, and vice versa.

409 Simondon, *On the Mode of Existence of Technical Objects*, p. 252, translation modified.

410 See Lotka, 'The Law of Evolution as a Maximal Principle', p. 188.

411 See Georges Canguilhem, *The Normal and the Pathological*, trans. Carolyn R. Fawcett and Robert S. Cohen (New York: Zone Books, 1991), p. 200.

412 Georges Canguilhem, *Knowledge of Life*, trans. Stefanos Geroulanos and Daniela Ginsburg (New York: Fordham University Press, 2008), p. xviii: 'In concrete terms, knowledge consists in the search for security via the reduction of obstacles; it consists in the construction of theories that proceed by assimilation. It is thus a general method for the direct or indirect resolution of tensions between man and milieu. [...] [I]ts end [...] is to allow man a new equilibrium with the world, a new form and organization of his life. [...] [K]nowledge undoes the experience of life, seeking to analyze its failures so as to abstract from it both a rationale for prudence (sapience, science, etc.) and, eventually, laws for success, in order to help man remake what life has made without him, in him, or outside of him'.

413 This will be analysed in greater depth in a forthcoming work.

414 This confusion is the expression of suffering in the post-truth age, whose herald is an electronic histrion produced by the transformation of noetic functions arising from the industrial exploitation of analogue and digital tertiary retentions.

415 Vladimir I. Vernadsky, *The Biosphere*, trans. D. B. Langmuir (New York: Copernicus, 1998), pp. 60–61, my italics for 'inexorable and astonishing mathematical regularity'.

416 John L. Pfaltz, 'Entropy in Social Networks' (2012), available at: <https://arxiv.org/pdf/1212.2917.pdf>. Thanks to Johan Mathé who drew my attention to this article.

417 This will be studied in depth in Bernard Stiegler, *La technique et le temps 6*.

418 Auroux refers to linguicides in Sylvain Auroux, *La Révolution technologique de la grammatisation. Introduction à l'histoire des sciences du langage* (Liège: Mardaga, 1994), p. 116.

419 William J. Ripple et al., ‘World Scientists’ Warning to Humanity: A Second Notice’, *BioScience* 67 (2017), pp. 1026–28, available at: <https://academic.oup.com/bioscience/article/67/12/1026/4605229>.

420 Intergovernmental Panel on Climate Change, ‘Global Warming of 1.5°C: An IPCC special report on the impacts of global warming of 1.5°C above pre-industrial levels and related global greenhouse gas emission pathways, in the context of strengthening the global response to the threat of climate change, sustainable development, and efforts to eradicate poverty: summary for policymakers’ (6 October 2018), available at: <http://report.ipcc.ch/sr15/pdf/sr15_spm_final.pdf>.

421 World Meteorological Organization, ‘WMO Statement on the State of the Global Climate in 2018’ (2019), available at: <https://library.wmo.int/doc_num.php?explnum_id=5789>.

422 Anthony D. Barnosky et al., ‘Approaching a State Shift in Earth’s Biosphere’, *Nature* 486 (2012), pp. 52–58.

423 *Translator’s note*: As with Peter Thiel’s investment and interest in ‘seasteading’.

424 *Translator’s note*: As with Elon Musk’s investment and interest in colonizing Mars.

425 Karl Marx and Friedrich Engels, *The Communist Manifesto*, trans. Samuel Moore (London: Penguin, 1967), p. 82.

426 Martin Heidegger, *The Essence of Truth: On Plato’s Cave Allegory and the Theaetetus*, trans. Ted Sadler (London and New York: Continuum, 2002).

427 *Translator’s note*: See, for example, the discussion in the Eighth Lecture of 2018 concerning the respective flying dreams of Leonardo da Vinci and Clément Ader.

428 Alfred Sohn-Rethel, *La pensée-marchandise*, trans. Gérard Briche and Luc Mercier (Broissieux: Croquant, 2010), p. 74. *Translator’s note*: Where an English translation has not been found, translations are directly from the French translation.

429 Theodor W. Adorno, *Negative Dialectics*, trans. E. B. Ashton (London: Routledge, 1973), p. 206.

430 Alfred Sohn-Rethel, *Intellectual and Manual Labour: A Critique of Epistemology*, trans. Martin Sohn-Rethel (London and Basingstoke: Macmillan, 1978), p. 19.

431 Sohn-Rethel, *La pensée-marchandise*, p. 41.

432 Ibid., p. 47.

433 Ibid.

434 *Translator's note*: See, for example, Stiegler, *Technics and Time, 3*, pp. 140–41.

435 *Translator's note*: See ibid., esp. pp. 213ff.

436 Walter Benjamin, *The Work of Art in the Age of Its Technological Reproducibility, and Other Writings on Media,* trans. Edmund Jephcott et al. (Cambridge, Massachusetts and London: Harvard University Press, 2008).

437 Sohn-Rethel, *Intellectual and Manual Labour,* p. 190.

438 Sohn-Rethel, *La pensée-marchandise,* p. 40.

439 *Translator's note*: As described in Jakob von Uexküll, *A Foray into the World of Animals and Humans, with, A Theory of Meaning,* trans. Joseph D. O'Neil (Minneapolis and London: University of Minnesota Press, 2010).

440 Sohn-Rethel, *La pensée-marchandise,* p. 41.

441 See Stiegler, *Technics and Time, 3,* pp. 52–54.

442 Sohn-Rethel, *La pensée-marchandise,* p. 47.

443 Karl Marx, *Capital: A Critique of Political Economy, Volume One,* trans. Ben Fowkes (London: Penguin, 1976), p. 165, quoted in Sohn-Rethel, *Intellectual and Manual Labour,* p. 78.

444 Sohn-Rethel, *La pensée-marchandise,* p. 47.

445 Ibid.

446 See Karl A. Wittfogel, *Oriental Despotism: A Comparative Study of Total Power* (New Haven and London: Yale University Press, 1957).

447 Kojin Karatani, *The Structure of World History: From Modes of Production to Modes of Exchange*, trans. Michael K. Bourdaghs (Durham and London: Duke University Press, 2014).

448 Jean-Paul Bronckart, 'Vygotsky, une oeuvre en devenir', in Jean-Paul Bronckart and Bernard Schneuwly (eds), *Vygotsky aujourd'hui* (Lausanne: Delachaux & Nietstlé, 1985), p. 14.

449 *Translator's note*: See Stiegler, *Technics and Time, 1,* pp. 205–6.

450 Karl Meyerson, *Les Fonctions psychologiques et les oeuvres* (Paris: Albin Michel, 1995), p. 9.

451 Ibid.

452 Ibid., p. 10.

453 Ibid., p. 194.

www.ingramcontent.com/pod-product-compliance
Lightning Source LLC
LaVergne TN
LVHW062028051126
851858LV00005B/118